The Return of the Theorists

The Return of the Theorists

Dialogues with Great Thinkers in International Relations

Edited by

Richard Ned Lebow
King's College London, UK

Peer Schouten
Danish Institute for International Studies, Denmark

and

Hidemi Suganami
Aberystwyth University, UK

Softcover reprint of the hardcover 1st edition 2016 978-1-137-51644-2

First published 2016 by
PALGRAVE MACMILLAN

Palgrave Macmillan in the UK is an imprint of Macmillan Publishers Limited,
registered in England, company number 785998, of Houndmills, Basingstoke,
Hampshire RG21 6XS.

Palgrave Macmillan in the US is a division of St Martin's Press LLC,
175 Fifth Avenue, New York, NY 10010.

Palgrave Macmillan is the global academic imprint of the above companies
and has companies and representatives throughout the world.

Palgrave® and Macmillan® are registered trademarks in the United States,
the United Kingdom, Europe and other countries.

ISBN 978-1-349-57788-0   ISBN 978-1-137-51645-9 (eBook)
DOI 10.1057/9781137516459

This book is printed on paper suitable for recycling and made from fully
managed and sustained forest sources. Logging, pulping and manufacturing
processes are expected to conform to the environmental regulations of the
country of origin.

A catalogue record for this book is available from the British Library.

Library of Congress Cataloging-in-Publication Data
The return of the theorists: dialogues with great thinkers in international
relations / [edited by] Richard Ned Lebow, King's College London, UK, Peer
Schouten, Danish Institute for International Studies, Denmark, Hidemi
Suganami, Aberystwyth University, UK.
pages cm
Includes index.
1. International relations—Philosophy.   I. Lebow, Richard Ned, editor.
II. Schouten, Peer, editor.   III. Suganami, Hidemi, editor.
JZ1305.R462 2016
327.101—dc23   2015025952

Typeset by MPS Limited, Chennai, India.

Contents

v

List of Contributors

Rita Abrahamsen, Professor, Graduate School of Public and International Affairs, University of Ottawa.

Lucian M. Ashworth, Professor and Head of Department of Political Science, Memorial University of Newfoundland.

Robert Ayson, Professor of Strategic Studies, School of History, Philosophy, Political Science and International Relations, Victoria University of Wellington.

Bertrand Badie, Professor of International Relations, Institut d'Etudes Politiques de Paris; Associate researcher, Centre d'études et de recherches internationales (CERI), Sciences-Po.

Richard Beardsworth, Professor of International Politics, Department of International Politics, Aberystwyth University.

Erica Benner, Fellow in Political Philosophy, Department of Political Science, Yale University.

David Boucher, Professor of Philosophy and International Relations, Cardiff University, Distinguished Visiting Professor, University of Johannesburg, South Africa.

Christian Bueger, Reader in International Relations, Cardiff University.

Ariane Chebel d'Appollonia, Professor of Public Affairs and Administration, Division of Global Affairs, School of Public Affairs and Administration, Rutgers, State University of New Jersey.

Christopher Coker, Professor of International Relations, Department of International Relations, London School of Economics and Political Science.

Michael Cox, Professor of International Relations, Department of International Politics, London School of Economics and Political Science.

James W. Davis, Professor of Political Science with focus on International Relations, Director of the Institute for Political Science, University of St. Gallen.

Ian Hall, Professor of International Relations, Griffith University.

Jan Willem Honig, Senior Lecturer, Department of War Studies, King's College, London.

Adam Humphreys, Lecturer, Department of Politics and International Relations, University of Reading.

Kimberly Hutchings, Professor of Politics and International Relations, Queen Mary University of London.

Beate Jahn, Professor of International Relations, University of Sussex.

Caroline Kennedy-Pipe, Professor of War Studies, Head of the School of Politics, Philosophy and International Studies, University of Hull.

Friedrich Kratochwil, Emeritus Professor, European University Institute.

Anthony F. Lang, Jr, Professor, School of International Relations; Director, Centre for Global Constitutionalism, University of St Andrews.

Andrew Lawrence, Visiting Professor, Vienna School of International Studies.

Anna Leander, Professor (MSO), Department of Management, Politics, and Philosophy, Copenhagen Business School.

Richard Ned Lebow, Professor of International Political Theory, Department of War Studies, King's College London; Bye-Fellow, Pembroke College, University of Cambridge; James O. Freedman Presidential Professor, Emeritus, Dartmouth College.

Andrei S. Markovits, Arthur F. Thurnau Professor and the Karl W. Deutsch Collegiate Professor of Comparative Politics and German Studies at the University of Michigan.

Seán Molloy, Reader in International Relations, School of Politics and International Relations, University of Kent.

Rens van Munster, Senior Researcher, Danish Institute for International Studies.

Iver B. Neumann, Montague Burton Professor of International Relations, Department of International Relations, London School of Economics and Political Science; associate of the Norwegian Institute of International Affairs.

Louis W. Pauly, Professor and Chair, Department of Political Science, University of Toronto.

Simon Reich, Professor, Division of Global Affairs and Department of Political Science, Rutgers Newark.

William E. Scheuerman, Professor, Department of Political Science, Indiana University.

Peer Schouten, Postdoctoral fellow, Danish Institute for International Studies.

Joshua Simon, Assistant Professor of Political Science at Columbia University.

Jens Steffek, Professor, Institut für Politikwissenschaft, Technische Universität Darmstadt.

Tracy B. Strong, Professor, University of Southampton and Distinguished Professor of Political Science, University of California, San Diego, emeritus.

Hidemi Suganami, Emeritus Professor of International Politics, Department of International Politics, Aberystwyth University.

Casper Sylvest, Associate Professor in History, University of Southern Denmark.

Michael C. Williams, Professor, Graduate School of Public and International Affairs, University of Ottawa.

Huw L. Williams, Coleg Cymraeg Cenedlaethol Lecturer, Cardiff University.

Pichamon Yeophantong, Lecturer (Asst Prof), School of Social Sciences, University of New South Wales.

Chen Yudan, Assistant Professor of International Politics at the School of International Relations and Public Affairs, Fudan University.

Introduction

Richard Ned Lebow, Peer Schouten and Hidemi Suganami

How would Kant or Weber respond to contemporary debates about epistemology? What would Hume say to critiques of his 'constant conjunction' and recent approaches that try to finesse causation? What would Hobbes, Machiavelli, Clausewitz and Morgenthau think about the quasi-integration of Europe or the rise of China, or Rousseau, Adam Smith and Norman Angell about globalization? How would any of these thinkers respond to positivism, constructivism, postmodernism, rational models and feminism? Could Plato and Aristotle have interesting conversations with Durkheim, Foucault or Bourdieu? Anyone who has had to struggle seriously with the work of dead theorists will have had moments when they would have liked to talk to these thinkers. Perhaps some have given into these musings and conducted imaginary conversations in the solitude of their offices or while on a walk through the woods. To write perceptively about these theorists we need to get inside their minds, and what better way than through imagined dialogues?

One of us – Ned Lebow – did a postgraduate political theory seminar with Isaiah Berlin in the mid-sixties. Berlin asked his students to write a course paper in the form of dinner party conversation with some prominent political thinker from the past. Ned chose Mozart and his librettist Lorenzo da Ponti as his guests and encouraged them to talk about their critique of the Enlightenment identity project. Prof. Berlin was amused, and told him how lucky he was that the statue of the Commendatore had not marked his paper.

In the decades since, Ned gnawed away at the prospect of imaginary conversations with great figures of the past. What fun it would be to ply them with good food and wine and prod them to hold forth on their works, how they have been interpreted since, and what they think about the contemporary world. These fantasies remained unrealized until Hidemi sent Ned a paper he had written about an imaginary conversation with David Hume. In it, he assumes the role of Hume's professor, and he and 'Dave' discuss the latter's idea for a dissertation on causation. He offers 'Dave' avuncular advice and tells him how he should proceed. They have a second conversation years later, when 'Dave', now a recognized authority, reflects back on his earlier work.

Hidemi's piece is thoughtful and amusing, and encourages readers to think about the development of Hume's thought and the ways in which strands of it connect. It was the catalyst for Ned to suggest that the two of them edit a book in which they would ask colleagues to interview other thinkers. Ned took the next step and conducted an interview with Thucydides. Ned and Hidemi then began to sound out friends in the discipline and were amazed to discover how many identified theorists with whom they would like to have a dialogue. After having recruited some dozen participants, Ned received an email from Peer Schouten inviting him to contribute a chapter to a book he was planning. Peer had for years been toying with the idea of interviewing dead International Relations (IR) theorists as an extension of his *Theory Talks* project. This was indeed a remarkable coincidence. Hidemi and Ned promptly invited Peer to merge his project with theirs and become a co-editor. A dozen participants quickly turned into a few dozen.

Two premises firmly unite all contributions. First is the tacit agreement that contemporary IR is as much a conversation between the living and the dead as it is among the living. Contemporary debates on international politics are thoroughly rooted in and shaped by the thought of many bygone minds, ancient and modern. The commitment to knowledge in international relations is that of the fox, rather than the hedgehog, to speak with Isaiah Berlin and Archilochus before him. In lieu of any kind of unified, authoritative truths, the real voice of International Relations theory is a web of conversations and unresolved debates that span centuries and continents.

We did not interview Sir Isaiah, as he had little to say about IR. We think, however, that he would be pleased with our enterprise, although it is more a feast than a dinner. We have invited some forty thinkers to engage in dialogues with us. They run the gamut from Homer and Confucius to Hedley Bull and Jean Bethke Elshtain. They span almost three millennia of human history and include representatives of Western and Chinese culture, but, like IR theory, are heavily weighted towards the former. The 'us' consists of forty International Relations scholars and political theorists. They too cut across cultures, continents and almost three generations.

There is a method and madness in our selection. We were committed to framing International Relations broadly. We would include, as far as it proved feasible, thinkers, or their precursors, from multiple paradigms. We would commission dialogues not only with mainstream International Relations scholars, but also with political theorists, historians and others whose ideas had influenced the development of the theory and practice of international relations.

We tried to match thinkers with scholars, and *vice versa*. Some of the contributors we recruited were very keen to conduct dialogues with specific thinkers. Their interest led us to include some theorists not on our initial wish list, and to search for colleagues who would be willing to interview those theorists we had previously identified as central to the enterprise. Our final table of contents deviates in some ways from our original design. The table of contents is more than double our original draft. This expansion reflects the surprising interest in our project throughout the profession. People from all over contacted us asking us if they could participate, and we only said no when additional chapters would have made the book more difficult to sell to a publisher. We also permitted two interviews with Immanuel Kant. He is such a towering figure for modernity and two of the colleagues we contacted were keen to write about him in very different ways.

We insisted that every interview be with a dead thinker. This is a distinguishing feature of the volume, and is what makes our dialogues imaginary. More than a series of séances – in which the spirit invoked speaks with an authority unmediated by the invoking agent – we offer fictional dialogues, dialogues informed by intimate knowledge of the thinkers in question. Interlocutors attempt to elicit their views about their works and to probe ambiguities, tensions, connections in their writings and the evolution of their views. Some are asked what they think about subsequent readings of their works, a question that provoked more than a few angry replies. Some insist on talking about present day international relations. Almost all think their ideas are still relevant. Their words are, of course, those of our interviewers, and the way in which they interrogate, criticize and defend the ideas of the thinkers they engage tells us something interesting about them and our world. Many thinkers find our world depressing; some because their predictions have come true and others because they have not. Far and away the most enthusiastic response to the present came from Karl Deutsch when he learned about the internet.

The personalities of some of these thinkers come across strongly. Plato is arrogant, Kant is crotchety, Marx is confident and arrogant, John Herz is a soft-spoken gentleman and Bourdieu is touchy. We know this from their

writings and first-hand accounts of contemporaries. Some of our thinkers died in the recent past and were personally well-known to those who
interview them. Ariane Chebel d'Appollonia was a student of Raymond
Aron, Andy Markovits of Karl Deutsch. Their acquaintance lends verisi-
militude to their dialogues, as does feedback from the two older editors
who knew casually to well most of the recently deceased thinkers.

The second premise that sets this volume apart from other explora-
tions of the firmament of classical and modern political thought is our
commitment to dialogue. We believe it is a unique and necessary vehicle
to understanding political thought. Since Plato, conversation has been a
central philosophical method, and in presenting the forty dialogues we
hark back to this method. To understand thinkers one must get inside
their heads, so to speak. One way to do this is through imaginary dialogues, and we suspect that they have been conducted by many serious
scholars in the course of their research and reflection. We make this process visible, and develop goals for our contributors who conduct them.

Our book is an amusing *jeu d'esprit*, but also a serious contribution to
the scholarly literature in political theory and international relations.
In this regard, the current volume should be seen as extending the
ambition of such efforts as Harry Kreisler's *Conversations with History*
and Peer Schouten's *Theory Talks*, both of which share a commitment
to knowledge production in International Relations by making public
conversations with some of the foremost thinkers in and around the
discipline, to the past.

Texts inevitably speak beyond the intentions of their authors as they
are read in novel contexts and against the works of their predecessors,
contemporaries, and successors. Our dialogues permit great thinkers to
reflect upon – albeit through the medium of our interviewers – subsequent
readings of their works and the concerns that led to them. It allows these
thinkers to participate, and possibly help shape this process, through the
questions and imagined answers of their interlocutors.

Dialogues are not necessary to identify tensions, contradictions or
other problems in important texts. However, they do provide a vehicle
for the thinkers we interrogate to respond to these criticisms, many
of which may not have been apparent at the time they wrote. Fritz
Kratochwil's discussion with Immanuel Kant, Hidemi Suganami's with
David Hume and Josh Simon's with Karl Marx are cases in point. This
kind of interrogation is also useful for probing the imagination, open-
ness and closure of thinkers, and styles of reflection and argument.

Dialogues bring dead thinkers into our world in ways that are otherwise impossible. They are compelled to address a context many could

not possibly have imagined, or extensions of their world in the case of those only recently deceased. Even some of these thinkers must contemplate new worlds, as Hans Morgenthau would the end of the Cold War. So too would earlier thinkers who expired on the eve of major changes in politics and international relations – for example, Max Weber, who died as Weimar was born and thirteen years before Hitler's dictatorship. Familiarizing great thinkers with events that post-date them and the new questions they generated about the past provides new and important challenges to them. It allows us to explore novel features of their thought, or features we know about in novel ways, and allows them to participate, albeit vicariously, in contemporary debates.

Finally, dialogues that pose similar questions to diverse thinkers encourage comparisons. They are an excellent way of drawing out the ways in which these thinkers agree and disagree, and just as importantly, what features of the world strike them as important. Political theorists and historians of political thought invariably approach the latter question by looking at what these thinkers have chosen to write about. Another method, and one that has the potential to elicit different answers, is to think about how they are likely to respond to the present.

For all these reasons, we believe that this collection of dialogues will be of interest to scholars and students. For the former, it raises new questions that can be addressed by more traditional modes of research. For the latter, it provides straightforward and engaging introductions to diverse thinkers and encourages them to think about their relevance to our world. It has the potential to open new horizons for all those students of International Relations who have been exposed only to works by acknowledged IR scholars and not to those thinkers who provided the intellectual foundations of our enterprise.

We thought at length about the appropriate format for the conclusion. An academic-style summary followed by some 'lessons' for IR seemed inappropriate and ill-fitting. Instead, we settled on an imaginary panel at the 2016 annual meeting of the International Studies Association. The real one is in Atlanta, and ours in Atlantis. The panel is entitled: 'Has There Been any Progress in International Relations Theory since Thucydides?' The presenters are Thucydides, Thomas Hobbes, Hans Morgenthau, Karl Deutsch and Hedley Bull. There are questions from the audience, which includes some of the thinkers interviewed in the book and a graduate student.

We hope you enjoy our book and find it provocative and intellectually stimulating in equal measure.

1
Homer (c.850 BCE)

Richard Ned Lebow

Thank you for agreeing to meet with me, even if it is so early in the morning that not even Starbucks is open.

Rosy-fingered dawn is the best time of day.

It also seems to be your favourite epithet. If you are blind, how can you appreciate a sunrise?

Ah, you are a breaker of poets, not of horses. For ancient Greeks, blindness is associated with seers and wisdom. Think of Tiresias in *Antigone* or Oedipus after he pokes out his eyeballs. They bring light to deathless gods and mortal men.

But what about you? Are you really blind as legend has it? Does everything look like the wine dark sea?

Careful how you use my lines, young man.

Sorry, but I'm curious to know if you are really the blindest of Achaeans.

There you go again!

Do you really need those shades in Hades?

Next are you going to ask me if I am really Homer?

You really are a seer. You read my mind. The consensus among classical scholars is that the *Iliad* and *Odyssey* are the product of multiple bards, composed over the course of centuries until a final version was committed to writing sometime in the classical era. I hesitate to say this, but some scholars doubt if there ever was a Homer, and a conveniently blind one at that.

Then why did you appeal to Apollo the far shooter to ferry you across the Styx to meet with me?

I think you're Homer, all right. I credit you with these epics but I would like to know how your versions differ from what follows, and whether the *Iliad* is based on a real war. And those are just the beginning of my questions.

It really doesn't matter if there was a Trojan War, or a swift-footed Ahkileus (Achilles), Agamemnon, a brave man at close-fighting, Odysseus, much beloved by Zeus, or Penelope, the most faithful of wives. It's what we think about sacred Ilios that counts, and our thoughts are shaped by stories that make an impression on us. My epics shaped a culture because the war caused by Ares, breaker of cities, and its sharp-speared heroes were real for generations of Greeks. Their 'facticity' – to use one of your fancy terms – is irrelevant. Consider your own so-called factual events. They too are only known through stories told by politicians, journalists and your intellectuals. They create reality, not represent it, and, unlike my epics, never rise to the level of poetry.

Surely your stories have changed in their telling?

Indeed. It wasn't until proud-hearted Nietzsche that you moderns came to the realization that authors don't own texts; they take on a life of their own. We Greeks always knew this truth. Texts are like gifts, they pass from giver to receiver in a long, perhaps even endless, chain. Each time they change hands they assume a new context and come with stories of their previous owners and why they gave them away. So it is with my poetry. I created a gift for my companions, which subsequently passed through many other mouths to become a treasure for all god-fearing Greeks. Am I troubled that others changed and added lines, adapting these epics to the needs of the merging polis? No, my words remain an endless spring that trickles down a rock face to be lapped up by the thirsty below.

I know you moderns think writing a great advance. Plato, student of the splendid Socrates, had his doubts and I remain unconvinced. Stories stagnate when they are committed to writing. You and your colleagues argue endlessly about what they mean rather than assimilating them and using them to give purpose and direction to your lives and helping you live them wisely and honourably. A text is a living resource, not a mud-encrusted fossil to be carefully brushed off and studied under a magnifying glass.

I'm conducting this interview for a book on International Relations theory, so I hope you won't mind if I focus my remaining questions on that subject?

Feel free, but understand that your interstate relations are markedly different from those of so-called Bronze Age Greece. And the *Iliad* offers a different kind of account of them than your modern historians or theorists. It offers what the far-seeing Max Weber would call an ideal-type representation of warfare, its causes and consequences.

You've read Max Weber?

No, I can't read. Never learned how. But I chat with him now and again, although it is not easy.

Why is that?

For a start, all his talk about a 'place in the sun' for Germany. And here he is in Hades. He doesn't appreciate the irony, but then he has no sense of humour. He speaks in long and convoluted sentences not connected or held together by metre or signifiers. I'm told his writing is worse. He's a profound but sloppy thinker, a breaker of concentration, not of horses.

If I can return to the *Iliad*?

Of course.

War in the *Iliad* is between Menelaus of the long-shadowed spear, supported by his revenge-seeking Danaans, and the honourable Priam of Dardanus's line and his Trojans. Each has numerous allies duty-bound to support them, but happy to do so because they see the war as a means of gaining *aristeia*, or honour, on the battlefield. This is why individual combats feature so prominently and why combatants pro-claim their lineage and accomplishments to each other. *Aristeia* is won by defeating an equally honourable adversary, and more so if they are invited to throw the first spear. Real war was never like this, but there were elements of it in ancient Greek and Roman warfare and in Europe up to the First World War. In the *Iliad*, there is no distinction between the honour of the individual warrior and that of the *ethnos*, which today you might describe as the state or nation. Honour remains alive at the platoon level, however, modern wars are not started by warrior-kings intent on upholding their personal honour, but by leaders moved by national honour and interests.

On the subject of other goals, security never appears to be a motive in the *Iliad*, except perhaps where the Greeks are desperate to prevent the Trojans from setting their ships on fire. Following the advice of the Geranian horseman Nestor they devise an appropriate strategy. In contrast, Hektor and other Trojans reject the sensible advice that they wage a defensive war behind their walls once Ahkileus has rejoined the fighting.

This is correct. Honour trumps other considerations in this war, secu-rity included, for the Trojans. You have many modern examples. At the end of World War I, Ludendorff wanted the German army to conduct a suicide offensive in the West to preserve its honour, and his naval coun-terpart wanted the German fleet to do the same. Honour among combat-ants was only possible when they regarded one another as equals, as did the Greeks and Trojans. This survived in your culture up until, and even through WW I, where class solidarity among aristocratic officers often trumped national differences. Officer prisoners of war were invited to dinner and sometimes given paroles. In World War II, a kind of camaraderie between some Luftwaffe officers and their RAF counterparts – although the latter were largely middle class – was maintained through the Battle of Britain. German ace Adolf Galland notified the British that their ace Douglas Bader had lost his prosthesis escaping from his burning aircraft and offered safe passage for the RAF to drop a replacement. It is reminiscent of Glaucus, son of Hippolochus, and Diomedes, master of the war cry, exchanging their armour.

Today, adversaries are not equals. Leaders and complicit media demonize the other side to mobilize public opinion and sustain combat morale. The inevitable outcome is mass bombings, Abu Ghraibs, mutilation of prisoners and beheading of journalists. This is not unlike the wars the Greeks fought against local tribes where no quarter was asked or given. In the modern era war has become more institutionalized and legalized, but, alas, more barbaric.

Aren't you forgetting what happened to broad-streeted Troy and its people once it was defeated, or to the peaceful villages where Ahkileus and his friends killed the men and made off with women and booty?

True. This is one important reason why I end my tale with the return by Ahkileus, son of the lovely-haired Thetis, of Hektor's body to Priam, noble king of Troy. He regains his humanity, and Trojans and Greeks show respect for one another when Priam breaks his fast and dines with Ahkileus. I agree that the theft of Briseus, the killing of her husband and brother and levelling of her village are acts of barbarism, but her father, with the help of Mars, is able to retrieve her in the end. This doesn't happen with hostages today, unless vast ransoms are paid.

How did either side feed themselves during ten years of war? Karl Marx was amazed that there is no mention of commerce or logistics anywhere in the *Iliad*.

Yes, he used to pester me about these omissions. I countered with the observation that there is no mention of honour in *Das Kapital*. This is in sharp contrast to Schumpeter, whose words are like honey-sweet wine and who believes that entrepreneurs are driven by honour, not profit. They seek to achieve immortality by this means, as Ahkileus did through warfare.

Let's turn to the rage of Ahkileus and his conflict with Agamemnon, which quickly equals, if not replaces, that between Greeks and Trojans as the focus of the epic. Drawing on the language of modern social science, I would describe their conflict as the inevitable product of the divergence of ascribed and achieved status. Agamemnon is *wanax*, something like a king, and therefore at the top of the ascribed hierarchy. He is supposed to be the bravest and best leader, but he is not. He's selfish, gives in to the wrong instincts, and does not set a good example for his fighters. Ahkileus, whom you frequently describe as 'the best of the Acheans', is the best warrior and most admired Greek, and at the top of the achieved hierarchy. This is signalled by the decision among the Greek warriors to reward him with Briseus. Agamemnon wants her for this reason, and in the false belief that he can impose himself at the top of both hierarchies, thus restoring their expected unity.

You could put it this way, if you must. In a more general sense, ambitious men – ambitious people – in your era, will always find grounds for resenting one another. However, it is certainly true that swift-footed Ahkileus had no chip on his shoulder and would have accepted Agamemnon's leadership if he had not behaved in such an insulting manner.

As you were careful to use gender-free language in your last reply, could I close with a question about women?

Why not? After fighting and horses, they are men's favourite pastime. In my day they talked endlessly about the first two and little about the last. Lovely-cheeked Helen was the exception, and nobody had anything good to say about her, in contrast to Andromache and Penelope, loyal wife and mother of Telemachus, who was greatly admired, but never mentioned in conversation.

Do you think women are inferior to men?

Certainly not. Nor were Greeks superior to Trojans. Both races are equally commendable and the differences in character, intelligence and bravery are not between the well-greaved Acheans and the Trojan breakers of horses but among them. Hektor of the glinting helmet, and Priam, and Menelaus and the huge Aias, are truly admirable, whilst god-like Alexandros (Paris) and Agamemnon are reprehensible. So it is with women. Alexandros and the Argive Helen together – not just Helen – are the cause of the Trojan War and suffering, just as Clytemnestra and Aegistus are in the War's aftermath. Andromache and Penelope – like Electra and Medea for the later playwrights – are intelligent women. The first two pursue their ends by acceptable means. Indeed, Penelope uses those practices to keep her suitors at bay and remain faithful to the crafty Odysseus, the sacker of cities. She is in every way his worthy counterpart. In my day it was convention, not anything essential about women, that relegated most of them to inferior positions, just as it was for men not of aristocratic birth.

You realize your *Iliad* has been used to sustain misogyny over the ages? It is an illustration of the truth to which I earlier referred. People turn to my epics for varied purposes over which I have no control. Sometime they are used sagaciously, but often stupidly. *Xenia* – guest friendship in your language – is the oldest and most honoured of customs, and the father of the gods is frequently described as Zeus Xenios. Guests must be housed and fed and they in turn must honour, not abuse their hosts. Paris violates guest friendship by running off with Helen and her jewels, and Priam makes war inevitable by honouring this deed, that is by giving refuge to Paris and Helen. He had no choice but to offer refuge as Paris is his son. The other Trojans treat them well although they fully recognize that they are the cause of war and their loss and suffering. What can I do if some readers single out Helen and ignore Alexandros, or for that matter, invent out of whole cloth a lowly trade dispute to explain war between the Greeks and Trojans?

Are you suggesting this is yet another way in which warrior-based honour cultures generate tensions that threaten to destroy them?

It is self-evident that first the abuse and then the forthright practice of *xenia* were responsible for the Trojan War, just as the intense competition for standing among warriors was an underlying cause of the conflict between Agamemnon and the swift-footed Ahkileus. In a deeper sense, war is a boon and a curse. It allows young men to distinguish themselves and gain honour, but wars that are not quickly resolved threaten to undermine the structure of the society that enables honour and its recognition. This is most apparent in the character of Ahkileus, who rages like a lion, mistreats Hektor's body, sacrifices young Trojan boys, and only adheres to *nomos* again when he meets Priam and imagines his father grieving over his body.

Would it be fair to say that Ahkileus and Priam both recognize their imminent deaths and struggle to find a discourse that would allow them to create new selves that would free them from their responsibilities and known fates? In this sense, one could read the epic as the first anti-war literary work.

Ahkileus and Priam struggle to reconcile themselves to their fates rather than to escape them. This heightens the poignancy that brings the epic to a close, and is another reason why it had to end here, *before* either hero dies. To the extent that there is a search for a new language, it is a task left to listeners – today, readers. Indeed, some of the bards who followed me, who tried to adapt the epic to the polis, strengthened this implicit plea in their treatment of Ahkileus and Agamemnon. There is a parallel here to Aeschylus's *Oresteia*, which makes explicit the need to give the city a monopoly over violence to stop, among other things, family feuds. Shakespeare advances a similar argument in *Romeo and Juliet*, and hints at the connection to the *Oresteia* by naming the prince of Verona, who outlaws feuds, Escalus. Max Weber would practically equate the state with violence. As when the sea's swells hurl on the booming shore, wave after wave of the West wind's stirring, his definition of the state shouts out from every International Relations text.

I'm limited to 3,000 words so I must end here. I am very grateful to you for giving me your time and promise to represent your words as accurately as I can.

No need to do that, as I've explained. But why am I limited to 3,000 words? Greeks would sit around heart-warming fires after sending the smoke from fat-wrapped loins of sheep to the gods and listen to my words for hours.

I'll try telling that to my editor.

2
Conversations with Confucius (551–479 BCE)

Pichamon Yeophantong

28 August 2013. I travelled from Beijing to the Temple of Confucius (Kongmiao) in the historic town of Qufu, Shandong Province. Celebrated for being the hometown of Confucius, the town exudes a quiet charm, which contrasts sharply with the cacophonous hustle and bustle of Beijing. Seeking inspiration for my research on Confucian political thought, I quickly made my way to the Confucius Temple, which is known as China's largest and oldest. The vast temple complex, together with the Cemetery of Confucius and the Kong Family Mansion, has been listed as a UNESCO World Heritage Site since 1994. Walking through the well-kept courtyards, I could not help but wonder if this was the same path trodden by those who had sought to desecrate the memory of Confucius here in 1966.[1]

I soon arrived at the temple's main hall – known as the Hall of Great Perfection (Dacheng). After duly paying my respects, I walked towards the Xingtan *(Apricot Altar), erected to commemorate Confucius' teaching of his disciples under an apricot tree. A warm breeze swept past as I seated myself on the platform's white steps. There, I closed my eyes and cleared my mind.*

I don't know how much time had elapsed before, amidst the rustling of leaves, I heard a faint voice that slowly grew louder. Half-awake, I saw the blurry outlines of a robed figure walking towards me.

I am certain that what followed was not a dream.

(*The ensuing dialogue is translated from the original Chinese.)

'I heard you calling me.'
'Kongfuzi?[2]' I replied, incredulous.
'Yes. And who are you? Why have you called upon me here?'
[Silence]
'Well?'
'Oh, my name is Sydney, and I've been studying Chinese political philosophy – Confucianism, in particular – for the past year. I just have

so many questions to ask you! Like what do you really mean by *ren*? And what are your thoughts on human nat–'

'Speak slowly. Do not be so excited. First, explain to me how exactly you have been "studying" my work.'

'I've been reading the *Analects (Lunyu)* – the collection of your sayings, of course – and I've also been trying to read, or rather decipher, the *Book of Songs (Shijing)* and the *Book of Rites (Liji)*. I haven't quite gotten to the other books yet, but I intend to read through the *Spring and Autumn Annals (Chunqiu)* soon. I know how important it is to take into consideration the historical context and all...'

'To learn but not think is fatal.'[3]

'And "He who thinks but does not learn is in great danger".'[4]

'Good. Then tell me, what is it that you are seeking to "learn"?'

'I suppose I'm trying to learn from the ancients.[5] I want to see how Confucian, I mean, *your* ideas from the past can help to illuminate and guide China's present. And to do this, I intend to focus on the influence of Confucian political thought on the evolution of Chinese conceptions of responsible leadership over time. Though my supervisor'll have to sign off on this topic first...'

'I see. Well then, proceed with your questions.'

'Um, if you don't mind, I'd like to begin by asking you some rather basic questions about your teachings. I don't know if you've kept abreast of the changes over the past 2,566 years, but Confucianism has undergone quite the revival (*fuxing*) of sorts in recent years, and talking about you and your ideas has become quite fashionable. In fact, a growing number of psychologists and political scientists are now trying to systematically study Confucianism's effects on contemporary Chinese culture and society.[6] There have even been attempts to reconcile Confucianism with other schools of thought like Legalism (*Fajia*) and socialism.

But it seems to me that despite the really interesting work being done, some have managed to misrepresent – or is it misinterpret? – the core principles of Confucianism, essentializing it to the extent that the traditions and attitudes you espoused are used to merely evoke politicized ideas like "harmony" and validate China's "pacifist" image abroad.'

'I am not surprised. To find a true *junzi* (superior person)[7] who cultivates *ren* (Goodness)[8] and is respectful of the *Dao* (the Way) is hard indeed! The world I see now bears some semblance to the world I knew.[9] The technological advancements and commercial exploits to which your generation cleaves and holds in such high regard are no more than a veneer that covers up deep-seated social and political fragmentation and the looming spectre of moral decline.

I trust you will have heard of the hubbub surrounding the enactment of the "Elderly People" law last month?'[10]

'Yes, of course. The public furore it elicited was really, quite divisive. Some agreed that the law was necessary to reinstate a modicum of morality in Chinese society, but others just thought it was a big joke. I was wondering whether you'd agree with this law.'

'Zixia once asked me about the treatment of one's parents.'

'Oh yes, I remember reading a passage about that in the *Analects*.'

'Then you will remember what I told him. Filial piety (*xiao*) goes beyond merely ensuring that one's parents have enough to eat or that one's elders are served with wine and food first. It is the demeanour that is difficult to attain.[11] Visiting one's parents often does not amount to filial piety. With "no feeling of respect",[12] such actions are empty gestures.

So no, I am not convinced that this law will be able to engender any meaningful change. Besides, I squarely disagree with Han Fei and those Legalists on the use of law as a tool to control and coerce.'

'Ah! This is one of my favourite passages in the *Analects*: "Govern the people by regulations, keep order among them by chastisements, and they will flee from you, and lose all self-respect. Govern them by moral force, keep order among them by ritual and they will keep their self-respect and come to you of their own accord."[13]'

'Good! Good! So you understand. External regulation can only go so far; what is needed is internal regulation of the self. Look at the current Chinese government. No matter how much those misguided officials try to control the internet, at the end of day, people are still able to find a way around those restrictions and access Facebook or Gmail. *Ren* is an inherently moral quality – you might even say a "perfect virtue" (*pinde wanmei*)[14] – from which the values of filial piety, *zhong* (loyalty) and the like flow. The *junzi* can only cultivate *ren* from within; it cannot be imposed from without. If the Chinese state – the ruling elite – seeks to reform the behaviour of the people, then it must govern by example, not by punishment or force. If social order is to be safeguarded, if the Way is to prevail, it is a prerequisite for the state to enforce the rules of ritual propriety (*li*) and exercise self-restraint.'

'Gosh, I daren't ask what you think of the notion of *"Ru biao Fa li"* (Confucian inside, Legalist outside)!'

'Ha! Governing through such means simply makes one neither Confucian, nor Legalist!'

'But hold on. How is it that you know about the Legalists, and Facebook, and G—?'

The Master laughed. 'There is still much that *you* do not know.'

'... I suppose if I could go back a bit then, I've always wondered why is it that you place so much importance on filial piety and the family unit?'

'Why ought one not place importance on family and devotion to one's parents?'

'Well, I suppose if one were to look to the ancient Greeks – let's say, Plato's *The Republic* – it's suggested that the state should stand over the family, given how personal loyalties to one's own family could potentially override one's loyalties and obligations to the state. In this sense, there would appear to be the possibility of a role conflict arising?'

'My response is simple: the reason why the cultivation of such virtues is deemed so crucial is because these serve as the fundamental building-blocks for orderly human relationships. As you are aware, a person cannot claim to be a *junzi*, a moral exemplar to others, if they fail to observe *li*. The maintenance of orderly relationships is, in turn, central to the establishment of a well-functioning social system – one that aligns with the Good. Imagine a series of concentric circles. The bonds of moral responsibility should be conceived as emanating from the self to family, to state and, finally, to All-under-Heaven (*tianxia*).[15] There is no inherent incompatibility between one's private and public duties. You need only to respect and treat others' interests as your own.

Do note, though, that these bonds run not just from the individual to the state, but likewise from the state to the individual. The incumbent ruler must be governed by the same rules of propriety and Goodness that govern the individual. Do you recall what I advised Ji Kangzi[16] when he asked me about how a ruler gains the respect and loyalty of the common people?'[17]

'Ah yes. I think I see what you mean now.'

'I assume you are familiar with the importance of *zhengming* (rectifying names)[18]?'

'When governing, "Let the prince be a prince, the minister a minister, the father a father and the son a son".'[19]

'Insofar as each person fulfils their responsibilities as accorded to them by their position within society, benign government and order will thrive, and the people will be happy. This is what defines able statecraft.'

'But aren't you overestimating human rationality? You acknowledge in the *Analects* that although every person has the potentiality to become a *junzi*, it is not everyone who succeeds in becoming so. You yourself bemoaned how you struggled to find a truly superior person.[20] So while I agree that good government should be dependent upon a ruler that has gained through "moral force" (*de*) the consent of the governed – that is, legitimacy derived from the Mandate of Heaven (*tianming*) – isn't "good government", as you've described it, still more of an ideal state that is exceedingly difficult to achieve in the real world?'

'Ha! You sound almost like a Legalist. The Daoists kept poking fun at me for not being "transcendental" enough in my depiction of humanly virtues; the Mohists accused me of "ruining the world".[21] But among my most ardent and vehement critics were those Legalists!'[22]

'And don't forget those New Culture youths[23] and Hegel – his criticisms of your teachings were most scathing.'

'While I admit that I am not very systematic in my arguments, Hegel lost sight of the bigger picture – of the social system I sought to explain. The same can be said of Weber too. Labelling my instructions as religious, "primitive rationalism",[24] when in fact my chief concern was always with the webs of obligation that exist between people, not with spirits.[25]

But to get back to your point, it would appear that we are entertaining different conceptions of human nature.'

'I've always wanted to ask you what your thoughts were on this!'[26]

'Mencius saw human nature as inherently capable of good; Xunzi saw humans as predisposed to being bad.[27] I am less inclined to provide such a definitive view on humanity. Through education, culture (*wen*) and cultivation of the *ren*, any individual can become a "rounded man" (*chengren*) or even a *junzi*, fit to contribute to their state and society. But without proper education and respect for the ways of propriety, then they will surely be destined for a different path. A similar logic applies to states and their rulers. Safeguarding the Way and governing by moral force will lead to prosperity; governing by penalties and repressive laws will result in eventual ruin.'

'So human nature, from your perspective, is basically malleable?'

'Yes, I suppose you could say so. This is why I believe education is a necessity for all: a person's worth ought never to be determined by their social status, but solely by their abilities and virtues. Only when you discriminate a person on the basis of their merit does this serve as the necessary foundation for an orderly society.'[28]

'What about their gender?'

'I am aware that some consider my views as being deeply gendered. You must understand, however, that women scholars such as yourself were far from the norm back then. So whilst I should like to think otherwise, I remain in part a product of my times. I still cannot help but admire the feats of the Duke of Zhou or those of Kings Wu and Wen.

Even so, gender cannot serve as a sound basis upon which to judge a person's character or their potential to contribute to society. Although the prevailing social norms of my day made it more probable for a man to become a *junzi*, there is in fact no natural predisposition that make men any more likely to possess such moral excellence. My failure to find a man, a ruler, worthy of the title *junzi* attests to this. And by the same token, there is no inherent quality that renders women incapable of cultivating Goodness and becoming a superior person.

Regrettably I cannot control how others interpret and appropriate my words. However, contrary to what some may say, *ren* as a virtue is not in itself hierarchical or gendered. These are prejudices which come with the individual, not with the idea.

So it is as I have told you: every individual deserves to receive a well-rounded education, regardless of their social position or gender – to contend otherwise would obviously make me a raving hypocrite! A society permeated by inequality, lacking in righteousness and propriety, is bound to falter. We already see this in certain parts of the world.'

'You really were – I mean, are – quite the innovator. What you've said sounds a lot like an exposition on human rights: a far cry from the feudalistic ideas of your time! The fact that you were reflecting on all of this during times of grave political instability and civil strife is truly remarkable.'

'I am no innovator.'

'Then are you "reactionary" as your critics claim you to be?'[29], I enquired jokingly.

'I am neither. I merely transmit what I have been taught.'[30]

'Speaking of transmitting, I wonder if I might bring up a question I asked you earlier – that is, the matter of modern-day interpretations of your teachings.'

'You mean those spiritual, self-help books?'

'Um... I was thinking more along the lines of, for instance, recent efforts to synthesize Confucianism with socialist thought or, more specifically, with official state rhetoric.[31] Some say that your teachings rationalize subservience to authority.'[32]

'They misunderstand. It is not subservience that I advocate. The ruler, like the father, is not beyond remonstration. If he behaves reprehensibly, then it is the duty of his ministers to rectify his ways. Blind obedience to what one's elders or superiors command is neither filial, nor righteous (*yi*).

I must say that I am worried, though. While I am pleased that the Chinese leadership no longer regards me in such adversarial terms as before, I am not entirely comfortable with certain aspects of this "Confucian revivalist" business. Not that I particularly mind Xi Jinping quoting from me[33] – he will still need to prove himself in practice – but I question the utility of such things like those Confucius Institutes. I trust you are aware of the controversy?'[34]

'Of course.'

'It is an unfortunate affair, isn't it? I should think that if the Chinese leadership seeks to truly spread *ren* and its attendant virtues to other parts of the world – and in effect, realize the "Chinese Dream" (*Zhongguo meng*) of a prosperous society and harmonious world – then it behoves them to observe and cultivate these values within themselves first.[35] Were they to succeed in doing so, they would have no use for these institutes. After all, "He who rules by moral force is like the pole-star, which remains in its place while all the lesser stars do [sic] homage to it".'[36]

'I see. But so, what do you envision to be China's future?'

'Over the past two millennia, China has borne witness to the rise and fall of great dynasties and ancient empires, and its people have persevered through the disorder wrought by countless wars, famines and revolutions. In the face of hardships, the Chinese people have exhibited resilience, each time rising up to shoulder their burdens. China – its people and culture – will surely continue to persevere.

Though the country may face a crisis of faith and legitimacy,[37] the Chinese people and their leaders still have at their disposal a vast repository of classical knowledge and wisdom, from which I hope they will find both solace and counsel. In looking forward, China's ruling elite must not hesitate to look back and learn from the Ancients. Attempts in recent years to relate classical Chinese political thought to the country's modern identity and encourage "national learning" (*guoxue*),[38] whilst promising, are not sufficient.'

'And what about the future of Confucianism?'

'It does not surprise me that "Confucianism", as you call it, has stood the test of time. Like the ancient trees of Mount Tai,[39] it sees the growth of new branches, yet its trunk and roots remain thick and deep, impervious to the storms that seek to fell it. You may consider myself and my teachings "feudal", "backward", "unrealistic", "unsystematic", or hopelessly "naïve". However, the virtues and traditions I have sought to transmit are unchanging, and have been deeply woven into the fabric of modern Chinese civilization. In due course, as the observance of *li* and knowledge of *ren* spreads, the same will be true of other countries and civilizations. And the Way will, at last, prevail in the world...'

No sooner had the Master finished his sentence than I 'awoke' from my meditation to the vociferous chattering of a little magpie that had perched itself, quite comfortably, on the stone railing beside me.

Notes

1. I refer here to the 'Annihilate the Kong Family Business Rally' in Qufu, which took place during the Cultural Revolution. See Sang Ye and Geremie R. Barmé, 'Commemorating Confucius in 1966–67: The Fate of the Confucius Temple, the Kong Mansion and Kong Cemetery', *China Heritage Quarterly* 20 (December 2009), available at <http://www.chinaheritagequarterly.org/scholarship.php?searchterm=020_confucius.inc&issue=020> (accessed 30 October 2014).
2. Literally, Master Kong. This is the appellation from which the Latinized name of 'Confucius' is derived.
3. Confucius, *The Analects of Confucius*, trans. Arthur Waley (New York: Vintage, 1989), Bk. II:15, p. 91.
4. Ibid.
5. See Arthur Waley, 'Introduction', in *The Analects of Confucius*, p. 46.
6. See Daniel A. Bell, 'What can we learn from Confucius?', *Guardian* (26 July 2009), available at <http://www.theguardian.com/commentisfree/belief/2009/jul/26/confucianism-china> (accessed 10 November 2014).
7. There are several possible translations for the concept of *junzi*. 'Gentleman' is normally one of the most frequently used, having also been used by Arthur Waley in his seminal translation of the *Analects*.
8. Also translated as 'human-heartedness'.
9. This refers to the Spring and Autumn period.
10. In full, the 'Protection of the Rights and Interests of Elderly People' law. Edward Wong, 'A Chinese Virtue Is Now the Law', *New York Times* (2 July 2013), available at <http://www.nytimes.com/2013/07/03/world/asia/filial-piety-once-a-virtue-in-china-is-now-the-law.html?_r=0> (accessed 20 November 2014).
11. *Analects*, Bk. II:7, 8, p. 89.
12. Ibid.
13. *Analects*, Bk. II:3, p. 88.
14. Fung Yu-lan, *A Short History of Chinese Philosophy* (Tianjin: Tianjin Social Science Press, 2008), pp. 69–70.
15. See Raymond Dawson, *The Chinese Experience* (London: Phoenix Press, 2005), p. 75.
16. Also latinized as 'Chi K'ang-tzu'. He was the head of the 'Three Families', who were the *de facto* rulers of the state of Lu.
17. 'Approach them [the people] with dignity, and they will respect you. Show piety towards your parents and kindness toward your children, and they will be loyal to you. Promote those who are worthy, train those who are incompetent...'. *Analects*, Bk. II:20, p. 92.
18. '*Zhengming*' has also been translated as 'correcting language'. *Analects*, Bk. XIII:3, p. 171.

19. *Analects*, Bk. XII:11, p. 166.
20. For outbursts of Confucius' disappointment, see *Analects*, Bk. V:26, p. 114; Bk. IX:17, p. 142.
21. Fung, *A Short History*, p. 84.
22. See Dawson, *The Chinese Experience*, pp. 108–115.
23. The New Culture Movement was an intellectual movement that unfolded over the course of a decade from 1916 to the mid-1920s. It involved prominent intellectuals such as Chen Duxiu who were disillusioned with traditional Chinese culture, including Confucianism, and believed that 'outdated' Chinese values were responsible for holding back the country's development vis-à-vis Japan and the West.
24. Feng Lan, *Ezra Pound and Confucianism: Remaking Humanism in the Face of Modernity* (Toronto: University of Toronto Press, 2005), p. 191.
25. Waley, 'Introduction', in *Analects*, p. 31.
26. See *Analects*, Bk. V:12, p. 110.
27. Mencius (c. 371–c. 289 BCE) was a Confucian philosopher and is often considered the 'second sage' of Confucianism. Xunzi (c. 300–c. 230 BCE) was also a Confucian philosopher – one of the most influential during the tumultuous Warring States period (479–221 BCE) – who further developed the works of Confucius and Mencius.
28. See *Analects*, Bk. I:7, p. 84.
29. See, for example, 'Carry the Struggle to Criticize Lin Piao and Confucius Through to the End', *Peking Review* 17:8 (February 1974), pp. 5–6.
30. *Analects*, Bk. VII:1, 2, 3, p. 123.
31. See Tang Yijie, '"Harmonious but different", "coexistence of civilization",' *People's Daily* (9 August 2005), available at <http://en.people.cn/200508/09/eng20050809_201195.html> (accessed 11 November 2014).
32. According to Henry C.K. Liu, 'The danger of Confucianism lies not in its aim to endow the virtuous with power, but in its tendency to label the powerful as virtuous'. Liu, 'The Abduction of Modernity: Part 3: Rule of law vs Confucianism', *Asia Times* (24 July 2003), available at <http://www.atimes.com/atimes/China/EG24Ad01.html> (accessed 18 November 2014).
33. See Wang Xiangwei, 'Xi Jinping endorses the promotion of Confucius', *South China Morning Post* (29 September 2014), available at <http://www.scmp.com/news/china/article/1603487/xi-jinping-endorses-promotion-confucius> (accessed 2 November 2014).
34. See 'China defends Confucius Institute after new doubts in U.S.', *Reuters* (5 December 2014), available at <http://www.reuters.com/article/2014/12/05/us-china-usa-education-idUSKCN0JJ0MC20141205> (accessed 6 December 2014).
35. See *Analects*, Bk. II:13, p. 91.
36. *Analects*, Bk. II:1, p. 88.
37. See, for instance, Will Hutton, 'Beyond the scandal lies a crisis at the heart of China's legitimacy', *Guardian* (15 April 2012), available at <http://www.theguardian.com/commentisfree/2012/apr/15/will-hutton-chinese-spring-inevitable> (accessed 18 November 2014).
38. See Amy Qin, 'China Weighing More Emphasis on Traditional Culture in Textbooks', *New York Times* (6 November 2014), available at <http://cn.nytimes.com/china/20141106/c06textbooks/print/en-us/> (accessed 7 November 2014).
39. Also known as Taishan. It is among China's most sacred and ancient mountains.

3
Lao Zi (6th–5th Century BCE?): Dao of International Politics

Chen Yudan

Seeing that the Zhou Dynasty is decaying, Lao Zi decides to leave the Central Kingdom and live in seclusion. When he arrives at the Hangu Pass, which holds the Western border, Yin Xi, the commander of the Pass, requests him to write a book which is later titled Lao Zi *or the* Sacred Book of Dao and De. *Having completed the work, Lao Zi goes further west and is never heard of again. The conversation is between Lao Zi and Yin Xi, when the former has completed his book and begins to leave. Though living in the 6th century BCE China, both men have a wide knowledge both of the Western tradition and international politics today.*

Yin Xi: Master, now you are leaving for the unknown West. It is our first, I am afraid, as well our last meeting. After you walk through the Pass, no one will find you. Fortunately, you wrote the book upon my request. It will be an undoubted classic, ensuring that your name and thoughts are remembered forever.

Lao Zi: My friend, why do you think that fame is important to me?

Yin Xi: I have heard that 'the highest meaning of immortality is when there is established an example of virtue; the second, when there is established an example of achievement; and the third, when there is established an example of wise speech'.[1] Your work establishes both examples of virtue and speech. Aren't you proud of this lasting possession?

Lao Zi: No, I am not interested in that. I wrote the book only because of your firm request, not for my fame. The greatness as examples of virtue and speech, as well as achievement, is vain.

Yin Xi: I don't understand, Master. You mean neither a man nor a state should strive for greatness?

Lao Zi: As I said, 'The Dao of the sage is that with all the doing he does not strive'.[2]

Yin Xi: So what is this 'all the doing' all about?

Lao Zi: It means doing nothing.

Yin Xi: Doing means doing nothing ... Master, I am confused.

Lao Zi: Think about international relations. They say that the best way to maintain peace is the balance of power. But wars break out between alliances carefully built for that purpose, not to mention the sufferings of small states from big powers' balancing games. They say that a league of nations can prevent great wars. But the artificial creature has proved ineffective. A respectable state complying with Dao, therefore, does not strive to lead, to govern, or to reform the international society, let alone to struggle for power.

Yin Xi: But don't you think that global issues like poverty, human rights, the environment ... all these still need active governance?

Lao Zi: It was exactly 'active governance' – the active colonization, the active exploitation of the earth, etc. – that all these problems came from. However, when there is abstinence from action, good order is universal.

Yin Xi: Interesting. Then the best way[3], or Dao, of big powers is to stay unconcerned? It sounds quite different from the Confucian teachings of *Ren* (benevolence).

Lao Zi: The Confucian school always asserts that *Ren* is a defining character of the sage. However, the real sage never acts from any wish to be benevolent. If he did, he would obviously send many his precepts to the world, only leading to quick decay and exhaustion. As happens to the big powers.

Yin Xi: But if neither the sage nor the big powers do anything good to the world, how can they be called sage and responsible states?

Lao Zi: Good question. Let me make a 'water' analogy. Water benefits all things and all people, but it never strives to do this. Its way is to occupy the low place which all men dislike, instead of doing something to rise. This is the advantage or benevolence of doing nothing. In this sense, the way of water is near that of Dao, since Dao in its regular course does nothing on purpose, and thus achieves everything. The way of responsible powers is laissez-faire for the sake of a well-ordered world. Doing nothing and doing all, they are two sides of the same coin, a unity of contradictions.

Yin Xi: If it is reasonable that the greatest services of the big powers is doing nothing on purpose, don't you think that all the states in the international society must actively struggle for power for the sake of survival, position and interests?

Lao Zi: Survival, position and interests, much resemble the three motives of the Athenians in Thucydides' work – namely fear, honour and profit. Striving to get rid of fear, achieve honour and gain interests, they struggled as enthusiastically as they could, but were eventually defeated in the Peloponnesian War. The popular term 'Thucydidean trap', which is little different from the power transition theory cliché, is very far from what the Greek writer would like to tell us. To me, the real trap here is the illusion that a state is able to control everything and reap all the advantages. Solon, a Greek sage, while answering a question about the 'happiest' man, said that 'the power above us is full of jealousy and fond of troubling our lot'.[4] Dao, as 'the power above us', is not personified as to be jealous, but it does similarly 'diminish where there is superabundance, and supplement where there is deficiency'. The most dangerous thing for a state, therefore, is the fetish of powerfulness. The Greeks call it 'hubris', that which made the Athenians lose the Peloponnesian War. That is why I argue that 'what makes a big power is its being like a low-lying, down-flowing stream', and 'a big power must learn to abase itself'.

Yin Xi: It seems like a paradox, that too much power brings about powerlessness.

Lao Zi: Power is just as the cargo of a ship. It is better to leave the vessel unfilled, than to carry it when it is full. How many possessors of a large wealth can keep it safe? A state's power and wealth will bring retribution if they lead to arrogance.

Yin Xi: Do you mean that a state should rather accept its weakness than endeavour to be powerful? But what if the weak meets the strong? You know what the Athenians said in the Melian Dialogue: 'The strong do as they can and the weak suffer what they must'.[5]

Lao Zi: What do you think is the softest and weakest in nature?

Yin Xi: Water maybe.

Lao Zi: And the firmest and strongest?

Yin Xi: Rock I think.

Lao Zi: When water meets rock, given enough time, the former will wear away the latter. This also applies in gender relations. Females are physically weaker than males, but always overcome the males by their feminine stillness, and usually have a higher life expectancy. Sweden is a case in international relations. It reached two peaks of power in the early 17th century under the rule of Gustavus Adolphus and the early 18th century when Charles XII was the King. As a great power, it did not hesitate to attend to the power struggles in Europe, only resulting in the death of the two great kings. However, Sweden has been cautious about getting involved into big power contentions since the nineteenth century, and thus hard to be regarded as a great power. But it has enjoyed a better life from then on than the superpowers rising and falling in the past two centuries. We all know that daring to do something is boldness, but few notice that 'not daring to do' is another way of braveness. The former appears to be injurious and is put to death, the latter to be advantageous and lives on.

Yin Xi: So your point is that small states must avoid any chances of strife, and thus they overcome big powers without direct conflicts?

Lao Zi: Note that what I say is 'weakness', not 'cowardice'. The reason that 'the soft overcomes the hard, and the weak the strong' is not the timidity of the weak and the soft, but rather its persistence of its own way. May I draw on the 'water' analogy again? How can soft water penetrate the firm rock? Because the water drips consistently and 'there is nothing (so effectual) for which it can be changed'. To sum up: 'The movement of the Dao by contraries proceeds; And weakness marks the course of Dao's mighty deeds'.

Yin Xi: Sounds reasonable, but I am afraid few will accept your idea. To the majority of states and peoples, the most glorious moments in their collective memories are when they are strong and powerful, when they lead the region or the world, and especially when they win critical external wars.

Lao Zi: Right. That is exactly one of the reasons why human beings have not been able to get rid of war. As you said, states delight in telling how powerful and wealthy they are, or have been, in certain historical moments. But he who carries a sharp sword at girdle and has a superabundance of property and wealth is no more than a robber and boaster. This is contrary to the Dao, surely.

Yin Xi: Since you attach so much importance to peace and condemn the wagers of war, are you going to declare that no war is good, just or legitimate, and appeal for renunciation of war?

Lao Zi: Few, if not any, of the wars people have conducted have been just. But I am not so radical as to oppose all violence in international society. The key point here is that states should be very, very cautious about war and use it only as a last resort. I condemn the people 'who carry a sharp sword at girdle' – 'carry' here meaning they are always ready to use or threaten to use it – but would not ask them to give up the weapons. They can keep buff coats and sharp weapons, but should have little occasion to don or use them.

Yin Xi: Can I understand your words as the strict criteria of *jus ad bellum*?

Lao Zi: Yes. War is a necessary evil. Thus, it is just only as an instrument to maintain peace. To end war by means of war, sounds peculiar, doesn't it? But imagine the pattern of the character 武 'Wu' (force/martial/military) in Chinese. It is a combination of the two characters 止 'Zhi' (stop/end) and 戈 'Ge' (dagger-axe/weapon). The use of military force, therefore, is by definition a way to stop violence and make sure that the weapons are not used again.

Yin Xi: When commemorating war, we should actually remember the misery instead of the victory?

Lao Zi: Exactly. I cannot agree more with Thucydides when he said 'in peace and prosperity both states and individuals are actuated by higher motives ... but war ... is a hard master and tends to assimilate men's characters to their conditions',[6] which is echoed in Henry V's well-known monologue, though in another tone, that 'In peace there's nothing so becomes a man/As modest stillness and humility/But when the blast of war blows in our ears/Then imitate the action of the tiger ... Disguise fair nature with hard-favour'd rage'. You may consider it as a *jus in bello* issue, that war, as organized killing, can hardly be justified. I see the weapons as 'instruments of evil omen', which decent people only use on the compulsion of necessity. To glorify war is to delight in the slaughter of men. The victor, though with a right intention to conduct a war, has nevertheless killed multitudes of men, and thus should be treated with a rite of mourning rather than with triumph.

Yin Xi: But how should international society be structured to secure peace?

Lao Zi: My utopia is little states with small populations, an international system characterized by absolutely independent, instead of interdependent, units. For such a state, 'a neighbouring state is within sight, and the voices of the fowls and dogs can be heard all the way from it, but the people to old age, even to death, do not have any intercourse with it'.

Yin Xi: Master, I don't see any feasibility in the idea.

Lao Zi: You may think of it as a Platonic Form or Idea. The entire world says that, while my Dao is great, it yet appears to be unlike any object in reality. I say that it is just its greatness that makes Dao 'unlike'. If it were like any specific object, for long would it have been less and small.

Yin Xi: With such an interesting discussion about Dao of international politics, Master, I have to say, well said, but as for Dao, what is it? Is that the objective law of international politics, or the moral imperative of international agents, or something else?

Lao Zi: Dao is somewhat like the Stoic concept 'nature' (*phusis*), which refers to both the essence of the well-ordered cosmos, and the innate endowment of human beings. The ultimate goal of the Stoics is to live in agreement with nature. Similarly, I say that 'Man takes his law from the Earth; the Earth takes its law from Heaven; Heaven takes its law from Dao; The law of Dao is its being what it is'.[7] The great Dao is all-pervading. Its outflowing operation in everything, including human beings, is De (morality, virtue, or *aretē*, its equivalent in Greek), which nourishes us all. Dao and De, in the universe and human society, and thus in international politics as well, is in the sense of both 'is' and 'ought to be'.

Yin Xi: If Dao is the law of international politics, isn't the mission of scholars to reveal and explain the law, by which theory of international politics is built?

Lao Zi: Theory is the explanation of laws ... This is a popular 'social science' statement. I am afraid it has no reference to Dao. The very first line of my book is that 'the Dao that can be told or explained is not the enduring and unchanging Dao'. There is, however, nothing related to mysticism or agnosticism in it. The social science way presupposes the distinction between the observer as a subject and the observed as an object, while for understanding and following Dao, one needs to 'experience', to break the border between self and other, between subject and object. The term 'theory' looks scientific in its modern sense, but you know its Greek root is *theorein*, to spectate. To understand Dao is like appreciating a painting: there is no reason to keep yourself outside or distance yourself from what you observe. Instead, you must have an empathy with

	your object, or as Chinese always say, 'forget yourself and your object alike'.[8]
Yin Xi:	Last question, Master, which chapter or paragraph in your book do you think is most worth reading to students of IR?
Lao Zi:	Chapter fifty-four maybe. Most of the IR scholars today hypothesize an independent domain of international politics with its own laws, and thus observe the world from the per-spective of inter-national interactions. My advice in this chap-ter is to observe states from the perspective of states, while observing the world (all under heaven) from the perspective of the world, which signifies a holistic approach to and a cosmopolitan vision of world politics.
Yin Xi:	Thank you, Master. On your farewell, I wish you all the best and promise to preserve your great book and spread your thought.
Lao Zi:	Take it easy, my friend. Always remember that 'Dao in its regular course does nothing (for the sake of doing it), and so there is nothing which it does not do'.

Notes

1. The cited words are from *Chun Qiu Zuo Zhuan (Commentary of Zuo on the Spring and Autumn)*, a classical Chinese work compiled in the 5th or 4th cen-tury B.C, which was actually later than the era of Lao Zi. However, the history recorded in *Chun Qiu Zuo Zhuan* was from as early as the 7th century B.C., ear-lier than the dialogue in this chapter. I use James Legge's English translation here, with slight changes when necessary.
2. See previous note.
3. Dao in Chinese language has its original meaning of both 'way' and 'say'.
4. From the story of Croesus recorded by Herodotus in his *History*, translated into English by George Rawlinson.
5. The famous statement made by the Athenian envoy should not be under-stood as the opinion of Thucydides himself, however. The Athenians at the moment of Melian Dialogue were rather driven by 'hubris' than interests or fear, which led soon to the tragedy of the Sicilian expedition. Therefore, 'The strong do as they can and the weak suffer what they must' could be seen as a pathology of the powerful, instead of the doctrine of what powers should do.
6. Here I use the English translation of Benjamin Jowett.
7. 'Its being what it is', in the original Chinese text of Lao Zi, is 'Ziran', which is here used as an adjective, meaning 'for-itself and in-itself', usually trans-lated, however roughly, as 'spontaneous'. It is noteworthy that the same word 'Ziran', as noun, means 'Nature' in Chinese.
8. It is no surprise that Daoism is the school of philosophy most influential in Chinese classical arts (music, painting, calligraphy, etc.). Lao Zi's work might shed some light on a 'methodology of arts', instead of the methodology of social science, in international studies.

4
Thucydides (c.460–c.395 BCE): A Theorist for All Time

Richard Ned Lebow

'Thucydides son of Olorus thank you for agreeing to meet with me. It's only my second trip to the underworld and forgive me if I still find it disorienting.'

'I find it a strange place too, although for different reasons. You have more life to live. I'm in the shadows for eternity, although 2,500 years has passed more quickly than I imagined.'

'What do you do to kill time, so to speak?'

'For centuries, I kept busy avoiding Pericles, Cleon, Alcibiades and other people I would find it unpleasant to encounter. These days I spend a lot of time talking to old and new friends, observing the world above and deriving equal doses of amusement and frustration from how my text is read.'

'I understand why you would not want to engage Cleon and Alcibiades, but why Pericles?'

'For a long time he was very angry with me, always wanting to defend his decision to go to war and convinced that Plato and I were conspiring to blacken his reputation and deny him the honour he deserved. The honour extended to Demosthenes only made it worse, but Pericles has become friendlier of late. As you must know he's about the most unsociable of Greeks, so it is ironic that he seeks out my company, if only to complain.'

'What about your standing in the world above? You have certainly become a possession for all time, as you intended.'

'This pleases me, but I often get attention for the wrong reasons. My work is a possession for all time because there will always be powerful leaders and political units who succumb to hubris. Tragedy is an Athenian invention but a feature of the world. I'm always amazed by just how universal it is and at how little people learn from the past.

More troubling still is when they cite or quote me in support of policies I think almost certain to lead to catastrophe. Guilt is a Christian concept, so I feel none of it. But disappointment and sadness are another matter. I described how politicians distort language to justify actions that would otherwise be thought of as unjust, and how over time language changes to accommodate and normalize such behaviour. In the wildest dreams I never thought this would happen to my own words!'

'I started a controversy with my interpretation of your claim that your account of the Peloponnesian War was a possession of all time.'

'Why do you and everyone else keep calling it the Peloponnesian War? There were two wars, the Archidamian and Peloponnesian, just as there were two World Wars in the twentieth century.'

'Don't you agree that one was a continuation of the other?'

'Yes, but this is true of the World Wars as well.'

'There are some historians who treat them as part of a longer European civil war.'

'Not only do they use the Peloponnesian War as the title to my work, they describe it as a history – in almost all Western languages. This pisses me off. I was very clear that I was not writing a history, but an account of what I had seen and heard. Much of it is first hand.'

'Did you really hear or get reports of all those speeches? Are they accurate?'

'Even my friend Aristotle now explicitly acknowledges that *ta deonta* – what is necessary – should have led him to finally say what he only hinted at in his writings: that poetry truly is a higher form of truth than history. It tells us what should have been, whereas history is restricted to what actually happened.'

'So you put words in peoples' mouths?'

'That's a very narrow formulation of the truth! Surely, people read my account in part because my speeches led them to insights that would have been otherwise unattainable.'

'What about the introduction of books, paragraphs and sentences? Do you approve of these modern inventions? They certainly make your text easier to read.'

'For people too lazy to figure it out for themselves. Worse still are the translations. Even good ones cannot capture the meanings I embedded in the characteristic "men … de" [either, or] structure of Greek sentences. I also construct what you call paragraphs and books this way. It's only with extraordinary effort that I have learned to dumb myself down and speak in the simple declarative sentences necessary to make myself understood by moderns. Old Pericles can be a pain in the arse and pompous at times but he speaks wonderful, educated Greek. Usually, all I have to do is raise my bushy eyebrows to make him remember that he is having a conversation in the underworld, not giving a speech on the Pnyx. He really misses audiences and frequently tells me he could have taught modern politicians a thing or two about radio and television. I egg him on by asking how good his tweets would be and he predictably flies into a rage. "What sort of civilization", he growls, "would limit its messages to 140 characters?" Even a Spartiate would be appalled!'

'If I can return to your expectations about readers. Did you think they learn anything from your account of the Archidamian and Peloponnesian Wars? And could awareness of hubris and its likely consequences reduce its frequency? My critics accuse me of hubris by even raising this possibility.'

'Sophocles, Euripides and I have often have this debate. They take opposing sides. Sophocles is convinced that tragedy has great pedagogical – there's an honest Greek word for you – value. He wrote Oedipus with this end in mind. He was a synecdoche – I'm on a roll here – for Athens and intended to question faith in the conquering power of reason. Euripides never tires of reminding Sophocles of what little effect the play had, his personal theatrical triumph aside. But then Euripides is a curmudgeon and a product of his time perhaps who sees only the darker side of human nature. He never stops telling us both how modern history amply confirms his pessimism.'

'Where do you stand?'

'Depends on the day. When I think about all the folly that has occurred since I came here I'm tempted to side with Euripides. But I remain hopeful that some lessons have been learned, or could be, by people that count. Having to cater to the demos and big business only makes it more difficult. The former is moved by its emotions and the latter by its purse. It's a most unusual politician who can safely sail the ship of state between these two dangerous reefs. Look at the way your country responded to the events of 9/11 by invading Afghanistan and Iraq, and how that Russian Putin is playing up to nationalist opinion to advance his personal goals and the expense of regional peace. And then there's global warming. Many of your compatriots deny it is happening. I give my fellow Greeks credit for at least recognizing their failures. Poor Oedipus put his eyes out, not to deny, but to see better.'

'Surely Aristotle believed that tragedy could teach ethical lessons? The Viennese Freud thinks the first step towards Enlightenment is understanding the scripts you enact and developing a commitment to avoid destructive ones.'

'Yes, Aristotle has had further thoughts on this subject – and every other subject for that matter. We tease him about just how wrong his scientific writings have proven and he keeps reminding us of how on target he was with aesthetics, ethics and politics. Look, I did write with the idea that successful societies would always overreach themselves but also with the hope that it might sometimes be prevented from studying the past. I was certainly right about my first prediction and alas, have seen little evidence in support of my second. Could we change the topic?'

'Yes, of course. You died before you could complete your account. How would you have ended it?'

'Therein lies a tale. I've thought and rethought about this so much, to be frank, I no longer know what I originally intended. I'm not alone in feeling this way. I attend a bi-weekly seminar on the subject.'

'A seminar? On what subject?'

'Unfinished works. Clausewitz, Mozart and Schubert are among the regulars, and so are a few artists like Dante who now have second thoughts about having finished their works.

Those most troubled are those whose works have disappeared. Sappho and Heraclitus never stop lamenting their fate. Sappho has written a couple of odes on the subject. She keeps hoping new papyri will be discovered in Egyptian sands with more of her lost poems. It's rumoured that Democritas got into big trouble for making contact with a visitor and bribing him to bring copies of some of his best writings upside. He's absolutely furious at what people read into the few fragments they possess, although he never stops saying nice things about Diels and Krantz for collecting and publishing what was preserved.'

'How does Mozart feel about Sussmayr's completion of his Requiem?'

'Let's stay on topic, shall we, as my handlers will soon whisk me away.'

'Okay, back to the conclusion of your masterwork. What do you think you intended to write?'

'I was deeply conflicted. I naturally wanted to finish my account, but the closer I came the more painful did it become. I just did not want to describe my city's final defeat and humiliation. Giving an account of the Sicilian expedition was bad enough. When illness overtook me I was still alert but did not have the emotional energy to push ahead. I put my stylus down and thought about more pleasant things: my youth, symposia, flute girls, feasts of freshly smoked eels....'

'Now you're wandering from the topic.'

'Young man, behave yourself. You asked what I would have written and I'm trying hard to recapture my self of the moment. Do you often think about women and eels?'[1]

'Less about eels, although I adore Unagi.'

'Unagi?'

'Japanese freshwater eels on a bed of sushi rice. I think about women all the time, but I don't want to change the subject. So tell me more about your conclusion.'

'Well, I faced a couple of problems. I thought about stopping my narrative with the failure Sicilian expedition. The rest was just the inevitable aftermath and, as you recognize. It was the second *hamartia* [an old Homeric word for missing the mark in archery], the first being the alliance with Corcyra. My framing still sticks in Pericles' craw. The defeat in Sicily was the consequence of overextension and there was really no reason to continue my narrative. It's not unlike the problem Mozart and Da Ponte confronted with Don Giovanni. Once he was carried away by the Commendatore – to our underworld, not Christian hell – the drama is over and the opera is resolved with a final D-minor chord. Yet, he felt compelled to write a final scene in which the surviving characters lament their fate and mouth platitudes about the Don and his lifestyle. Thank Zeus and Athena we Greeks didn't have to cope with moralistic, Christian censors the way Enlightenment artists did! On another visit, I'll introduce you to some of the later – they're my buddies.'

'The other problems?'

'I've already told you about the angst of confronting the final defeat, occupation, tyranny and near-stasis of my beloved city. Another difficulty was intellectual. Once the two acts of hubris were resolved and my double tragedy was concluded I had no framework to encompass what would have followed. Herodotus, Plato and Aristotle, and more recently, Hobbes, Gibbon and George Grote, have suggested narrative strategies they think would do the trick. I'm not persuaded by any of them, but pleased that they have made the effort to work them out. I'm starting a collection of alternative endings and perhaps could convince a publisher, or at least post my text on a website along with a ranking of these endings. We could do an experiment and see what people like the most and why.'

'So you get to meet all kinds of modern people?'

'Only those who request an audience. Some are really interesting and others are tedious, sometimes in the extreme. There are the so-called realists – speak of gross distortion – who insist – and refuse to be persuaded to the contrary – that I intended the Melian Dialogue, not as a pathology, but as a description of reality and a guide for others. A while back I received a visit from a very well-dressed wife of one of your former presidents who thought I was another Greek shipping magnate. For some reason, she insisted that we chat in French.'

'If you had to write an ending?'

'I'll tell you what I wouldn't do. There would be no conclusion. I can't get over the simplistic and boring format used by your historians and social scientists. They have introductions and conclusions that tell readers what the work is about and what lessons they should come away with, all in the authorial voice. Neither Plato nor I could abide the sophists, but they did develop a sophisticated format that compels readers to use their minds to get beneath their texts and, if done well, convince themselves that they conclusions they formulate are original rather than those they are intended to reach. Those sophists could teach Madison Avenue a thing or two about persuasion!'

'Without a finished narrative or conclusion you give readers the opportunity to impose almost any interpretation they want on your work.'

'They would do this anyway. Look at all the nonsense that's been written about Virgil, Shakespeare and Pushkin. And I'm not talking student essays! There are postmodernists who think they can do anything with a text, and that everything is a text. I don't get angry on the rare occasion I read them because I can't understand what they are trying to say, and I'm not sure they do either.'

'Realists aside, are you unhappy with other readings of your work?'

'For the most part no. I find them endlessly fascinating. I learn something about myself from reading what others fathom about my intentions – even when they are completely wrong. I quiz myself about my response. Then there is Nietzsche, who put in language something Greek authors already knew and counted on: that our texts extend beyond ourselves. Not only does every generation read them in light of their concerns, there is ever greater distance between them and texts they read. Maybe I need to find another word; 'text' has lost its appeal given how postmodernists abuse it.'

'Do you think at least some of these readings are worthwhile?'

'All readings tell us something, and Herodotus and I can be read against each other and the tragic playwrights. Later interpreters put our works in perspectives that were unavailable to us. We keep learning from these readings, and Herodotus finds many of them flattering. He always resented being dismissed as unprofessional and a myth-teller and is pleased that in recent years his reputation has been resurrected – better if I say "restored".'

'Herodotus is easy to flatter, unlike me. But I anger more easily, and especially when those realists take my Melian Dialogue out of context and use it to teach their students to formulate interests narrowly and violate norms whenever it appears to suit their purposes – which it rarely does. I'm afraid my time is up.'

'I'm very sorry you have to go. You said your handlers would be here shortly?'

'Yes, that's right. They know how keen I am to see the last episode of Wolf Hall and the programme is about to begin. I can't keep Aristophanes and Brasidas waiting. They're already mixing the wine.'

Note

1. Athenians were fixated on eels as a culinary and quasi-erotic treat.

5
Discussing War with Plato (429–347 BCE)

Christopher Coker

In 1947 the philosopher Alfred Whitehead, ten years after retiring from Harvard, meets up with Plato in a dream.

Whitehead: '… Well, at least I think this is a dream. Of all the philosophers who have lived, or so I have told my students, you were the most important, you know. I even told them that all other philosophy was merely a footnote to your work.'

Plato: 'I'm not sure what a footnote actually is. But please don't bother to tell me. Consider yourself fortunate that I'm willing to talk to a barbarian at all. The conversation we're having may prove interesting, but from my point of view it's hardly likely to be instructive. Where did you say you come from?'

Whitehead: 'It's a country in what you would call the "northern world".'

Plato: 'I suppose you're what Herodotus calls a Hyperborean, one of the peoples from the back of the North Wind? Barbarians aren't great thinkers. You produce charms and enchantments, not arguments. You're not a philosophical people … So you come from the future, you say? What's it like? I suppose it is just like the past. Nothing ever changes, you know; everything that will happen has probably happened before.'

Whitehead: 'Well, the country in which I was born and the one to which I have moved – we call it America – are both democracies. You would recognize us as such, I suppose. You Athenians, after all, invented the concept before it vanished for almost 2,000 years.'

Plato: 'And much good it did us! You can only have a work-
                 able democracy, I have always insisted, if the soul of the
                 demos is cultivated. And it became clear to me early in life
                 that a city that chose Alcibiades to lead the expedition to
                 Syracuse in the Great War, and later condemned Socrates
                 to death, was lacking in such cultivation. For me, both
                 events were proof enough that democracy is corrupting.
                 It all went wrong anyway, long before Salamis. The vic-
                 tory of the oarsmen proved to be the victory of the worst
                 kind: the poor landless people to which Athens in its
                 infinite wisdom still sees fit to pay a pension for life. And
                 do you think democracies can fight wars? Look what
                 happened at Aegospotami – they executed twelve of our
                 admirals – the best and brightest, well certainly the best,
                 for not rescuing the sailors who drowned in a storm at sea.
                 Do you know that but for that we might even have won
                 the war? Anyway, I suppose you'd tell me that democracy
                 flourishes in your world?'

Whitehead: 'I wish I could. Twenty years ago we fought a war to make
                 the world safe for democracy. I lost my son Eric to it. It
                 didn't quite work out as we hoped. In the years that fol-
                 lowed most democratic societies in fact seemed to go into
                 retreat. We have just fought another war. When it began
                 there were only 12 democracies left in the world. And
                 soon we're likely to find ourselves locked into another
                 internecine conflict with a former ally, Russia.'

Plato: 'The Scythians, again, hey?'

Whitehead: 'Well, anyway, not quite the ones Herodotus tells us
                 about.'

Plato: 'I fear that war in your world is a constant? Unfortunately,
                 the same is true of ours. Every Greek city is in a state of
                 permanent war with another.'

'Whitehead: You are very interested in war, aren't you, more so than
                 most philosophers? I used to tell my students that there
                 are more references to war in *The Republic* than there
                 are to any other phenomenon; even the word "peace"
                 appears it would seem only to amplify war's absence.'

Plato: 'How could I not be interested? It robbed me of the
                 political career that was my due. But I don't regret that.
                 Philosophy is the only calling. But can you imagine what
                 might have happened if Socrates, the noblest man I have

ever known had died on the battlefield of Delium, which he nearly did. I was only five years old at the time. I probably wouldn't have embarked on the life I did. Of course, the battle made Socrates famous for his bravery and especially his presence of mind in standing his ground against the Locrian horsemen.[1] Had he tried to flee like the generals in command he would have been cut down.

The task of a philosopher is to explain how the world works, to mobilize the power of argument and reason, to understand the logic behind things. Not that as a barbarian you'd recognize this. We fight war quite differently from you. I did concede in *The Republic* if you care to look for the passage, that courage is not unique to Greeks; barbarians show it too, but the desire to learn, I'm afraid, is unique to us, and it's only through instruction that we learn the prudent use of bravery. Courage should be a matter of practical intelligence, not passion.'

Whitehead: 'Didn't you make this point in *The Laches*? I recall that Socrates tells the sons of Aristides and Thucydides of Melissia that their fathers had sadly neglected their education.'

Plato: 'Glad to see you know my work so well. Yes, Socrates tells them that their fathers might be great generals, but they had neglected to pass on their skills to their sons. One of the parties to the dialogue, you may also recall, is Nikias, who originally opposed the expedition to Syracuse, even though it was his fate to have to command one of the forces that sailed there. The whole debate in the Assembly was a generational conflict between the old and the young, Nikias representing the former and Alcibiades of course the latter, with the young as always anxious to prove themselves, at the cost of being reckless. You may also recall that Aristides and Thucydides tell Socrates that one day they will want their own sons trained first in the art of fencing. They missed the point entirely, didn't they? What's the point of swordplay if you don't know the true nature of courage? Philosophy is deadly serious because the consequences of not philosophizing can be just that – deadly'.

Whitehead: 'And you were also the first writer, as far as I know, to attach as much importance to numeracy as to language; you are the very first to insist on the importance of mathematics. In *The Protagoras* you make much of the superiority of *techne* which I suppose can be translated as the development of foresight over *tuche*, which is usually translated in my world as "luck" or "fate". And *techne* of course, in your eyes, is a branch of mathematics.'

Plato: 'Yes, I wanted to show how through the study of philosophy and mathematics you can manage your own needs and to some extent order the future.[2] What I'm trying to say is that ethics and strategy can be quantified. It's possible to gauge in each situation the quantity of a single value (like courage) and maximize it. And, mathematics to be sure has a more practical use as well. Geometry enables the formation of an army in battle, and arithmetic is useful for a soldier because it enables him to marshal all his forces.'

Whitehead: 'And you think these rules allow for moderation?'

Plato: 'No, they permit thoughtfulness. The problem with the Great War was that it threatened to turn "war" (*polemos*) into *stasis* (internecine conflict). That's why I argued in *The Republic* that we Greeks needed more codified rules of behaviour. Our conflict with Sparta was really a civil war, a domestic quarrel. I propose the only way to avoid another such conflict would be to see conflict between Greeks as similar to a philosophical dialogue. Defeat and victory would then be seen as a way of bringing an opponent round to one's own point of view, getting him to see reason, or at least to concede the argument for the time being. I would like war to be more reasonable, by which I mean not more humane, but more rational.'

Whitehead: 'Well, we trusted to the same principles in our own Great War (which one of our historian-philosophers, a man called Arnold Toynbee, compared with your Great War – it was one of his more inspired thoughts). I doubt, however, whether you would warm to him. He's a great reductionist. But, there's something I'd like to pursue a little further. What I find interesting about your views on war is the way in which you try to tame the warrior.'

Plato: 'Of course. A state needs warriors but not Homer's heroes. What I find most dangerous about our great poet's depiction of Achilles is the latter's intense self-absorption. He may be a hero, but his single-minded pursuit of reputation blinds him at times to the world he shares with others. Of course, if he were totally undeserving of admiration we wouldn't revere him at all. I go out of my way to show he has a number of virtues that are admirable, such as honour and undeniable bravery. But his spirit is disordered; he is clearly very unhappy and he is unhappy because of his inability to forge lasting friendships. Remember in *The Iliad* even Nestor says of him that he will enjoy his valour in loneliness. Paradoxically, it's because he has no friends that he's too much in love with life. He really cannot imagine the value of other people and therefore what value his own death might have for others. He's not willing to sacrifice himself for anyone else.

I make it a point to say that the warriors of the future should be trained by those who know about intellectual pursuits such as arithmetic and geometry. Not that I am against physical strength, by the way. Gymnastics is important too; warriors have to be healthy both in body and soul. You have to know when to run, and when to hold your ground, as Socrates did at Delium. But you can only be in harmony with yourself if spiritedness is distinguished from desire. Otherwise, spirit will be infected by desire soon enough.'

Whitehead: 'Indeed, I think this is your great contribution to our understanding of war: the wish to bring spirit, desire and reason into balance. Sometimes, I can't help thinking you take it a little far, particularly when you suggest young boys should be taken onto the battlefield to learn about war at first hand. We have an author who wrote a book called *Brave New World* – a really frightening vision of the distant future, in which young boys are brought to hospital to see the old dying.'

Plato: 'But the death of an old man from illness has little to tell us about life; the death of a young man in battle tells us everything. We seek the "good" in order to live a better life on the understanding that it is the only life we live. But if you are a warrior by calling you can find death life-affirming. Death can even settle the account. That's why I discourage excessive mourning (like Achilles' mourning for Patroclus). In suggesting that children should be allowed to witness battles early in life I wanted them to grasp the fact that courage is aroused in those who believe they are fighting in defence of their city.'

Whitehead: 'You know, in my world your reputation has suffered from your wish to ban Homer from your ideal city. But I think I now understand why you do.'

Plato: 'I have no quarrel with Homer as a poet but I do as an instructor of morals. I am, I like to think, something of a poet myself – my metaphors are praised by many. I am also a supreme stylist, unlike some I could mention. Have you tried reading Thucydides? I even cast my own thoughts in the form of dialogues you could re-enact on stage, I suppose, but for the crucial fact that the parties to the dialogue have no real character of their own – but then why should they? I want my readers to see themselves in the characters I portray, and they may not always like what's reflected back. But my quarrel with Homer is that we are seduced by his artistry to admire even a man who is in no way admirable, even a man such as Achilles who we would be ashamed to resemble in real life.'

Whitehead: 'I have to disagree, I'm afraid. I grant that as you say the artist makes "the soul relax its guard". We can indeed be seduced by our stories but a great artist can show us aspects of the real we don't always see. Art, after all, doesn't offer an escape from reality; surely it animates it?'

Plato: 'Whatever.'

Whitehead: 'Might I ask why you cast your arguments in the form of dialogues, by the way?'

Plato: 'At the risk of belabouring the point, a dialogue, you should understand, is not a trial in which two protagonists make equally strong cases and a jury in the end has to decide which to believe. Both parties must be prepared to recognize the superior arguments of the other, and find their positions reversed, or simply to find at the end that they are left without an argument which is believable. The purpose of a dialogue, after all, is not to produce a consensus – the gods forbid – but to strengthen the bonds between the participants through a free exchange of ideas. The decision to abide by the result shows respect for the dialogue itself and the people one's in conversation with.'

Whitehead: 'And that I suppose is why Socrates always has the last word? Or perhaps, if I may be bold, I should say you do.'

Plato: 'What are you implying?'
Whitehead: 'Well, surely the Socrates that makes an appearance in
                your work is actually *you*? There's a Greek philosopher
                called Diogenes who will follow you who claimed that
                Socrates once heard you reading *The Lysis* and com-
                mented, "by Herakles, what lies this young man is telling
                about me!".'
Plato: 'And did this Diogenes witness this episode or report what
                he was told. Don't listen to tittle-tattle.'

*(at this point, Whitehead overhears himself thinking: this conversation itself
is becoming a bit like a Platonic dialogue)*

Whitehead: 'But, if I may continue with my line of enquiry. You are
                the first person and the last for about 2,000 years, who
                suggested that women could serve as soldiers. Were you
                being disingenuous?'
Plato: 'Remember, I said that physical fitness has no bearing
                on what seems to be an almost universal reluctance –
                amongst Greeks and barbarians – to prevent women from
                serving as soldiers. Why is that so? Take the case of guard
                dogs: both male and female are equally efficient, from
                which one can conclude that any educational system
                should be able to produce female warriors, too. To the
                objection that different sexes have different innate abili-
                ties, I would concede only that people are obviously dif-
                ferently inclined, but that their inclinations have nothing
                to do with any innate ability'.
Whitehead: 'So I suppose you would be seen as an early feminist?'
Plato: 'What do you mean by that?'
Whitehead: 'Well, we now allow women to vote, you may be surprised
                to hear, though we don't allow them to bear arms.'
Plato: 'But don't be obtuse, I'm not arguing that most women
                are capable of bearing arms. I'm only arguing that in the
                case of a few it may be possible to cultivate manly virtues –
                because you know, there are manly souls in some female
                bodies. I don't think you can train out natural desires, but
                masculinity in a woman, if it exists, can be brought out.
                Anyway, if I were you, I wouldn't take it too seriously.'
Whitehead: 'Anyway, you will probably be glad to know that even in my
                century women won't be donning uniform anytime soon!'

(It was at this point that Whitehead himself woke up, just before he could ask Plato whether he was indeed the author of the Seventh Letter. He died a few months later still wondering whether he should not have insisted on explaining what a footnote actually is).

Notes

1. See Victor Davis Hanson, 'Socrates dies at Delium', in Robert Cowley (ed.) *More What If: Eminent Historians Imagine What Might Have Been* (London: Macmillan, 2002).
2. See Martha Nussbaum, *The Fragility of Goodness; Luck and Ethics in Greek Philosophy and Tragedy* (Cambridge: Cambridge University Press, 1986), p. 95.

6

Aristotle (384–322 BCE): The Philosopher and the Discipline

Anthony F. Lang, Jr

International Studies Association Convention, Big US City, sometime in the future

Chair:	Welcome, ladies and gentlemen, to this Senior Scholars Panel. If you could please find your seats, we can begin.
Aristotle:	Oh my goodness, this is just wonderful. I can't believe this. This is wonderful.
Chair (quietly to Aristotle):	Professor ... er Mr ... Aristotle, could you please get off the floor? We need to begin.
Aristotle:	I'm sorry, it's just that this, what did you call it, 'electricity' is simply amazing. The concept behind it is incredible. You said something about positive and negative electrons alternating? I want to know more about electrons. I need more information on this. Can we simply hold off until later? [He goes back beneath the panel table and looks carefully at the wires.]
Chair:	I promise, we can discuss this later. Can you please be seated? [Louder] So, we can begin, I think? Today, we are lucky to have a guest from our collective past, Aristotle, who will be the subject of our Senior Scholars Panel. If I can please introduce our guests: First, we have Professor Realist, who comes from University Ivy and has published widely on power, institutions and war. Second, we have Professor Positivist from University Midwest, who has published

on methods, statistics and foreign policy analysis. Third, we have Professor Critical, from University Europe, who has published on international political theory, securitization and constructivism. Next we have Professor History from University England who has published on international society, imperialism and responsibility. Finally, we have Professor Gender from University Australia who has published on gender, critical theory and poststructuralism. Welcome to you all. Can I first ask our guest of honour to say something about his orientation to the field of International Relations?

Aristotle (fumbling with convention computer on the table): Ah, yes, I would like to use this machine here if I could? Does it project some kind of light or substance on the wall behind us? I saw someone else using it. Can I learn to use this, please?

Chair: Aristotle, we are more interested in your ideas about international relations? Or even politics?

Aristotle: Oh, of course, politics. Yes, I have much to say about this. But we can return later to the electricity and machines, yes? I do so wonder at the world around me, and your world is immensely wonderful.

Chair: [Somewhat annoyed] We only have 10 minutes for an opening, so perhaps we could hear your ideas?

Aristotle: Minutes? I'm not sure I know what you mean there? Well, in any case, let me begin. As you know, it is nature that begins and ends our inquiries. I have spent much of my efforts in studying the works of nature. My teacher, Plato, was more interested in the world of ideas, but I wished to see the world as it is, the real world. I spent many long days in the lagoon in Pyrrha, a wondrous place filled with fish, scallops, birds, molluscs, simply an abundance of life. Have you ever wondered about the shape of the nautilus shell? Why is it curved in the way it is? Empedocles and others had their theories, but of

	course I realized that it must relate to the way in which it moves upon the waters. This locomotive effect, then, is what defines the nautilus in terms of its peculiar features. As I investigated further, I realized that the reasons must be deeper still, related to the difference between living on land and sea and how an animal, a living creature, could be able to do both. I then …

Professor Realist: I'm afraid I don't see how this is relevant. I have a celebration of my life thrown by my influential students to attend in a few hours. In what ways does this relate to the nature of conflict and war?

Aristotle: Nature of conflict and war? Well, I will get to conflict and war eventually, but, again, I think we might first seek to explain what we mean by nature, should we not? For me, nature defines our investigation, for within nature there is meaning. But that meaning will not be found by simplistic reflections on ideal types as Plato suggested. No, we must look to the reality around us, we must compare like and unlike, and from this comparison we can create our categories by which we continue our investigations.

Professor Positivist: Precisely! Only through a rigorous comparative method can we find the answers to the fundamental questions of why there is war.

Aristotle: Excellent, a fellow comparativist! What do you compare, if I may ask?

Professor Positivist: Well, I have recently added to the Correlates of War database a new category of analysis, one that should hopefully solidify our findings on democracies and war.

Aristotle: Indeed, you have also found that democracies are warlike? I have only comparisons from Greece, but perhaps you can add others. It seems the world has grown a great deal since my time, or at least more of the world has been discovered.

[Awkward silence]
Professor Positivist: Well, in fact, we have found that democracies do not go to war with each other in our comparisons.

Aristotle: So, is that common wisdom according to you? I think we ought to begin with that, though I'm not sure we should trust it.

Professor Realist: Yes, I agree, we certainly should not trust this. It may be common wisdom among some, but I do not think it is correct. Power differentials are a better predictor than domestic structure for determining war.

Aristotle: It appears the common wisdom is not shared by all. This is quite a good beginning point for our investigation. So, how should we proceed? Perhaps we need to determine what is the essence of war? And of democracy?

Professor Realist: According to Clausewitz, war is the continuation of politics by other means, i.e., violent means.

Aristotle: Yes, perhaps. Though, I am not sure this is how we ought to define politics. Is not politics the activity of ruling and being ruled? And, does it not entail, ultimately, the use of reason and language to persuade our fellows?

Professor Realist: I am only appealing to the authority of one of the greatest writers on war who has ever lived. Is that not how scholarship ought to progress, by turning to the greats? We could even go to one of your colleagues, Thucydides. Did he not teach us that war comes from fear of the other in a system of anarchy?

Aristotle: That disgraced general who sought to justify his views in his disputed history of the war? His ancestor of the same name was a great man, one who was essential in moving Athens toward its constitutional order. But the Thucydides to whom you refer, well, I'm not so sure he has much to tell us. Perhaps he might be relevant in our investigation, as would your friend Clausewitz. At the same time, while we ought to respect authority, we also ought to observe, compare and analyse in order to come to some conclusions about war and democracy. So, to return to our question, do democracies go to war with each? You have offered us one definition of war, that of politics by violent means. I do not think this is the essence of war. It would seem that war is better understood as conflict and competition. And, we know of course that it allows men to practice their virtue, the virtues of courage and wisdom. So, perhaps it is an activity in which might teach us how to act politically, in that some of the virtues are shared by both?

Professor Realist: Hmmm. Perhaps.

Professor Critical: I would just like to interject here, if I may? Is not war something that we construct? Is it real in the sense in which you are both discussing it? I think that–

Professor Realist: Here we go ...

Professor Critical: I am sorry you still feel that investigating the nature of language and its relation to international politics is so unimportant. But, I think Wittgenstein and Giddens and so many others have demonstrated its centrality to our investigations that we must take them seriously.

Aristotle: Yes, yes, of course language is important.

Professor Critical: As you can see, our guest agrees with us.

Aristotle: Language, or reason, what we call *logos* in my tongue, defines the nature of what it means to be a person. For it is language that differentiates us from all other animals, is it not? Without it, we could not understand the nature of the universe and our place in it.

Professor Critical: Yes, indeed, language is central. So, we can then conclude that any investigation into the question of war and democracy is in fact an investigation into the ways in which these words, this language, constructs the reality of democracy and war. And, ...

Aristotle: Ah, excuse me. I am not sure what you mean there. Language does not construct our world, does it? Language and our ability to rationalize about the world is the first and primary element of our nature as humans. But, language is simply a way to categorize the reality of our world. The words we use can be made to construct either a proposition, which can be true or false, or a judgment, which is located in the mind of the individual person. So, when you speak of language constructing

	the world, you must be speaking of judgments not propositions? But, if so, science should begin with propositions not with judgments.
Professor Critical:	True and false are simply judgments, are they not? They have no actual foundation in reality.
Aristotle:	Hmmm. I am not sure what you mean by this, though perhaps we are using language differently here. Let me suggest a different way of approaching this. So, we might begin by seeking to discover the primary elements involved in war and democracy. In terms of war, we might begin with the element of the army or weapons, could we not?
Professor Critical:	But a weapon is not real unless we define it as a weapon. A gun is simply a piece of metal with gunpowder and a spark to make the bullet fly forward. This is not necessarily a weapon, but only a weapon because we define it as such. It is our discourse that turns the metal into a weapon.
Aristotle:	I am quite interested in this thing you call a gun; I assume it shoots out some sort of a projectile? As an arrow?
Professor Critical:	Yes, sorry, I forgot you may not know what that is. We might consider a sword instead.
Aristotle:	Yes, a sword, I know this. But, it is not my perception of a sword which makes it a sword. There are, I would suggest, four causes to this thing. There is the material from which it is made, the bronze, wood and twine; there is the blacksmith who made it; there is the form of it, which can vary but which must include a blade and a handle in some configuration; and, most importantly, there is its purpose, which is to cut and kill in battle.
Professor Critical:	But you know it could be used for other things, such as cutting down a tree or slaughtering animals, yes?
Aristotle:	I am afraid not. For that you would either use an axe or a butcher's knife. The sword is for fighting in battle. It may share the form of the butcher's knife, having a blade and a handle; indeed, they may be almost identical. But in the end it is the purpose, its *telos*, its final function that defines it

Professor Critical: as a sword. The sword is for fighting and killing in battle, nothing more nothing less.

Professor Critical: Well, then, what is the purpose of war? It cannot be so simply defined as the purpose of sword, can it? And what is the purpose of democracy? I'm afraid I simply cannot accept your move to some sort of mystical ontology from what is essentially a matter of epistemology.

Aristotle: But there is nothing other than ontology, is there? The nature of being is what we are trying to discover here. And, I do not think my ontology is mystical, not at all. Compared with Plato, well, I am much more grounded in the nature of reality than he and perhaps many others. The causes of which I speak are readily evident in the natural world that surrounds us. As to the nature of war and democracy, I thought that is what we were seeking to investigate. I do not have the final answer to this, but I think we are moving forward. I am still intrigued by the question of whether or not democracies go to war. I see that received opinion suggests that they do not, but I do not quite agree with this. So, we need further discussion and debate about this.

Professor History: Could I perhaps take us into slightly different territory? I understand the importance of the war and democracy question, though this has become a bit of a preoccupation with my friends in the United States. Might I suggest a different question?

Aristotle: Well, if we might come back to the war and democracy question later, yes, of course. What do you wish to discuss.

Professor History: I am curious, Aristotle, whether you think an imperialistic foreign policy is justified? In light of the history of not only Athens but Macedon too, I would think this would be something you have considered?

[Awkward silence]
Aristotle: As you know, my pupil, Alexander, went on to become a rather strong, ah, advocate of expanding the Greek world. I believe the best political order is one that enables a form of civic friendship, one

	in which all citizens know and interact with each other. So, it would seem that such a thing is not possible in an empire.
Professor History:	But our world does not contain such polities; the smallest has more than 100,000 people.
Aristotle:	What of the largest?
Professor History:	More than one billion.
Aristotle:	This surely must be a disordered polity. It cannot function. How does political life take place? There can be no deliberation. Individuals could not become citizens, for they would have no chance to rule, much less learn how to be ruled. I simply cannot envision such a political community.
Professor History:	But Alexander created an empire with very large numbers. And even the Amphictyionic League? This brought together a great group of Greek city states, did it not?
Aristotle:	Yes, of course, but this was a religious league, one designed to protect the temples in times of war. It did not create citizenship or allow individuals to rule. It had a diplomatic function, to be sure, but it was no polity, I can assure of that.
Professor History:	I am sorry, Aristotle, but polities as you envision them are simply not applicable in our world. The size of the world and the technology that has been created to enable greater interactions – these are radically different than your day. I do not think your reflections on politics have relevance any longer.
Aristotle:	Well, I hope that is not the case. Perhaps I might ask a few questions, though, to see if my reflections still remain relevant?
Professor History:	Of course, please do. It's your panel, after all.
Aristotle:	If you are correct, and the world has changed so radically, we might well want to consider the nature of change. Is it not the case that all things change?
Professor History:	Indeed, they do. This is what history tells us.
Aristotle:	But, is there not a worry that too much change, particularly in political life, will be a problem? For rapid change in politics leads to revolution, and revolution is not conducive to a life of thought, pleasure and the development of the virtues. So, I would

	think we want to identify those things in political life that might hinder revolutionary change.
Professor History:	I'm afraid that is impossible. All things change, the human person evolves.
Aristotle:	Indeed, I would not deny some elements of this. But, does the human person change? Does he truly evolve? I would think there is something essential about the human person, something that does not change. If we can identify that, can we not protect ourselves against the dangers of rapid, revolutionary change?
Professor History:	Well, perhaps you are right. But I think it may well be difficult, if not impossible, to find any unity across the diversity of the human condition.
Aristotle:	This may be the case, but because political life is about the human person, should we not begin there? Has the human person changed?
Professor History:	From your day, perhaps not. In terms of evolution, the great changes happened far previous to that.
Aristotle:	Good, so we can start here. What differentiates the human person from the rest of reality?
Professor History:	Well, I'm not sure. This seems a question more for biologists and other scientists than it does for us.
Aristotle:	But, my good man, is it not the case that we are all scientists?
Professor History:	I am not scientist, I can tell you that. I believe in a humanistic approach to knowledge, one that refuses to use quantitative methods or other such nonsense.
Aristotle:	I am not sure what you mean by quantitative methods, but if you mean measuring things with numbers, I'm not sure why you would object to that.
Professor History:	They cannot capture the reality of the human condition, and they distort the reality they seek to measure. Consider the question of democracies and war – there is no way to quantitatively measure how many democracies there are in the world. There are simply too many differences and divergences to capture that reality. The entire exercise is flawed, I'm afraid.
Aristotle:	I am not sure I agree; science is merely ensuring that our propositions are true and that they reflect

	the reality of our world. But, in any case, let us go back to the question of the human person. If we consider reality, there does seem something that makes us different. We are active in the way that rocks, earth, water and air are not. True?
Professor History:	I suppose so.
Aristotle:	We are part of those things that are living, plants and animals. Plants do not move, animals do. So, this makes us part of the animal world.
Professor History:	Yes, proceed.
Aristotle:	But, we clearly differ from animals, do we not? No animal thinks or communicates as we do? Is this not so?
Professor Gender:	May I please jump in here? I've been listening so far very carefully to you, Aristotle, waiting for us to get close to my own concerns, which I will get to in a moment. But, at this point, I must disagree with you. Dolphins and monkeys communicate in ways that are not dissimilar from us. Further, there is no good reason to believe that animals don't have the same rights as we do, in terms of not being subject to pain.
Aristotle:	Ah, so, I was not entirely sure who you are. [To the chair] Do women usually participate in such deliberations? This is, ah, different from my world, I must say.
Chair:	Yes, of course, Aristotle, women are full-fledged members of our academic community.
Aristotle:	But, you only have one on the panel. Are there others?
Chair:	Yes, well, true, our ideal is that women are full members of the community, but of course, we have not quite achieved that yet in our numbers.
Professor Gender:	I am finding this conversation rather offensive, for many reasons. However, perhaps we can return to the question of animals and persons before proceeding further with the question of women?
Aristotle:	Yes, of course. To be honest, if you have evidence that dolphins, monkeys and other animals share the ability to communicate, this would be important. But, I'm afraid that it is not simply

	communication on its own. It is, what I mentioned earlier, *logos*, and the ability to combine the spoken (and written) word with reason. Do these animals share this? Do they reflect on themselves and what they are doing? Can they articulate issues within the form of a syllogism, the master concept of scientific investigation?
Professor Gender:	Well, I doubt that. But the fact that a person cannot reason does not make her any less a person. So, that alone cannot be what differentiates us.
Aristotle:	Yes, I agree, that there are some who reason better than others. But this simply means they are more virtuous than their fellow persons. So, I would suggest that there is the potential for reasoned speech and discourse among all persons, even if it is not fully developed. Could we agree on this?
Professor Gender:	Yes, I suppose we can.
Aristotle:	There is, then, one more element that differentiates us from other animals. We live in communities, political communities, ones that are designed to advance our good as persons. Do animals have this?
Professor Gender:	Well, animals do live in community. Dolphins swim in pods with some evidence that they have the ability to structure their interactions in accordance with forms of hierarchy.
Aristotle:	Yes, but they do not deliberate about the nature of their political structure, do they? Further, I am not convinced, unless you have learned otherwise, that they structure their interactions in such a way that allows for true political community, a political community dedicated to the good.
Professor Gender:	No political community is dedicated to the good, at least none that I know of. Moreover, the good means nothing. My friend, Professor Critical, might argue that the good is something we construct together and so exists.
Professor Critical:	Indeed, I believe moral norms are central to political life.
Professor Gender:	I do not. The good is nothing more than something used by the powerful, by men, by the wealthy, by

	all with power to disempower the weak. It is a failed concept that we must abandon.
Aristotle:	But, certainly, every political community is devoted to some good, or it would not exist. All things, all persons, all activities seek toward that which is good for them. And, if we agree that what is good for persons is the pursuit of knowledge and living together in community, then a political community is necessarily devoted to a good. It may not be a good about which we all agree, but it must be a good.
Professor Gender:	I do not understand.
Aristotle:	Consider yourself. You come here, at this table before this audience, in pursuit of some good. What is it?
Professor Gender:	I would not call it a good, I would call it my role as a scholar/activist.
Aristotle:	I think there is something worth pursuing here. So, it is a good, a good of some sort. Now, we then need to consider whether or not that good is a true good or a distorted one. Is your good something that reflects the good for the human person, or an individualized, particular good?
Professor Gender:	Well, I believe that we should all be pursuing our roles as scholars and activists.
Aristotle:	I completely agree! You have captured the nature of the political life precisely. We should orient our political communities toward creating spaces in which we can think and act. This is the good of the political community. I am so glad I have someone with whom I agree on this panel.
Chair:	I believe we are almost out of time. I know there are many more questions to ask our guest, but perhaps we can give him some time to raise any issues we have not brought up?
Aristotle:	Yes, I did have an important question. Are you not all teachers?
Chair:	Yes, almost all of us teach at colleges or universities. Why?
Aristotle:	We have not spoken of your educational methods or beliefs. Is this not the most important element of the political? Should we not orient our communities toward education?

Chair: Well, you know, there are a great many pressures on our time. Most of us have graduate students helping us with teaching and, well, it is just a bit more rewarding to have that article published or book come out. I'm not sure I get much pleasure from teaching anymore. I've got more important things to do.

Aristotle: I am a bit shocked to hear you say this, especially if you are interested in politics. Should you not be teaching your youth to be good, to rule and be ruled? What of music? Do they listen to music?

Chair: Oh, do they ever.

Aristotle: Do you ensure the music connects them to the centrality of the soul and its relation to the political life? What forms do they use? Are they taught to play music? What of athletics? Do they learn to compete and excel on the field of play?

Chair: Ah, I would think this is something for the student life programmes?

Aristotle: Well, I feel you must rededicate yourself to this. Your political life, no matter the size of the polity or the gender of the persons, must begin and end with education. My teacher, Plato, felt all education should be left to the polis. I am not sure I would go that far, but certainly you, as teachers and scholars of the political life, should have education as your first and foremost concern. If you do not, well, you simply do not understand politics.

Chair: Ah, well, that's all we have time for. Aristotle, thank you very much for your participation. We hope to see you at some future conference.

Aristotle: Thank you! Now, can someone explain to me how these lights upon the wall work without any flame ...

Note

Thanks to Chris Brown, Laura Sjoberg, Cian O'Driscoll, Nicholas Onuf, Hidemi Suganami, Ned Lebow and Peer Schouten for helpful comments on the text.

7

Niccolò Machiavelli (1469–1527): Two Realisms

Erica Benner

Lou, a present-day student, meets Niccolò Machiavelli at his old workplace inside the Palazzo Vecchio in Florence, where the Florentine government was based in his day.

Lou: Thanks so much for agreeing to see me, Signor Machiavelli. There's a crowd of tourists out there hoping to meet you.

Machiavelli: My pleasure, and please call me Niccolò. I've never been one for titles and ranks. When I worked for the Florentine government, some of the great gentlemen I worked with constantly complained that I showed them too little reverence.

Lou: They'd be amazed to see how popular you've become 500 years after you wrote your *Prince*. People here keep saying they've never seen a longer queue in Florence than the one outside your door, even to see the Mona Lisa. You've become quite a rock star over the centuries.

Machiavelli: I doubt that most of those people are my adoring fans – I've always been more notorious than loved. But I can't complain. Notoriety has made my afterlife rather interesting.

Lou: Well, I personally am a great admirer, not just of your *Prince* but also your *Discourses* and *Art of War* and other works, though I confess I haven't read them all cover to cover. And a few months ago I performed in a student production of your comedy, *The Mandrake*. That was the most fun I've had in ages. A few puritanical spectators were shocked by the risqué subject-matter and hard-hitting jokes, but most of the audience loved it.

Machiavelli: In my own time, you know, I was far more famous for that play than for my political writings. The *Prince* and *Discourses* weren't even published until after my demise. I wanted to make a gift of the *Prince* to the princely rulers of Florence, the Medici. But my friend Francesco Vettori advised me not to send it to them.[1]

Lou: Why not?

Machiavelli: He knew how much they mistrusted me. They thought I wanted to get rid of their family dynasty and restore a republican form of government. For 14 years, you see, I'd been Secretary – a sort of high-up civil service post – to the Florentine Republic. I worked like the devil to defend my city's popular constitution against its enemies, mostly upper-class types who wanted to turn it into an oligarchy or a principality. Then the year before I wrote my *Prince,* a foreign-sponsored coup swept the Medici princes into power. They let most people keep their political posts, but I was dismissed and banned from these government offices. Those were hard times for me, and for my family. My wife Marietta was pregnant with our third or fourth child ...

Lou: And things went from bad to worse, didn't they? A few months after you lost your job, weren't you imprisoned and tortured on suspicion of conspiring to overthrow the new rulers?

Machiavelli: I was. The charges were based on the flimsiest evidence. They released me after a few weeks, after ripping my shoulders from their sockets. But for years after that, the Medici and their partisans remained suspicious of anything I wrote about politics. No matter how extravagantly I seemed to praise their princely style of government, they were convinced that I wanted to bring back a republic with elected leaders and a popular assembly.

Lou: But they liked your comic plays, didn't they? Though I think I detect some similarities between your *Mandrake* and the *Prince*. The *Prince* tells men who want to become absolute one-man rulers how to fulfil their dreams, even if they have to use unscrupulous methods. Your *Mandrake*'s protagonist is a rich young man, Callimaco, who returns to Florence from abroad – a bit like the Medici princes, who were in exile under your republic.

Using every dirty trick in the book, he connives to go to bed with a virtuous married woman, Lucretia (I played her in our student production). Between all the laughs, some of those Medici must have wondered if you weren't offering a sneaky commentary on how they wangled their way to power.

Machiavelli: Ah, the goddess Fortuna has decided to smile on me today! At last she sends me an interviewer who doesn't expect me to talk like some cold-fish political scientist, rattling off ruthless how-to maxims! And such a pretty interviewer, if you don't mind my saying so.

Lou: Considering your well-known weakness for the ladies, and – if you don't mind *my* saying so – your venerable age, I don't mind at all. But I still want to ask you some hard questions.

Machiavelli: Please do.

Lou: As you know, people these days tend to use the word 'Machiavellian' as a synonym for 'unscrupulous' or 'cynical'. The lecturers in my university courses tried to get beyond the crude stereotypes. They had us read parts of the *Discourses* where you praise republics and the rule of law. We learned that even the *Prince* contains some surprisingly moral-sounding advice. Still, most people who write about you seem to agree that you're a clear-cut Realist. Do you accept that label?

Machiavelli: I'm not very up-to-date with these modern terms, you know.

Lou: Well, most Realists think self-preservation is a basic good that may conflict with moral concerns like justice or freedom. They say that individuals and states sometimes have to set moral ideals aside for the sake of security.

Machiavelli: Now I remember. Back in the 19th century, some Germans – first Fichte and Hegel, later Meinecke – started citing me as a champion of *Realpolitik*. They invoked some of my arguments to call for national unification, if necessary by means of blood and iron.[2] Then various Italian nationalists, of both the left and right, followed suit. I was happy to lend my name to support their more reasonable aims. Like them, I wanted Italians in my day to stand up against foreign invaders. I thought they'd only succeed if the separate Italian states – there were quite a few of them in those times, always at each other's throats – put aside their rivalries and made some sort of league for countrywide defence. But I never said this could be done by blood and iron, or that a single great man could save Italy, if he were sufficiently ruthless.

Lou: So what is the key to defending a state, or a divided country?

Machiavelli: One's own arms. Instead of relying on foreign mercenaries or begging for military help from abroad, train your own citizens to defend their country. When I was Secretary I persuaded the Florentine government to create a militia of peasants recruited from our countryside. If other Italian cities had done the same and formed a defensive confederation like the Swiss, Italy might not have been torn apart and occupied by foreign powers until the mid-19th century.

Lou: If you make an army of ordinary people, won't the upper classes and princes worry that the lower orders might turn their arms against them?

Machiavelli: Indeed. My colleagues and I met with ferocious resistance to our militia plans from Florence's so-called great men, I can tell you! They were too scared to arm ordinary people inside our city walls. So we started with a few peasants in the countryside. Then before we could take things further, the Medici came in and abolished our people's army altogether.

Lou: It must be easier to set up those armies in popular republics, where the people who fight also have a large role in government.

Machiavelli: Absolutely. That's one reason why the best-defended states are republics of that kind. But there's another reason why your Realists should prefer republican forms of government, since they care so much about security. People fight more fiercely to defend their country when they have a real stake in its way of life: when they can make a decent living, feel that they're treated with respect, and take part in politics.[3]

Lou: Is that how the ancient Romans organized their defences and grew so strong?

Machiavelli: I do think the Romans got more things right than wrong, until they grew too great for their own good and started handing too much power to their generals and other overambitious men. But I had contemporary models too.

While I was Secretary we Florentines fought a long war with Pisa after the Pisans rebelled from our little empire. They'd been under Florentine control for 100 years and were desperately weak, impoverished, and depopulated. But they'd never forgotten their proud old traditions of republican government and independence.[4] Fired up by the memory of their fathers' freedom, they armed and trained every man, woman and child to defend their liberty. Their wealthy men agreed to share power with the lower classes and the peasants, inspiring everyone to fight for the common cause.[5] For 14 years they fought us off and made life very, very hard for us Florentines. On paper we were far stronger than them, but they had something we lacked: a burning popular will to defend their own power of self-government against our efforts to stifle it. Though we eventually re-conquered Pisa with the help of my new citizen militia, the whole world saw how useful the love of freedom is to anyone who wants to build good defences.

Lou: It sounds as if you think some ideals are needed for self-preservation. The kind of republican government you want is an ideal, isn't it? In one of your less well-known writings you say that the best way to defend any state is to establish a 'true republic' inside, organized so that what you call 'the generality of people' have a major share of power.[6] In the *Discourses* too, you claim to be setting out general standards of government and foreign policy for 'any city whatever.'[7]

Machiavelli: I find it a bit baffling when people think it's easy to draw a line between political 'ideals' and 'realities'. As I see it, the most realistic solution to the problem of insecurity inside and among states *is* a well-designed republican government defended by its own people. And if that's an ideal, it's one I anchor in a certain understanding of basic human realities.

Lou: I wonder if your basic realities are the same as those of many modern Realists? I'm thinking of the ones who say that the instinct for survival is the main reality that drives human beings. It seems to follow that it's realistic to seek safety, and idealistic to want to live free. The practical conclusion is that safety has to come before freedom or republics.

Machiavelli: I say safety and freedom have to go together. Of course human beings have a powerful drive to preserve themselves, like all other animals. But we're thinking animals, and it doesn't take much deep thought to understand the advantages of a free way of life, especially for our own security.[8]

Lou: All right, but now I'm wondering how all this fits with what you say about human nature in the *Prince*. Here's a quote: men generally are 'ungrateful, fickle pretenders and dissemblers, evaders of danger, eager for gain.'[9] Your point is that most people can't be trusted; human untrustworthiness is, one might say, a basic reality. If you can't trust other people, don't you have to watch your own back *before* you can think about living with them in some high-minded republic?

Machiavelli: Yes you do. That's why I advise the founders of new states to make a thorough, honest study of human shortcomings before they set to work. But if you get too fixated on other people's untrustworthiness, you might not try hard enough to work out ways to make them deserve your trust.

Lou: I'm not sure what you have in mind.

Machiavelli: Take my citizen militias again. As we said earlier, upper classes tend to mistrust their armed plebs and peasants; and so long as they use them as cheap cannon fodder, they have good reason to worry about a possible rebellion. But if things are organised in a state so there aren't extreme inequalities, economic or political, and so that ordinary people can feed their families and win public respect, they'll become its stoutest defenders.[10] With the right policies, it's possible to turn people you mistrust into reliable partners.

Lou: But what happens when trust and civil order collapse, as you say they eventually always do, since no state can last forever? Then isn't it every man and state for him – or itself?

Machiavelli: In my books I talk about two possible responses to political collapse, or indeed to any serious threats. One is to go it alone, ignoring the moral scruples that restrain us in quieter times and learning 'not to be good.'[11] The other is to tackle threats by building new, collaborative relationships to help you feel safer. Romulus, Cyrus, and other famous empire-makers did the former. Other ancient city-founders, such as Aeneas and Dido, did the second. Cast out of their homelands, they had to work *by way of friends and confederates* to build their new cities, winning *the consent of neighbours where they settled.*[12] Another example is Hiero of Syracuse. After his tyrannical predecessors destroyed trust within Syracuse and with its neighbours, Hiero rebuilt it. He rose to authority by being chosen for his merits, not by money, cunning, family connections, foreign armies, or brute force ...

Lou: I'd never heard of him before reading the *Prince*. I sort of skimmed the parts where you mention him,[13] assuming that the other big names you mention are more important role models.

Machiavelli: That's probably because Hiero didn't found a sprawling new empire, or get elevated to the rank of a god. He merely helped his countrymen throw off a decadent tyranny, replaced useless mercenary forces with a strong civilian army, forged new alliances that made for stable peace and strengthened his country's shattered ties with their fellow Greeks. That might not sound as impressive as the grandiose conquests made by Romulus or Cyrus or Theseus. But unlike those princes – whom ancient writers criticized for their excessive personal ambitions – Hiero won the unqualified praise of his chroniclers.

Lou: I'm not sure this makes sense, but could we say that your writings actually set out two kinds of Realism: one unilateral and amoral, the other collaborative and more concerned with how to treat other people – and states – when seeking security?

Machiavelli: That sounds like a fair description. I don't like to tell my readers which methods they should imitate. I'd rather they use their own brains to decide what's the surest route to long-term safety. They also need to think hard about which *ends* are compatible with lasting security. Yes, Romulus became a big *padrone* and conqueror. But Plutarch tells us that his bullying methods made him so many enemies that his own Senate had him murdered as a tyrant.[14] And the virtuous Roman republic became horribly corrupted after it started expanding beyond Italy, and soon died a violent death.[15]

Lou:	You've got me thinking now about how to build trust among people who start off suspicious of one another. I see how you can do this inside a state, as you tried to do with your militia. But isn't it a different story in international relations, where there's no central force to back up the institutions that are supposed to foster trust?
Machiavelli:	It can be harder, but the basic methods of persuading people to act as your co-defenders are the same inside or among states. If you want to be sure of a foreign ally – that he won't abandon you when you're down, or if he grows strong enough to threaten you – what's the most effective way to secure his loyalty?
Lou:	Money and favours? Fear?
Machiavelli:	Money buys you poor-quality, fair-weather friends. Allies who support you out of fear are unreliable too: too much fear makes people hate you, and when they hate you they conspire against you.[16] No, your safest bet is to act in ways that inspire trust in yourself. If you take clear sides and stick by friends through their defeats as well as victories, there's a more than fair chance that they'll reciprocate and help you out when you're down. In response to your firm commitments they form *an obligation to you and a contract of love for you*. Even if your allies are much stronger, this obligation restrains them from taking advantage of your weaknesses. After all, *men are never so indecent as to crush you with so great an example of ingratitude*. And *victories are never so clear that the winner does not have to have some respect, especially for justice*.[17]
Lou:	It seems your view of human nature isn't as pessimistic as people say. Still, don't you argue that justice plays a very limited role in international relations?
Machiavelli:	Do I? Perhaps you've forgotten that episode in my *Discourses* where three Roman ambassadors violated the law of nations in their war against the Gauls. When the Romans rebuffed their requests to punish the miscreants, the Gauls swept down on Rome in a rage, nearly wiping the city off the map. *This ruin*, I remark, *arose for the Romans only through the inobservance of justice*. I also say that nothing could restore Rome to safety unless the Romans pulled *back to the limits* defined by

the customary law of nations.[18] In other words, injustice makes you less safe, because it's both natural and reasonable for human beings to seek to punish it.

Lou: But you also say that when the safety of one's fatherland is at stake, 'one ought to follow entirely the policy that saves its life and maintains its liberty,' without considering justice or injustice, praise or shame.[19]

Machiavelli: Look again. I call that a 'saying' that different people invoke to justify various policies, some more reasonable than others. In my examples, the reasonable ones don't use that rhetoric to excuse injustice; they save their country from being crushed by accepting 'shameful' terms of surrender when they're on the verge of defeat.

Lou: I hope you don't mind my saying this, Niccolò, but you can be a really slippery writer. At first glance your language seems so refreshingly clear. But whenever I try to pin down your main ideas, I get confused. It's as if you write in two voices. I read somewhere that quite a few of your earlier readers, including Spinoza and Rousseau, suspected you're being ironic when you praise violent princes like Cesare Borgia or recommend breaking faith and the like. They thought you were exposing and slyly criticizing the cynical methods of over-ambitious men, not recommending them in earnest.[20]

Machiavelli [grinning enigmatically]: One of my very first critics, Cardinal Reginald Pole, insisted that the devil's-spawn author of the *Prince* couldn't seriously be advocating oath-breaking and cruelty, since any politician who does these things will make swarms of enemies and self-destruct. What later generations call 'Machiavellian Realism' looked thoroughly *un*realistic to Cardinal Pole.[21] If I were being ironic, of course, I wouldn't want to be too obvious about it. Let's just say I want my readers to do a bit of work. Sometimes I tease them by switching from one position to another, or between tough-talking and moderate 'voices', as you put it, so they're forced to think. The best brains grasp things by themselves; they don't need me, or any authority, to tell them how to judge the facts and arguments placed before them.[22]

Lou: Thanks so much for this chat. I've learned that I shouldn't
                trust first appearances, or judge great men or writers by
                their reputations.

Machiavelli: That's one lesson I'm never ashamed to lend my name to.
                Addio.

Notes

1. Vettori was a Florentine statesman and Machiavelli's close friend. The two men conducted a wonderfully rich correspondence after the Medici coup of 1512; see *Machiavelli and His Friends: Their Personal Correspondence*, trans. ed. James B. Atkinson and David Sices (DeKalb, IL: University of Northern Illinois Press, 1996).
2. Johann Gottlieb Fichte (1971/1807), 'Über Machiavelli' in *Fichtes Werke*, vol. 11, ed. Immanuel Hermann Fichte (Berlin: Gruyter), pp. 400–453; G.W.F. Hegel (1999/1800–2), 'Die Verfassung Deutschlands' in *Werke: Frühe Schriften*, vol. 1 ed. Eva Moldenhauer and Karl Markus Michel (Frankfurt: Suhrkamp) pp. 451–620; Friedrich Meinecke (1998/1925), *The Doctrine of Raison d'État and Its Place in Modern History*, ed. Werner Stark (New Brunswick: Transaction Publishers).
3. *Prince*, chapters 10 and 12; *Discourses* I.60, II.2.
4. *Prince*, chapter 5.
5. Michele Luzzati (1973), *Una Guerra di Popolo* (Pisa: Pacini Editore).
6. Machiavelli, 'Discursus on Remodelling the Government of Florence' in *Machiavelli: The Chief Works and Others* ed. and trans. Allan Gilbert, vol. 1, 101–115.
7. *Discourses* I.1 (title: 'What have been universally the beginnings of any city whatever, and what was that of Rome').
8. *Discourses* I.16, II.2.
9. *Prince*, chapter 15.
10. *Prince*, chapter 10.
11. *Prince*, chapter 15.
12. *Prince*, chapter 6; *Discourses* II.8. Machiavelli's original words are in italics.
13. *Prince*, chapters 6 and 13; *Discourses*, Dedicatory Letter.
14. Plutarch, 'Life of Romulus' in *Plutarch's Lives*, vol. 1, trans. Bernadotte Perrin (Cambridge, Mass.: Harvard University Press, 1998).
15. *Discourses* I.18, III.24, II.2, II.30.
16. *Prince*, chapters 17 and 19.
17. *Prince*, chapter 21. Machiavelli's original words in italics.
18. *Discourses*, II.28, III.1. Machiavelli's original words in italics.
19. *Discourses*, III.41.
20. Jean-Jacques Rousseau, *Social Contract* (1762), III.6; Benedict Spinoza, *Tractatus Politicus* (1677) VI.4–5, VII.1. X.1.
21. Cardinal Reginald Pole (1536), 'Apology' in Jill Kraye, ed. (1997), *Cambridge Translations of Renaissance Philosophical Texts* (Cambridge: Cambridge University Press), vol. 2, pp. 274–85.
22. *Prince*, chapter 22.

8
Thomas Hobbes (1588–1679)

Michael C. Williams

It is 1675. Thomas Hobbes is sitting on a bench in the gardens at Chatsworth, the country house of the Cavendish family, by whom he has for decades been employed as a tutor, secretary and intellectual. Hobbes has just returned from his daily walk when he customarily does his initial thinking for the day. He is 87 years old and remarkably spry for his age. His mental capacities remain as sharp as ever, and his tongue, renowned for its droll wit, but also prone to giving vent to his exasperation at misunderstandings of his position, is likely even sharper. As he enjoys the warmth, a modern scholar (MS) appears, asking if he may join him in conversation. Showing his customary civility, Hobbes chooses to humour his visitor, granting an interview and ignoring his guest's absurd claim that he comes from the future.

MS: Good afternoon, Mr Hobbes. I trust you enjoyed your walk.

TH: Good day to you, sir. As to my walk, indeed I did enjoy it! I have always held that activity is necessary for good health, and I hope to have lived long enough to prove it as best I may. I do miss the court-tennis that I used to play until recent years, but we must be grateful for the pleasures given to us. Pray, tell me who you are, and your reasons for wishing to speak with me. I am sorry to be abrupt, but even as an old man I have little time, and much pressing correspondence to attend to.

MS: I am a university professor, Mr Hobbes, and I would like to ask you about international politics.

TH: Ah, you are one of them, are you?

MS: One of them?

TH: Professors. Schoolmen. I fear I have little other than vexing experience with most of them, both when I was a student at Oxford, and ever since. Vain pedants – most of them foolish, seditious, or both. Filling the heads of their students with nonsense, and casting their writings about with scant regard for the quality of their reasoning or their baleful impact on the public.

MS: In the universities where I come from, we like to believe that we have moved beyond that situation.

TH: Oh, you do, do you? (grinning wryly). I would like to believe you, and I sincerely hope that it is true, though I confess my doubts. I have seen too many Professors in my time to share your optimism. But let us err on the side of optimism. Now what was the topic you wished to discuss? International ...?

MS: International relations. The relations between states.

TH: These are not terms I am familiar with. And words are vital to understanding. One must always be clear in one's meaning and definitions. So, to be clear, is it relations between sovereigns that you mean?

MS: Yes. I suppose so. You see, you have become quite famous – not just as a theorist of sovereignty, but also as a theorist of relations between sovereign powers, what we call international relations.

TH: Really? That is pleasant to know. As a thinker on sovereignty, well, I can understand that my ideas might be compelling. I spent a great deal of time endeavouring to make them so. But I do not recall ever having written much about the topic you mention. And I am reputed for the quality of my recollection.

MS: Well, you see, in my time a great many people have adopted your claim that relations between sovereigns should be understood as a 'Hobbesian' state of nature ...

TH: Please, let us pause a moment before we go any further! For I am already somewhat puzzled. Who says this, and where do they believe that I say such a thing?

MS: Many scholars claim it – indeed they take it as close to common sense, or even as axiomatic. Surely in *Leviathan*, particularly in chapter 20, you argue that sovereigns exist in a state of war, whether actual or potential.

TH: The latter point is quite true. But your use of the term 'axiomatic' is significant, for I take it seriously. My terms and conclusions are rigorous, not random. In this case, the state of war is not at all the same thing as a state of nature, however much it might superficially resemble it.

MS: Could you please explain that?

TH: I do tire sometimes of having to clarify points that are perfectly obvious, if only people would read carefully and think clearly ...

though it is true that these issues are not simple – and as I have often said, getting people to think calmly and carefully is one of the greatest challenges in politics. At any rate, let me explain as directly as I can. In the state of nature individuals – note, *individuals* – exist in a war of each against all. They lack natural means of agreeing on what is good and bad, true and false; they are driven by diverse appetites and aversions that influence their understanding of these things; they are vain, believing that their own ideas are correct; and they live in perpetual fear of others and of violent death at their hands. All of this is familiar to you from my writings, is it?

MS: Yes.

TH: Fine. Now forgive me, but these next points may take some time to explain. I will be as brief as possible. The state of nature is a condition where there is no order, and where there can be no stable order. It is also a condition of equality. No individual can impose their will upon the others. All have different strengths and weaknesses; all must sleep, and can thus be overcome; and all must die – and thus with them any order that even the strongest might conceivably produce and maintain. In such a condition, the natural condition of mankind, there is only chaos. It is this condition – the constant fear of violent death, especially at the hands of others – that drives men to use their reason to seek escape from it. The Covenant or social contract that they enter into creates a sovereign that overcomes this situation. The sovereign provides the laws, providing common principles of good and bad by which the citizens shall live, and it alleviates fear by providing an authority that can punish transgressors.

To turn to the question you ask, entry into the social contract creates collective agents, sovereigns, who stand in quite different relation to each other than do individuals in the state of nature. As collective persons, if I can use the term, sovereigns vary in size and strength, they do not sleep, nor, unless dissolved by internal or external actions, do they die. Since they differ in size, some sovereigns are also capable of imposing or trying to impose order upon weaker sovereigns. The extreme fear and chaos of the state of nature does not exist amongst sovereigns, which differ from individuals in the state of nature. It is a state of war, but not a state of nature.

Finally, there is another set of differences that are important to recognize. As collective persons created by reason, reasonable sovereigns should recognize limits on their decisions. In principle, decisions of the sovereign are final and must be obeyed. But one must remember that individuals never give up their natural right – the right to defend their own lives – that, after all, was why they entered the social contract in the first place. Thus, sovereigns should be very cautious about going to war, where they are commanding citizens to put their lives at risk, since their citizens retain the right to disobey without acting against natural right. A reasonable sovereign will recognize this, and will be very cautious in resorting to war. Reasonably understood and acted upon – by which I mean understood through reason – sovereigns can exist in a state of war, which is a constant disposition to fight without actually doing so.

MS: I'm sorry, but may I stop you at this point? I understand your argument so far. But several centuries from now, many influential thinkers who claim to admire you greatly – particularly two whose names are Carl Schmitt and Leo Strauss – will argue that this is precisely the weakest point in your thinking. If individuals retain the right to defend their own lives, and can with perfect right refuse to support their sovereign in war if they think it likely to cost them their lives, then how can the sovereign defend itself? Does not your entire argument falter at this key juncture – on the question of war and relations between sovereigns?

TH: These are good questions, but the criticisms are mistaken. When I say that persons are driven by their fear of death, by the desire to preserve their lives, I do not mean that this is a mechanical reaction without a role for reason. It is true that I have compared this desire to the force of gravity. What I mean is that the fear of death is a continual tendency to be appreciated, not that it is a simple necessity. There are many situations in which individuals overcome their fear of death for other things they value. People will die for each other in certain situations. Courage, properly defined, is precisely the overcoming of the fear of death. The question is not the possibility of them doing so. The most important question becomes the reasonableness of their reasons for doing so – their principles and their consequences. Those who run from battle do not act wrongly. Yet they do act *dishonourably*: and dishonour is a failure to understand the importance of defending one's sovereign.

MS: But isn't a concern with higher values and ultimate ends, with actions based on religious enthusiasm or courtly 'honour' for example, exactly what you tell us we need to discard if we are to avoid conflict? Your explanation of the Civil War, for instance, seems constantly to show these kinds of beliefs and values were central elements in that bloody conflict.

TH: That is true. And it makes it all the more important that we are able to distinguish between those things that we can rationally know, and those things which we can reasonably be obligated to do, and those that we cannot. The reason that I spend so much time on the question of knowledge in my writings is because mistaken or mischievous claims about what we really can know can easily become sources of fear of conflict.

In a Commonwealth based on the reasoning that I develop, citizens will understand why they must obey and defend the sovereign. Moreover, the sovereign will understand that even though its power is absolute, it should attend to the good of the citizens. The possibility of war reinforces this conclusion, since citizens' commitment to defend the sovereign even at risk of their lives is more readily produced under sovereigns that recognize the need to promote the good and the safety of their citizens, and that use their authority to this end. Thus the most secure sovereign is that which acts in accordance with the laws of reason – what I call the laws of nature – for the good of the state as a whole.

MS: You seem almost to be saying that although belief is dangerous, the sovereign's power rests on the people's beliefs? In my time, we might call this a 'social constructivist' position.

TH: Social constructivism? That is a strange term, and if I may say so, a rather infelicitous one. Words matter. I would recommend you study them further. Rhetoric, as Thucydides well knew and taught us, stirs the passions and calls to action. And understanding can be aided by the passions that rhetoric stirs, even if understanding cannot be directly guided by those passions alone. This is why, to the degree possible, the people must be taught the reasonable vision of politics, which is what I attempt to do in my writings. In fact, one of the reasons that I wrote *Leviathan*, where I restated many of the arguments that I made in my previous book *De Cive*, is that I wanted to phrase them in a more evocative language. Indeed, and I hope this is not too vain, the rhetorical style of *Leviathan* – the description of life in the state of nature as 'solitary, poor, nasty, brutish, and short', for instance – is something I am rather proud of. At any rate, forgive me, for I am an old man and tend to digress somewhat.

To return to your question: in a very particular sense, yes, beliefs matter; as I wrote in *Behemoth* 'the power of the mighty hath no foundation but in the opinion and belief of the people'.[1] One can, to use your term, 'construct' one's understanding and actions in an infinite number of ways, generally corresponding to the infinite variety of appetites and aversions that move individuals. Even fear, that most powerful of motivations, is marked by the variety of the objects to which it is attached and the responses it provokes. My account of the state of nature is in part intended to demonstrate this. Yet to recognize this diversity is alone insufficient; it remains little more than the scepticism of the ancients. If actions are driven in large part by opinion, then those opinions must be judged in terms of their adequacy to reason, and in light of their consequences. This is what I have done.

MS: I would like if I may to return to the issue of fear, since much of your account relies upon it? In my time, fear is much derided in politics. It is seen as something dangerous, a tool of manipulation or a source of irrationality and violence; in sum, something that we need to avoid. You seem to have a less negative view of fear.

TH: Fear is something that must be handled with care. It is complicated; yet no vision of politics can be sufficient if it fails to account for it. Let us first agree that the mistrust of fear of which you speak is not without foundation. Fear is dangerous, and that danger must always be reckoned with. This said, the inescapability of fear must be accepted, and its positive political potential recognized. Human life is a life of fear. We fear not just the evils we know – potential harm from others, for instance. We also fear what we do not and cannot know: the future. Fear of the future gnaws at us continually, and ceases only when we die. There being no escape from fear, we must appreciate its influence and counter its more baleful consequences. This is yet another of the many advantages of the social contract: it provides the greatest possible degree of predictability in life, and sovereigns and citizens should recognize the value of this predictability inside the commonwealth and, in a different way, in relations between sovereigns.

Fear of the sovereign is also essential for political order. Without it, citizens will be tempted to disobedience, and to substituting their own reason for that of the sovereign. This is disastrous. Potentially equally disastrous, however, is an excess of fear. As I mentioned earlier, a sovereign that puts its subjects continually in fear of their lives risks having those subjects question their obligation and obedience. To state this in more practical terms, let us say that a people does not know its duty, that the citizens fail to obey and refuse to obey the laws and defend the sovereign. What, then, shall make them do so? You might well answer, 'the army', and you would be in part correct. But again as I once wrote in a dialogue similar to that which we are having now, you must then answer the question, 'and what shall force the army?'[2] If the sovereign is personated by a single Monarch, or even a group of persons in a Parliament, it shall never be of sufficient force to compel an army to do its duty through fear alone. And, as our own sad Civil War shows, an army alone is often insufficient to impose order upon a restive people. The people and the army must know their duty. Fear of punishment alone cannot provide this. Only when mixed with understanding, with reasoned belief, can it be reliably achieved.

MS: You seem to be saying that there is no way to understand what we call international relations without understanding political theory and the connections between politics within sovereigns and politics between them.

TH: I think that a fair assessment. I cannot imagine how it could be otherwise.

MS: I fear that this leaves me quite confused about what people in my time so loosely call a 'Hobbesian' theory of international relations. What you have said about the state of nature does not seem to support the claim that world politics is akin to 'Hobbesian anarchy'.

TH: Yes, it seems so. That is a challenge I am afraid I cannot help you with. But there it is. Now, if you will forgive me, I fear that I must leave you. I no longer have quite as much energy as once I had. And as your questions show, there are many misunderstandings and partial understandings of what I have to say that need to be confronted or corrected. My critics are fierce, rarely just, and even more rarely correct! One must be as vigilant in response as one is in reasoning. I have enjoyed our conversation, even if I am well aware – as my reason must tell me – that it has been little more than a phantasm conjured in the reverie of an old man dozing in the sun.

Notes

1. Thomas Hobbes, *Behemoth*, (Chicago: University of Chicago Press, 1990), p. 16.
2. Hobbes, *Behemoth*, p. 59.

9

An Interview with John Locke (1632–1704)

Beate Jahn

Angela: Mr Locke, I am so grateful that you are ready to talk to me. My name is Angela and I am a PhD student in International Relations. I want to write my thesis about the importance of your work for understanding international politics and I hope that you can clarify a few issues that puzzle me.

Locke: You are very welcome, young lady. I will do my best. Please proceed.

Angela: While political theorists engage regularly and thoroughly with your work, it does not play much of a role in International Relations. Is your work only or largely relevant for domestic politics?

Locke: Well, I have to admit that this distinction between domestic and international politics puzzles me a bit. It was the general religious, political, economic and intellectual crisis of the 17th century that motivated me to write about politics – and there was nothing 'domestic' about it. All of Europe had lived through civil wars; the economic downturn had a lot to do with bullion coming in from America; the ancient Greek writings that the Arabs had brought to Europe as well as the discovery of the New World and its peoples undermined traditional intellectual certainties. I myself lived through the English civil wars, Cromwell's Protectorate, the execution of the King and what you now call the Glorious Revolution. Much of the fortune of my esteemed employer, the Earl of Shaftesbury, was made in overseas trade and I was secretary to the Lord Proprietors of Carolina and to the Council of Trade and Plantations, a member of the Board of Trade, and I also had some money invested in the Royal Africa Company, the Company of Merchant Adventurers to Trade with the Bahamas and the East India Company.[1] It was the fact that the old order had completely broken down that motivated me to try and sketch a new political order.

Angela: Very interesting – I think I'll have to come back to the distinction between the domestic and the international later. For now I am curious how you went about developing a new vision of politics.

Locke: Well, traditionally, people had studied empirically the diversity of God's creation. Alas, this interest also encouraged the diversity that then led to religious and political fragmentation and ultimately the complete breakdown of political order. So we, I and many of my contemporaries, were approaching the problem of political order in a different way. We tried to identify a self-evident basic principle of human life. This would be our starting point. And we then proceeded to sketch the laws and institutions that were logically necessary for the maintenance of that principle. In other words, unlike our predecessors, we began with a theoretical principle rather than empirical observation.

Angela: This is fascinating! Is this why so many political theorists in your day base their work on the 'state of nature'?

Locke: Indeed, the state of nature always entails the first and most self-evident principles about human life.

Angela: But different authors came up with different ideas about the state of nature. What did you think was the most important principle about human life?

Locke: Well, young lady, for me the most fundamental and first principle is that all human beings are born free.

Angela: Yes, of course, but what other institutions were necessary to uphold this freedom?

Locke: First of all, in order to enjoy this freedom, human beings had to keep themselves alive – and this meant that they had to eat and drink, and needed clothes and shelter. So human freedom was based on material conveniences and it is obvious that a human being is not free if it is dependent on others, employers or charitable institutions, for the provision of these necessities. This is why I argued that individual freedom requires private property. And this freedom in turn calls for government by consent. Moreover, imagine a government made up of individuals (or their representatives) whose freedom rests on their private property – this government will have as its chief aim the protection of private property which in turn underpins individual freedom.[2] I have to admit that I was really rather pleased with the core of my theory – with the way in which each element was absolutely necessary for the other elements to exist and for the whole system to work: private property constitutes individual freedom and that leads to government by consent which in turn protects private property.

Angela: Yes, it really is cool – and I actually think we can see the system at work today. But this in itself is curious because you said that you developed this vision deliberately in abstraction from practice. And, indeed, most people in your day were poor, most were dependent for their livelihood on others and there were no governments by consent: so how did you bridge this gap between theory and practice?

Locke: Yes, this was indeed a problem. I had to explain the disjuncture between my theory and reality and I had to identify policies that could bridge this gap.

Angela: So how did you explain the gap between theory and practice?

Locke: Well, I had been really, really interested in the discovery of the New World and its peoples for as long as I can remember. I used to buy every book that came out on the topic and read them all. So I knew there were indigenous societies that were ruled through councils of equals. These tribes, moreover, appeared to represent humanity in its infancy – today you would say they were not yet very developed – and this proved that individual freedom and government by consent were indeed in line with human nature. I then developed a historical narrative that explained how this natural law had been forgotten, leading to the constitution of despotic governments. The most likely starting point for that development seemed to be the invention of money. On the one hand, it put an end to poverty since it made surplus production possible which could then be exchanged for non-perishable metal. On the other, it led to struggles over land and the need for government to settle property rights – which meant that now the struggles over land took place between political communities and hence required the settling of boundaries. And it was these wars that brought rulers to power who did not respect the property of their citizens but pursued their own interests – justifying such policies with reference to tradition and culture. So I speculated that this is how, over time, people simply forgot their natural rights to private property, freedom and government by consent. Of course, having rediscovered these natural rights, we could set out to realize them again.

Angela: Yes, I do recognize the story about the self-serving and corrupt governments. This is exactly the story the World Bank tells about poverty and corruption in Africa – and its solution is the 'good governance' agenda.[3] In practice, this means that aid and loans for African countries are made conditional on the implementation of certain policies: the privatization of state-owned industries, the opening of markets, and democratic elections.

Locke: This is absolutely fascinating! It really means that they are doing now what I suggested at the time as a practical way to realize my political vision. I basically argued that providing people with private property constitutes them as free individuals. The problem was that there were huge numbers of poor people in the country and private property was, well, private, and therefore had to be protected. So I suggested that we can generate private property through the privatization of common property. Though this involved expropriation of communities in the short run, I argued that private property is more productive than common property and so in the long run generally beneficial. Of course, there was nowhere near enough common land in England to provide all the poor people with private property. But, again it proved fortuitous that I had been reading so much about America: there was enough common land there for everyone. So I advocated colonialism.

Angela: Are you saying that the privatization of common property is the most fundamental policy for turning 'nonliberal' into 'liberal' individuals and communities? Wouldn't the communities that depend on the common property for their livelihood object?

Locke: Yes, the privatization of common property is, indeed, the most fundamental 'liberal' policy. The suggestion was taken up by my esteemed employer, the Earl of Shaftesbury, and many of his rich friends in the Whig movement. Under the old regime, their fortunes were not safe, their individual freedom was jeopardized – both Shaftesbury and I spent time in prison and exile – and they had no say in government at all. They used my theory to demand political rights based on their property and once in government they embarked on concerted policies to privatize common land – this was called enclosures. They also followed my argument for colonialism which is nothing else, in the end, but the privatization of other peoples' land. But, of course, you are right: these policies could only be pursued if the poor people at home and weak indigenous populations abroad were denied political rights. So I argued that political rights had to be tied to property and abroad only the political rights (to sovereignty) of communities based on private property needed to be recognized.

Angela: Wow, so your theory actually played a crucial role in the constitution of the distinction between the domestic and the international sphere in the modern states system! In order to realize individual freedom in the domestic sphere and to establish a government that would protect that freedom, you needed to advocate colonialism as the material basis for these policies. Now, I know you justified that by arguing that the common property regime in indigenous societies was not as productive as the private property regime – but with all due respect, Mr. Locke – your arguments here do not stand up to scrutiny. First, given your voracious reading on the New World, you must have known that there was a great variety of economic and political orders amongst indigenous communities – including many that engaged in agriculture and trade (with the equivalent of money). More importantly, secondly, you noted yourself that even in England there existed common property in land that outsiders could not simply appropriate. This is why you ultimately argued that it was the overwhelming power of the English that allowed them to deny weaker communities political recognition.[4] And this, Mr. Locke, essentially amounts to the establishment of the international sphere as a realm of power politics in the modern period in contrast to the domestic sphere which is, at least in principle, ruled in accordance with natural rights.

Locke: Yes, but this denial of political rights was only ever meant to be temporary. Once private property had spread more widely, the franchise could also be extended.

Angela: I see. Well, in the long run you were, of course, right. Democratization in the domestic sphere and decolonization in the international sphere meant that political rights were indeed extended. Does this mean, as liberals argue today, that liberal principles were realized?

Locke: I wish you were right, young lady. But if we look more closely at the historical development – I have just had the chance to read up on this – we find that the policies I advocated actually established both liberal and nonliberal actors. Expropriation and political oppression led to impoverishment and alienation; it constituted worker's movements, communists, fascists, independence movements in the colonial world and led to social upheavals, revolutions and wars of independence. These political actors actually fought for their political rights, and ultimately they won. In fact, the core liberal policies of expropriation and political oppression continue unabated to this day – they were simply adapted to the shifting power relations. The establishment of the Bretton Woods institutions after WW II institutionalized liberal principles for the world economy and thus provided continued access for core liberal states to resources, labour and markets abroad – even in the absence of formal imperial rule. And the recent period of neoliberal policies basically consisted of the privatization of common property – of state-owned industries, health and education, the extension of intellectual property rights. Furthermore, today as in the past, these policies constitute resistance. And wherever that resistance emerges, the political rights of the relevant actors are denied. You can see this clearly during the Cold War when interventions were consistently undertaken against 'nonliberal' actors. The same is happening today. Where democratic elections produce 'nonliberal' outcomes, they are not only not recognized but actively undermined and states that challenge the rules, rogue states, are excluded from equal political rights.

Angela: Yes, I can see what you mean. Today we use democracy promotion and humanitarian intervention to deny people equal political rights if and where these do not lead to 'liberal' outcomes. But how do you explain this development? Was your theory wrong?

Locke: Well, I would like to say that my followers did not pay enough attention to the fact that I insisted that privatization could only be pursued as long as enough was left to provide all people with the means to work for their subsistence.[5] If this rule had been followed, then people would indeed be free, though inequality would still abound. Instead, the relentless and unchecked drive towards privatization has produced exactly the opposite: It has made almost all people unfree. Alas, I fear that my commitment to logic and honesty does not allow me such an easy way out. In fact, I was disastrously wrong when I assumed that the reality could be shaped to match my theory. Bridging this gap required power politics and I overlooked that power politics would shape political actors and the political environment as much as my emancipatory policies did. And I don't really see a way of overcoming this problem.

Angela: Oh dear, though I think your reasoning is sound, this is nevertheless devastating for me and my thesis – which was after all supposed to be about the importance of your work for international politics.

Locke: But my dear young lady, you must not make the same mistake I made. I thought that I had solutions to offer to concrete political problems – and in that I was wrong. But this does not mean that my work is entirely useless. In fact, it has been instrumental in shaping politics ever since the end of the 17th century. The Whigs and their successors actually quoted me in parliament in support of their enclosure acts – and did so for over a century.[6] The British colonists in America and also later in Australia, New Zealand and Canada used my arguments to justify the expropriation of the indigenous populations.[7] Hence, you can use my work to explain and understand the dynamics of modern politics.

Angela: Yes, but here's the problem: I wanted to write about contemporary international politics and your work may have been cited widely in the past, but this is not the case any longer. On the contrary, in International Relations in particular everyone refers to Immanuel Kant and nobody wants to be associated with you.

Locke: Slow down, my dear, you panic and so you lose sight of the bigger picture. If people today are citing my esteemed colleague Immanuel Kant, they do so precisely because his work has not had the same influence on the making of modern politics as mine – and so he is not easily associated with its shortcomings. The very fact that people shy away from using my work tells you that it offers an extremely useful way to understanding and analysing the working of modern politics – including its dark side. If you'll allow me to dispense with modesty for a moment: I was right to argue that our actions constitute the world around us – and since my theory motivated such actions, it can be used to analyse the workings of this world.

Angela: You are right, of course. Thank you so much! I will just have to remind myself that the purpose of my thesis is analysis, not the provision of political solutions. Thank you so much for your time and the privilege of talking to you!

Locke: You are very welcome, my dear. It was a pleasure to get the chance to reflect on my own work with historical hindsight – but also quite taxing. So, I think if you don't mind I shall now retire again and leave you to take up the baton.

Notes

1. Tully, J., 1993, *An Approach to Political Philosophy: Locke in Contexts*, (Cambridge: Cambridge University Press), 140–1; Tuck, R., 1999, *The Rights of War and Peace. Political Thought and the International Order from Grotius to Kant*, (Oxford: Oxford University Press), 167; Jahn, B., 2013, *Liberal Internationalism. Theory, History, Practice*, (Basingstoke: Palgrave), 42.
2. Locke, J., 1994, *Two Treatise of Government*, (Cambridge: Cambridge University Press), 351.
3. Williams, D. and T. Young, 1994, 'Governance, the World Bank, and Liberal Theory', *Political Studies* 42:1, 84–100.
4. Locke, *Two Treatises*, 292.
5. Locke, *Two Treatises*, 288.
6. McNally, D., 1988, *Political Economy and the Rise of Capitalism. A Reinterpretation*, (Berkeley: University of California Press), 62, 8–9.
7. Arneil, B., 1996, *John Locke and America: The Defense of English Colonialism*, Oxford: Clarendon Press, 169; Ivison, D., 2003, 'Locke, Liberalism and Empire', in P. R. Anstey (ed.), *The Philosophy of John Locke: New Perspectives*, (London: Routledge), 93.

10

Two Days in the Life of 'Dave' Hume (1711–1776)

Hidemi Suganami

In what follows, David Hume first appears as 'Dave', a PhD student supervised by 'Prof'. Dave is excited about the progress he has made over the summer and Prof asks some searching questions. Forty years later, Hume, now an Emeritus Professor of Psychology (EPP), gives a piece of advice to a Promising Young Academic (PYA) from the United States.

Prof: Hello Dave, come in; how are you?

Dave: I am fine, thanks; how are you, Prof?

Prof: I am doing all right, thank you. I can't grumble; I'm still in fulltime employment! Anyway, what can I do for you today?

Dave: You said to come and see you for supervision.

Prof: Ah, right, OK; so, what have you been up to over the summer? Or, more to the point, what is your research question? You know the one with a question mark at the end? Have you found what that is for you yet?

Dave: Yeah, I know; I've been thinking about that a lot over the summer and I think I've fixed it. It's 'What is causation?'.

Prof: That's a big one, Dave. Hmmm … [*Pause*] Do you mean 'what is the meaning of the word *causation*?'; or do you rather mean 'What happens in the world when what we call *causation* happens?'

Dave: I haven't thought quite in those terms. But as far as the first one goes, I already know the answer: 'causing' means 'bringing things about'.

Prof: I see; is it the second question, then, you're asking?

Dave: Well, not quite. I got the impression from my reading over the summer that there is a problem, quite a serious one, arising in relation to the first question.

Prof: But Dave, you just said you know the answer to that; have I misunderstood you?

Dave: Well; you see, philosophers say that all our ideas stem from what we see or experience. And here we seem to have an idea that when something causes something else the first thing *brings about* the second thing. But I am pretty sure that we don't see this strange thing called 'bringing about' or 'forcing' or 'necessitating'. So, I am curious about where we get that kind of idea from. How is it that we come to think about the world in causal ways?

Prof: I see; but are you sure, Dave, that we can say of *all* our ideas that they stem from our experiences? And are you really sure that we have no experience of causation? What if someone pushes me? Don't I feel the pressure, the *forcing*? Or what if someone makes me angry? Don't I experience someone *making* me angry?

Dave: Hmmm. I haven't thought about all that. But I am pretty sure that if a billiard ball hits another and makes it move, all I see is the first one moving and the second moving on contact. I definitely don't see 'causing' as an in-between sort of thing.

Prof: You mean 'causing' isn't an event in its own right?

Dave: Precisely.

Prof: Alright; please proceed. Where do *you* think our idea of 'causing' comes from?

Dave: I've thought a lot about that over the summer. And my hypothesis is that we have *instincts*. And by instinct we tend to expect something to happen when, again and again, we have seen it happen when something else happens. This 'again and again' is the important bit. We come to expect some kind of thing to happen because we got used to seeing that kind of thing happen repeatedly after seeing another kind of thing happen. Our idea of 'causing' as some kind of necessitating stems from that experience, I believe.

Prof: You mean we are like what's-his-name's dog? I mean, Pavlov.

Dave: Precisely – except, of course, dogs won't develop 'ideas' as we do.

Prof: That's very pertinent. But do you seriously mean that this thing we call 'causal power' is just in our thinking and never, ever, actually, in the world? Do you mean to say there is no 'gravity' if we don't think about it? There is some more explaining to do there, Dave.

Dave: Well, we all know of Zack's work on that subject. He is brilliant. He's got a nice position in Cambridge even without a PhD, you know.

Prof: I do; people like him don't need a qualification. Mind you, Ludwig's got one of those.[1] Anyway, Dave, you were saying ...

Dave: So, anyway, I read Zack's work and daresay I understood most of it. What he is saying is this: that there is what he calls 'the force of gravitation'; but there is not much he can find out about it; yes, he knows the law; he has identified it; but over and above that knowledge – and that, on its own, is a tremendous achievement – he is saying he can't find out anything by the method he is using. He calls it the 'experimental' method; maybe it's better to call it 'observational'. Anyway, I believe him. We can find the laws of nature but we can't unlock the secrets of nature beyond that. We have no way of finding out what causes things to obey Zack's law other than just calling it 'gravity'.[2]

Prof: Alright; so, according to you, and you are happy to follow Zack on this, we can't be sure what 'causation' really is; all we can know is, if we are lucky, the laws according to which nature works. Hmmm. [*Pause*] I am getting a bit lost here, actually. You seem to be saying this: (1) we know that 'causing' means something like 'necessitating'; let's call this 'the operation of causal powers'. But (2), we can't ever find out what really goes on when this 'necessitating' happens, apart from, if we are lucky, the laws that such powers seem to obey when they do operate. Is that right? But you have your answers, then, at least to the two questions I raised earlier. Just remind me again what you are asking in addition. I don't always remember everything my students tell me, you know.

Dave: What I really want to do is say something about *us* that is as clever as what Zack said about *nature*. You see, I am interested in *us*, our way of thinking, how we think, how we come to understand the world.

Prof: And ...?

Dave: As I said, I want to solve this puzzle; where does our idea of causal necessitation come from when we don't see or experience it at all? I do think that all our ideas are, and have to be, rooted in our experiences. And, over the summer, I have come up with a solution. And I can tell you what my definitions of 'a cause' are.

Prof: That's awesome, Dave; 'definitions', eh? That's quite a lot to expect of a PhD student. What are your 'definitions' of 'a cause', then; I'd be curious to learn.

Dave: I thought you'd be interested; I have written them down to make sure I get them right. Here they are:

> We may define a cause to be *an object, followed by another, and where all the objects similar to the first are followed by objects similar to the second.* Or, in other words, *where, if the first object had not been, the second never had existed.*

And we may also define 'a cause' as:

> *an object followed by another, and whose appearance always conveys the thought to that other.*[3]

Prof: Interesting. I don't think anyone else had come up with that. Hmmm … But can you explain to me how you arrived at these, what you are calling, 'definitions'? How are you going to defend your reasoning at your *viva* – and you know you must go through that in just over a year – that these are the *correct* definitions? I feel nervous when someone just gives me such things.

Dave: Well, this is a bit complicated. And I'm going to stake my claim to originality on my reasoning here. So, I hope I can explain this to you clearly and win you over.

Prof: I am listening.

Dave It goes like this. Ideas are difficult to define outside geometry and things like that. Especially when we come to my kind of enquiry …

Prof: Enquiry concerning human understanding?

Dave: Yes, nicely put, when it comes to that, we just have so many ideas floating about which are really quite faint and obscure. That's especially true of an idea like 'cause'. What can we really mean by that? Now, I have a solution, a way of addressing such difficulties.

Prof: That's very exciting; I don't like leaving things vague, as you know.

Dave: I do; and so, when in doubt, when you are uncertain, because there are so many vague ideas floating about, I say, trust your experiences, what you see, feel, etc – because, because, I tell you, all these sensations are vivid; they are, aren't they? They are certainly more vivid than the sensation you get if you imagine or remember something; you know getting wet is getting wet;

remembering getting wet is not quite as vivid; and the idea, just the thought, of getting wet, well, you can *think* that but not really *feel* it in any vivid way. So, in my view, the way of defining an idea, when we are uncertain about it, because we don't have any sensory experience that seems to match it, that backs it up, if you like – and remember we don't have a sensory experience of that in-between thing called 'necessitating' – then, and then, I would suggest we try to look for something else, something we can really feel that may have given rise to that otherwise inexplicable idea, such as, as in this case, causal necessitation.

Prof: You are doing well; please continue.

Dave: Well, I've given you my answer already. That feeling, the experience, rightfully regarded as lying at the root of our idea of what we call 'causation', is really that Pavlovian dog thing; our expectation that Y will happen when we see X when we have seen Y follow X again and again.

Prof: And so?

Dave: And so, that's what my definitions of 'a cause' say. We can define a term firmly only with respect to the experience underlying it; unfortunately, we don't experience or feel 'causal powers' at work; but, fortunately, we *do* feel our mind expecting things.

Prof: Like Pavlov's dog, salivating?

Dave: Precisely!

Prof: That's certainly very innovative, Dave. But why do you call what you have formulated 'definitions'? Is that quite the right word for the kind of thing you are doing? It seems a bit strange that we arrive at a definition of a word by looking at our experiences. Hmmm … [*Long pause*] Might it not be the case that what you were arguing about would be best expressed in terms of something looser than 'definitions'? Let's say, how about, 'the best take' we can come up with about this thing called 'causation' over and above what Zack had told us about it?[4] You had agreed that there is not much even he could say about it, let alone people like you or me. We just have to accept what people like Zack say when it comes to physics – although I suspect there is some more to come in that field, maybe when another genius like Zack turns up – you know, someone who can think 'outside the box', as they say. [*Pause*] In fact, we will have to think outside of our box, I mean, our space and time, if we want to explain something like gravity, which is everywhere in that box but no explanation is found anywhere in it. Hmmm ... that's a thought. Hmmm ... Oh, well, never mind; you are interested, you said, in finding out how our understanding works. And you are, basically I believe, saying that our minds work, by instinct, like that of the dog; we get conditioned into expecting things. And that's the best take we can offer, the most insightful thing we can say about – well, not about causation in the world, that's a separate issue, but about how we come to think causally about the world. Call this a *definition* if you will but what you are really producing is an *explanation*, from the viewpoint of the science of human understanding, of our way of making sense of the world in causal terms. And so, when you say you are looking for a definition of an idea in our experiences, what you are really doing, it seems to me, is this; you are trying to identify our experiences that you think have given rise to our idea of causation and making our idea of causation a bit more intelligible than before. 'Making it a bit more intelligible'; well, you know, I once called it 'intelligibilifying'; nobody liked that.[5] Anyway, all the time you are acknowledging that we have no comprehension of what goes on in the world when 'causing' goes on beyond what Zack had said about that subject; no intelligibilifying beyond Zack, we might say. So, yes, I am getting the picture now. [*Prof now clears his throat.*] There are two ways of understanding about causation at stake here; Zack's way and Dave's way, each dealing with a specific question about that subject matter. Zack's way has to do with what causation really is in the world. Gravity is a causal force, of course. But we don't have any understanding of it – other than to say that it works according to a formula, for which Zack is rightly famous. So, that's shown in your first 'definition'; causal-relations-in-the-world can only be known to us as law-like relations. And then, of course, there's Dave's way. This has to do with how our mind works, how the human mind comes to make sense of what happens in the world in terms of the idea of causation – understood, of course, as the operation of causal powers. And that you say is based on our instinct, our innate tendency to expect Y when we see X, that is, if we have repeatedly witnessed Y follow X. That's what your second 'definition' is about, isn't it? And, may I perhaps add, just as Zack has no explanation of what causes gravity, so you can't say, either, can you, what causes instinct. Am I right; or am I right?

Dave: Well, thank you, that's *amazing*; you've nailed it – though, you've heard of an HD screen, no doubt; high *definition*, that's what I am after; you know the one that makes things look really vivid?

Prof: Oh yes, I've heard about it; maybe I should get one. It's kind to your eyes, my son tells me. Hmmm ... But ...

Dave: But what?

Prof: But, are you really sure about your substantive claims? Apart from the method issues, you will, of course, be asked about those. I mean Pavlov's dog and all that. I recall reading Durkheim years ago – you know his work on primitive religions – I think he was arguing that our awareness of causality has *social* origins.[6] If you are asking 'where does our idea of causation come from?', you can't just assume 'it comes from within us individually, and commonly, due to our makeup'; there may well be something about the way our society is organized which gives rise to our notion, or understanding, of this thing called 'causation'. And even if you decide to stick to individual psychology, I remember glancing at a book by Michotte, who actually talks about 'causal impressions', based on some rather clever psychological experiments.[7] Have you done any experiments in your research, by the way?

Dave: Ah, no; but I am only a philosopher; and, surely, the examiners would understand I can't do everything.

Prof: You are right there but I am a bit concerned; what you are calling 'philosophy' isn't actually what I tend to think of as 'philosophy'; but then, well, who am I to say what 'philosophy' really is? In any case, there is at least one thing we can agree philosophy tries to do – making our thinking a bit clearer and tighter; and you are trying to make a contribution there. [*Prof gives a big smile.*] OK; that's enough for today. Let's meet again in two weeks. I suggest you take a look at Roy's work before then. He has done some interesting stuff on causation but does a different kind of philosophy from yours.[8] And, yes, you were saying something about the 'experimental' method; you will find something interesting about that in his work. Take a look. By the way, when you get your thesis done, you could call it *An Enquiry concerning Human Understanding*.

Dave: Thanks, Prof; I'll bear that in mind. I'd better be going.

Forty Years Later. Having duly defended his doctoral thesis, Dave obtained a lectureship in the Department of Moral Philosophy up North, awarded a personal chair in recognition of his work on human understanding, and is now Emeritus Professor of Psychology. His 'definitions of cause' came to be widely quoted in various disciplines, including IR, though mostly out of context and misunderstood. One day, a Promising Young Academic pays him a visit from the United States.

EPP: Oh, hello, come in. You are the young man from I.N.I.S.O.S.[9] I've been expecting you this afternoon. Welcome! Sit yourself down. Yeah, take that comfy chair. And what can I do to help?

PYA: It's a great honour to meet you, Professor. I have come to see you for some advice.

EPP: I am not sure if I can be of much help there but let's see; what is your problem?

PYA: Well, I have a project – to write a book relating to your great work on causation from many years ago.

EPP: Ah, yes, a book on causation. Well, I can tell you now, it's very tricky; if I were you, I wouldn't go anywhere near it. [*Pause*] You see, I hit upon that subject over one summer – when I was very young and imprudent – without, in fact, seeing my supervisor about it beforehand. Good old Prof let me get on with it because, I rather think, it was a bit too late to change my topic by then; I had only a year left to go. These things happen, you know. I had many other interests – Physics, History, coffee houses and the College Snooker Club. I daresay they all helped me in the end. But ... but you already have your PhD; so you are in no hurry. Why don't you take your time and come up with something less tricky for your book project?

PYA: But, Professor, what seems to be such a huge problem with 'causation'?

EPP: I can tell you what the problem is. It's that we can't *see* it. So, people have very different ideas about it, without ever being able to *show* conclusively what it *really* is. And so, what happens is – well, I can tell you what *really* happens because I have *seen it again and again*. There is no *necessary connection* that anyone can *see* between writing a book on that dreaded subject and being misunderstood and got at by everyone, even by friends and colleagues in your own department. But, my experience tells me, there is a *constant conjunction!*

PYA took heed, wrote many books and many articles over many years on many subjects, but could not in the end resist the temptation to do one on 'that dreaded subject'.[10] He is probably safe in his belief that, in the social world, there are no constant conjunctions – *but, of course, there is* always *causation.*

Notes

1. G. E. Moore, an examiner of Ludwig Wittgenstein's *Tractatus Logico-Philosophicus*, wrote in his report: 'I consider that this is a work of genius but, even if it is not, it is well above the standard required for a PhD degree'. Alastair MacFarlane (no date), 'Brief Lives: Ludwig Wittgenstein (1889–1951)', *Philosophy Now* http://philosophynow.org/issues/87/Ludwig_Wittgenstein_1889-1951 (accessed 17/10/2013).
2. Isaac Newton, *The Principia*, tr. Andrew Motte (New York: Prometheus, 1995), 442–43.
3. David Hume, *Enquiries Concerning the Human Understanding and Concerning the Principles of Morals*, 2nd ed. L. A. Selby-Bigge (Oxford: Clarendon Press, 1962), 76–77.
4. See Galen Strawson, 'David Hume: Objects and Power', in Rupert Read and Kenneth A. Richman (eds), *The New Hume Debate*, rev edn (London: Routledge, 2007), 31–51 at 47.
5. Hidemi Suganami, 'Agents, Structures, Narratives', *European Journal of International Relations* 5(3) (1999): 365–386 at 367.
6. Emile Durkheim, *The Elementary Forms of the Religious Life, with a New Introduction by Robert Nisbet* (London: Allen & Unwin, 1976), 362–69.
7. Albert Michotte, *The Perception of Causality*, tr. T. R. Miles and Elaine Miles (London: Methuen, 1963).
8. Roy Bhaskar, *A Realist Theory of Science*, 3rd ed. (London: Verso, 2008).
9. Isaac Newton Institute of Strictly Observational Sciences.
10. Richard Ned Lebow, *Constituting Cause in International Relations* (Cambridge: Cambridge University Press, 2014).

11

The Dangers of Dependence: Sultan's Conversation with His Master Jean-Jacques Rousseau (1712–1778)

David Boucher

Jean-Jacques Rousseau (1712–1778) is one of the most misunderstood and reviled philosophers of the 18th century. Rousseau was born in Geneva in 1712 to a family of middle-class connections, which was forced to flee Geneva when Rousseau was ten years old. After many years of an itinerant existence Rousseau fled to England to escape persecution. He was a hypochondriac and paranoiac, exacerbated by the fact that he was often ill and had many enemies. In 1762 with the publication of Émile *and* The Social Contract *Rousseau was denounced both in France and Geneva for his unorthodox and heretical views on religion, despite describing himself as the only man in France who believed in God. From then on he lived a somewhat nomadic existence. In exile in England, accompanied by his beloved dog Sultan, Rousseau felt extremely vulnerable because of his dependency on David Hume. Rousseau's views on a wide range of issues, including international relations, may be attributed to his morbid fear of dependency and his attachment to his dog Sultan astonished his acquaintances. David Hume commented that Rousseau's affection for that creature is 'above all expression and conception'.[1] After Rousseau publicly vilified Hume, Hume described him as a 'pernicious and dangerous' man who 'lies like the devil'.[2] He died on 2 July 1778 at Ermenonville. During the French Revolution, hailed as a towering inspiration, his body was exhumed and transferred to the Panthéon.*

Sultan: You have now been dead for over two centuries master. There have been unimaginable advances in science and technology. Do you think that you may have been rather hasty in claiming that such advances in your day contributed nothing to human moral progress?

Rousseau: Progress, my faithful canine, is illusory and the so-called sciences caused and are still causing the ruin of mankind. The more sophisticated a culture, the more corrupt it becomes. Just look at how the establishment in Britain ignored serial child abuse among their numbers; the reports on how prevalent the practice of torture by the United States was during the first decade of this century; and, how French society has been rocked by attacks from within on its traditions of citizenship and freedom of expression. Modern culture contributes nothing to the greater happiness, nor to a more virtuous life. We are enslaved by the complexities of modern societies, and here I agree with Gadamer's condemnation of the subversion of reason by science, and our dependence on so-called experts.[3] Simple societies in which citizens live a Spartan existence provide the only environment in which virtue may flourish. Plato had it right in identifying the danger of allowing poets and artists to live uncensored in the *Republic*. They should be exiled. I was completely opposed to the establishment of a theatre in Calvinist Geneva on the grounds that it invited immorality and constituted an affront to republican virtue. Free entertainments such as games, athletics, dances and concerts were much more appropriate for the idea of republican virtue.

Sultan: Are you suggesting, then, that a world populated by small republics, living in relatively Spartan conditions, is more conducive to peace and harmony?

Rousseau: I am suggesting exactly that, Sultan. Since my death in 1778, critics failed to get the irony and satire in my characterization of the Abbé de St. Pierre's Project for Perpetual Peace.[4] I have been portrayed as a miserable pessimist, and a realist who understood power politics all too well. I understood it all right, but I did not advocate or encourage it. My opposition to the position exemplified by Kantian idealism was not because I believed that realism would inevitably prevail.[5] It is also true, as Kenneth Waltz suggests, that I may be called a structural or neo-realist who portrays war as endemic in the international system.[6] The qualification I would make to Waltz's view is that I am simply giving an explanation of the international system as it is, and I am far from advocating that is how it should be. Nor would I agree with Waltz that I think the solution is a federation of states.[7]

I want to deny that I am a realist in any meaningful sense of the term. I do not subscribe to the idea of reason of state, or the equation of might with right. Right cannot be derived from might. Force is a physical thing and it cannot create moral obligations. Right becomes superfluous if we believe that force creates and sustains right. If it were so we would have to come to the ludicrous conclusion that without force men would feel no obligation and cease to obey the ruling power. The idea of Right on this view would add nothing to force. Authority arises from convention, not force. Indeed, I offer a credible alternative to realism that will almost completely eradicate international conflict.

Sultan: That sounds wonderful. Why were your recommendations not accepted and acted upon?

Rousseau: They never got them, Sultan. Even today my critics think I am a deranged madman, a modern day King Canute, deluded into thinking that I can stem the tide of progress. They equate economic growth and interdependence with progress. Advances in the arts, letters and sciences have generated not happiness, but misery, moral corruption and greed, precariously built on a foundation of sand.

Sultan: Aren't you being a little pessimistic and over-dramatic? Isn't it rather perverse to think that the great advances in economic growth and technological innovation have been destructive rather than productive of moral progress?

Rousseau: You too, Sultan, have been taken in by the propaganda of the rich and powerful, who have structured the world to their own advantage and to the detriment of humankind. You of all people (if you excuse the expression) should have observed how human nature is corrupt and depraved, all stemming from the invention of private property, and the consolidation of the unnatural inequalities among men that it generated, and which are structurally embedded by the rich in the social and legal apparatus of the state. That natural pity I detected in the state of nature, long before the emergence of rationality, and which Hobbes failed to see, had the propensity to make us far better than we have actually become. It is instrumental rationality, alien to our natural condition, that taught us to deceive and dominate. I offered the world salvation, the elevation of the subject to the status of citizen, in a polity where the people are sovereign. In substituting representative democracy for direct democracy, in polities that are far too large to generate national patriotism, we are free only at elections, and even then we cannot rise above self-interest and comprehend what is good for us all, both within and between polities. Only through small city-states in which citizens directly participate in the political process can the world escape the vested interests of corporations, and other particular interests that subvert the general will.

Sultan: I see what you are saying, master, but I am not entirely clear on why you are saying it. What is the driving principle behind all this?

Rousseau: Dependence is the problem, Sultan. A state that becomes dependent loses its freedom and becomes vulnerable to exploitation and servitude. A republican like myself is free only when free of dependence. This is why I was so annoyed with David Hume who took pity on me when I was impoverished and in Britain. He secured for me a pension from the King of England. By making me a dependent upon the King, he enslaved me. I tried to spell out my objections to dependency in *Discourse on the Sciences and the Arts* (1750); *Discourse on the Origin of Inequality* (1754); *Discourse on Political Economy* (1755); *The Social Contract* (1762); *Émile* (1762), *Constitutional Project for Corsica* (1765); and *The Government of Poland* (1772).

Sultan: With Thucydides and Machiavelli, I think we are hard-wired to compete and enter into conflict with each other, both at the state and inter-state levels. It is just human nature that humans try to subdue and dominate each other.

Rousseau: What do you know about human nature? You are a dog. I can't understand why I am so fond of you, Sultan, given that we seem to have diametrically opposed views on most things. Or are you just playing Devil's advocate? I reject Pufendorf's view that men are naturally social, but that does not mean I accept Hobbes' contention that men are self-seeking and competitive by nature. There is nothing inherent in human nature which inevitably leads to the war of all against all that Hobbes so erroneously talks about. Things could have been and may yet with be very different. In the states system as it stands, with the personal interests and capricious whims of governments acting like monarchs, it is impossible to detect consistent principles of state behaviour. We can't presume that the interest of the state and that of its government coincide. There will be no improvement in international relations until there is a transformation of the modern state. Even if states embody the General Will, the problem of international conflict will not be resolved. In relation to each, states will still exhibit particular wills, or to put it more simply, self-interest, or national interest. Only when men in their relations, and states in theirs, cease to be dependent, will international peace be possible. The resolution for me is for men to become not dependent on each other but upon the whole community, and not subjugated to the particular will of a superior, but instead to follow the general will, which means obedience to the law that reflects his own real interest. At the international level, commerce is the main source of dependence. States have to become self-supporting and withdraw from relations with other states. Withdrawing from the European Community is not the answer. Withdrawing from all but essential trade relations is what must be achieved.

Sultan: That is an even more extreme position than the United Kingdom Independence Party puts forward. Who exactly are going to be the agents of change to bring about the radical transformation you propose, Jean-Jacques?

Rousseau: I acknowledge that is a serious problem. In a world in which morality has become so corrupt and depraved, it is asking a great deal of individuals to acknowledge the error of their ways, renounce their self-seeking and desist from the competition of the satisfaction of one desire after another. I know you will think it dangerous because of the examples of Stalin and Hitler, but what is needed are charismatic leaders who are able to rise above the fray and offer a vision of leadership that persuades and convinces without force. In other words, such leaders must claim to be inspired by a higher authority and convince citizens of the necessity for a transformation. Stalin and Hitler did not have this vision. They were blinded by self-interest and had no conception of the general will for their states. They were megalomaniacs afraid of losing their grip on power. The leadership of which I speak is that of persuasion. It is people such as Moses, Numa and Jesus who hold out the promise of salvation from our current predicament, and they are likely to arise at times of extreme crisis. It is only a matter of time before the fragile global capitalist system collapses under the weight of its own greed.

Sultan: You seem to want to deny that there is anything like a universal moral community, a thin universalism to which all states minimally adhere. Are you a relativist, suggesting that each society develops its own morality?

Rousseau: No I am not a relativist. Even John Rawls recognizes that in taking one of my main objectives for his own understanding of international relations. What drives his study is something that he attributes to me. That is, uniting what right permits with what interest prescribes. What this means is that neither individuals nor states can act consistently on capricious whim, nor can they act according to abstract principles in denial, or ignorance, of their interests. I thought when he talked of peoples rather than states he was going to renounce the principles of modern international relations. Liberal peoples and decent hierarchical peoples, however, exhibit the same self-interested principles, tempered by human rights, as states in the modern state system always did. Rawls' peoples are just as dependent upon each other in terms of commerce and international relations as states always were. Rawls has been criticized for resting his arguments on a very shaky or incomplete understanding of the relevant history.[8] I cannot help but concur. Anyone who thinks he can reconcile Kant's project for perpetual peace with what I was trying to do must be fundamentally confused.[9] I reject Kant's belief that progress in international relations will develop out of greater interdependence. It is interdependence that creates the conditions for international conflict.

Sultan: I think I am clearer now on what you are arguing. You are equating virtuousness and morality with a very strong sense of patriotism. It is not a form of insidious nationalism which harnesses the love of one's country to assert superiority over other countries or nations. It is a patriotism that promotes community and a strong sense of shared identity. You are a proto-communitarian!

Rousseau: Yes, that is right, Sultan. We are virtuous only when our wills are in conformity with the General Will. Patriotism promotes our sense of community and identity. When we love our fellow citizens we readily want what they want. The sympathy, sentiment and obligations we feel towards our fellow citizens are all the more powerful in being bounded by community. The moral rights we acquire as citizens arise out of conventions. Conceptions of a universal moral order of humanity arise out of our bounded communities, and do not exist prior to them. I admire Pericles' funeral oration because he is expressing exactly what love of one's country entails. It is a sort of erotic, ardent love, 'a hundred times more ardent and delightful than that of a mistress'.[10] The community of the whole world dilutes the sentiment of humanity and provides little or no foundation for obligations to each other as fellow human beings rather than citizens. If a state maintains its independence, it will neither need to conquer nor will it be vulnerable to conquest. Education 'must give souls a national formation' by instilling in the young the whole cultural heritage of its people. A people whose love of liberty and country has been brought to the 'highest pitch' will not easily be conquered.[11] I told both the Corsicans and the Poles that if they wish to be self-sustaining, happy, free and peaceful nations, they must revive and cherish the most praiseworthy of their customs. The performance of great deeds should not be motivated by financial gain, but instead by a love of one's country, a love filled with ardour and passion.[12] I am inspired by Machiavelli in suggesting that they should establish a citizen militia in order to promote a healthy and courageous warrior spirit, free of ambition. They must return to the old ways of life, respecting traditional trades and agricultural development. This is the only way to make a state independent in external affairs. No amount of wealth is a substitute for self-sufficiency in the production of food. To be dependent upon another state for imports of food is to be at its mercy. Commerce, while it produces wealth, leads at the same time to dependency. Freedom and agriculture go together hand in hand. The allure of the city must be tempered by superior attractions to be achieved by remaining on the land. If land is made the foundation of citizenship rights and social status, and if close family ties are encouraged by the equation of paternity with the ownership of land, the flow from the countryside to the city will be stemmed.[13] Natural resources are exploited and depleted by individual greed, to the detriment of society. The use of natural resources must be intelligently managed and meticulously planned. The current emphasis on global warming and environmentalism is a consequence of my warnings having gone unheeded in the 18th century. I argued then that there was no other answer but the sustainable exploitation of such resources as the forest. It is national traditions and institutions that shape the character of a people and give rise to its genius. A free nation is not dependent upon any other nation for anything.

I see your eyes glazing over Sultan. Time for a walk.

Sultan: Woof.

Notes

1. Cited in David Edmunds and John Eidinow, *Rousseau's Dog: A Tale of Two Great Thinkers at War in the Age of Enlightment* (London: Faber and Faber, 2006), 5.
2. Letters from David Hume to Richard Davenport, 8 and 15 July 1776, in *Rousseau's Political Writings*, ed. Alan Ritter and Julia Conway Bondella (New York: Norton, 1988), 198.
3. Hans-Georg Gadamer, *Reason in the Age of Science* (Boston: MIT press, 1982).
4. Kenneth N. Waltz, *Man the State and War: A Theoretical Analysis* (New York: Columbia University Press, 1959), 6–7 and 165–86. F. Melian Stawell, *The Growth of International Thought* (London: Thornton Butterworth, 1929), 140–168 and Howard P. Kainz (ed.), *Philosophical Perspectives on Peace* (London: Macmillan, 1987), 39. Also see the introduction by G. Lowes Dickinson to Rousseau's, *Project for Perpetual Peace*, trans. E. M. Nuttall (London: Richard Cobden-Sanderson, 1927), xxii.
5. Stanley Hoffman, *The State of War: Essays on the Theory and Practice of International Politics* (New York: Praeger, 1965), 54–87.
6. Waltz, *Man the State and War*, 6–7 and 165–86.
7. Waltz, *Man the State and War*, 185.
8. Martha Nussbaum, 'Women and the Law of Peoples', *Politics, Philosophy and Economics*, 1 (2002), 287.
9. John Rawls, *The Law of Peoples* (Cambridge, Massachusetts: Harvard University Press, 1999), 10 and 13.
10. *Discourse on Political Economy*, in *Rousseau: The Basic Writings*, 121.
11. Jean Jacques Rousseau, *The Government of Poland* (1772), trans. Willmoore Kendall (Indianapolis: Hackett, 1985), 190.
12. Rousseau, *Government of Poland*, 177. Cf. Jean Jacques Rousseau, *Constitutional Project for Corsica in Rousseau on International Relations*, ed. Stanley Hoffmann and David P. Fidler (Oxford: Clarendon Press, 1991), 143. Includes the Geneva Manuscript of *The Social Contract*; *Considerations on the Government of Poland*; *The State of War*.
13. Rousseau, *Constitutional Project for Corsica*, 155.

12
Immanuel Kant (1724–1804): A Little Kantian 'Schwaermerei'

Friedrich Kratochwil

This story might seem more like an encounter of the third kind than an actual conversation with Immanuel Kant. But since it provided me with some answers to several questions which have troubled me, it could be of interest to others.

The setting was my study where I worked on the Stoic notion of cosmopolitanism and had just reread Cicero's 'Dream of Scipio',[1] aptly accompanied by an early composition by Mozart with the same title. It was one of the first hot days in summer and I must have dozed off, as suddenly I found myself in a big hall with Corinthian columns and thought at first to have been transported to antiquity. But then I realized that outside there was not the sun of the Mediterranean but some flat summery landscape and inside I saw an inscription: Republic of Letters: Hall of the Dead White Males, *over a door, where some person was persistently knocking. In frustration he turned around towards me. I was flabbergasted: the man wore a wig, was clad in late 18th century garb and had an uncanny resemblance with Kant, as I knew him from portraits.*

When he greeted me, I hesitantly queried: 'Professor Kant, I presume'. He nodded and looked up, surprised by my strange outfit and said: '… and who are you and what do you do?' I noticed the Baltic accent with which I was familiar from many encounters with refugees of East Prussia after the War. I pulled myself together and mumbled:

FK: Friedrich Kratochwil, *angenehm* … I have been looking for the moral politician in whom you *placed* so much hope. Unfortunately, I have not found him although as a *Privatgelehrter* I even travel abroad in this search.

IK: Yes, travelling …. I would have liked that! But I never made it beyond Koenigsberg. However, I read a lot and gave courses on geography, rather successful ones I might add. But on the matter before us: Do you know why this door is locked? There was supposed to be a hearing this afternoon on my complaint against John Rawls. Nice fellow, but, of course, totally wrong.[2] To make me a liberal, as if I were one of the 'felicific calculators'. This is – with due respect to Mr. Bentham – nothing but 'nonsense on stilts', bah .... To make *me* serve in the chain-gang of so-called 'liberals' who elevated the satisfaction of desires to the main end of human existence. Their projects all ended up – if they were lucky – in some form of benign despotism, which had little to do with my idea of the 'kingdom of ends' and the notion of freedom and publicity under a self-imposed law, constitutive of the individual, the state and their relations.

FK: With all due respect, does liberal theory not also comprise the rule of law and a theory of (human) rights?

IK: Of course, the notion of a *Rechtsstaat* and that of the rule of law are overlapping but they are not the same. When it comes to the rights of a human being, my notion of 'human rights' is, rather different from all those 'interests' which have made the human rights agenda.[3] Thus there cannot be a right to democracy as a human right or a 'right to the internet' even if many people believe this and this strange association, called the United Nations – not what I had in mind when I talked about the League of Republics – endorses it. The point is not that some of these things are desirable but they cannot be *human* rights.

Besides, how anybody can miss the main point that my practical philosophy begins with *duties* and not rights, desires, or preferences, as liberals are wont to, I cannot fathom. There are many things which might be 'right', without being subjective rights. Take the police powers of the state as an example – there cannot be a subjective right to drive on a one-way street downtown when it has been designated as going only uptown. My good friends, the clever Scotsmen David Hume and Adam Smith had some interesting things to say on this, without making out of those 'charges to the government' a simple 'market failure'.[4]

FK: Permit me to interrupt here. Doesn't the 'market' also play an important role in your dialectics of separation and unification of mankind since it is the *douce commerce* and the cosmopolitan right of visit and carrying on trade that figures prominently in your *Perpetual Peace*?[5]

IK: Yes, there is some parallel to the general 'natural histories' tracking the development of the human species, topics, which were the rage of my times. Smith and others, as well as I, were interested in finding some ways of understanding the historical progression of different forms of human association, as mankind had been dispersed, separated by languages and religions, but then again was being increasingly drawn together through 'discoveries', the overcoming of distances and through commerce, even if the latter often implied exploitation. I have taken up these themes not only in the *Perpetual Peace* but also in the *Idea of a Universal History with a Cosmopolitan Purpose*. They were to provide an 'enlightened' account of human development in which God no longer actively interceded through wonders or signs showing his *manus gubernatoris* – a notion which the clever Smith then appropriated for his 'invisible hand' – but in which religion as God's direct message has been replaced by universal human reason. All different religions are then seen as only different forms of one 'natural religion'. This was my intent in both my writings on Religion and the State, since the enlightenment project saw the autonomy of the individual reduced to tutelage by the perhaps well-meaning but disastrous efforts of both the throne and the altar.[6]

FK: Ah, I see now that your 'List der Natur', the *natura daedala rerum* of Lucretius,[7] has to fulfil this task of giving meaning to human existence. Man no longer has one well-defined 'essence' but man's variability and 'progress' is now the dominant theme.

IK: That's right and Hegel, this imperious philosopher, made out of it the *List der Vernunft* and was not that mistaken. By the way, Hegel never gave me full credit for this nice catchword but changed it slightly so that it would not show up as plagiarism. But let me come back for a moment to the *douce commerce* thesis as it has inspired some controversies recently among liberals and post-colonialists.[8]

There is, of course, a way in which the argument by that man of great esprit, Montesquieu, can be read as a celebration of the progressive function of commerce that subdues the military spirit and leads mankind to a closer and more peaceful form of interaction, allowing also for the further cultivation of the spirit. However, such a course of events is by no means inevitable. The dispossession of the native Americans by the Spaniards, the English and Portuguese, later followed by the atrocities of the Dutch private companies in the East and West Indies show this. Over the years I got increasingly convinced that the 'right to visit' and to a *commercium* had to be limited[9] to safeguard the local populations and their autonomy. Nobody who carefully reads my *Perpetual Peace* and my comments on Japanese and Chinese counter-measures, can believe that I was a friend of unrestricted free trade. This is why the third preliminary article speaks only of a 'cosmopolitan' right of visit but not of settlement, notwithstanding the recent attempts of grafting a whole host of individual rights on this tender reed. Your contemporary colleagues should not read into the texts of my contemporaries things they did not contain. Thus for Smith, members of the Scottish enlightenment and myself, the notion of the 'economy' as a separate sphere with its own logic and a general equilibrium is entirely outlandish. Of course we knew of avarice, and benevolence, and were even sensitized to the odd effects that vices and virtues create in social interactions, as Mandeville had suggested.[10] But even Smith's notion of 'innate tendency to truck and barter' remained part and parcel of a wider social understanding[11] or a 'theory' of action and society. It links this tendency to socially shared 'sentiments' (rather than idiosyncratic desires) and to possibilities of their cultivation by the institutional order.[12] After all, my friend Hume had introduced 'utility' into that discourse but what he meant is entirely different from what the 'economists' of your age mean by that.[13]

FK: A useful reminder that works cannot be broken down and reassembled as if they were stones or ornaments from antique temples or theatres which have become part of our palaces, houses or churches. Let me ask about the tension between your argument about 'nature's design' and the question of freedom of action. Here two major problems arise; one, the issue of how the transition from the 'unsocial sociality' in the original state to a society occurs in persons who subject themselves to the law. How do we get then from the self-interested actor to an autonomous and moral person? The other – but not unrelated – one is of how the change from the state of perpetual war to a perpetual peace is supposed to come about. Having perhaps abandoned your earlier position of a teleology of nature by the time of the *Third Critique* there is a surprising reappearance of a teleological argument in the *Perpetual Peace*, even though it is no longer ascribed to nature but to the 'history' of mankind. This might seem to press a barely disguised secularized version of Christian eschatology into the service of relieving you from the dilemmas you had raised. But it was precisely this synthesis to which the enlightenment from Hume to Voltaire, Rousseau and you had objected.

IK: Ah well, the question of God and of revelation is indeed a tricky and unanswerable one.[14] As the shrewd Hobbes already remarked, the problem is simply that we always can only discuss the 'messages' that come to us by the word of a 'prophet' or a tradition *claiming* to have received or collected it. But we have no way of knowing whether what they say is indeed the 'truth' transmitted to them, or whether they just misheard or misunderstood the message, or had had a bad day or were even delusional. In a way, the notion of a 'natural religion' is another attempt to come to terms with the tension between our inability of knowing and the insatiable desire to 'know'. Thus, I took the admittedly ambivalent concept of 'nature' and ascribed to it some 'teleology' that works itself out behind the back of the particular agents. And, I found a compatibilist solution with the freedom of will – by leaving the notion of the 'task' or destiny of mankind to nature while changing, so to speak, the 'mechanism', i.e. substituting freely-willed action of the agents for nature's predestined 'design'.

FK: But did you not reject this 'solution' in your *Third Critique* of 1790? There you make the cryptic remark that it is the power of 'Judgement [that] will bring about a transition from the pure faculty of knowledge, the realm of natural concepts, to the realm of the concept of freedom, just as in its logical use it makes possible the transition from Understanding to Reason'.[15] You develop this thought by analysing aesthetic judgments. When we say that Boticelli's *Birth of Venus* is 'beautiful', we claim general validity for our judgment although we do not arrive at that conclusions by the usual steps of inference. Hannah Arendt[16] has seen the wider implications of this argument for politics, but ....

IK: *Gemach, gemach!* There might be certain parallels between aesthetic and political judgments but it is simply not true that we have to go to aesthetics in order to understand politics. What else do I do in the already mentioned *Rechtslehre*, or in my *Dispute among the Faculties* where I develop the notion of 'publicity' further ... even though I must insist that the ideas developed there have again little to do with the later notion of publicity and with the vulgarity and garishness of its presentations in the modern media. And that holds for both, the circus-like atmosphere that has taken hold of our *public* debates, as well as for the obscene exhibitionism one encounters in the new '(a)-social media'. When I advocated – in a way – 'transparency' as a means of insuring publicity, I did not think of 'letting it all hang out' or making every move or action a matter of 'record' so that the 'data' can be used by allegedly benign but actually increasingly tyrannical sovereigns for 'managing' their subjects, or by any 'private' *Zwangsbegluecker* (coercive felicifier) who can get their hands on data. Similarly, when I said that 'ought implies can' I did NOT say that 'can implies ought', i.e. simply deriving policy from 'capabilities'.

How anybody who has read my *Perpetual Peace* can see in it the outline of a political project for justifying outside interventions for protecting basic rights or for imposing a 'regime change', escapes me. But I guess, this is just to show that a little bit of knowledge might be a dangerous thing and I probably was too sanguine when I believed that the spread of ideas was bound to have emancipating consequences, by entirely discounting the possibility that a lot of people might be educated – nay let's rather say: might be 'trained' – far beyond their capacities.

FK: Well taken, and consistent with your earlier objections to being inducted into the 'liberal chain gang'. But let us come back to the point about your conception of teleology. On the one hand, sections 83 and 84 of the *Third Critique* contain again teleological arguments. But you also illustrate: the fact that driftwood which falls into the water somewhere in the tropics and is transported by sea currents to polar regions, so that the people there are supplied with the necessary wood for tools, tents or heating *does not entitle us* to infer that a teleology is here at work. With good reason you warn us: 'even merely to demand such a predisposition and to expect such an end of nature would seem to us *presumptuous* and ill-considered.'[17] But this argument makes it impossible to ascribe any strong form of teleology to nature. After all, we would not accept as an explanation the following: When little Johnny wants to know, why the sun is so far away from the earth and his mother answers to him by saying that is because if the sun were nearer, all the trees and animals would die. While mom's assertion is certainly true, it cannot be adduced as a cause, reason or purpose.

IK: I understand that there remains a difficulty, but what I was actually after was to show that somehow the inference from purposes to outcomes which we use when we reason in practical matters – an idea that is already as old as Aristotle's *hou heneka* (for the sake of what, or for which reason do we act) – can also be useful when we use it analogously for our heuristics of nature, without, however, forgetting the limitations of this analogy. One consequence is that the gravitational centre of philosophy moves from epistemology to the 'science' of morals and thus willy-nilly we have then to accept by implication that the Newtonian attempt of providing the paradigm of our understanding as a whole has failed because of its too-demanding conditions. But for a careful reader it becomes clear (after proper reflection) that it is now more the 'practical' rather than the theoretical reason that serves as the 'court' to which we appeal when making knowledge claims.[18]

A second, and interrelated corollary is that with the *Third Critique* the emphasis slides from nature to history, i.e. from a concern with the teleology inscribed in nature 'forcing' mankind by pushing and shoving into a certain direction, to a concern of man as an artificer of his own world and thus to a focus on how he uses his intelligence 'to give to nature and to himself a relation to an end that can be sufficient for itself and independently of nature.'[19] To that extent 'culture' rather than the teleology of nature becomes the focus for the 'history'. Its political project is the creation of a cosmopolitan order whose 'signs' we perceive, but which have no longer any causal powers to 'guarantee' the outcome, to which we are, however, committed as humans endowed with practical reasons. Thus I wrote: 'The human being, through the freedom from causality finds things in nature completely advantageous' and 'knows how to bring things into correspondence with his own arbitrary inspiration, to which was by no means predestined by nature'[20].

FK: Oh I see, that is indeed an interpretation that fits well with your emphasis on human freedom while preserving the notion of an a priori duty to work towards the goal of securing these conditions for the preservation of freedom and autonomy through the institution of *a Rechtsstaat*. It also justifies a cosmopolitan legal order, consisting of a league of republican states, and their commitment to forgo the use of force and opting instead for a lawful resolution of conflicts. This vision is, of course, the topic of your *Perpetual Peace* and in greater detail of your *Rechtslehre*.

But then I still wonder about the actual way of bringing this about. As I remember you entrust this feat in the *Perpetual Peace* to a somewhat heroic 'moral politician'. In the *Rechtslehre* you deal with it somewhat differently by broaching the idea of how the heteronomy of law and the autonomy of moral action can be brought under practical reason, and how publicity secures 'right' (rightful) political choices. There, morality, law and politics seem to be mediated in a more explicit fashion instead of expecting the moral politician as a *deus ex machina*.

IK: That's right!

FK: But then I want to explore a bit further the question of 'transition' which occurs when people enter into the civil state and when the properly constituted states, based on the idea of the *Rechtsstaat*, are taking steps in order to 'guarantee' the conditions for a 'perpetual peace', a peace which does not resemble the one of a graveyard to which you ironically refer to in the opening of your *Perpetual Peace*.

Let us begin with the first transition: what ultimately engenders the 'shift' from a rather unstable arrangement for the preservation of public order to a shared 'commitment' to the moral law, or to what your colleague Rousseau called the 'alienation totale' in his *Social Contract*? With Rousseau, this radical transformation to the 'moral being' is necessary when the actors leave the state of nature by contracting with each other, so as to make out of the *volontée de tous* a *volontée generale*. But how does this transformation occur in your case?

IK: Ah well, I advanced a couple of solutions to this conundrum. One is the argument that people when provided with security will have the opportunity to discover the principles of right and act out of some feeling of enthusiasm or awe before the law. This feeling is, however, inspired by the principle of right and not some psychological idiosyncrasy. The other is the notion of 'publicity', as elaborated in the *Dispute among the Faculties*[21] and the Second Appendix to the *Perpetual Peace*.[22] While I do not address in the former pamphlet the larger question of a 'public sphere' and of political deliberation, as some of my later followers have,[23] I do insist that in a *Rechtsstaat* legislation has to issue from the people while the possible enlightenment under present circumstances has to issue from the State and its officials. But in their decisions they have to take into consideration the proposals discussed by the philosophers, as they are the ones who are concerned with practical issues, even though not in the same way as the 'service' faculties are, be they medicine or law, which are tending to their particular patient or the client. The philosophers' view is rather directed at how the particular choice impacts on the whole community and the future of mankind.

FK: May I interrupt here?

IK: By all means, if you have a question.

FK: I do … actually, I have several. How is it that your solutions sit well with some form of strong teleology to which you come back in the *Perpetual Peace*, as well as in your *Dispute among the Faculties*?

The *Dispute among the Faculties* preserves the move from nature to history and to culture. But it displaces the familiar contradiction of nature as a 'guarantee' on the one hand, and of freely willed actions, on the other hand, by reintroducing the same contradiction in the disguise of a secularized version of the prophetic and New Testamentarian eschatology (minus the Last Judgment which was cancelled due to lack of interest). But I am getting ahead of myself. Let me come back to your First Supplement of the *Perpetual Peace* where you argue again that even without the efforts of conscious agency mankind will reach a stable state within a cosmopolitan order that includes individuals and states, as well as 'others' (such as non-state societies) under a common regime of law. As you surmise: 'Nature comes to the aid of the universal and rational human will ... and makes use of precisely those self-seeking inclinations in order to do so'.[24] This seems to square well with Hobbesian, or better still, with Lockean presumptions, but it is difficult to see what that has to do with a respect for law and for human autonomy.

Does the argument of 'awe' before the law to which you then appeal solve this problem? There is the famous remark in the *Second Critique* on this 'awe': 'Two things fill the mind with ever new and increasing admiration and reverence, the more often and steadily one reflects on them: the starry heavens above me and the moral law within me.'[25] But then in the *Perpetual Peace* and the *Dispute* you again fall back on your already repudiated natural teleology or some 'miracle', even if it is presented in the cultural form of a powerful narrative.

IK: Oh, *mon Dieu!* You want to make me into a theologian?

FK: Not necessarily, but I did not chose the word 'miracle' factitiously since its persuasive pull rests on the ability to read the 'signs' of the times, which has an uncanny resemblance to biblical prophesies. Only from this prophetic perspective can we postulate an 'a-priori duty' to work for the 'kingdom of ends'. This raises the further question of whether the similarity of your expression of the 'kingdom of ends' and of the biblical 'kingdom of God' (or of heaven[26]) is merely coincidence? The notion that man is the 'crown of creation'[27] also points to specific religious roots of your speculation, not to some 'universal reason'. Finally, I do not want to go so far as to maintain that Matthew 1:23 provides additional 'supporting evidence'[28] for my thesis because in that case I would become factitious. But is this not a 'Schwaermerei' *par excellence*?

Here we suddenly got interrupted, as more and more people entered into the room opposite us. The door had opened and people began to flock in. At his point something cold hit my face. I woke up and before me sat Ulysse, my dog, bright-eyed and bushy tailed, waiting for his evening outing. What a difference a day makes! I started with the Stoics, being transported to Carthage and then I entered the halls of the Republic of Letters, only to be transported back not to Ithaca, but to my home and to Ulysse.

Notes

Kant calls 'Schwaermerei': 'The principled transgression of the limits of human reason', *Critique of Practical Reason*, Akademie Ausgabe II, 109f. Roman numbers indicate volume of the standard text of Kant's work in German, as published by the Prussian Academy.

1. Marcus Tullius Cicero, *De re publica*, Bk VI.
2. See John Rawls, *A Theory of Justice* (Cambridge, MA: Harvard University Press, 1971) where Kant's moral theory is re-interpreted in terms of a rational choice approach bringing it nearer to the liberal intuitions of morality. For a later, more nuanced 'political' notion see his 'Kantian Constructivism in Moral Theory', *The Journal of Philosophy*, vol. 77 (1980): 515–72.
3. See Friedrich Kratochwil, *The Status of Law in World Society: Meditations on the Role and Rule of Law* (Cambridge: Cambridge University Press, 2014), chaps 8 and 9.
4. See Friedrich Kratochwil, 'Problems of Policy Design based on Insufficient Conceptualization: The Case of "Public Goods"', in Ernst Ulrich Petersmann (ed.), *Multilevel Governance and Interdependent Public Goods* (Florence: European University Institute, 2012/13) Robert Schumann Center Working Paper Global Governance Program 18, pp. 61–72.
5. Immanuel Kant, 'Perpetual Peace: A Philosophical Sketch', in H.S. Reiss (ed.), *Kant: Political Writings* (Cambridge: Cambridge University Press, 1991), pp. 93–115.
6. See Immanuel Kant, 'An Answer to the Question: "What Is Enlightenment?"', in *Kant's Political Writings* op. cit., 54–60. Immanuel Kant, *Religion within the Boundaries of Mere Reason (1793): And Other Writings* (Cambridge: Cambridge University Press, 1999), pp. 31–192. Immanuel Kant, *Metaphysische Anfangsgruende der Rechtslehre* (VI 203–372), 1797.
7. Lea Ypi, 'Natura Daedala Rerum? Justification of Historical Progress in Kant's Guarantee of Perpetual Peace', *Kantian Review*, vol. 14 (2010): 118–48.
8. See e.g. Sankar Mutu, *Enlightenment against Empire* (Princeton: Princeton University Press, 2003).
9. See Lea Ypi, 'Commerce and Colonialism in Kant's Philosophy of Nature and History', in Katrin Flikschuh and Lea Ypi (eds), *Kant and Colonialism: Historical and Contemporary Perspectives* (Oxford: Oxford University Press, forthcoming), ch. 4.

10. Bernard Mandeville, *The Fable of the Bees or Private Vices, Publick Benefits,* (1714) 2 vols., ed. F.B. Kaye (Indianapolis: Liberty Fund, 1988).

11. See Stefano Fiori, 'Adam Smith on Method: Newtonianism, History, Institutions and the Invisible Hand', *Journal of the History of Economic Thought,* vol. 34 (2012): 411–35.

12. Adam Smith (1759), *The Theory of Moral Sentiments,* ed. A.L. Macfie and D.D. Raphael (Oxford: Clarendon, 1976).

13. David Hume, *A Treatise of Human Nature,* ed. David Fate Norton and Mary J. Norton (New York: Oxford University Press 2000). Introduction, 10, p. 6.

14. See *Critique of Pure Reason,* A VII: 'Human Reason has this particular fate that in one species of its knowledge it is burdened by questions which, as prescribed by the very nature of reason itself, it is not able to ignore, but which, as transcending all its powers, it is not able to answer'.

15. Immanuel Kant, *Kant's Critique of Judgment,* trans. with Introduction and Notes by J.H. Bernard (2nd ed. revised) (London: Macmillan, 1914). III: Of the critique of judgement as a means of combining the two parts of philosophy into a whole.

16. See Hannah Arendt, *Lectures on Kant's Political Philosophy,* ed. Ronald Beiner (Chicago: University of Chicago Press, 1989) p. 61.

17. Immanuel Kant, *Critique of the Power of Judgment,* ed. Paul Guyer (Cambridge: Cambridge University Press, 2001), p. 241.

18. See Kant's argument that since we cannot attribute 'purposefulness to nature but for practical purposes it is 'dogmatic and well founded as to its reality' *Perpetual Peace* VII 362; 332.

19. Kant, *Critique of Judgment, op cit.* at 240 V:369

20. Kant, *Critique of Judgment,* p. 298, V:431.

21. Immanuel Kant, 'The Contest of Faculties' in *Kant: Political Writings,* op.cit, pp. 176–190.

22. See Immanuel Kant, *Perpetual Peace,* in H.S. Reiss (ed.), *Kant: Political Writings,* op.cit. Appendix 'On the agreement between politics and morality according to the transcendental concept of public right', pp. 125–130.

23. See Juergen Habermas, *The Structural Transformation of the Public Sphere: An Inquiry into a Category of Bourgeois Society,* trans. Thomas Burger (Cambridge, MA: MIT Press, 1991).

24. Immanuel Kant, *Perpetual Peace,* in H.S. Reiss (ed.), *Kant: Political Writings,* op.cit. First Supplement, at p. 112.

25. *Critique of Practical Reason* V, 161–62.

26. See Kant, *Grundlagen der Metaphysik der Sitten,* IV: 430.

27. Immanuel Kant, *Kant's Critique of Judgment,* trans. with Introduction and Notes by J.H. Bernard op. cit. § 84.: Of the final purpose of existence in the world, i.e. of creation itself.

28. It reads: Behold a virgin (young woman) shall be with child and bear a son and they shall call his name Immanuel, which is translated 'God with us'.

13

A Fine Bromance: Immanuel Kant (1724–1804) and Niccolò Machiavelli (1469–1527)

Seán Molloy

Immanuel Kant awoke with a sense of something having changed radically overnight. First, the confusion and incapacity that had dogged him these past few years had lifted and he felt restored to the full extent of his intellectual powers. Those powers led him to his second insight of the morning: he was not in his bed and judging by the flora and fauna that surrounded him, nor was he in his house. Quickly, he rose to his feet. That rascal Lampe was no doubt behind this practical joke, Kant fumed, but then he remembered that Wasianski had already dismissed Lampe. Perhaps this was his idea of revenge? Whatever the motivation of whoever had placed him in this strange position, Kant realized that *his* motivation was fairly clear and simple: to return home and to resume his ordered existence. With his powers newly restored, it was time to finally complete the project of unifying and systematizing all the threads of his philosophy.

Picking his way through the thickets that surrounded him, Kant found a wide path that seemed to have been made by the passage of many feet over countless years. Reasoning that this must be the path back to civilization Kant elected to follow its course. On he walked through the dim light that never seemed to get any darker or brighter. Kant could not make out the sun in the sky, even when the woods ended and he found himself on a very unprepossessing plain dominated by a tall mountain. He made his way towards the mountain intending to climb it (why not? He was full of vigour!) and from the top survey his surroundings and determine how far exactly he was from the nearest town, which he hoped would be his own dear Königsberg.

As he approached the hill he noticed an interesting feature: there was a large cave at the bottom of the mountain. Kant could not help but notice that the path he was on led inexorably to its entrance, there were no trails deviating left or right away from the entrance to the cave as one would expect. It must be a site of pilgrimage, or some kind of tourist attraction, thought Kant with a sinking feeling: there was no such site in the forests around Königsberg, and certainly none on this scale, or he would certainly have heard about it by now. No, he reasoned, he must be very far from home indeed.

He resolved to make his way to the entrance: perhaps someone visiting the cave could provide him with instructions as to how to get to the nearest town, or failing that he could sleep in the cave if he felt it necessary. Through the dim light he could make out that the entrance was completely covered by a large gate. They must charge entry, Kant thought, and sought for a couple of *thalers* in his pockets to pay the custodian.

Kant reached the gate, which was truly impressive in both its size and the perfection of its construction. Surely the fellow that built this gate knew what he was doing! – no army could ever force its way through such a barrier, or, it occurred to him oddly, none would ever be able to force its way out from the inside either. Before he could pursue this thought fully, Kant was distracted by an almost imperceptible creak as a small door within the gate opened and a shaft of lamplight burst through the gloom. A man of average height, wearing good clothes, but of very antique design, stepped through the door and into the space separating Kant and himself. *'Salve, professore!'* the man said and offering his hand in friendship he introduced himself: 'My name is Niccolò di Bernardo dei Machiavelli ... welcome to Hell!' In the fraction of a second between hearing this news and the loss of consciousness it provoked, Kant knew that it was true: he was dead and would return to Königsberg no more.

'You must forgive my somewhat melodramatic greeting, *professore*', Machiavelli said to Kant on waking, 'it is true that you are in Hell, but you have been allocated to Limbo, the most pleasant circle. It's not so bad: a temperate climate, the finest minds of antiquity for company and myself as your guide and interlocutor.'

'I postulated an afterlife in the first two *critiques*, but I had no idea that Dante's vision was quite so ... accurate. But what have I done to be denied access to purgatory and heaven? And I would have thought that you would be somewhere a little more, shall we say, subterranean.'

'In truth, *professore*, we weren't entirely sure what to do with you. We could not even decide if you were a Christian or not. In ambiguous cases like yours, Limbo is the safest option for everybody. As for me, I'm a Florentine who opposed neutrality – it pleased both the Maestro and the True Powers to give me the run of the house', Machiavelli said with a sweep of his arm to indicate his free rein within Hell.

'But what do you find ambiguous about me and my works, Herr Machiavelli?'

'Pretty much everything, *professore*, but let's begin with your decidedly odd work on politics, and the pamphlet *Toward Perpetual Peace* in particular. It is supposed to be one of your more popular, easy to read pieces and yet it is slippier than a bagful of eels. If I could report back to the Powers that preside over this place that we had cleared up even that portion of your *oeuvre*, then that would be most appreciated by both them and myself.'

'My approach to politics is directly related to, and derived from, my critical philosophy.'

'I was afraid you were going to say that ...'

'In the first *critique* I ask three questions: What can I know? What ought I to do? What may I hope? I later added another question, a master question, which, with the others, permeates all my work, including, and especially, *Toward Perpetual Peace*: that question is, What is man?'

'So your approach is fundamentally anthropological, *professore*?'

'Yes, but I employ two levels of analysis to the question "What is man?" The first level of analysis views the human being as a product and part of nature. In this understanding, man is a cog in a machine that continues on its course indefinitely and for no apparent purpose, save – perhaps – its own propagation. Nature may have ends but we cannot *know* them. This version of man is, like all animals, motivated by fear for its own safety and desire for material comfort. This creature operates according to sensibility, the understanding and the insights of technical practical reason. Ultimately human beings develop societies out of self-interest informed by prudence and what I call their unsocial sociability – human beings are social animals who, despite their mutual antipathy, tend to form groups.'

'This sounds very familiar!'

'Yes, your work is quite accurate in describing the nature of mankind as a species of political animals, although even you admit that mankind cannot be reduced to the ability to calculate political advantage without regard to a wider moral purpose.'

'Indeed, *professore* – I differentiate between Agathocles, who though a brilliant warrior and politician, deserves no respect and is not fit for emulation as his actions were solely in his interest and not in the service of the state and Cesare Borgia, no less ruthless, but whose actions brought justice and improved government to the people of the Romagna. Commentators often forget that in *The Prince* I promote the liberation of Italy from the barbarians and peace and unity under an Italian redeemer.'

'Well, I take it a bit further than that, Herr Machiavelli. I propose independence from nature itself! Nature is a despot who uses mankind without any real concern for its wellbeing. Yet nature is only one part of mankind: reason offers another perspective on what man is, what he can know about himself, how he ought to act and for what he may hope. In *The Groundwork* and the second *Critique*, I explore what reason, distinct from nature and appearance, reveals about humanity as a *moral* species. Reason has this advantage over nature, Herr Machiavelli: it reveals the *singular* truth about how we *ought* to act. Reason allows us to uncover the genuine principles of moral behaviour and how we ought to live, both as moral and political agents.'

'Now, *professore*, you sound uncomfortably like Fra Girolamo Savonarola, who wanted to remake Florence according to Christian virtue. Surely, your project, like his, will fail as you do not recognize that to live virtuously is to invite your destruction in the political realm. The best we can do in terms of political morality is to preserve order and seek the welfare of our citizens or subjects, by any means necessary'.

'Savonarola's problem, Herr Machiavelli, is that he tried to do too much, too soon in circumstances that were not ripe. The beauty of my political system as explored in *Toward Perpetual Peace* is that it is composed of two eventually converging teleologies, one natural and political, and the other rational and moral. What I argue is that nature will ultimately exhaust itself and in doing so it prepares the way for the moral reorientation of mankind. The key to understanding my work is to bear in mind that there are two paths to perpetual peace, the path laid by nature is built on a foundation of fear and desire, the path laid by reason on duty and observance of the moral law. I also admit that the failure of mankind is entirely possible and that the peace of the graveyard may be the fate of the species if we cannot realize our moral and political destiny.'

'You say that nature will exhaust itself: what do you mean by this?'

'Nature undoubtedly dominates human existence, Herr Machiavelli – that was as true in your day as it is in mine. Yet if we compare the wars of your day to the Thirty Years' War or the wars of my era, then it is obvious that the latter are more destructive of both wealth and persons. Extrapolating to the future, which is an important part of my argument in *Toward Perpetual Peace*, one can hypothesize wars of such destruction that mankind would eliminate itself if such a war was to be fought. This fear of destruction, wedded to the desire for material goods and comfort, present two natural impetuses to peace. Trade and war are incompatible – it will be in the interests of states to preserve the peace effectively in order to minimize any potential disruption to their commercial activity.

Realizing the destructive potential of war, political leaders would not wish to jeopardize peace. In such circumstances, the observance of moral norms and legal restrictions on the behaviour of states would be of paramount importance as states seek to avoid antagonizing one another. We can hope that in such an era, the *pretence* of virtue based on the self-interest of survival, may eventually become true virtue as generations become educated and acculturated to the prevailing condition of peace.'

'This is a very optimistic vision, *professore*, I still don't understand *how* it will come about. The moral actor will find himself at the mercy of the immoral, and the immoral will show no mercy in the gladiatorial arena of politics and war.'

'This is a good point, which I address in my work through the person of the moral politician. The moral politician is capable of surviving in the realm of politicians who eschew rational morality. The moral politician combines moral ends with moral means but within a political context. The moral politician is bound by one constraint: he must always act according to the guideline of the categorical imperative, i.e., act in such a way that you can wish your maxim could become a universal law. There is no mistaking the difficulty of the moral politician's task: he must be tactically astute enough to deflect the schemes of his immoral adversaries, but all the while remaining within the parameters of the moral law. But we must remember that eventually the operation of nature will circumscribe everyone's actions and that there are social and political advantages in such circumstances in *appearing* to be virtuous. The preliminary articles of perpetual peace are designed to create the conditions in which the moral politician can prosper. The definitive articles outline the system in which all levels of politics are resolved according to the satisfaction of both technical and ultimately pure practical reason. Interest and right combine with and reinforce one another in my analysis.'

'But let us say, *professore*, that I renounce your ideas of reason and morality? That I find them too constrictive and I simply wish to live in the here and now, securing my rule, enjoying what I will and taking what I want or what I believe is necessary. Let us say that rather than project into an uncertain future, we restrict our analysis to what history and the present reveal of human nature and its attendant political behaviour?'

'It is true, Herr Machiavelli, that one could certainly live one's life in such a manner. It is for this reason that I seek to incentivize good behaviour through the postulates of practical reason, i.e., the existence of God and the afterlife. We cannot (at least when we are alive) *know* that God exists, or that we are the subjects of a rational plan of nature of His design, but we are, I argue, forced to *believe* that is the case. For the sake of our salvation we must believe, if only on a regulative basis, in that which pure practical reason points us toward, i.e., that God exists and we should orient ourselves to the moral law. Without this belief hope exits human existence.'

'The foundations of your project, then are hope and belief in both God and Man, *professore*? These are commendable virtues surely, but are they enough to serve as a basis for understanding political life? Surely, it is better to recognize the nature and limits of human beings and to ask what can be done within those boundaries?'

'Your position, Herr Machiavelli, is one of despairing denial to which I offer, by way of contrast, a stance of benign hope. I concede that *knowledge* of human beings as they appear to themselves and each other leads one to conclusions similar to yours, but this is why (among other reasons), in the first *Critique*, I make it clear that it is necessary to sacrifice knowledge to make room for *faith*. Like all 'pragmatic' politicians, you profess to know what human nature is, but not what *may be made* of humanity. I merely point toward an asymptotic ideal, that though it may never be reached, allows us to hope for an escape from the despotism of nature and the negative effects of our defining characteristic as a species, i.e., the radical evil of a race that misuses its freedom. If it is true that from the crooked wood of man, no straight thing can be made, we can at least hope to improve that timber sufficient to *approximate* an order in which rational morality replaces, or at least tempers, the excesses of mankind.'

'I have my doubts, *professore*, but time will tell ...'

'Your doubts stem from your anthropology, Herr Machiavelli. The elements you neglect in your treatment of political life are the necessity to view human existence in terms of an *anthropodicy* and the requirement to *believe* (without ever knowing) that God has arranged matters such that mankind can, by its own capabilities, find its way back into conformity with the divine will and the harmony of the universe. All that is necessary is that mankind should cease to abuse its freedom, but this in itself is ultimately dependent on a leap of faith. One thing is certain, the path to peace, although *guaranteed* by nature, is *completed* only by accepting a providential interpretation of human destiny. Any gains secured under the aegis of nature are reversible, the ceaseless judgment required of technical practical reason in a purely political environment leads to unpredictable outcomes, and nobody can guarantee that prudence will be sufficient to find a solution to the spiralling series of crises that each judgment itself entails. By contrast, rational morality offers an impeccable basis for lasting peace under the aegis of providence. In terms of our practical interests as a moral species we are condemned to believe in God and ourselves or face the abyss of a meaningless existence in a Godless universe in which the human being is nothing more than an animal deluded by its accidental and deceitful reason as to its status in a cosmos that is perfectly indifferent to its survival or extinction.'

'Bravo, *professore*, that makes things much clearer. Now, if you will excuse me I must usher in an impressively moustachioed chap called Nietzsche. I believe he has much to say about this abyss you have mentioned. It has been decreed that you two must spend eternity in conversation with each other, *professore*. Although this is the first circle, it nonetheless remains Hell.'

With that, Machiavelli retrieved the lamp from Diogenes and left Kant puzzled at the table. Machiavelli made haste to the door: Nietzsche was banging on the gates of Hell and demanding entry...

14

G.W.F. Hegel (1770–1831) and International Relations

Richard Beardsworth

Student: Good evening, Herr Professor. I am writing my thesis on the contemporary crisis of liberalism? Can I ask you a few questions?

Hegel: It is indeed a fine sunset. Do come in. How can I help?

Student: Well, your name often comes up in international theory as someone who helped lay the intellectual foundations for the school of IR Realism, and yet the person who most refers to you in the discipline as a whole, Francis Fukuyama, uses you to affirm, *contra* realism, the liberal 'end of history' with the final advent of liberal democracy.[1] This seems contradictory. Furthermore, twenty-five years on from the end of the Cold War, liberalism is considered in crisis. So, I am wondering who you are with regard to my adopted discipline, and, if Fukuyama's interpretation of you is basically correct, whether the contemporary dynamics of history have in fact destroyed your intellectual framework for reflecting upon history, religion, politics and the present. To converse with you, and precisely you, about these issues would considerably help me to frame my research question.

Hegel: Do you see the deep-pink hues of the sun? What a fine sunset indeed … Ah yes, your questions. There seem to be four in all: 1) Am I a proto-realist? 2) Do I agree with Fukuyama's interpretation of my reading of history and politics? 3) Is 'the West' in decline? And 4): If it is, does Hegelian philosophy still have anything to say of interest (particularly to the Global South?); and, if it is not, are people like Fukuyama right to say that the ideological future of the world is settled and, therefore, boringly *bourgeois*?

Student: Yes, these questions are about right. My generation is deeply frustrated by the present poverty of domestic and international politics. Can you help us in this context? Or should we write you Hegelians off (as, I gather, has happened before)?

Hegel: Well, let's proceed in order of the questions. Am I a proto-realist? I am uncertain that the question has much meaning, but let me try. As a philosopher concerned with the objectification of what I call *'Geist'* (truth or being, for short), politics deeply interests me. It is only through politics that the fundamental human value of freedom has any concrete meaning; indeed, because I am an evolutionary thinker, freedom only has objective meaning, for me, *through* the institutions of politics. I work on this development of the concept of freedom in my *Philosophy of History* and *Philosophy of Right*.[2] Now, since, first, it is only through the nation-state that the principle of freedom has acquired objective meaning (neither in the subjective realms of art or religion nor in pre-modern political forms, but in the differentiated organization of the modern state), I focus on the state as the rational site of freedom.[3] In this sense my contribution to thinking politics is state-centric. Freedom cannot be thought objectively outside the state. Since, second, there never will be a site for freedom outside of, or above the state, there will never be an arbiter of freedom between or beyond the state (a 'world government' or whatever).[4]

Student: Hence you are a realist ...

Hegel: ... In these terms, yes, my political philosophy can certainly be harnessed to IR Realist tenets of state-centrism and anarchy. This harnessing, however, makes little sense. My concern is the objectification of freedom in the world. For me, history is not cyclical, but has a direction with regard to this objectification. Basically, unlike the arts (Samuel Beckett is no better than Sophocles) the human institutionalization of freedom improves over historical time. And, in that sense, while there is no court of world government worthy of the idea of freedom (my liberal colleague on the top floor, Immanuel Kant, did understand that), history will decide.[5] Hegelianism and IR realism are accordingly two very different readings of freedom, history and their relation to one another. IR realism, with its tenets of anarchy and power politics, is one essential part of what makes up the real; but it only one part of a larger whole.

Student: Do these remarks make you, then, a liberal, as Fukuyama argued in 1989?

Hegel: This is complicated. Let's go slowly, turning, as we do, to question two: to what extent do I agree with Fukuyama's use of me regarding history and politics? IR realism is born in response to the failures of 'liberal internationalism' (ineffectiveness of the League of Nations, etc.). My critique of Rousseau and Kant in both my early work up to the *Phenomenology*[6] and in my last lectures *Philosophy of Right* is useful to spur this response, for two reasons. First, the early liberals propose a legal formalism (equality before the law) that, while effectively critical of all forms of political hierarchy, ends up 'empty' of content and, therefore, prone to political abuse. The Terror of 1792–5 is, in this sense, the historical truth of unorganized or undifferentiated concepts of freedom and equality.[7] We sadly see this logic again at work today when democracy is imposed from above: it leads to chaos and domination.

Student: This is the realist critique of moralism.

Hegel: I prefer my terms since they keep ethics alive in politics: it is the fate of formal freedom. Second, undifferentiated, liberal freedom leads to the domination of one part of the social whole upon another. Modern freedom is subjectively rooted in the choices of the market. Before institutional objectification, its site is the town. The market leads, in turn, to civil society into which the middle-class is born and thrives. Now, civil society is for me one part of the state. If it comes to dominate the terms and principles of the state as a whole (as can happen under liberalism, particularly its Anglo-American variety), the state is thought and practised in contract terms particular to market society.[8] One result is the 'marketization' and 'financialization' of society where little philosophical and political distinction is made between public and private goods and where state leaders are either captured by, or themselves behave like, the business class. This second 'fate' of liberalism is not only domestic, and this is where realists find me useful for their cause.

Student: Why?

Hegel: Kant, the liberal, believes that a 'perpetual peace' (a definitive end to war) can be found between states if they form a 'league' of like-minded polities.[9] This idea reproduces, for me, contract thinking, specific to civil market society, at the international

level. Liberals, that is, take one part of the whole within the
modern state up to the world level in the belief that a social
contract can be formed between like-minded states to form
a world government that would regulate state behaviour.
Given, however, the spatial and temporal differences between
states, such a contract could *never* be guaranteed, but only
imposed, leading to new forms of domination. This is the irrational nature of liberal formalism, taking one part of the social
whole for the whole. (*Pause*) So you see, I am, at one and the
same time, critical of realism's refusal to consider freedom one
motor of an evolutionary history and of liberalism's formal
understanding of political freedom, an understanding that
in the international realm leads in the twentieth century
to the school of IR realism (starting with scholars like Hans
Morgenthau and E.H. Carr). This oscillation between liberalism and realism is actually all part of the *show* (*Schein*) of
international history, but let's not go there this evening.

Student: Well, as you know, at the end of the Cold War Fukuyama
argued that history had come to an end with the twentieth-
century victory of liberal democracy over authoritarianism
(fascism and communism). He used your philosophy of history to make the argument that the meaning of history is
freedom and that history has, therefore, a direction.[10] And
yet you speak with as much ambivalence of liberalism as of
realism. To have your thoughts on his *End of History and the
Last Man* would be very helpful in this context?

Hegel: It is an interesting book, and its general thesis is certainly not
superseded by the present economic (and military) decline of
the West. So, regarding this second question, let's again go
slowly. First of all, Fukuyama explicitly says that he is working with an interpretation of my philosophy by Alexander
Kojève.[11] Now, Kojève underestimated the 'speculative' nature
of my thinking and overemphasized its 'dialectical' synthe-
ses. For example, the modern state brought together for him
subjective and objective freedom (the dignity of the 'I' and
institutionalized rights and duties) whereas my *Philosophy of
Right* develops the intellectual rationale of the modern state,
not its immediate presence (which constantly falls back into
new forms of misrecognition and domination).[12] By making
Kojève's interpretation his own, Fukuyama makes me a liberal democrat and liberal democracy the end of history. He

thereby oversimplifies the relation between philosophy and actuality: the task of philosophy is to apprehend what is, but 'what is' constitutes a complex *whole*, the parts of which try to substitute for the whole.[13] Liberal democracy cannot stand for the whole of the modern state; if it attempts to do so, it engenders its own fate.

Student: We see this today with neo-liberalism?

Hegel: Absolutely. That said, Fukuyama is asking an essential question *via* my dialectical philosophy. Is there a better alternative to liberal democracy *as* an ideology? In historical terms, is there a nation-state that has come up – or is likely to come up, as we comprehend the 'what is' of our age – with better principles of political organization than those, under liberalism, of *liberty* and *equality*? Following Hegel-Kojève, Fukuyama responds negatively and argues, therefore, that the end of the Cold War marks the 'end of history'. Although historical time will continue, there will be no new set of principles by which to organize human freedom. In this sense History (history as a process of meaning) has finished. At the level of ideology (subjective spirit), I consider Fukuyama correct. How these principles are *organized* (objective spirit) remains, that said, a constant historical struggle. And this is where his book lacks an understanding of speculative totality.

Student: Just on the first point for now since it is also my third question: does this mean that for you, as for Fukuyama, the West is not in decline *despite* its relative material decline and despite recent events (the loss of international legitimacy following the Iraq and Afghan wars and the financial crisis of 2007/8)?

Hegel: If new principles informing political organization do not arise, the West is, strictly speaking, not in decline. In this subjective sense history has indeed ended. For example, and as many IR scholars have remarked, despite setbacks and digressions, the principles of the West – the state, market society, constitutionalism – are becoming global. The West is, therefore, only in decline because all parts of the world are becoming Western.[14] This process could produce major tensions, if not war and destruction (I don't agree with Fukuyama's democratic peace theory here). But again, the modern principles of freedom and equality will not have been superseded; rather, they will have been generalized. I do not see this basic Fukuyamean thesis as incompatible with my philosophy of history. If I glanced at the end of *Philosophy of History* towards America as the new dawn of *Geist*, the generalization of 'liberal democracy' is one interesting interpretation of that glance.[15]

Student: And yet many on the Left have criticized Fukuyama for making no distinction between liberal and social democracy and, therefore, for promoting a neoliberal version of liberalism. Since the legitimacy of neoliberalism probably came to an historical end in 2007/8, how can you say his thesis is compatible with your historical conception of objective freedom?

Hegel: This is again complicated. I think the balance between liberty, on the one hand, and equality on the other is the issue (*die Sache selbst*) for democracy in general. I did not focus on this balance in my writings because, when writing, the franchise was not yet universal. Although it was already posited in the idea of equality before the law, equality was, therefore, not developed. Today it is much more objectified, at least in the West, although neoliberal doctrine has brought about several major regressions in the last thirty years. If one emphasizes equality more than freedom, one is a social democrat; if one emphasizes freedom more than equality one remains a liberal. The point is twofold here. I think Fukuyama was right not to have over-worried about the distinction between liberal and social democracy since they both work *within* the liberal and democratic principles of liberty and equality.[16] Second, the next stage of *objectifying* equality remains a task for humanity *as a whole* and for the states that organize this humanity: radical global inequality constitutes a major misrecognition of freedom. For a dialectical Hegelian like Hegel-Kojève-Fukuyama, this stage is post-historical. For a speculative Hegelian like myself (!), this objectification of freedom may be understood as post-historical at the ideological level; but since the institutional forms of freedom and equality are, precisely, *critical* to these very principles, History is still at play. In this sense, history has both ended and continues (I call the apprehension of this historical relation of identity and difference 'speculative thought'). This is necessarily complex, but I hope you can see here where and why I am agreeing with Fukuyama's thesis and, at the same time, where and why I am not agreeing at all.

Student: Yes, some might argue that you are having your speculative cake and eating it, but, as a student of IR, I appreciate the point about Western decline as a generalization of the West. Russia and China are authoritarian states and will probably remain so for some time. To follow you, they offer no better alternative to the ideas of freedom and equality, and, in this sense, are not on the rise. China could of course become more efficient at dealing with climate change than the West (itself a debate), but from your perspective, this functionalist approach to politics will not offer new principles of political organization. The human species may, in the meanwhile, perish from the existential threats of climate change or a nuclear explosion, but the principles of human dignity and their objectification will have remained intact. I hear you well, Professor, on the fallacy of Western declinism; indeed I sense your philosophy still offers an interesting approach to it, to one side of postmodern and postcolonial critiques of you. You have made my understanding of the present crisis of liberalism more sophisticated, thank you.

Hegel: Philosophy helps us not to 'shoot from the hip'.[17]

Student: That said, I still think that your directional theory of freedom and history rides roughshod over the cultures of other states and regions of the world. After nineteenth-century imperialism, twentieth-century decolonization and, now, an age of increasing interdependence, we simply cannot say, for example, and as you do, that Christianity provides the terms of ontological truth.[18] Furthermore, what makes you so sure that this generalization of the West is not simply *another* story of the 'West' (who, after all, is loudly saying it in the 'Global South')? And, what makes you so sure that your narrative of the history of freedom has simply forgotten its condition: un-created nature?

Hegel: I never said that the Christian religion was the truth, but that it was the truth in subjective form. The concept of the 'Son of God' provides the terms through which the infinite (God) is related to the finite world and the finite world is related to the infinite: after the life and death of Christ, it is impossible, as a thinker, not to think the two together.[19] When Tunisian or Egyptian Muslims ask for dignity from their political dictators and are willing to die in the name of this dignity and for the sake of its practice, they are, of course, not interested in Jesus Christ, and their religion provides them with a fairly strong notion of equality (all humans, including Pharaohs, in submission to God). That said, I am arguing that, at the level of thought, this 'dignity' of humanity is best articulated in the notion of the 'the speculative good Friday'[20]: in the simple sense that we, following Christ, are both infinite and finite; that we are free, but free only *through* institutional practices, practices that, at the same time, can come to dominate us. It is these notions of truth and of freedom (the speculative marriage of the infinite and the finite) that Christianity formulated and embodied for the first time in history. They allowed Christian Europe, at the level of ideas at least, to develop modern science, modern technology and the modern economy. *My philosophy simply attempts to understand this singularity.* That these developments, now global, clash with the cultures of peoples that are not Christian is, I agree here with you, not something that I ever thought essential. As Fukuyama understood, these clashes are in the realm of contingency: what is necessary remains the idea of freedom.

Student: This is where the postcolonial critique of your Western metaphysics remains important, and very important today as power shifts eastwards. I understand, and admire, your refusal of Western declinism as well as your speculative development of historical and contemporary liberalism. That said, Professor, you seem always to begin from where you are, Christian Europe, and say ultimately that what it drove forward was, from the beginning, necessary (Spirit, Freedom). This conveniently ignores the necessity, not simply the contingent fact, of other cultures and of (pre-spiritual) nature. In an age of increasing interdependence and existential threats to the human species, is your argument for freedom not intolerant both of other humans and of nature? Can we afford this intolerance today? And is this not the *real* crisis of liberalism today despite everything you have said?

Hegel: I do not think my speculative philosophy is intolerant. It is a philosophy of freedom, pitched against all forms of ideological domination. In today's globalized context, it *certainly* has to be argued differently but the essential points remain. The task of thought is to apprehend 'what is': 'what is' is, precisely, complex. But rather than, *à la* Waltz, using theory to simplify the real with ideal-types (human anthropology, the state, the system of states) in order to have instrumental purchase upon it, I am interested in placing freedom at the heart of world politics and discussing freedom and its institutionalization in as upfront a way as possible. If I consider that Christianity did this better historically than other religions, then let me argue it, and let the better argument win. But let us have the argument. Despite postmodernism, I am not sure we have had this deep cosmopolitan conversation yet. My major hesitation here is, however, *nature*. As ecological thought suggests, by making nature part of the development of human freedom, we have run the risk of nature destroying us. This 'fate' cannot be ignored today in any theory or practice of freedom. You are right: I did not anticipate this irony at all. It is probably *the* challenge of political thought today. There's your thesis on the speculative futures of liberalism!

The sun has set. I must get home before darkness falls.

Student: Good night, Herr Professor.

Notes

1. F. Fukuyama, 'The End of History', *National Interest* (Summer 1989) and *The End of History and the Last Man*, (New York, Macmillan, 1992). This position has since been revised by Fukuyama.
2. G.W.F. Hegel, *Philosophy of Right* (trans. J. Sibree, revised), (Mineola, N.Y.: Dover Publications, 2004); G.W.F. Hegel, *Philosophy of Right* (trans. T.M. Knox), (Oxford, Oxford University Press, 1968).
3. *Philosophy of Right*, ## 257–259, #347, pp. 155, 160, 217.
4. Ibid., ## 341–353, pp. 216–20.
5. Ibid., # 340, p. 215.
6. G.W.F. Hegel, *Phenomenology of Spirit* (trans. A.V. Miller), (Oxford, Oxford University Press, 1979), 'The Enlightenment', pp. 324–65.
7. Ibid, 'Absolute Freedom and Terror', pp. 355–64.
8. *Philosophy of Right*, # 258, pp. 156–160.
9. Immanuel Kant, 'Perpetual Peace Essay', in *Kant's Political Writings* (trans. H.B. Nisbet), (Cambridge, Cambridge University Press, 1991).
10. *End of History*, pp. 45–6 and p. 136.
11. Ibid., pp. 200, 204
12. On this, see G. Rose's classic, *Hegel Contra Sociology*, (London, Athlone, 1981).
13. *Philosophy of Right*, Preface, p. 11.
14. See, for example, E. Harrison and S.M. Mitchell, *The Triumph of Democracy and the Eclipse of the West*, (New York, Palgrave Macmillan, 2014).
15. *Philosophy of History*, p. 441.
16. For his own comments, see *End of History*, p. 293.
17. *Phenomenology of Spirit*, Preface.
18. *Lectures on the Philosophy of Religion*, vol. 1. Introduction, ed. Peter Hodgson, (Oxford University Press, 2008).
19. G.W.F. Hegel, *Science of Logic* (trans. A.V. Miller), (Oxford, Oxford University Press, 1981), 'Determinate Being', pp. 138–156.
20. *Lectures on the Philosophy of Religion*, vol. 3, ed. Peter Hodgson, (Oxford University Press, 2008), pp. 216–23.

15

A Brief Encounter with Major-General Carl von Clausewitz (1780–1831)

Jan Willem Honig

We speak in German. 'General, I am not the first person', I venture, 'who can claim to have communed with you beyond the grave. There is something of a tradition of officers who have enjoyed this very special privilege – from Captain von Pönitz of the Saxon Army who, in the 1840s, published five volumes of letters you wrote to him from here on Mount Olympus, to a Lt. Col. Freudenberg who interviewed you in the 1970s for the US Army's *Military Review* on the Vietnam War.[1] I notice, however, that these men generally professed to be on familiar terms with you – a right to which I could not wish to make an honest claim. I beg forgiveness for my ignorance, but would you allow me first to clarify what form of address *der Herr General* prefers?'

My use of the third person, formally adopted in the German Army in the later 19th century, elicits an immediate retort, as caustic as it is dismissive: 'I do not wish to be associated with a *Generalität* whose own pretensions to exalted exclusivity took pride of place over the interests of the German nation.'

Before I can ask whether he means that the generals should have involved themselves more directly in national politics to restrain war or whether they should have driven the national cause further than *Kaiser* or even *Führer* did, Clausewitz adds: 'The appropriate form, *Herr Doktor*, is *Herr General*. But as I presume you will be translating my words into English and since you yourself retired from military service only with the rank of hussar third class, the alternative of "your excellency" may present a more straightforward choice.'

I am tempted to click my heels in speedy acknowledgement but realize that this was not yet customary in the General's own day, and of course inappropriate given my present civilian status.

'But as you well know, *mein ehrenwürdigster Herr Doktor*,' the General continues in a more conciliatory tone, 'the English language is not the best vehicle for the transmission of my ideas. You have, I believe, pointed out as much and suggested that my work should only be read in the original German,[2] especially by my Anglo-Saxon "fans".' – I am sure the General, who seems to have lost little of his penchant for sarcasm and intellectual arrogance, chooses this English word because of its association with 'fanatic'. Before I can mumble that that is perhaps a somewhat exaggerated conclusion to draw from my writings, Clausewitz carries on by stating that knowledge of the German language by itself is of little use to access his ideas, without an understanding of the philosophical language of concepts and method that underpins his analysis of war. I sense a veiled reproach, but try to humour the great man by saying that he must surely be pleased with the great renown that his name and work have achieved across the globe?

His answer once again surprises: 'Far too many people read my work and expound on it, who shouldn't. I am quite pleased with the cartoon that circulates among students of the US Army War College, likening reading my *On War* to taking a lozenge that is guaranteed to induce sound sleep. That is how it should be for them. One cannot be surprised that the average officer, and academic for that matter, is not up to the task. Who really understood my ideas during my lifetime? Did any of the royals in Prussia or Russia, or their senior advisers, civil and military? Even those whom I directly taught war, the crown prince and his younger brother, the later Kaiser Wilhelm I, struggled! The relationship between simplicity and complexity – which I tried to catch in my dictum that 'everything is very simple in War, but the simplest thing is difficult'[3] – was clearly so baffling that they could only take in either the first or the second half. Consider the state of military theory as I found it. I had to dismiss it all and was forced to develop what you would call an interdisciplinary approach, which took from other disciplines a critical method and framework for analysis that made sense of war in a revolutionary new way. Did I therefore not also, as director of the War College in Berlin, advocate the introduction of a curriculum that focused on vocational training?[4] But Rühle, who was my director of teaching at the War College, thwarted me and maintained a liberal arts programme.'[5]

'In our discussions here on Mount Olympus,' Clausewitz continues, 'Rühle now cites Moltke's generalship as proof of the success of his educational approach, and Moltke's legacy of a technocratic general staff as proof of the disastrous military and political effects of a narrow vocational officer education.[6] Bah, I say, Moltke's example merely proves how difficult it is to understand and teach war properly and what blockheads most students and generals are. Yes, mine may be the most widely read, cited and studied text on war but how well are my ideas taught and understood? When I said that my work should not accompany soldiers on the battlefield,[7] I did not mean that they should then all carry it around in their briefcase at military college instead. *On War* was only really intended for the private reflection and self-study of those in high command or senior staff positions. I thought it too revolutionary and difficult for wider dissemination.' Clausewitz's face took on an ironic condescending grimace: 'Or would you say that my ideas are today so commonplace amongst enemies across the world that no one any longer manages to draw on the advantage of a superior understanding of war, and as a result they are fighting themselves to all these politically and militarily indecisive standstills in these so-called "new" wars?' With that remark, the General retreats into a sulking silence.

Marie Countess von Brühl, whom I had of course found close by the General's side but whom both of us had otherwise ignored, now speaks up and gently rebukes her husband: '*Mein liebster Carl*, the gentleman has made an arduous journey and takes a sincere interest in your work. We all know how worried you were about your ideas being misunderstood, how you continuously tinkered with *On War* and never came close to considering publication. I published what there was soon after your death because I sincerely believed that there was enough coherence and clarity to occasion the revolution in military theory that you intended to bring about. Posterity has proved me right. The understanding and, dare I say, the practice of war were fundamentally transformed as the result of your work, my most wonderful and dear husband. No other theory of war exists that rivals yours. You literally defined war. Few authors have been as fortunate as you. You have now had another two centuries to observe and reflect further. Here is an opportunity to give some idea of the results to the world below.' 'As always, Marie, you are completely right. But,' asks the General contemplatively, 'where shall I start?'

This is my chance. I had naturally prepared a very long list of written questions but it is rather dark on gloomy Mount Olympus and I seem to have forgotten my reading glasses. I try to recall and rephrase my biggest question from memory: 'Would you permit me to make a suggestion, Your Excellency? Your Excellency appears to have maintained, from your early writings onwards, that war is a political instrument. A critically distinctive element of your method, however, is that you take your subject of study – war – and in the first instance attempt to define it in its pure form, to the exclusion of everything else. This allows you to lay bare the inner nature of war and set up an argument that permits rigorous discrimination between those things that are extraneous to the workings of war and those that are intrinsic to it. What follows in your case, if I may say so, is a remarkably parsimonious, elegant and truly insightful theory on which you claim to be able to base the effective practice of war. Yet, this very method, or perhaps your definition of it, seems to have introduced a problem into your overall theory, one that ultimately amounts to a contradiction with the idea of war's political instrumentality.'

After a deep intake of fresh breath I continue: 'Permit me to recall your definition as it appears on the second page of *On War*: "War is [...] an act of violence intended to compel our opponent to fulfil our will." The definition seems to marry three things: the elements of instrumentality and interaction between contending actors – but the critical, exclusive element which sets war apart from all other forms of social intercourse is the use of force. War understood as force, and force as a physical capacity to kill and destroy, leads to a peculiar interaction between the antagonists. You claim that it is the element of instrumentality, the desire to win if you like, which blends naturally with force's ability to denude the enemy of his capability to make war as it is the only thing protecting him from unwelcome demands. Defencelessness thus quickly and logically appears as the natural aim to be pursued in war. Now, you recognize that willpower plays a major role throughout war.[8] Enemies can decide to give in or give up well before they've lost the physical ability to continue resistance or pursue their attack. However, a red thread throughout your work is that one should not, as a matter of course, trust that the enemy's willpower shall break – and you include political moderation here as a weaker form of will as well, or am I mistaken? – before his physical, military power breaks. Physical destruction of the enemy's means of resistance is the surest road to success and constitutes the regulative principle of war.[9] Political or any other form of moderation is a hostage to fortune.[10] Can one not find this belief continually re-asserted in the final sentences of your later chapters in *On War* when you increasingly struggle to reconcile the demand for escalation with the possible desire for limited political objectives? By the way, Your Excellency, I've long enjoyed and admired your mastery of the art of the concluding sentence. The great novelists may have laboured to perfect the opening sentence, but you certainly turned, if I can put it like this, the closing salvo into as high an art form as the one you desired decisively to end the act of war.'

'Anyway, Your Excellency, let me not digress: this whole theory of yours is very clever, of course, but ultimately it seems to make policy if not wholly subordinate to the dynamics of war, then at least a mere accessory to war. Even your most famous dictum, "war is a continuation of politics by other means", arguably seeks to safeguard war's distance from politics and its special violent character, does it not? As you well know, this understanding, clearly directly inspired by your work, has had terrible results in practice. The short 20th century started with a mad and murderous search for decisive, destructive battle and progressed to a stage that allowed the man who lost World War One for Germany, General Erich Ludendorff,[11] and a French philosopher, Michel Foucault, to invert your dictum to politics being a continuation of war by other means. Surely, the better approach for you would have been to pre-empt the radical irony of Foucault and let your work be guided by the idea that politics and therefore war also were socially constructed "realities". You could then also have given your book the better and clearer title "On Politics and War". That way, you would also easily have countered modern critics, who claim that your theories are fatally compromised by an increasingly anachronistic inter-state warfare paradigm.'

'Another academic pedant, *der Herr Doktor.*' I hear the General whisper under his breath to his wife. Clausewitz turns to me and says: 'Bah, new-fangled *French* theories. Clearly, there is a correlation between their theorizing and their real-world struggle to obtain military success since Napoleon. What is war without violence? War *is* violence. One therefore must first of all account for this fact and its implications. I stand by my theory and by my method. Permit me to add that you modern liberals may think that I would have habitually sided with the civil, and political, over the military, and militarism. That would be wrong. Yes, the politician Bismarck had a point in the Franco-Prussian War in wanting to over-rule the general Moltke who advocated carrying on the war to decisive victory – but only because the immediate internal turmoil and revolution tormenting the French people in 1871 prevented them from escalating the war and defeating the newly proclaimed German Empire.[12] However, the terrible price of that compromise peace had to be paid forty-three years later with the outbreak of a much bigger, world war. A half-hearted prosecution of that war accompanied by offers of compromise peace would have been signs of weakness that the associated powers would have taken advantage of to outfight and defeat Germany because they *could* and because they *must.*[13] Militarily and also politically a compromise peace no longer made sense in the era of democratic nation-states. The involvement of the people in politics and war did not mean that politics overwhelmed policy but that policy was brought into line with politics, and rightly so. The democracies – Britain, the United States and even France – realized that better than autocratic Germany and their militaries played the game of chance and probability better on the battlefield than Ludendorff and his emperor. This is clearly explained by my celebrated trinity of passion, reason, and probability and chance, or as many think of the people, government and military. One can bewail the carnage and blame everything on "militarism" but the game of politics and war is more dirty and complex than that.'

This is not going well and there are so many tricky questions yet to explore: how would Clausewitz then precisely define *Politik*? Would he favour 'policy' or 'politics' in English translation? Or, as his outburst now suggests, would he have clearly differentiated between them? Surely, the trinity and his celebrated formula that war is a political instrument privilege reasoned and reasonable state policy and limited war? Is the first chapter of book I of *On War* really a finished product, despite its odd draft-like structure with numbered sections and these little *aide-mémoire* summary titles? Did he really begin to employ Hegelian dialectics to resolve the contradiction between war's inherent violent dynamic and its subjection to political purpose?[14] What does he think of the "new wars" debate and the continuing relevance of his ideas? What role did his wife play in his intellectual development and the genesis and gestation of his works?

I decide on a gambit. In his own day, reading one's work out loud in a small social gathering was a common practice for disseminating ideas. Much was written with this express purpose in mind. Such opportunities also counted as a mark of respect. The crown prince, whose not altogether easy relationship with Clausewitz was already alluded to, invited him nonetheless to read several of his works to him between 1827 and 1829 – generally on Mondays and Thursdays at 10 o'clock. I hope that a similar request now might also have a beneficial effect on our relationship, and might moreover give me an inestimable opportunity to hear in the author's voice how his work should be read. The General's face indeed lights up, and so does his wife's: 'I would do so with pleasure, as I have all the time in the world.' My gambit proves something of a mistake nonetheless. 'The work I would recommend is my 1799 campaign history.[15] As you well know, this was the last work I wrote and I put off completion of *On War* for it.' I also recollect it was a major effort, clocking in at 947 pages in the first edition, only a little under the 1,047 of *On War*. 'It is strangely ignored in the world of Clausewitz scholarship, which almost exclusively concentrates on my unfinished

On War, though I am sure, *Herr Doktor*, that a man of your erudition will have little difficulty in divining the relevance of this study to the progression of my ideas on the relationship between war and politics.' I want to ask whether he means here *policy* or *politics*, but quickly think the better of it. The General from the first word quickly gets into the flow of things and he is clearly enjoying himself. No longer used to this means of communication, I soon struggle to stay focused. Although the author's voice brings out the fluent cadence behind his written word and its astonishing clarity of thought and reasoning, my mind begins to wander. Strange, I never imagined the great thinker to be so cantankerous and, frankly, so illiberal.[16] I fully expected him to dazzle me instead with his wit and insight. I also presumed he'd immediately take to someone who took his ideas so seriously. But then perhaps the social and intellectual conventions of two centuries ago do present an easily underrated barrier to modern engagement and understanding. Or perhaps, he just had had a bad day on Mount Olympus, which does appear to be a crowded place with rather a lot of argumentative prima donnas. I sink into sleep. My last distinct memory of the encounter is another strange one. I am sure I hear the General read out the very same word that so memorably concludes *On War*: 'Fool.'

Notes

1. [Karl Eduard von Pönitz], *Militärische Briefe eines Verstorbenen an seine noch lebenden Freunde, historischen, wissenschaftlichen, kritischen und humoristischen Inhalts. Zur unterhaltenden Belehrung für Eingeweihte und Laien im Kriegswesen*, 5 vols (Adorf: Verlags-Bureau, 1841–5); and G. F. Freudenberg, 'A Conversation with General Clausewitz', *Military Review*, Vol. 57, No. 10, October 1977, pp. 68–71.
2. Jan Willem Honig, 'Clausewitz's *On War*: Problems of Text and Translation', in Hew Strachan and Andreas Herberg-Rothe, eds, *Clausewitz in the Twenty-First Century* (Oxford: Oxford University Press, 2007), pp. 57–73.
3. Carl von Clausewitz, *On War*, tr. J. J. Graham, introd. Jan Willem Honig (New York: Barnes & Noble, 2004), Book I, Chapter 7, p. 58.
4. Carl von Clausewitz, 'Denkschrift über die Reform der Allgemeinen Kriegsschule zu Berlin', 21 March 1819, in Clausewitz, *Schriften, Aufsätze, Studien, Briefe*, ed. Werner Hahlweg (Göttingen: Vandenhoeck & Ruprecht, 1990), Vol. II, 2, pp. 1151–63. See also Peter Paret, *Clausewitz and the State: The Man, His Theories, and His Times* (Oxford: Oxford University Press, 1976), pp. 272–80.
5. Lt. Gen. August Rühle von Lilienstern (1780–1847) was a noted polymath as well as military theorist who ended his career as Inspector-General of Military Education. Rühle was on friendly terms with Jomini until he wrote a negative review of one of Jomini's major works, followed by a very positive one Clausewitz's *On War*.
6. Field Marshal Helmuth von Moltke (1800–1891) was Chief of the Prussian (and later German) General Staff from 1857 to 1888 and is regarded as the

architect of the military victories in the wars against Austria and France that led to the unification of Germany in 1871. He was educated at the War College in the mid-1820s when Clausewitz was director and Rühle director of education.

7. Clausewitz, *On War*, Book II, Chapter 2, §27, p. 82.
8. Clausewitz, *On War*, Book I, Chapter 1, §5, p. 4.
9. For examples, see Honig, 'Clausewitz's *On War*', pp. 62–3 and 66–9, esp. p. 67 n. 32.
10. E.g., Clausewitz, *On War*, Book I, Chapter 2, p. 33; Book VI, Chapter 30, p. 555; Book VIII, chapter 2, p. 644; chapter 3B, p. 660. For examples from Clausewitz's other works, see Jan Willem Honig, 'Clausewitz and the Politics of Early Modern Warfare', in Andreas Herberg-Rothe, Jan Willem Honig and Daniel Moran, eds, *Clausewitz, the State, and War* (Stuttgart & New York: Franz Steiner Verlag, 2011), pp. 44–6.
11. General Erich Ludendorff (1865–1937) ran Germany's war effort together with Field Marshal Paul von Hindenburg from 1916 to 1918. In 1935, he published a military theoretical work under the title *Der totale Krieg*, which became an international bestseller and popularized the term 'total war'.
12. The clash between Prussian Prime Minister Otto von Bismarck and Moltke during the Wars of German Unification is usually seen as an example of soldiers' tendency to subordinate political objectives to purely a military demands and an offence against Clausewitz's dictum: e.g., Gerhard Ritter, *The Sword and the Scepter: The Problem of Militarism in Germany*, Vol. I: *The Prussian Tradition, 1740–1890*, tr. Heinz Norden (Miami, Fl.: University of Miami Press, 1969), pp. 187–260; Gordon A. Craig, *The Politics of the Prussian Army, 1640–1945* (London: Oxford University Press, 1964), pp. 180–216, and Volker R. Berghahn, *Militarism: The History of an International Debate, 1861–1979* (Leamington Spa: Bergham, 1981).
13. Cf. Clausewitz, *On War*, Book VIII, chapter 2, p. 644.
14. Youri Cormier, 'Hegel and Clausewitz: Convergence on Method, Divergence on Ethics', *International History Review*, Vol. 36, No. 3 (2014), pp. 419–42.
15. *Hinterlassenes Werk des Generals Carl von Clausewitz*, Vols V and VI: *Die Feldzug von 1799 in Italien und der Schweiz* (Berlin: Dümmler 1833–4).
16. C. B. A. Behrens, 'Which Side Was Clausewitz On?', *New York Review of Books*, 14 October 1976.

16

A Conversation with Karl Marx (1818–1883) on Why There Is No Socialism in the United States

Joshua Simon

Below, I reconstruct as accurately as possible a remarkable conversation I happened to have while walking with my dog today on Hampstead Heath. Barrington (my dog) is a sweet but strong-willed terrier, prone to pursuing his own inclinations. This afternoon, we were taking advantage of a rare break in the clouds, following one of the Heath's many improvised paths when Bear (as he is affectionately known) suddenly broke away, dashing through a hedgerow and barking with great animation. Giving chase, and incurring some minor scratches on the way, I was relieved upon emerging from the brush into a small clearing to find Bear retrieving a tennis ball thrown by a girl of around ten, much to her delight and that of her two younger sisters. Near where the girls were playing, a middle-aged man with a heavy beard sat on a blanket, surrounded by the remains of a picnic and several newspapers. I apologized for Bear's poor behaviour, and was trying to bring him to heel when the man put down the volume from which he had been reading aloud (Shakespeare if I'm not mistaken) and addressed himself to me.

Marx:	I perceive from your accent that you are, like me, an exile on this island. Tell me, was it political dissent that forced you to depart your native land?
Me:	Well, no, not really. I'm an academic, you see – a political scientist to be specific – and when I was offered a position here in London I decided to move, but I have to say I really like –
Marx (interrupting):	A political *scientist*, really? What an intriguing field! And from America? A longstanding of interest of mine, as it happens. I've even thought of moving there myself.[1] Please, sit with me for a moment. My daughters seem to be enjoying your hound more than my

134

	bard. Have a glass of this good *bier,* and tell me, how fares the workingman in America?
Me:	The workingman? Not too well, I'm afraid – at least relatively speaking. From what I've read, unemployment is down a bit since the last recession, and corporate profits and the stock market have recovered famously, but real wages haven't grown in at least fifteen years, and income and wealth inequality are as high as they've been in a century.[2]
Marx:	Hmm. Yes. Well, I'm not surprised. These trends are expressions of the tendencies inherent in the capitalist mode of production itself. You see, the capitalist's insatiable appetite for surplus value and the scourge of competition drive him to pursue the expansion of his productive power through accumulation and technological improvement. This has, of course, a most revolutionary effect upon society, enormously increasing social output and average consumption, but there are other consequences. The development of the productive power of labour cannot keep pace with the advance of accumulation and technological improvement. Thus, the organic composition of capital changes. The ratio of constant to variable capital grows,[3] and as a result – I say, you're looking a bit dazed. I thought you said you were a political scientist! Are you following me at all?
Me:	Uh, yes, I think so. The ratio of organic to variable capital grows –
Marx (interrupting):	The ratio of *constant* to variable capital grows! Machines replace men, dead labour overwhelms the living! More and more can be produced in fewer and fewer hours by fewer and fewer labourers. This is progress, no? But there's the rub. As the contributions of variable capital – labour – decline in the production function, giving way to capital, the rate of profit must also decline, and this breeds over-production, financial speculation, and finally, crisis.[4]
Me:	So, the recession in the United States –
Marx (interrupting):	Represents only the latest in a long line of crises: a violent and forcible solution to inevitable contradictions, which swells the ranks of the reserve army of unemployed workers, reduces wages, raises rates of

	exploitation, and thus, for a time, restores the disturbed equilibrium.[5]
Me:	'For a time', you say?
Marx:	In the aftermath of each crisis – during the period the bourgeois political economists brazenly term a *recovery* – the same tendencies that precipitated the prior breakdown return and intensify. Accumulation and centralization leap ahead, but along with the constantly diminishing number of capitalists, who usurp and monopolize all the proceeds of this process of transformation, the mass of miserable and exploited labourers grows. However, with this too grows the revolt of the working class. With each crisis, the knell of capitalist private property sounds. One day, the expropriators will be expropriated.[6]
Me:	But surely we are very far from that day.
Marx:	In America, capital accumulation has proceeded further than anywhere else in the world. The capital stock is the most technologically advanced in the world. And the ratios of constant to variable capital are the highest in the world. The rate of profit declines, the periodic crises worsen, and the struggle between capital and labour intensifies. With every turn of the screw, the workingmen of America come closer to understanding the true conditions of their own existence. They will be the first to recognize that capitalism has outlived its usefulness, and show the rest of the world the image of their own future: socialism![7]
Me:	It does sounds very convincing when you say it, but there is one problem.
Marx:	What problem?
Me:	There is no socialism in America.
Marx:	No socialism? That's preposterous. I've read myself about the Workingmen's parties, the Railroad Brotherhoods, the Knights of Labor, and all the rest.[8]
Me:	Well, yes, there is a strong tradition of industrial militancy in America, and there have been some prominent American exponents of revolutionary socialism, but the labour movement has never produced a competitive political party. In this sense, the United States is somewhat exceptional. Britain has the Labour Party,

	France the *Parti Socialiste*, and Germany the SPD, but in the United States neither of the political parties is a party of the working class, and neither party incorporates any commitment to socialism, revolutionary or reformist, in its platform. If socialism is going to overtake the world, it seems unlikely that it will emerge first in America.
Marx:	I must admit, that does come as something of a surprise, and a rather disappointing one at that. But you're a political scientist, so please explain it to me. Why is there no socialism in the United States?
Me:	I think many Americans would say that they have ideals and beliefs that are simply inconsistent with socialism. They are generally suspicious of the state and of state authority, and they are particularly opposed to state intervention in the economy, because they believe that a free market reliably rewards hard work and stimulates innovation.
Marx:	Truly a world seen in *camera obscura*. But, surely, this can only be part of your explanation. Life is not determined by consciousness, but consciousness by life.[9]
	If we grant, for the moment, that American capitalism has proved uniquely resistant to socialism because Americans are uniquely committed to bourgeois institutions and ideologies, it is still left to you to explain why they are so committed. What accounts for the unusual strength of their beliefs?
Me:	A fair question. The answer might lie in the unique conditions surrounding the country's founding. As I am sure you know, the settlers that colonized North America fled economic limitations and religious persecution in Europe, and they did not duplicate the European class system in their colonies. Instead, they created a novel, truncated society – one without a landless peasantry or hereditary aristocracy, only a universal middle class of small property-owners and labourers who aspired to be small property-owners. The availability of land across the frontier of settlement made even the most destitute labourer's economic aspirations seem achievable. At the same time, the early abolition of property qualifications for the franchise after

independence seemed to confirm the impression that there were no classes in the United States. In these conditions, the ideals and beliefs I mentioned became reflexive for Americans, and as a result, they were as indifferent to the challenge of socialism in the later era as they were unfamiliar with the heritage of feudalism in the earlier one.[10]

Marx: No feudalism, no socialism, is that it? Well, that's a theory, anyway, but not a very good one.

Me: Where does it go wrong?

Marx: It explains, perhaps, why the emergence of socialism was delayed in the United States, but not why it failed to emerge as capitalism matured. The conditions surrounding primitive accumulation in a colony such as the United States *are* unique. With the relative scarcity of labour and relative abundance of land, the social dependence of the labourer on the capitalist, that indispensable requisite of exploitation, is torn asunder. So long as the settler can escape the workhouse to begin an independent existence, he cannot be exploited to the same degree as his metropolitan counterpart, a result as frustrating to the socialist organizer as to the grasping capitalist.[11] But these days are fleeting. Capitalism compels all nations, on pain of extinction, to adopt the bourgeois mode of production; it compels them to become bourgeois themselves. In short, it creates a world after its own image.[12] The American frontier has vanished. The safety valve is closed. American capitalism has advanced in great strides, overtaking even its English predecessor. So, to understand the persistent absence of socialism in the United States, we must consider other factors.

Me: I suppose you're right. But what do you have in mind?

Marx: To describe the pre-history of the United States as simply 'not feudalism' is rather narrow, isn't it?[13] It is true that the pattern of primitive accumulation in America differed from Europe's but we must think more broadly about the idiosyncratic class system of a settler colony. While the settlers themselves enjoyed more opportunities to own property and labour independently than they might have in Europe, their privilege came at others' expense.

Me: That's true! The frontier wasn't really uninhabited at all, and settlement entailed the forced removal or elimination of millions of people –

Marx: Precisely. Consider also that America's problematic deficit of labourers was met, not by the natural increase of the original settler population, but by the introduction of new peoples – Africans, southern and eastern Europeans, and Asians – transported voluntarily or involuntarily to North America to fill out the sparse ranks of the working class.

Me: That's also true. But what does it have to do with the absence of socialism?

Marx: Racism and nativism have persistently split the American working class into hostile camps. The Anglo, Protestant labourer resents his African, Asian and Catholic counterparts as competitors who threaten to lower his standard of living. The material advantages and personal dignity he derives from the relative oppression of darker-skinned and newly-arrived workers lead him to regard himself as a member of the ruling class. Consequently, he becomes a tool of the capitalists, strengthening their domination over himself as well as the others. He is repaid with interest by the objects of his disdain, who see in the Anglo, Protestant worker an accomplice and a tool of their oppressors. This antagonism is kept alive and intensified by the political parties, by the press, the pulpit, the comic papers, in short, by the entire ideological apparatus at the disposal of the ruling classes. It is the secret of the impotence of the American working class. It is the secret by which the capitalist class maintains its power.[14]

Me: I think there's a lot of truth in that. It is clear that throughout the nineteenth and early twentieth centuries, despite the earnest efforts of some socialist leaders, nativism and racism impeded the formation of a unified working-class politics in the United States, while at the same time helping legitimize the repression of labour activism.[15] From the middle of the twentieth century up to the present day, civil rights legislation and immigration policy have proven to be effective partisan wedges, splitting the American working class between the two dominant parties, and thus reducing demands for the redistribution of income and wealth through taxation and government spending, to say nothing of socialism.[16] But one issue still bothers me.

Marx: What issue?

Me: The absence of socialism makes America exceptional
                   in comparison with Europe, but the *Americas* are
                   another story altogether. Nearly every country in the
                   New World, except the United States, has a com-
                   petitive socialist or social democratic party. In Latin
                   America and the Caribbean, quite a few countries are
                   currently governed by socialist parties. And for over
                   half a century, Cuba has offered the world an exam-
                   ple of actually existing socialism! So the United States
                   is exceptional even within its own hemisphere, but
                   here its idiosyncrasies cannot be explained as effects
                   of the absence of feudalism, or as results of racial and
                   ethnic divisions within the working class, because
                   those factors are present throughout the Americas,
                   and for the same reason they are present in the
                   United States: a history of primitive accumulation, as
                   you put it, under colonial rule.

Marx: Well that is truly surprising. I never imagined *Latin*
                   America in the global vanguard. I must confess
                   that, frankly, I have never given much thought to
                   the region at all.[17] But now I must ask, how do you
                   explain the extraordinary success of socialism in
                   Latin America?

Me: That's a question as big as the one we began with,
                   but I'll give it a try. The domestic divisions you've
                   described in the American working class exist within a
                   broader, international division of labour. This is impos-
                   sible to understand if one assumes that the emergence
                   and development of capitalism follows the same pat-
                   tern in every country – one must think, instead, of
                   capitalist development as proceeding within a world
                   system, which integrates different parts of the world in
                   different ways. The United States, along with Western
                   Europe, formed an industrial core of this system,
                   while Latin America, along with Eastern Europe, most
                   of Asia, and Africa formed a primary-goods produc-
                   ing periphery. The spoils of this system were and are
                   divided unevenly, not only within the core and the
                   periphery, but between the core and periphery. The
                   working classes of the core, though they are exploited,
                   enjoy a much higher standard of living than those of
                   the periphery. This produces antagonisms analogous

to the domestic ones you described, and with analogous effects. The international division of labour invests the North American working class with a material interest in the maintenance of the capitalist world system. They not only fail to support the revolutionary socialism of their Latin American counterparts, they also work actively against it, helping to elect governments that have violently suppressed socialist movements and deposed socialist regimes. While these interventions have limited the success that Latin American socialists have had in implementing their programmes, they have also provided a powerful impetus to socialism itself in Latin America, allowing socialist parties to present themselves as the enemies of Yankee imperialism as well as capitalist exploitation. In this sense, the absence of socialism in the United States and its strength in Latin America could be seen as two sides of the same coin.[18]

Marx:	A very intriguing concept, this world-system – and one that rather fundamentally revises the terms in which I've thought about capitalism. But I am prepared to endorse its implications.
Me:	What implications do you mean?
Marx (standing and gesturing with great emphasis):	Well, comrade, this means that the revolutionary struggle cannot succeed – until the WORKERS OF THE WORLD UNITE!
Epilogue:	

As my new acquaintance rose to his feet, and punctuated this striking insight with emphatic gesticulations, we were joined by a woman, apparently returning from a walk. She seemed unsurprised by the man's excitement, and, after introducing herself to me, chided him affectionately for forcing me to endure his lecturing. She then instructed the girls to begin packing up their things. After a few pleasantries, we parted ways and Bear and I set off for home.

Notes

1. For Marx's interest in America, see: Karl Marx and Friedrich Engels, *Letters to Americans, 1848–1895: A Selection* Leonard Mins, trans., (New York: International Publishers, 1953); Robin Blackburn, *An Unfinished Revolution: Karl Marx and Abraham Lincoln* (London: Verso, 2011). For Marx's thoughts

on moving to the United States, see: Jonathan Sperber, *Karl Marx: A Nineteenth-Century Life* (New York: W.W. Norton, 2013), 185–6, 258–60.

2. David Leonhardt, 'The Great Wage Slowdown of the 21st Century', *The New York Times*, 7 October 2014, A3; Thomas Pikketty and Emmanuel Saez, 'Income Inequality in the United States, 1913–1998', *Quarterly Journal of Economics*, vol. 118, no. 1 (February 2003), 1–39; Emmanuel Saez and Gabriel Zucman, 'Wealth Inequality in the United States Since 1913: Evidence from Capitalized Income Tax Data', NBER Working Paper 20625 (October 2014).

3. Here, and at several points below, I take some licence in mixing direct quotation, sincere paraphrase and shameless misrepresentation from Karl Marx, *Capital*, vol. 1, chapter 25.

4. Marx, *Capital*, vol. 3, chapter 15.

5. For an account of the financial crisis of 2007–8 by reference to Marx's comments on the 'law of the tendency of the rate of profit to fall' see Andrew Kliman, *The Failure of Capitalist Production: Underlying Causes of the Great Recession* (London: Pluto Press, 2011). For a modified version of the argument, written before the crisis, which emphasizes the effects of globalization on declining profitability, see Robert Brenner, *The Economics of Global Turbulence* (London: Verso, 2006). For critiques, see also: Nicholas Crafts, 'Profits of Doom?', *New Left Review*, no. 54 (November–December 2008), 49–60; Michael Heinrich, 'Crisis Theory, the Law of the Tendency of the Profit Rate to Fall, and Marx's Studies in the 1870s', *Monthly Review*, vol. 64, no. 11 (April 2013), http://monthlyreview.org/2013/04/01/crisis-theory-the-law-of-the-tendency-of-the-profit-rate-to-fall-and-marxs-studies-in-the-1870s/; and David Harvey, 'Crisis Theory and the Falling Rate of Profit', unpublished manuscript (2014).

6. Marx, *Capital*, vol. 1, chapter 32.

7. Marx, *Capital*, vol. 1, Preface to the First German Edition.

8. For Marx's optimism regarding the American labour movement, see Davis, *Prisoners of the American Dream*, 3–5.

9. Marx, *The German Ideology*, part 1.

10. Hartz, *Liberal Tradition*, 5–6.

11. Marx, *Capital*, vol. 1, chapter 33.

12. Marx and Friedrich Engels, *The Communist Manifesto*, part 1.

13. Rogers M. Smith, 'Beyond Tocqueville, Myrdal, and Hartz: The Multiple Traditions in America', *The American Political Science Review*, vol. 87, no. 3 (September 1993), 549–66.

14. Marx to Sigfrid Meyer and August Vogt, 9 April 1870.

15. Davis, *Prisoners of the American Dream*, 16–50; David R. Roediger, *The Wages of Whiteness: Race and the Making of the American Working Class* (London: Verso, 1991).

16. John Roemer, Woojin Lee, and Karine Van der Straeten, *Racism, Xenophobia, and Redistribution: Multi-Issue Politics in Advanced Democracies* (Cambridge, MA: Harvard University Press, 2007).

17. See José María Aricó, *Marx y América Latina* (Mexico City: Alianza Editorial Mexicana, 1982).

18. Theotonio Dos Santos, *Imperialismo y Dependencia* (Mexico City: Editorial Era, 1978); John Toye and Richard Toye, 'The Origins and Interpretation of the Prebisch-Singer Thesis', *History of Political Economy*, vol. 35, no. 3 (2003), 437–67; Immanuel Wallerstein, *World-Systems Analysis: An Introduction* (Durham: Duke University Press, 2004).

17
Friedrich Nietzsche (1844–1900)

Tracy B. Strong

This interview takes place in Sils Maria in the Engadin section of the Graubünden canton, Switzerland and on a walk to and back from Lake Silvaplana. The date is 6 August 1888, Transfiguration Day on the Catholic calendar. This was to be the last summer Nietzsche spent in Sils.

Strong: My dear Professor Doctor Nietzsche – I am deeply grateful that you have acceded to this interview. This village of Sils Maria is a wondrous place. Are you here often?

Nietzsche: I have relatively few visitors here and at times need human company. As you come well recommended from my dear friend Köselitz, I am especially delighted to make your acquaintance. You ask about this village. Since I have resigned from the University of Basel – my eyesight and recurrent migraines made continuing impossible – I have been spending summers here for several years. I always stay in the same villa – right next to the Hotel Edelweiss, though I take my lunch at the Hotel Alpenrose – the food is preferable. The clarity of the air and the sublime mountains invigorate me: we are almost nineteen hundred meters above men and time. I am able to go for long walks and find that my best thoughts come while I am on them. I walk every day both in the morning and afternoon. Follow me and I will take you on one. We must head in the direction of Silvaplana – it is only about two kilometers. The terrain is flat between the Sils lake and that of Silvaplana.

Strong: As we walk, let me ask you this. Here you are so far away from all culture. I spoke with your friend Erwin Rohde as well as with our musician friend Köselitz about your interests. Rohde mentioned a letter you had written him some years back in which you said that if only a few hundred of the next generation could take from music what you take you would expect that there develop a completely new culture. Music seems very important to you; the subtitle of your first book speaks of the birth of Greek tragedy from the, how did you put it, the 'spirit' of music – and yet here there is not even a concert hall.

Nietzsche: True, but in the winter months I am in Nice or Turin where there is no lack of venues. And I can play the piano here. There are some concerts in St. Moritz. But mostly I walk and write.

Strong: Still, let me ask you about that first book. I am no expert, but I believe that very few pieces of actual Greek music have been recovered and that we have no sense of how they might have sounded. How can you claim to find the origins of Greek tragedy in something about which we know almost nothing?

Nietzsche: I will come to that but, see – the lake has come to us. We must go up the East side here, towards the area of Surlej. I like how the woods come down so dark right to the water. Now we emerge from the forest. Indeed, I tremble when I approach this spot. Do you see that running stream with its falls – what in their medieval Latin the local people call an 'ova' – we will follow it to the water's edge. I am always entranced by the combination of movement and frozen stillness of these waterfalls. I often linger here like the waterfall, which lingers even while it plunges.[1]

Strong: That feels like a lonely song. It would appear though you find meaning in this nature.

Nietzsche: Indeed. When we look at the waterfall, its countless twists and turns, the bends, loopings and breakings of its waves of water, we believe that we can see in it a freedom of will, a kind of autonomy of choice. However, everything about it is necessary: every motion can be calculated mathematically.

So it is with human actions: if one were omniscient, one would be able to calculate every action ahead of time, including all progress of knowledge, every error, every piece of malice. To be sure, the one who acts is himself stuck in the illusion of autonomy. Yet if the wheel of the world stood still for a moment, and if an omniscient, calculative intellect were on hand to take advantage of this moment, that intellect could tell the future of every creature into the most remote of times, marking every track on which the wheel would roll. The illusion the actor has, the supposition of free will, is itself attributable to this utterly calculable mechanism.[2] I have thought long about the supposition of free will ...

See this pyramid of a stone right on the shore: I have spent many hours on it with the falling water sounding behind me and the utter calm of the lake before me. It was here that my most profound idea came upon me.

Strong: Pardon me, but what was that? can you tell me about it?

Nietzsche: Not easily. Like the music of the Greeks you will only grasp it if you are able to make the experiences it engenders available to yourself.

Strong: You are calling for a kind of phenomenology?

Nietzsche: That is not a word I use – perhaps the association is too strongly to Hegel and the idea of dialectical progress. I suppose there could be another meaning, perhaps one that reflected more clearly the Greek word that it is derived from – *phainómenon* – we could then have a science of that which appears. One should always consider the Greek understanding.

Strong: You are not fond of Hegel?

Nietzsche: Well, he got music wrong. Do you know that in his lectures on aesthetics he mentions Beethoven not at all and prefers Rossini to Mozart? He shows no understanding of the possibility of hearing the words as music. For him – I think I quote him accurately – 'the character of great music is that it does not stream forth desiringly in a Bacchic manner but rather in such a way that the mind is also in itself soulful'.[3] And not surprisingly and more importantly he thus got the

Greeks wrong. For him they are an occasion for celebrating *Geist* and dialectical unity – I celebrate Dionysos and disindividuation. Let me put it like this. If on finishing his work, Hegel had declared it to be all a joke, he would have been the greatest philosopher ever. But he was serious about it. In fact, most philosophers have gotten music wrong: think of Kant who compares it to perfume. Only Schopenhauer has come close before me.

Strong: Please then go on with your insight at this rock.

Nietzsche: Well, think of yourself confronted with this test: What, if some day or night a demon were to steal after you into your loneliest loneliness and say to you: 'This life as you now live it and have lived it, you will have to live once more and innumerable times more; and there will be nothing new in it, but every pain and every joy and every thought and sigh and everything unutterably small or great in your life will have to return to you, all in the same succession and sequence – even this spider and this moonlight between the trees, and even this moment and I myself. The eternal hourglass of existence is turned upside down again and again, and you with it, speck of dust!' Would you not throw yourself down and gnash your teeth and curse the demon who spoke thus? Or have you once experienced a tremendous moment when you would have answered him: 'You are a god and never have I heard anything more divine'. If this thought gained possession of you, it would change you as you are or perhaps crush you. The question in each and every thing, 'Do you desire this once more and innumerable times more?' would lie upon your actions as the greatest weight. Or how well disposed would you have to become to yourself and to life *to crave nothing more fervently* than this ultimate eternal confirmation and seal?[4]

Strong: I must admit that this test leaves me confused. If I experience everything I have experienced in the same succession and sequence, how is it that I am, as you say, changed?

Nietzsche: Here you must be careful. It is true that when 'you incarnate the thought of thoughts it will transform you'.[5] You have to make this thought part of your flesh – that is what incarnation means. I am reminded of a phrase in the American Emerson about Montaigne – both writers I greatly admire – 'if you cut his words they would bleed'. But you 'must guard against thinking of eternal return on the example of a false analogy of the stars, or the ebb and flow, day and night, seasons ...'.[6] Eternity does not mean forever, but of and only of the present.

Strong: I begin to see. Perhaps your teaching is something like that we find in a great Austrian-English philosopher who writes: 'If we take eternity to mean not infinite temporal duration but timelessness, then eternal life belongs to those who live in the present'.[7]

Nietzsche: I should like to have known this thinker. There are so few in my world .... The individual has always had to struggle from being overrun. If you try to resist, you will be lonely often and sometimes frightened. I know this, too well ....

But you were asking about my doctrine. My teaching says the task is to live such that you must wish to so live again. You will in any case! ... This is not a doctrine of superiority. To whom striving gives the highest feeling, let him strive; to whom peace gives the highest feeling, let him be peaceful; to whom ordering, following, obedience give the highest feeling, let him obey. May he only become conscious about that which gives him the highest feeling, and not baulk at any means. It is a matter of eternity.[8]

Strong: Did you perhaps have something like Kant's doctrine of the Categorical Imperative in mind?

Nietzsche: Indeed – but I do not share his dessicated notion of abstract universality. Something can appear as categorically imperative *to me* without this meaning that there is *a* Categorical Imperative.

Strong: I would like to bring you back to the importance of music. You were for many years associated with Richard Wagner – indeed, you seem even to have run errands for him.

Nietzsche: Ah! Really too much is made of that. Once when I was in Basel and he in Tribschen, Richard merely asked me to procure some silk undergarments for him from a store in Basel. A favour for a friend. I was as close to Richard – and to his wife, Cosima – as I have been to anyone. He was a genius – and not a bit of an actor. It is an infinite sadness that my hopes for our relation did not materialize.

Strong: Yes – that relation soured.

Nietzsche: Indeed it did. In the end I was mistaken – I had hoped that we would be partners in bringing about a cultural revolution in Germany and Europe. But he really needed me more as a propagandist while I saw him more as my *Vorkämpfer*.

Strong: How do you mean, *Vorkämpfer*?

Nietzsche: I wrote that about him at the end of my dedication of my first book to him. It means something like an 'advance scout', one who would prepare the way. I thought of myself as, shall we say, the heavy artillery – but I had to be careful not to be too obvious: all geniuses have very high opinions of themselves. I never forgave Wagner because he *condescended* to the Germans – he became *reichsdeutsch*.[9] And then there was *Parsifal*.

Strong: Did you perhaps have the sense that Wagner through his music – perhaps with your help or with your ideas? – might be able to achieve something for our culture like what you had argued the Greeks achieved through tragedy?

Nietzsche: Yes! And the music was a centrally important component. But it is important to realize that the Greek language accomplished its musical effect naturally – the language was itself tonal and instead of the spoken stresses we use, it used pitch changes. This now answers your earlier question. The Greeks, we might say, sang as they spoke. Our language is not like that – so Wagner was obliged entirely to reconceive the relation of the score to the libretto and to construct a new design of performance space to make this real. This is one reason why when I republished my first book – inadequately written as it was – I suggested I should have sung it rather than written it. I worked out how ancient Greek sounded – its music – in my lecture courses – alas no one seems to read them.

Strong: Well, they are rather hard to come by. But perhaps one day they will be published.[10]

Nietzsche: I hope so. Perhaps I should have been more explicit in my first book – but then I had other, bigger and more important, aims than to impress the world of professional classical philology. A possible sub-title for my book had been 'Considerations on the ethico-political significance of drama'. I was and still am very disappointed at its lack of reception.

In any case, I found and showed that one could and should read the tragedies the way a musician reads a score. As I wrote in my *Zarathustra*, 'must one smash their ears before they learn to hear with their eyes'? – a phrase that few seem to have understood.

Strong: It is perhaps not an easy thought in not an easy book. But as you mention your *Zarathustra* book: what did you hope to accomplish in writing it? You call it 'a book for all and a book for none'.

Nietzsche: It is about the elements of the world in which we live – a kind of critique in verse. And it is to some degree also a parody of that which would teach lessons. It starts by a going down – surely that reminds you of a famous book?

Strong: I must assume that you mean the *Republic*? A book about politics and education.

Nietzsche: Quite so. But my book is that and also a journey, a set of wanderings, paths in several woods in search of a clearing.

Strong: You must here have the *Bildungsroman* in mind – something like *Wilhelm Meisters Wanderjahre*? But your style in *Zarathustra* is not that of Goethe – much of your German there is slightly archaic.

Nietzsche: You catch on quickly. The language pays tribute to and hopes to overcome the man who invented the German language by his translation of the Bible – Martin Luther. I have similar hopes for my work. Let us imagine an extreme case: that a book speaks of nothing but events that lie altogether beyond the possibility of any frequent or even rare experience – that it is the first language for a new series of experiences. Thus *Zarathustra* is a book for all as well as a book for none. In that case, simply nothing will be heard, but there will be the acoustic illusion that where nothing is heard, nothing is there. This is, in the end, my average experience and, if you will, the originality of my experience. Whoever thought he had understood something of me, had made up something out of me after his own image – not uncommonly an antithesis to me; for example, an 'idealist' – and whoever had understood nothing of me, denied that I need be considered at all.[11]

And there are more layers to my *Zarathustra*. I am after all trained in classical philology and rhetoric – which one should never forget in reading me. Few will notice it but *Zarathustra* is also modelled on Lucian of Samosata's dialogue *Kataplous he tyrannos* where he portrays the *hyperanthropos* – what you call the 'overman' – in a satirical way, a feeling I share.[12]

The book critiques and satirizes our various institutions – in the first book alone I deal with academia, criminality, the Church, warfare, the state, the economy, marriage, women, children, friendship and so forth. In some sense this book is also my understanding of why it is that most have so much trouble in understanding me.

Strong: This means, however, that contrary to what might seem to be the case, that your thought is centrally concerned with our social and political actualities and not just the isolated individual.

Nietzsche: Of course! I should have thought that any reading of my first book – the concerns of that book have stayed with me through my entire career – would have made that clear. I originally conceived of that book as accompanied by a project to reform educational institutions and another to understand what it would mean actually to do philosophy under the conditions of our world – and I do not mean by that to be a 'professor' of philosophy.

But perhaps to discuss this, we should return towards the world of men and women. If you don't mind let us continue up towards Silvaplana and go around its lake on our way back to Sils. See though how the snow and ice remains on the high peaks. And the sun's rays are so intense here – I almost always bring this umbrella, which I use to protect myself from them. The coat of arms of Sils has a sun over a trout – a bit literal, do you not think?

Strong: You have often addressed the question of the origin of morality as a human institution. Yet it appears to many that you are – how should I say it – opposed to morality.

Nietzsche: Not at all – although it is true that I am distressed about the possible consequences of the moralization of morality. Let me explain with a story. Imagine that there is a bird of prey who is fond of carrying off lambs. The lambs are obviously not happy with the situation. The bird of prey thinks to himself: 'I love those tasty little lambs'. He has the strength and will to continue carrying them off. The lambs however want the bird of prey to stop carrying them off, that is, not to act as what he is. I call the morality of the bird of prey 'master morality' – a kind of parody and critique of Hegel, if you will. I thus also call the morality of the lamb 'slave morality'. Note, however, that, contrary to Hegel, these are not in dialectical relation to each other. The bird of prey says 'I am good, you are not like me: you are bad'. Might one think here of Homer? The lamb says: 'you oppress me, you are evil, I am the opposite of you, therefore I am good'. Here – in slave morality *only* – is where the dialectic comes in – and you might see why I attacked Socrates in my first book. There are three important consequences to my little fable: first, moral judgments rest on considerations of relative power; second, in the end the victor will be the lamb who will get the bird of prey to stop carrying off lambs; and third, the self-understanding of the lamb depends on having an enemy.

Strong: But, still, does not even the morality of the lamb place restraints on human actions?

Nietzsche: Increasingly, I think not. We live more and more in an age where nothing restrains what humans can call 'good'. When faith in God was active and shaped human affairs, there was at least some possible restraint; after the death of God – after, that is, the erosion of the sense that our lives were constrained by forces that we could not comprehend – there are not such restraints. I fear that in the next century we shall see wars the like of which we have never seen.

But see – we have arrived at the small village of Silvaplana – or Silvaplauna as most people here still speak the Puter dialect of Romansch – that form of medieval Latin I referred to before. Perhaps we might stop for a glass of Asti Spumante.

Strong: I did not think that you drank alcohol.

Nietzsche: Rarely, but every so often a glass – what offends me is the kind of drinking they do in Munich. Besides this is a charming little tavern. I amuse myself by speaking Latin to the locals and find that I am not completely misunderstood. See over there is a very fine village church – it dates, I believe from the fourteenth century. And way up there, on the way back towards Sils, is the Corvatsch peak – I believe the highest around here. I have climbed part way up. I have also climbed up to the glacier of the Piz Chüern over there above Sils – that is a wonderful hike past a high mountain lake. The path starts at my villa but we, alas, do not have the time today.

Strong: The dire matters you predict seem very far away in a place like this.

Nietzsche: Yes, there is always calm before a storm – and in some places perhaps even in a storm. But I have no doubt that we are to see wars for the domination of the earth. You see, instead of there being wars like the one we fought against the French in 1870 – I was in that war, you may remember, as a medical orderly and was injured – wars will now become a *Geisterkrieg* – a war for the *Geist*, for the human spirit itself and not just for territory and wealth. We did already see the beginnings of some of this after the war with France: think of the Commune and then the cost in money and land imposed on France for reparations.

Strong: You were very distressed with the Commune in Paris.

Nietzsche: I do not like group psychology and mass movements – they are destructive of individuality. Nor did I much like the policy of Adolphe Thiers in massacring the Communards. I had thought, mistakenly, that the Communards had burned the Louvre museum – as a museum it lacks something, but the culture that is preserved there is beyond price. Happily, I was wrong. My point though is that whereas wars in the past were fought over the distribution of what there was, in the future wars will be fought to determine what there is to distribute and for the domination of the earth as a whole. We are approaching a century of total war that involves entire populations and not just soldiers.

Strong: But how does this relate to what you were saying about slave morality?

Nietzsche: I should have thought it obvious. Come, we have finished our glass; let us be on our way back to Sils.

Strong: I am sorry but I must insist on the question about slave morality.

Nietzsche: Everyone is fascinated by slave morality – yet that is what we all are. Very well. It is like this. Slave morality requires the continued presence of a foe, against whom one might define oneself. The logic of the coming wars – like the logic of slave morality – is such that there can be no logical way of bringing them to a final conclusion, nor a way of permanently stopping. Might one perhaps say that it is the moral and political equivalent of what Bruno Bauer – have you read him? an interesting man – sees as relations of exchange in our economy. You must understand: humans would rather will the void, than be void of will.[13] Slavely moral human beings are unable to stop willing, for willing is the faculty by which the future is constructed in the light of a given particular present – *our* present – and the nature of the present form of slave morality willing is nihilism or nothingness. Thus the will of the slavely moral person is to bring about *das Nichts* because that is all that there is for slave morality – after all, for two thousand or more years we have experienced *Einverleibung* – we have embodied the Socratic-Christian form of life and everything we do manifests that incarnation.

Strong: This is a very dark picture. Can nothing be done?

Nietzsche: Were I but in charge ... but that is madness. However, if we can forego wars, so much the better. I know of a better use for the twelve billions that the armed peace in Europe costs each year; there are other means to bring physiology to honour than military hospitals ... Well and good, indeed very good: I might say that after the old God is done away with, I would be ready to rule the world.[14]

Strong: Surely you are not serious?

Nietzsche: I do not know. If I could, I sometimes think I would have Bismarck and the emperor and all anti-Semites shot.

But see – we have now arrived back in Sils at my residence. I am most grateful for your company and your conversation. Perhaps if you pass this way again we can continue it, although I shall leave in three weeks for Turin. If you are staying the night, I recommend the *Edelweiss*. I must go now to my desk – I shall have some tea, some bread and honey and fruit and work until close to midnight. I have so much to set down – and I sense that time presses.

Strong: I thank you, Professor Nietzsche. It has been an honour and an education to spend this time in your company. Perhaps we might meet in Turin.

Notes

1. Nietzsche, 'The Night Song', *Thus Spoke Zarathustra*, Book II.
2. Nietzsche, *Human-all-too-Human*, I, # 106.
3. Professor Nietzsche is here prompted by Professor Babich. See e.g. G.W.F. Hegel, *Lectures on Fine Arts*, (Oxford: Clarendon Press, 1975), volume II, p. 90.
4. Nietzsche, *The Gay Science*, #341.
5. *Werke Kritische Gesamtausgabe* (Berlin: De Gruyter, 1965ff) volume V-2, 394. [WKG].
6. WKG V-2, 400.
7. Ludwig Wittgenstein, Tractatus Logico-Philosophicus (London: Routledge and Kegan Paul, 1963), 6.4311 (p. 147).
8. WKG V-2, 402.
9. *Ecce Homo*, Why I am so clever, 5.

10. They have been in the first sections of the *Werke Kritische Gesamtausgabe* from de Gruyter.
11. Ecce Homo, Why I write such good books, 2.
12. The only one to notice it is Babette Babich, 'Nietzsche's *Zarathustra* and Parodic Style: On Lucian's *Hyperanthropos* and Nietzsche's *Übermensch.'* *Diogène*, 58, 4 (November 2011 [March 2013]): 58–74.
13. Last sentence of the *Genealogy of Morals*.
14. WKG VIII-3 p. 460 (slightly modified).

18
Émile Durkheim (1858–1917)

Bertrand Badie

I had the pleasure and the great honour to meet Emile Durkheim who accepted to give this interview in his office, located in the Sorbonne. Even if the great sociologist had never worked on International Relations (which did not exist as a discipline in France at his time), the major role that he played in founding the French sociology and irradiating the discipline everywhere around the world urged me to have this chat with him.

BB: Professor Durkheim, it is an honour to meet you; I am really impressed. Do you mind if this interview is run in English?

ED: I am really so happy to go back to academic concerns! But I do not understand why to speak English ... Don't you speak French fluently enough? I have heard that you are a French academic?

BB: English is now a kind of common academic denominator and ...

ED: I am happy to hear that finally German did not predominate; but, sorry, young fellow, I will speak French, whether you like it or not ... English cannot exactly convey what French sociology means ...

BB: I understand. Please reply in French and I will do my best to translate it into in English ... We are used now to turn to English in all international conferences (*) ...

ED: Just as well I'm retired! But tell me, young fellow, what are you expecting?

BB: You did not write on International Relations, except a short book on the causes of the First World War: we would like to know your vision on international politics ...

(*)Emile Durkheim replied in French. Translation has been made by the interviewer under his own responsibility, even if this interview was a fiction! Wasn't it?

ED: First World War? Was there a second one or even more? Anyway, I am not sure that this topic is so relevant as such: international facts are social facts like the others. Aren't they? Why would you consider them as exceptional?

BB: The main stream in IR theory considers that inter-state competition is covering the game and makes it a power competition ...

ED: I do not see the point. First, I observe a growing social density in your world; it is clearly challenging international actors who are then less and less sovereign. Second, even in my time, non-state actors were playing an increasing role on the international arena. What I observed at the national (or local) level is more and more relevant at a global level: as far as I know, social density is getting stronger in your present world; division of labour is for the same reasons more and more active and obvious; people communicate amongst themselves from all the parts of the world. To say briefly, interdependence is now playing a role at the international level which could be compared with what happened in my time inside the nations. Interdependence contradicts sovereignty, doesn't it? But I am afraid that all of that is now well known in your world: even, in my time, one of my bright fellows, Léon Bourgeois, made the point and promoted on this line what he called 'solidarism' ... He carved out a terrific career ... However, we have to pursue this idea up to the end: it would be probably more important to stress that a division of labour does not directly lead to integration and may result in many social pathologies; as far as I know, your present world is affected by these tensions; my own sociology would help to explain this concerning situation ...

BB: Professor, may I interrupt you? Do you consider your vision as the opposite of Max Weber's vision: in fact, IR theory has been much more influenced by your German colleague ... It is not clear whether you could meet him and discuss with him on this point ... It's said that Weber came in Paris in 1912 to attend a performance at the Opera ...

ED: This anecdote really does not matter; anyway I am fed up with this reputed opposition between both of us. I don't wonder that Weber played such a role in IR: my distinguished colleague founded his sociology on power, when I promoted the concept of integration. I can understand that he was captured by those who conceived international arena as shaped and dominated by power politics! Integration was not really at stake in IR when this subdiscipline was created. However, in my time I heard of a British politician, named Norman Angell, who published *The Great Illusion*: I read this book with which I agreed particularly when Angell showed that a growing interdependence among states made war impossible ... In fact, he was contradicted in 1914, but valuable seeds were sown and prepared a new approach. The Weberian sociology is relevant as far as international relations can be reduced to the use of force and to the predominance of power. Now, I have heard that, in your world, conflicts are no longer promoted by the strongest and depend less and less on strategists: this is the clear evidence that we have to move to other paradigms and precisely to go back to the conditions of a real social integration, which I would call 'international social integration'. You know, I faced two big traumas in my life: I was 13 when 'La Commune de Paris' happened and I lost my son during this horrible World War ... I became convinced that something constitutes the essence of all kinds of conflict which can't be reduced to power competition.

BB: Actually, many scholars point that new conflicts are much more often the result of a lack of social integration, a fragile social network and a collapse of institutions: it's probably why wars are moving from Europe to African and Middle East countries ....

ED: Well, I hardly wake up to the idea that Europe is no more the battlefield of the world! Maybe it's the evidence that, in what you call a global world, power is much less decisive than the country's social fabric and its solidity. I was always convinced that social division of labour was enough for creating solidarity; I also ever argued that social bounds are not efficient if they are not moral bounds. In your world, economic and trade relations are not enough to create conditions of peace: you don't pay enough attention to the domestic solidarity inside the new (and fragile) nations nor to the minimal international social integration among deeply unequal States ... In my time, IR concerned a small number of equivalent States: now, your global world is reported to have so many economic disparities that global social issues are becoming the main source of wars.

BB: How can the international community promote peace in these conditions?

ED: 'International community'? I don't remember ever meeting this concept!

BB: Sorry: how can we manage this kind of threat?

ED: As I mentioned, I have always advocated moral bounds before utilitarian ones ... Inside developing and rising societies, I have understood that social bounds were too weak, while they were too vertical and coercive, even arrogant and humiliating, between 'Northern' and 'Southern' countries ... This lack of solidarity reminds me the way working class was treated at the end of nineteenth century. What was generating anomy inside domestic societies triggers anomy in the global world! But you cannot solve anomy only by using force and coercion: if you do that immoderately, you risk creating a 'war society' in which, paradoxically, fighting meets social needs .... For these reasons, I would say that peace implies a social treatment of the present conflicts.

BB: It's exactly what UNDP advocates with human security ...

ED: UNDP? I don't know, but 'human security' is an interesting concept that I would have loved to coin! Is Léon Bourgeois at its origins?

BB: He probably inspired it, but the concept is much more recent!

ED: More recent? You needed such a long time to create it?

BB: States are protecting their own sovereignty ... and human security is interfering with their domestic affairs ...

ED: It seems oversimplified ... Social issues are more and more interdependent, beyond the border-lines: when you speak of a global world I can't but imagine that there is an organic solidarity among the players ...

BB: By the way, what do you think about an 'international society'?

ED: I have never used this concept, young man, but it does not bother me ... From my point of view, a society is made of beliefs, values and collective representations which are commonly shared as social density grows. When you report that your global world springs from such a densification, I can conceive that this kind of society takes place. But I recently had a talk here with two bright British colleagues, Hedley Bull and Martin Wight, as they joined me in this other world. I was puzzled when Bull told me that international society resulted from an agreement among States, as I don't think that the State could be a resource of international integration. As for Wight, we both set together the question of a common culture which would organize this international society.

I told him that I would prefer the hypothesis of a collective consciousness which would grow with this globalization (as you say) and which does not imply a common culture. It's strange how you mobilize this concept which was reserved in my time for anthropologist colleagues. Someone even told me that a president in one American country wanted to promote a 'regime change' and organize the world according to his own vision and his own 'culture'; he was even mentioning his country as a 'good nation' and referred to God! But how to imagine that state-building could be possible without a social intervention coming from below? Social institutions, as I explained, are generated from religion, but I meant from *each* religion, as the expression of the common consciousness brought by each social collectivity. That's why I told Wight that a common culture was not possible nor functional ... To speak frankly, I was a little bit irritated!

BB: So, this so-called international society is not made of a common culture nor an interstate agreement?

ED: Please, my young friend, consider that collective consciousness is first of all an empirical concept which would imply empirical investigations in order to define from where it does come and to assess whether it could promote a real solidarity. Without this real solidarity, the world would be affected by conflicts: it's what I would consider as a world anomy ... Utilitarianism didn't consider this functional prerequisite: without moral bounds, people wouldn't be *solidaire* (sorry, there is no English word for that: it's meaningful, isn't it?). There is no special agent for that: neither 'superior cultures', nor 'elected nations'. We need then a real collective creation involving all the local actors and institutions, which would be able to teach morality ... I remember that Léon Bourgeois advocated for a League of Nations and ...

BB: A League of Nations was created but didn't work well ... It was replaced by the United Nations.

ED: Great: unity is better than league ... I would say more hopeful! Is there inside an agency devoted to international moral education?

BB: I am afraid not! Power is given to the P5, i.e. the five more powerful countries ...

ED: You mean France, Germany, Austria, England ... What about the fifth? Russia? Just before passing away, I heard that they were strongly involved in an overwhelming revolution ...

BB: Not exactly: USA, Russia, China, France, England ...

ED: What about the others?

BB: They are out ...

ED: Strange: the international division of labour would be successful only if those who are not properly integrated are real partners of ... what did you say? The 'governance' of the world? At my time, we called that 'oligarchy'; a young student of Weber was very fashionable at my time when using this word at parties ... But oligarchy does not fit with promoting solidarity ... I pointed out that an achieved division of labour implied moral solidarity, redistributive justice and common consciousness!

BB: Could it be an orientation for IR?

ED: Probably. The global world, as you say, seems to be less and less dominated by military issues, while social issues grow in relevance. The market is not able to regulate these new tensions ... I recently bumped into a lady who introduced herself as a former British Prime Minister: she strongly maintained that the global market was able to build up a new international order which would be more peaceful and less political. I told her that social contrasts which we experienced in each European nation at my time will be back now at the international level with much more dramatic dimensions. We could overcome these conflicts in my time by mobilizing daring social policies at the domestic level. You must now conceive three directions at the international level, which could be modelled on what I suggested back in the day for the nations: a global justice which would be more restitutive; a transnational moral solidarity among States; a priority given to social issues in the international agenda setting. It seems close to human security that you were mentioning!

BB: What do you mean by 'restitutive global justice'?

ED: Maybe you remember that I considered new organic solidarity as depending on redistribution and no more on coercion and repression. The present world is more and more shaped by a division of labour and a new organic solidarity: it will work better if we play the card of restitution and not the repressive one. However, I got the impression that old powers are commonly using force, power and coercion rather that restitution. I recently glanced at a newspaper and saw that even a French President spoke of 'punishment' about some conflict or other ... Punishment is not a therapy in a world of interdependence: quite the opposite, it's a way of strengthening abnormal divisions of labour ...

BB: How do you consider this 'abnormal division of labour' at the international level?

ED: I would use the categories that I coined for investigating this abnormal division of labour at a domestic level. Loosening interdependence and a constrained division of labour seem to be two meaningful factors of this 'abnormal division of labour' in a 'global world', as you say. As far as I know, your world is clearly affected by a new kind of 'sovereignism' and egoism, which contain the transnational solidarity which is needed. Use of coercion is also resulting in new tensions which entail this pathological division of labour. Now, it's clear that this process is much more difficult to conduct in the international arena. If we compare this with the domestic scene, several aspects jeopardize a functional division of labour at the international level: resilience of sovereignties, deeply rooted conflicts, capacity of nationalisms, absence of a 'global State' which would contain this radical neo-liberalism that I pointed out, when competing national States prevent an active international social integration ...

BB: You consider the State as emancipating at the national level and conservative at the international level?

ED: When it was invented, the State was planned for granting individual rights whilst protecting social order and thus social integration. This functional dialectic was possible due to the social contract. Such a contract does not exist in the international arena: quite the reverse, we have there to face a strong competition among States; this competition is especially strong since States pretend to be sovereign. Worse still, all the failures met by the States trigger ultra-nationalist and 'sovereignist' reactions. We are then in a pathologically vicious circle: the more we need international integration, the more we face a reluctance from the main international actors. The solution is to be found in international institutions which can't but grow from this international social densification: all the simple acts of daily life prompt the setting up of international agreements and conventions which are more and more needed; they then boost international cooperation. This trend would help to restore the state in this balancing role at the international level, between constraint and consent ... But, obviously, this would be possible only if an international substratum took root, made of an active international civil society, and new actors ... How do you call them now? NGOs? International law must also be promoted, beyond the inter-sovereign paradigm that we practice now.

BB: What about wars? Do you consider these 'new wars' as radically different from those you experienced?

ED: As far as I know, war has now deeply changed. I have in mind the nightmare of the World War that I experienced. It was then clearly a competition of powers, while your wars get settled among poor countries and are run by weak or (as they say) collapsed States. I guess that there are pathologies of the global world whereas they were at my time symptoms of strength ... The narratives on these new wars seem particularly dismaying: these conflicts take place where social bounds and social fabric are too much fragile or even ineffectual ... It's a paroxysmal abnormality of the division of labour at both levels: domestic and global; it's a kind of virulent anomy! But, in this kind of desperate weak integration, fighting and war can offer the only possible kind of integration ... So, as I understood, war societies are emerging, with warlords and new integrations through criminal networks, war economies and this abject practice of child soldiers that someone recently reported from your world ... We can't but admit that the violence market is for these young people their only chance to be fed, clothed and even considered! Keep in mind that this kind of conflict will never be solved by military instruments; they must be treated by mobilizing social policies ...

BB: Thank you very much, Professor Durkheim for your time.

ED: Time is meaningless in my realm, but I felt younger and even alive! Could you remind me the name of your publisher? Paul ...?

BB: Palgrave!

19

Theory Talk #-100: John Dewey (1859–1952) on the Horror of Making His Poetry Public

Christian Bueger and Peer Schouten

TT: Dear Professor Dewey. Thank you so much for your willingness to participate in this Talk. *Theory Talks* is an open-access journal, which contributes to International Relations debates by publishing interviews with cutting-edge theorists. It is not often that *Theory Talks* is able to overcome space-time limitations and conduct a Talk with a departed theorist.

I am sorry – I think I have to interrupt you there ...

TT: Well, all right?

Yes, yes, the fact of the matter is that I am not a theorist and refuse to be associated with that label! To purify theory out of experience as some distinct realm, sirs, is to contribute to a fallacy that I have dedicated my life to combat! I am afraid that this venture of yours, of involving me in this *Theory Talks*, is stillborn.

TT: Dear Professor Dewey – with all due respect, we are running ahead of matters here a little. The reason why we invited you is exactly for you to expound your ideas – and reservations – regarding theory, practice and international relations. Would you be willing to bracket your concern for a minute? We promise to get back to it.

Well my dear sirs – it is that you insist on a dialogue – that restless, participative and dramatic form of inquiry, which leads to so much more insight than books[1] – and that you have travelled from far by means that utterly fascinate me, so I will give you the benefit of the doubt.

TT: Thank you. And let us from the outset emphasize that by interviewing you for *Theory Talks*, we don't necessarily want to reduce your contribution to thought to the practice of theorizing. Isn't it also correct that you have written poetry?

Now I am baffled a second time! I have never publicly attempted my hand at the noble art of the poetic!

TT: It has to be said, Mr. Dewey, that the problem of what is and isn't public has perhaps shifted a bit since your passing. That's something we'd like to discuss, too, but the fact of the matter is that what you have consistently consigned to the trashcan of your office at Columbia University has been just as meticulously recovered by 'a janitor with a long view'.[2]

Oh heavens! You tell me I have been uncovered as a versifier? What of my terrible scribbling has been uncovered you say?

TT Well, perhaps you recognize the one that starts like:

I hardly think I heard you call
Since betwixt us was the wall
Of sounds within, buzzings i' the ear
Roarings i' the vein so closely near ...

... 'That I was captured in illusion/Of outward things said clear ...'[3] I well remember – a piece particularly deserving of oblivion. I wrote that in the privacy of lonely office hours, thinking the world would have the mercy not to allow a soul to lay its eyes on it!

TT: We are sorry to say that besides this one, a total of 101 poems has been recovered, and published in print[4] – and you know, given some advances in technology, circulation of text is highly accelerated, meaning that one could very well say your poetry is part of the public domain.

So there I am, well half a decade after my death, subject to the indirect effects of advances in technology interacting with the associations I myself carelessly established between roses, summer days, and all too promiscuous waste bins! Sirs, in the little time we have conversed, I see the afterlife hasn't brought me any good. Hades takes on a bleaker shade ...

TT: Well, in reality, the future has been good to you: you are firmly canonized as an authentic American intellectual, and stand firmly on a pedestal in the galleries occupied by the notables of modern international social thought. So why don't we explore a little bit why that is, within the specific domain of political theory? *Theory Talks* actually poses the same first three questions to every interviewee, followed by a number of questions specific to your thought. The first question we always pose is: What, according to you, is the biggest challenge or central debate in International Relations and what is your position vis-à-vis that challenge/debate?

I think that while it must have been noted by other interviewees that in fact this question is two separate questions – one about real-world challenges and another about theoretical debates – I would be the last to do so, and I am happy you mix concerns of theory and practice. I have always fought against establishing such a fictional separation between seemingly distinct domains of thought and practice. It is a dangerous fiction on top of it. The same goes for International Relations – while I have not dedicated myself to the study of the international as a discrete field of action, I do think that this domain does not escape some of the general observations I have made regarding society and its politics.

I hold that 'modern society is many societies more or less loosely connected'[5] by all kinds of associations. As I explain in *The Public and its Problems*,[6] a fundamental challenge of modern times is that the largely technically mediated associations that constitute society have outstripped the social mechanisms that we had historically developed on the human scale of the village to mitigate their indirect effects on others. During my life, I witnessed the proliferation of railway, telegraph, radio, steam-driven shipping, and car and weapon industries – thoroughly extending the web of association and affectedness within and across borders. This means action constantly reaches further. People close by and in far-off places are suddenly confronted with situations that they have to relate to but which are out of their control. This automatically makes them part of interested publics, with a stake in the way these mechanisations work. Now this perhaps seems abstract but consider: the spread of a new technology – I see you both looking on some small device with a black mirrored screen nervously every 5 minutes – automatically involves users as a 'stakeholder'. Your actions are mediated by them. You become affected by their design and configuration – over which you have little control. In that regard, you are part of a concerned public, but you have no way to influence the politics constitutive of these technologies.

I would say the largest challenge is to amplify participation and to institutionalize these fleeting publics. The proliferation of technologies and institutions as conduits for international associations has rendered publics around the globe more inchoate, while seemingly making it easier than ever before to influence – for good or ill – large groups through the manipulation of these global infrastructures of the public. We sowed infrastructures, we reap fragilities and more diffusely affected publics: each new technological expansion of the possibility to form associations leads to concomitant insecurities.

TT: How did you arrive where you currently are in your thinking?

I have had the sheer luck or fortune to be engaged in the occupation of thinking; and while I am quite regular at my meals, I think that I may say that I would rather work, and perhaps even more, play, with ideas and with thinking than eat.[7] I was born in the wake of the Civil War, and in times of a profound acceleration of technology as a vehicle of social, economic and political development. Perhaps, as in your own times, upheaval and change was the status quo, stability a rare exception. My studies at Johns Hopkins with people such as Peirce had tickled an intellectual curiosity as of yet unsatisfied. I subsequently went to the University of Chicago for a decade in which my commitment to pragmatist philosophy consolidated. Afterwards at Columbia, and at the New School which I founded with people such as Charles A. Beard and Thorsten Veblen, this approach translated into a number of books. In these I applied my pragmatist convictions to such disparate issues as education, art, faith, logic and indeed politics, the topic of your question. For me, these are all interdependent aspects of society. This interdependence and inseparability of the social fabric means that skewed economic or political interests will reverberate throughout. But I am an optimist in that I also believe in the fundamental possibility and promise of science and democracy to curb radical change and reroute it into desirable directions for those affected. Good things are also woven through the social and we should amplify those to lessen the effects of negative associations.

TT: What would a student require to become a specialist in International Relations or to see the world in a global way?

A question dear to my heart. You might know that throughout my entire life I have striven to transform our understanding and practice of education. Human progress is dependent on education, and as I have learned during my travels to Russia, reform is not to be had by revolution but by gradual education. Education is training in reflective thinking. The quality of democracy depends on education.

Towards the end of my life I witnessed the creation of the United Nations. This was a clear signal to me that 'the relations between nations are taking on the properties that constitute a public, and hence call for some measure of political organization'.[8] Having this forum implied that we saw the end of the complete denial of political responsibility of how the policies in one national unit affect another as we find in the doctrine of sovereignty. That the end of this doctrine is within reach means that we require global education, which will ensure the rise of informed global publics which can develop the tools required to respond to global challenges.

In a more substantive fashion, I would insist that students hold on to the essential impossibility to separate out experience as it unfolds over time. The divisions and preferences that have come to dominate academic knowledge in its 20th century 'maturing' are for me a loss of rooting of knowledge in experience.

TT: We're sorry, but isn't the task of social sciences to offer universal or at least objective analytical categories to make sense of the muddle of real-world experience? What you seem to be proposing is the opposite!

I align with Weber in lamenting the acceleration of the differentiation of understanding in society. This has made it difficult for your generations to address social, political and economic challenges head on while avoiding getting lost in one of its details or facets. Isn't the economic and the political, constantly encroaching on everyday life? In the end, this perhaps explains my insistence on democracy and schooling as the pivots of good society: democracy to reconstruct and defend publics, and schooling to defend individuals against (mis)understanding the world in ways that cannot be reduced to their own lived experience.[9] If students could only hold on to this holistic perspective and eschew isolating subject matters from their social contexts.[10]

TT: Throughout your 70 years of active scholarship you have written over a thousand articles and books. One commentator of your work suggested that your body of writing is an 'elaborate spider's web, the junctions and lineaments of which its engineer knows well and in and on which he is able to move about with great facility. But for the outsider who seeks to traverse or map that territory there is the constant danger of getting stuck'.[11] Many find your work difficult to navigate – what advice would you give the reader?

Sirs why would anyone want to engage in a quest of mapping all of my writings? You have to understand that thought always proceeds in relations. A web, perhaps, yes. A spider's web certainly not. A spider that spins a web out of himself, produces a web that is orderly and elaborate, but it is only a trap. That is the goal of pure reasoning, not mine. The scientific method of inquiry is rather comparable to the operations of the bee who collects material within and from the world, but attacks and modifies the collected stuff in order to make it yield its hidden treasure.[12] 'Drop the conception that knowledge is knowledge only when it is a disclosure and definition of the properties of fixed and antecedent reality; interpret the aim and test of knowing by what happens in the actual procedures of scientific inquiry'.[13] The occasion of thinking and writing is the experience of problems and the need to clarify and resolve them. Everything depends on the problem, the situations and the tools available. Inquiry does not rely on a priori elements or fixed rules. I always attempted to start my work by understanding in which problematic situations I aimed at intervening. Philosophy and academic, but also public life, in my time was heading in wrong directions that called upon me to initiate inquiry to resolve issues – *in media res*, as it were. When I wrote *Logic*, I tried to rebut dogmatic understandings. Now it appears that I am on the verge of becoming a dogma myself. In a sense, the most tragic scenario would be if people develop a 'Deweyan' perspective or theory. Now I am curious, what problem brought you actually to converse with me?

TT: Well, we are here today because we have been asked to contribute to an effort to collect the views of a number of different theorists, who, like you, live in different space-time. Now that we are here, could we ask you to tell us how you use the term 'inquiry'? It is one of your core concepts and in our conversation you already frequently referred to it. It is often difficult to understand what you mean by this term and how it provides direction and purpose for science ...

It's a simple one, provided you have not been indoctrinated by logical positivists. You, me, all of us, frequently engage in inquiry. There is little distinction between solving problems of everyday life and the reasoning of the scientist or philosopher. Most often habit and routine will give you satisfaction. Yet when these fail or give you unpleasant experience, then reasoning begins. Without inquiry, sirs, most likely you wouldn't have been able to speak to me today! You will have to explain later how you bent time and space and which technology allowed you to travel through a black hole. But Albert was right, time travel is possible! Could we converse today without Einstein's fabulous inquiry that led him to the realization of space-time? Until the promulgation of Einstein's restricted theory of relativity, mass, time and motion were regarded as intrinsic properties of ultimate fixed and independent substances.[14] Einstein questioned this on the basis of experimentation and an investigation of the problem of simultaneity, that is, that from different reference frames there can never be agreement on the simultaneity of events.

Reflection implies that something is believed in (or disbelieved in), not on its own direct account, but through something else which stands as witness, evidence, proof, voucher, warrant; that is, as ground of belief. At one time, rain is actually felt or directly experienced without any intermediary fact; at another time, we infer that it has rained from the looks of the grass and trees, or that it is going to rain because of the condition of the air or the state of the barometer.[15] The fact that inquiry intervenes in ever-shifting contexts demands us to restrain from eternal truths or absolutistic logic. Someone believing in a truth such as 'individualism', has his programme determined for him in advance. It is then not a matter of finding out the particular thing which needs to be done and the best way, and the circumstances, of doing it. He knows in advance the sort of thing which must be done, just as in ancient physical philosophy the thinker knew in advance what must happen, so that all he had to do was to supply a logical framework of definitions and classifications.[16]

When I say that thinking and beliefs should be experimental, not absolutistic, I have in mind a certain logic of method. Such a logic firstly implies that the concepts, general principles, theories and dialectical developments which are indispensable to any systematic knowledge are shaped and tested as tools of inquiry. Secondly, policies and proposals for social action have to be treated as working hypotheses. They have to be subject to constant and well-equipped observations of the consequences they entail when acted upon and subject to flexible revision. The social sciences are primarily an apparatus for conducting such investigations.[17]

TT: Doesn't such a form of reasoning mean we'll just muddle through without ever reaching certainty?

Absolutely correct! Arriving at one point is the starting point of another. Life flowers and should be understood as such; experimental reasoning is never complete. I can imagine the surprise you must feel at sudden unforeseen events in international political relationships when you hold on to fixed frames of how these relationships do and ought to look. That we will never reach certainty does not imply to give up the quest of certainty, however. We have to continuously improve on our tools of scientific inquiry …

TT: Sorry to interrupt you here. Now it sounds as if you have a sort of methods fetish. Do you imply that everything can be solved by the right method and all that we have to do is to refine our methods? That's something that our colleagues running statistics and thinking that the problems of international can be solved by algorithms argue as well.

It might be that mathematical reasoning has well advanced since my departure, and that the importance granted to the economy and economic thinking as the sole conditioning factor of political organization has only increased, but you haven't fully grasped what I mean by 'tools'. Tell your stubbornly calculating colleagues that inquiry is embedded in a situation, hence there cannot be a single method which would fix all kinds of problems. Second, while I admire the skill of mathematicians, what I mean by tools goes well beyond that. A tool can be a concept, a term, a theory, a proposal, a course of action, anything that might matter to settle a particular situation. A tool is, however, not a solution *per se*. It is a proposal. It must be tested against the problematic material. It matters only in so far as it is part of a practical activity aimed at resolving a problematic situation.

TT: You emphasize that language is instrumental and reject the idea of a private language. You also spent quite some energy on demolishing the 'picture theory' of language. These arguments form the basis of what we call today 'constructivism', yet they are mainly attributed to the *Philosophical Investigations* of the later Ludwig Wittgenstein.

Earhh, I am aware of this fellow. He is an analytical philosopher, so develops his argument from a different background. I started to work on the social and cultural aspects of language use from around 1916. I don't know whether Wittgenstein actually read my work when he set out to write *Philosophical Investigations*, but you are quite right, there are obvious parallels. I think my own term of 'conjoint activity' expresses pretty much the same, perhaps less eloquently, what Wittgenstein termed language games. I am pleased to hear, however, that the instrumental view on language, that objects get their meanings within a language in and by conjoint community of functional use, has become firmly established in academia. I'd have reservations about the term, 'constructivism'. It might be useful since it reminds us of all the construction work that the organization of politics and society entails. Indeed I have frequently stressed that instrumentalist theory implies construction. If constructivism doesn't mean postmortem studies of how something has been constructed, but is directed towards production of better futures, I might be fine with the term. But perhaps I would prefer 'productivism'.

TT: That is a plausible term, but we are afraid, the history of science has settled on constructivism. And you are right, the tendencies you warn us of are significantly present in our discipline.

172 Christian Bueger and Peer Schouten

Sirs, if you permit. I have to attend to other obligations. I wish you safe travels back. Make sure you pick up something from the gift shop before you leave.

Notes

1. John Dewey. (1929) 'From Absolutism to Experimentism', in *The Later Works of John Dewey, 1925–1953*, ed. Jo Ann Boydston (1989), vol. 5, p. 155.
2. Gibboney, Richard, & A.V. Christie. (2002) '*This Mixture is the Better Art:*' *John Dewey's Poems*. Education & Culture, XIX:2, p. 21.
3. *Ibid.*
4. Jo Ann Boydston, ed. (1977) *The Poems of John Dewey* (Carbondale: Southern Illinois University Press/London: Feffer & Simons).
5. *Democracy in Education*, 1997 ed., p. 21.
6. Dewey, John. (1927) *The Public and Its Problems* (New York: Henry Holt and Company).
7. Remarks by Dewey during historic address on his seventieth anniversary on 19 October 1929, as published by the *Harvard Crimson* (17 October 1959), accessible here http://www.thecrimson.com/article/1959/10/17/dialogue-with-john-dewey-pnext-tuesday/
8. Afterword to *The Public and its Problems*, p. 222.
9. See Dewey, John. (1916) *Democracy and Education: An Introduction to the Philosophy of Education* (New York: The Macmillan Company).
10. Dewey, John. ([1916] 2008) *Democracy and Education* (Radford, VA: Wilder Publications), p. 63.
11. Hickman, 1990, xi.
12. Dewey, John. (1920) *Reconstruction in Philosophy* (New York: Henry Holt and Company), p. 32.
13. Dewey, John. (1929) *The Quest for Certainty: A Study of the Relation of Knowledge and Action.* (New York: Minton, Balch & Company), p. 83.
14. *The Quest for Certainty*, p. 122.
15. Dewey, John. (1909) *How We Think.* (Boston: D. C. Heath & Co), p. 8.
16. *The Public and Its Problems*, p. 202.
17. *Ibid.*, 203.

20
Max Weber (1864–1920)

Richard Ned Lebow

Lebow: I am delighted to meet you Professor Weber. If Kant cast a long shadow over nineteenth-century German intellectual development, you did the same for twentieth-century social science.

Weber: I find that hard to believe, especially in light of what I learned about this century from the books you gave me. On my deathbed I was angry at dying relatively young, and worse still, at doing so at an important turning point in German and European history. In retrospect, fate did me a favour, and I know that Marianne would be upset if she heard this, but *it would have been even better* to have died in the early months of 1914.[1] I always thought it tragic that Nietzsche went mad, but now understand it as a courageous and sensible move on his part. But he was ahead of all of us in his thinking.

Lebow: You found the readings worthwhile?

Weber: Interesting but *horrifying*. The twentieth century was evidently the *worst* since the fourteenth century and the Black Death.

Lebow: Does it prompt you to rethink your idealization of the state, support of German imperialism and its support for Austria and invasion of Belgium in 1914?

Weber: It does, but this will take me some time to work through. My commitment to Germany, its state and *Kultur* was a given since my childhood memories of the Franco-Prussian War and unification. I am now beginning to feel as anchorless politically as I did intellectually when alive. In a demystified world all former certainties lose their hold on us. We must accept the impossibility of making sense of the world and come to terms with its meaninglessness – as far as we can. I once told the

173

jurist Richard Thoma that 'I want to see how much I can bear', by which I meant accepting personally and intellectually this uncertainty and its consequences.[2] Now in my second life – if that's what this is – I must face up to equally disturbing truths and acknowledge that my political commitments, perhaps liberalism aside, were a comforting delusion. This will take time.

Lebow: Turning to a less traumatic subject, what did you think of the scholarly journals I gave you?

Weber: They are also disturbing. Most of the articles are on narrow subjects and narrowly framed. The first one in the *American Sociological Review* is on light cigarettes, whatever they are, as an example of market categories that are taken for granted and how companies can exploit this phenomenon. Surely, there are more important questions to research? The *American Political Science Review* was a little better but still largely focused on voting behaviour. I was struck by how articles in both journals use, really *misuse*, the concept of rationality.

Lebow: Would you care to elaborate?

Weber: They assume that actors are rational, or more problematic still, that their societies are, and somehow make appropriate accommodations to changing conditions. Rationality is central to my analysis, but in a different way. I start with the concept of *Richtigkeitstypus* [right rationality]. It is 'the a priori' of interpretative understanding.[3] It is subjective because there are no rational ways to determine what is rational. This depends in the first instance on actor motives and their beliefs. If people are motivated by fear versus material gain, they will evaluate risk differently. If someone believes in the power of god or gods to produce rain or other boons, they will consider prayer or prescribed rituals rational while we do not. Even if we understand the goals actors seek – and they are by no means self-evident to them or us – right rationality requires us to determine the course of action that had the best chance of advancing them given their beliefs. How do we know what the most effective means are in the absence of controlled experiments? We fall back on our subjective estimates and perhaps counterfactual analysis. Judgments of rationality, even when evidence-based, involve leaps of inference at every step.

Lebow: So you consider rationality an ideal type rather than a description of reality?

Weber: That's right. Rationality is an ideal type that provides a clear
          and unambiguous – but purely theoretical – account of a causal
          relationship. It is nothing more than 'a methodological device'.
          It does not require, nor is it intended to suggest, 'a belief in the
          actual predominance of rational elements in human life'.[4]
          The closer any action conforms to right rationality, the less
          need there is to introduce 'psychological considerations' to
          comprehend it. The identification of 'irrational' processes
          [*Sinnfremd*] and their analysis also start with reason. We must
          'determine how the action would have proceeded in the limit-
          ing case of purposive and right rationality' and then account
          for the variation.[5] The rationalist models and arguments that
          I encountered in these journals err by confusing ideal types
          and reality. Reason is an assumption we make for purposes of
          analysis. Rational models cannot describe behaviour. They are
          merely starting points for studying it and must be followed
          by careful empirical analysis to see how and why behaviour
          departs from this norm.
Lebow: Doesn't this approach open its own can of worms? You insist
          in your posthumous *Grundbegriffe*, and argue now, that ideal
          types help us to understand the motives of actors. I find this
          difficult to reconcile with your insistence on reconstructing
          motivations from the point of view of an actor. Admittedly,
          some ideal types attempt to capture or build on commonly
          shared motives, but many do not. Injudicious use of ideal
          types is no different from 'assuming' motives in the way
          present-day rationalists do.[6]
Weber: I am skating on some thin ice here, but I won't fall through.
          The seeming contradiction is neither as sharp nor as irrecon-
          cilable as you suggest. By definition, any end-means, that is,
          causal, relationship *must attribute some rationality* to actors.
          Purposeful rational behaviour is that which 'is exclusively
          oriented towards means which are (*subjectively*) considered to
          be adequate for the attainment of purposeful goals which are
          (*subjectively*) unambiguously comprehended'. Mind you, here
          I refer only to instrumental rationality because any motive – it
          need not be realistic or ethical – can provide an incentive for
          acting. I try hard to exclude substantive rationality, which
          pertains to the ends actors seek, from my analysis.[7]
          Consider the practical aspects of this problem. The more
          an individual's deliberations 'have not been obfuscated by

"external" constraint[s] or irresistible "affects"', the more readily they submit to an ends-means analysis. I acknowledge that this condition is hardly ever met in practice, but we must nevertheless try to use what evidence we have about actors, their goals and behaviour and try to make the latter 'fit into a model of rational action'.[8]

Lebow: If I understand you correctly, you are saying that in the absence of instrumental rationality social behaviour would be entirely unpredictable and societies could neither form nor function.

Weber: Precisely. But we must be careful not to attribute too much rationality to actors. What is important is that *researchers* function in terms of rationality. Wearing my neo-Kantian hat I conceive of the world as one of logical behaviour and causal 'necessity', but in which such necessity is never more than guide. I'm also willing to admit that there is more unpredictability in human behaviour than in the weather.[9]

Lebow: Your last admission about unpredictability is not easily reconciled with the Kantian belief that the world is made accessible by reason.

Weber: It is if you consider that there is no better method for understanding the world. In my youth, Historicists and Dilthey put their trust in intuition, but that doesn't take you very far and it is even more difficult to justify or evaluate. Reason is, I admit, an imperfect and fallible guide, but it is the best we have. It has the additional advantage of compelling the researcher to be explicit about his or her assumptions and inferences, which allows for constructive dialogue. If you want, I might say the qualities of character – *integrity*, honesty – is a prerequisite to any claim of truth.

Lebow: I see your point. Your former student and my mentor, Hans Morgenthau, thought along these lines. He built a theory of international relations that gave great prominence to the balance of power. He recognized that this mechanism functioned to preserve the independence of states only some of the time. Among other things, it required actors who desired this end and understood and used the mechanism in question. He devoted a lot of attention to analysing why the balance of power failed in 1914 and 1939. It was a starting point for an analysis that took context, actors and confluence into account to explain specific historical outcomes.

Weber: I don't remember this Morgenthau, but his approach makes sense as you describe it.

Lebow: He was not strictly speaking your student, but audited your lectures in Munich.

Weber: At least one of these lectures I considered important enough to publish.

Lebow: Yes, *Politik als Beruf* [The Vocation and Profession of Politics]. It has become very famous. Everyone in political theory, and many university students, but alas, hardly anyone in politics, is familiar with your distinction between the ethics of conviction [*Gesinnungsethik*] and responsibility [*Verantwortungsethik*].[10] The former requires people to act in accord with their principles regardless of the outcome. You describe it an unaffordable luxury in a world where force must sometimes be used for survival or laudable policy ends. The ethic of responsibility focuses on the consequences of our behaviour, and you consider it more appropriate to politics, and presumably even more to international relations.

Weber: That is correct. And in an immoderate moment, I wrote that anyone who fails to recognize this truth 'is indeed a child in political matters'.[11]

Lebow: I think your formulation is open to challenge, and not only because you conclude your essay by arguing for a combination of the two ethics. The ethic of responsibility is problematic because, as you acknowledge, behaviour often has unforeseen and undesired outcomes. Policies can have horrible, unintended consequences that are not apparent beforehand. The European alliance systems before 1914 are cases in point. If you can't estimate policy outcomes in advance how can you possibly apply the ethic of responsibility?

Weber: The Oedipus problem, if you like, is undeniable, but may not be as common as you assume. In many cases, careful, rational analysis can give us some idea of the likely consequences of a course of action.

Lebow: We can agree to disagree on this one. But tell me how good politicians can treat ethics dialectically and act on some synthesis of the two seemingly opposed ethics.

Weber: Responsible politicians must carefully consider the conditions in which either ethic is most appropriate and the outcomes to which their initiatives may lead. A wise leader must 'be conscious of ethical paradoxes and of his responsibility for what may become of *himself* under pressure from them'.[12] He, or I suppose, she these days, from what I read, must think with the head, but also listen with the heart, because there are occasions where policy considerations trump ethics and vice versa. *The two ethics are more complementary than opposing* 'and only in combination do they produce the true human being who is *capable* of having a "vocation for politics"'.[13] I have always been moved by Luther's words in his defence at Worms.

Lebow: You put more faith in politicians than I do. Even in your time, and more so in mine, the profession of politics attracts the very kind of people who are unwilling or incapable of acting as you think they should. This is an empirical criticism, but I have a conceptual one too. You say nothing about the conditions that should govern the choice between the two kinds of ethics on the grounds that it is situation specific. In the absence of any criteria, leaders are left dangerously free to make choices of convenience. And I fear that most political leaders will make the wrong ones.

Weber: I can only hope that democratically elected leaders will make the right choices, but I appreciate your criticism because the choice and appropriate application of either ethic requires leaders with a conscience, courage and open minds.

Lebow: Can we return to epistemology again?

Weber: This seems to be my fate. Every time I engage in a substantive project I am compelled to write *another* epistemological essay!

Lebow: This won't be a long digression. I'm interested in your understanding of cause. As I understand the several essays you would have preferred not to write, you think all social science should aim for causal analysis. But that this does not entail a search for law-like regularities.

Weber: So-called 'cause' and 'effect' are *human creations*; they are not features of the world. Causal inference is *purely rhetorical* in nature and scholars must convince others of their claims, which they often do by appealing to common sense. In effect, they are asking others to accept their inferences on the ground that that they are based on shared assumptions about how the world works.[14] We can also evaluate these claims on the basis of logical consistency, empirical evidence and *Erfahrungsregeln* [rules of experience]. Researchers use reason to discover regularities, but also emotions that allow empathetic understandings of actor motives.[15]

Lebow: How do ideal types assist in this process?

Weber: To make causal inference we must posit events types and identify events that we might subsume them. Events are what we want to explain, and our categories the means we employ toward this end. Typologies of event types enable comparative study and nomological understandings in the form of very imperfect regularities. These associations are imperfect because events have many causes and we can only identify and study some of them. The context in which they unfold is also likely to differ across 'cases', making them far from comparable.

Lebow: How do you differ from regularity theorists?

Weber: I recognize the value of regularities, or at least the expectation that some kinds of behaviour are likely to produce certain kinds of outcomes. Knowledge of this kind can be *a useful starting point* for causal analysis. However, nomological knowledge for historians and social scientists are means, not ends, in contrast to the physical sciences. This difference derives from the former's interest in the particular and the latter's in the general.

Lebow: Am I right in thinking that regularities, or any other kind of understandings, are the foundation, but nothing more, for causal narratives that emphasize what is particular about the event in question?

Weber: We must construct narratives around imagined causal chains. I use the words *Verlauf* and *Ablauf* to describe the progression we offer of seemingly related actions and events. These actions and events that seem causally linked can also be manifestations of an underlying process. Either way, the narrative form encourages us to think about mechanisms that connect actions and events. Mechanisms are, of course, also figments of our imagination.

Causal narratives offer another advantage. They allow us to conceive of deeper levels of explanation. To provide the most compelling accounts of causation 'we have to refer back to other, equally individual configurations' that might account for the phenomenon in question. We must then try to account for these configurations. Ultimately, we hope to reach *underlying cultural explanations*. Consider the phenomenon of the market, which is now found almost everywhere. We want to know what changed in Western society to make this possible. These changes enabled the growth of a money economy and made it 'significant' and 'distinctive'.[16]

Lebow: How do counterfactuals assist in this process?

Weber: To determine if antecedent conditions are *objectively probable*
         and *adequate* we rely on counterfactual thought experiments.
         Here, I drew on the probability theory of Karl Knies and the legal
         analysis of Gustav Radbruch.[17] Radbruch sought to determine
         malfeasance or criminal responsibility by asking what the likeli-
         hood was that some negative outcome would have occurred in
         the absence of the agents or conditions alleged to be respon-
         sible. My reformulation would have us ask if 'elimination ...
         or alteration' of the putative cause 'according to general rules of
         experience' could have led to a different outcome.[18] Social sci-
         entists, like judges, must work backwards from what they want
         to explain to its possible causes. By removing one putative cause
         at a time and asking what might have happened in its absence
         we can evaluate its relative importance for an outcome.

Weber: My time is almost up. A man with pointed ears and a flat voice
         said at 5 p.m. he would 'beam me up', whatever that means.
         Do you think we could walk across the river and have a peek at
         my house before we reach the appointed hour? And who lives
         there now?

Lebow: Of course, Herr Professor. Your house is now part of the
         University of Heidelberg and often used to host seminars and
         training courses. Before we part, I want to thank you for being
         so accommodating.

Weber: You posed good questions and I would have been very content
         to have had you as a student.

Lebow: I can think of no higher honour.

Notes

1. Weber had the annoying habit of using italics frequently, often multiple times
   in the same paragraph, to emphasize certain points. I follow his practice by
   having him punctuate his replies.
2. Marianne Weber, *Max Weber: A Biography*, trans. Harry Zohn (New York:
   Wiley, 1974), p. 678. Lotte Kohler and Hans Sane, eds., *Hannah Arendt/Karl
   Jaspers Correspondence 1926–1969*, trans. Robert and Rita Kimber (New York:
   Harcourt, Brace, Jovanovich, 1992), pp. 660–62.
3. Max Weber, '*Objektivität*' and 'Kritische Studien auf dem Gebiet der kulturwissenschaftlichen Logik', in Max Weber, *Gesammelte Aufsätze zur
   Wissenschaftslehre*, ed. Johannes Winckelmann, 3rd ed. (Tübingen: J. C. B. Mohr
   (Paul Siebeck), 1968), pp. 170–72, 276–80. Cited henceforth as GAW. All trans-
   lations are mine unless otherwise noted.

4. Max Weber, 'Conceptual Exposition', in Guenther Roth and Claus Wittich, eds and trans *Economy and Society* (Berkeley: University of California Press, 1978), pp. 6–7.
5. Weber, 'Kritische Studien'.
6. Weber, *Economy and Society*, p. 22.
7. Max Weber, 'The Profession and Vocation of Politics', in Peter Lassman and Ronald Speirs, eds *Political Writings* (Cambridge: Cambridge University Press, 2000), pp. 309–69.
8. Weber, 'Roscher and Knies', GAW, pp. 67–70.
9. Ibid., pp. 127–31.
10. Weber, 'Profession and Vocation of Politics'.
11. Ibid.
12. Ibid.
13. Ibid.
14. For a contemporary version of this approach to causation, Richard Ned Lebow, *Constructing Cause in International Relations* (Cambridge: Cambridge University Press, 2014).
15. Weber, 'Objectivität', GAW, pp. 178–80.
16. Ibid, pp. 175–78.
17. Karl Knies, *Die Statistik als selbständige Wissenschaft* (Kassel: J. Luckhardt, 1850) and Gustav Radbruch, *Die Lehre von adäquaten Verursachung* [Theory of Adequate Causation] (Berlin: Abhandlungen des Kriminalistischen Seminars an der Universität Berlin, NF vol. 1, 1902).
18. Weber, 'Kritische Studien auf dem Gebiet der kulturwissenschaftlichen Logik', pp. GAW, pp. 282–83.

21

The Republic of Norman Angell (1872–1967): A Dialogue (with Apologies to Plato)

Lucian M. Ashworth

October 1963

I was relaxing in a café on London's Strand when a young journalist from The Observer *that I had met earlier in the month came rushing up to my table. 'Is it true?' she asked catching her breath, 'Were you at a dinner recently with Kim Philby and the new leader of the opposition?' Philby had defected to the Soviet Union earlier in the year, and Harold Wilson was the new leader of the Labour Party, and would be British Prime Minister in the following year. 'Yes, there was a dinner party where we were all present, Susan, but it wasn't this year. It took place in early October 1938, just after Neville Chamberlain returned from Munich. It happened at the home of Robert Cecil, the Conservative politician and League enthusiast. Wilson was the youngest Don at Oxford, while Philby had returned from reporting the war in Spain. But Wilson and Philby were not the main guests. That honour fell to Norman Angell, the recently knighted writer and former Labour MP, and Maurice Hankey, who had resigned as secretary to the Cabinet in August. There was also a young American from the US Embassy there, but it was Angell who dominated the proceedings'. 'Angell?' My friend looked puzzled. 'Oh! Great Illusion! There was a radio programme on him earlier in the year.*[1] *So'. She asked, 'What was discussed at this dinner?'*

October 1938

We had gathered at the London house of Robert Cecil. When I arrived Philip Noel-Baker, an old protégé of Cecil's and now a senior Labour figure, was already there with Wilson. I arrived with John, the twenty-one year old son of the American Ambassador, Joseph Kennedy. The novelist Margaret Storm Jameson and writer Vera Brittain arrived soon after, followed by Hankey and Philby. Talk before dinner was all about the new deal with the Germans. Just before dinner Angell arrived.

Angell: So what have you all been talking about?
Kennedy: Your deal with Hitler. Father is fulsome in his praise, but I have unanswered questions.
Angell: So do I young man. Tell me, where does that accent come from?
Kennedy: New England mostly.
Angell: I was a cowboy and homesteader near Bakersfield, California before the war. Always considered myself a little bit American, though I never managed to get my land claim accepted.[2]
Kennedy: I had hoped to study politics with Harold Laski at the LSE; unfortunately I fell ill and had to return home. What are your thoughts on the international situation, Mr Angell?
Cecil (jovially):   *Sir* Norman now, Mr. Kennedy.
Angell: Well, my boy, why don't we ask *Lord* Cecil (smile). He knows far more about foreign policy than I do. Cecil, was it a success?
Cecil: Carried out in secret without the support of the rest of the League and the international community? It worries me. We should deal with these dictators out in the open.
Angell: Given that the League powers failed to stop Japanese and Italian aggression, was open League diplomacy really an option?
Cecil: It was the governments of the great powers that refused to allow the League system to work.
Angell: I agree, but now that it has failed to work, should we not fall back on the next best thing: an anti-fascist alliance?
Cecil: That is what we need to do now, but it is a pity we never allowed the League to work.
Angell: Perhaps once we have confronted the dictators we can rebuild the League?[3]
Cecil: That is what we are reduced to. Still, the publics in the democracies seem more interested in peace at any price than they do with establishing an international order that would preserve security and peace.

Just then an angry Maurice Hankey intervened. I could see Hankey getting redder in the face as the talk had gone on, but unable to control himself he now blurted out his 'opposition to this nonsense!' He said that the Munich agreement was the best deal we could have got, and that any peaceful settlement had to be based on the balance of power between states. Anything else was just 'eyewash'.

Angell: Well, you know more about these things than I do, Hankey. After all, you have been involved in this government's foreign policy. Perhaps I could ask you some questions about this, since you know so much more than us? Does a stable and peaceful order in Europe need to be a just order?

Hankey: Well, the powers need to see it as just. Remember Herr Hitler's claims are based on his belief that Germany has been treated unfairly.

Angell: So to work it has to be at least seen to be just?

Hankey: Yes.

Angell: How does the balance of power work?

Hankey: The great powers weigh up their different levels of military power and potential, and form alliances on the basis of preventing any one state from having a preponderance of power. Ideally, diplomats work to guarantee that negotiations reflect those power arrangements, but if diplomacy breaks down the threat of force is the last resort.

Angell: So decisions are made on the basis of power and the threat of force?

Hankey: Largely, yes.

Angell: So the balance of power is about might, not right?

Hankey: We have to take power into consideration, yes. As we did at Munich.

Angell: But if the defining feature of the balance of power is issues of power, then surely issues of justice must be silent? If we side with a country for reasons of power balance, then the question of the rightness of that country does not enter into the equation? Yugoslavia might have a just cause against Italy, but if we need Italy to balance the power of Germany we will side with Italy against the just claims of Yugoslavia?[4]

Hankey: I suppose so.

Angell: Then how can we have a system based on justice? And without states believing that the system is just, do we not have an unstable system poisoned by claims for redress?

Hankey: Look, Angell, you miss the point here. Power and cabinets are the reality we have to deal with. If we want peace we need to take both these seriously. If that means we have to act unjustly sometimes then it is a price we pay.

At this point Margaret Storm Jameson and Vera Brittain both voiced their objection to Hankey's view, and Brittain graciously asked Jameson to speak for them both.

Jameson: Both of us are left cold by Hankey's view of international affairs, but we are not entirely convinced by your analysis either, Angell. As women we understand the world can change, and indeed if it had not we would not now be sitting here as equals with you men. The vote has given us a stake in the political game that we never had before. Our problem is, if the balance of power between great powers is unstable because it is unjust, how can we build a stable world? Is it possible to banish war from our lives forever? What should a new order look like?

Angell: Building a new global order? You have both set me a difficult task! Indeed, one it seems our own statesmen have failed to accomplish in the last twenty years. I don't think I can do it alone so you will need to help me. You too, Noel-Baker. Your knowledge of the League and disarmament will be vital.

Noel-Baker: Thank you, Angell, but if it is all the same to you, I will sit this out until you have something for me to comment on.

Brittain: I should be most happy to help, although I feel that our views on the role of war, Sir Norman, are not the same. I oppose war completely, and so I welcome the Munich agreement, but not for the same reasons as Hankey.

Angell: Very well. Shall we start with some basics? What was the purpose of war in the past?

Brittain: To steal someone else's land. Caesar's campaign in Gaul was about land, wealth and increasing his personal power.

Angell: Indeed it was. Wealth was in land and in goods you could take as booty. How would you advise me to invest my wealth now?

Brittain: Well, not in land! All the great landed estates seem to be in trouble these days. Despite the crash ten years ago,

	I would still say stocks and bonds, perhaps, sadly, stocks in armament firms.
Angell:	So the new wealthy are those who own bits of paper? We might add credit to that list too, as well as the trading system now that none of us are self-sufficient nations.[5]
Brittain:	This is obvious, and we already know this. You wrote about it in your *Great Illusion* before the War. The world has changed, and we express wealth in intangibles that can be so easily destroyed by war.
Angell:	Precisely. Modern war between great powers destroys intangible wealth, and as a result even the victors in war suffer the effects.[6] I think the last War is a good example of this, although I was more pessimistic. I thought a major war would destroy our fragile system of wealth, but instead government action managed to limit the damage.[7] Still, the war and capitalist trusts did destroy the *laissez faire* system that we had come to rely on for our daily bread before 1914.[8]
Cecil:	We are all socialists now, Angell. Government controls are a fact of life after the War.
Jameson:	But the fact that we had a war shows that our new forms of wealth and their vulnerability were not enough to prevent war. People went to war against their own interests.
Angell:	Indeed they did. This brings us to the human nature of the case. In *The Great Illusion* I had assumed that if we explained to people the realities of money and credit then they would see that war between great powers does not pay, and then they would follow their own interests and refrain from conflicts that would destroy their wealth. I was wrong. But why?
Jameson:	You should have asked a novelist, Angell. We could have told you. Also that Dr Freud whom the Woolfs have translated. Humans are not rational.
Angell:	Yet, can we not have a rational conversation between men and women of good will? Where is the irrationality here?
Wilson:	It is not here, Angell. When I am talking one-on-one with someone I disagree with we can both be rational. It is when I am in a group of like-minded people that the trouble starts. We Labourites can be very rude about you Conservatives, Cecil, when we are in a large group.
Kennedy:	The newsreels from Germany and Italy back you up here.

Angell: Indeed they do, my young friend. I wrote about this in
              my first book, *Patriotism Under Three Flags*.[9] The resort to
              blind nationalism in three otherwise very rational socie-
              ties – Britain, America and France – was so shocking to
              me back then. Yet, it was not until after the Great War
              that I realized how dangerous this 'public mind' was. You
              cannot just hope that groups of people will eventually be
              convinced of the rationality of your argument, because
              in groups they will act irrationally.[10] That is why the old
              liberal *laissez faire* order died, as I made clear in my *Fruits
              of Victory*.

Cecil: That is why we founded the League, Sir Norman. You
              have argued it yourself since the War. We need structures,
              some basic form of international government, to keep
              those dangerous group passions at bay.[11]

Noel-Baker: We return to the League. Again, it is our only hope for
              lasting peace.[12]

Brittain: Yet, the League also threatened supposed aggressors
              with war. I am thinking here of the excellent work of
              Mrs Swanwick, who has proved to my satisfaction that
              'League wars' for peace would be just as dangerous as
              wars of aggression, and anyway, the nations who ran the
              League were remarkably good at avoiding their legal com-
              mitments under the Covenant.[13] In this sense, perhaps
              Hankey is right about the ubiquity of power and interests?

Angell: I am not altogether in agreement with Mrs Swanwick on
              League wars. Nor, do I think is my friend Noel-Baker.

Noel-Baker: Indeed not! Fighting to maintain law and order – policing
              if you will – is not the same thing as aggression.

Angell: Yet, the League system, although so much better than what
              we had before 1914, has failed us. But who is to blame?
              Here at least I will agree with Mrs Swanwick up to a point.
              The League powers – their governments – failed us.[14]

Angell turned to me.

Angell: You have been very quiet my friend?
Me: Not because I have not been listening, and not because I have
          not found this conversation riveting. I think your public mind
          idea does explain why seemingly rational people blindly fol-
          low irrational ideas.

Philby: That describes pretty much everyone at my Cambridge college, and not a few of my friends at the Foreign Office. One of the reasons I like journalism: the freedom to think.

Wilson: There are a few people at Oxford that I would describe that way too.

Angell: The freedom to think strikes me as the missing ingredient here.

Wilson: So let me summarize here, Sir Norman. A changed world dominated by finance, credit and trade (I might add the white heat of technology here too)[15] means that war between great powers no longer pays. This means that the balance of power cannot function, and anyway its privileging of might over right makes it unstable. Because mankind is irrational in groups, states left to their own devices in an international anarchy will not learn from the economic realities of life. Instead they will follow policies that are actually incompatible with their true interests. As a result we need international institutions and agreements to rein in the passions of the public mind.

Angell: Ably summarized.

Jameson: Yet, the League did not stop aggression. The irrational public minds of Japan and Italy got away with it over Manchuria and Abyssinia. What are we missing?

Brittain: Can't international public opinion still be mobilized for peace? Like we did with the Peace Ballot three years back?

Cecil: Yes. That showed that the public mind is not all bad, surely?

Hankey: Nonsense. All Hitler respects is force, not the legalities of the League and the ballots of international public opinion. We threatened him with the spectre of war at Munich and he backed down. Here, at least, I agree with Sir Norman's view of the nature of the human mind.

Philby: I still think a few people of good faith can make a difference.

Angell: A good point, Philby. Are we stuck with the evils of the public mind? Certainly the League powers, especially Britain and France, made very wrong choices against their longer term interests by not fully backing a League solution in 1931 and 1935. Can we improve our knowledge to fight off these unseen assassins?[16] How can we make statesmen in an age of the common man realize the self-defeating nature of selfish national interests?

Jameson: The freedom to think and debate? To create spaces like this dinner in which rational argument can trump the passions of the group?

Angell: Yes, that is why freedom matters.

Brittain: But we have not really solved the problem yet. If the problem is controlling the public mind, how do we create institutions that will work for peace? League-pooled security did not solve the problem. I would back George Lansbury's call to refuse to play Hitler's game and to disarm on our own.

Hankey: Nonsense. A return to secret diplomacy between nations is the answer. Rational men using diplomacy to solve problems without public meddling.

Angell: The same men who failed to bring peace in 1914? Has not the recent past shown us that the old diplomacy can no longer work? I think young Philby is on to something here. Yes, we do need organizations like the League to provide legal structures to prevent the public mind from gaining the upper hand. In that sense Cecil and Noel-Baker are right. But the League is not enough. We also have to change the mindsets of our voters and politicians. This requires freedom of thought and the protection of the right of the individual to think what they like in the face of the irrational public mind.[17] We may not be able to change man's violent and greedy nature, but through education we can at least change his view of the world, and perhaps show him that there are better paths for his selfishness than war.

Jameson: But that will take a long time. What do we do now? We can hardly wait until Herr Hitler has seen reason, and with the League so weakened it is going to take a labour of Hercules to make it work properly again?

Angell: Yes. What I have been talking about are, of course, long-term goals.

Kennedy: Miss Jameson is right. What interests us Americans right now is not what we all may do in the future, but what England can do now. Is a partnership with Germany possible? What are your thoughts on the agreement with Herr Hitler, Mr Angell?

Angell: The dictators cannot be appeased.[18] I would agree with Hankey that it is now all about force, although I think the Prime Minister is deceiving himself if he thinks that this agreement heralds peace.

Hankey: I doubt that the Prime Minister sees this agreement as the last word. He is no enthusiast for Hitler.

Angell: Be that as it may, our best hope lies in rebuilding the League and collective security by bringing together those nations that are willing to pool their security to defend the ideals of the League.[19] This is why I support an alliance with France, and why we must rearm to face down the dictators. Here I find myself in agreement with my old friends Leonard Woolf and Henry Brailsford. We could have had this so much earlier and easier if we had stuck with the League, but now we must return to the jungle of the reason of state and rebuild what we had already built after the waste of the last war.

Cecil: Quite right. The future is the League.

Wilson: ... or whatever we build to replace it.

Brittain: But that still leaves the problem of war.

Angell: Sometimes war may be the only option, but hopefully we can at least fight it for nobler ends like freedom and internationalism. A war will not enrich us, but it might at least prevent a worse fate befalling us.

Brittain: I cannot accept that. War is always wrong.

Angell: I hope one day we will live in a world where that is true. Until then we may have to risk war to secure freedom.[20]

Jameson: I must admit my revulsion towards war is only exceeded by my revulsion towards the Nazis. I don't welcome war, but we may have no choice.

Brittain: That is where we differ, I am afraid. We all have a choice, and I choose peace.

Philby: What about an alliance with the Soviet Union?

Angell: I would not rule it out. Mr Brailsford seems to be positively inclined to just such an alliance. Although I cannot call myself an enthusiast for Comrade Stalin. My experience is that your communist is as much a victim of the excesses of the public mind as your fascist or Nazi.

Kennedy: ... and don't expect American public opinion to back a war in Europe.

Angell: A pity, Kennedy. With Britain and America working together who knows what we might accomplish in the world? I have high hopes for America and its democracy.[21]

At this stage I could see that we had exhausted the topic. Angell had diagnosed the patient, suggested the medicine that could be applied,

and finally offered his thoughts on what should be done to allevi-
ate the immediate symptoms. He had not convinced everyone, but
I could see that it had got John thinking about the wider problems of
appeasement.[22]

As we got up to go our separate ways Angell took me aside.

Angell: You were quiet tonight my friend. I hope nothing is wrong.
Me: I was listening. I just didn't think it was right for me to
        intervene.
Angell: Am I right, do you think?
Me: Well, I can't answer that, although you sometimes make
        leaps of logic that may not be warranted, and at others you
        do seem to contradict yourself. I do think many of the ideas
        that you have will survive you. The importance of what
        Americans are calling interdependence; the damage that
        war does to prosperity, even to the wealth of the victor; the
        problem of the public mind, which has also been recognized
        by others. Sadly, though, I fear your current fame will not
        outlive you.
Angell: Well, I would rather my ideas survived my fame than the other
        way around. These issues are more important than any one
        person.
Me: It will be a problem of success. So many people will become
        interested in international affairs that their fame, research
        output and intellectual prowess will tend to obscure those who
        came before.
Angell: Well, if our civilization survives these current difficulties, and
        is still talking about the issues that I have raised in my career,
        then I suppose I am content.

October 1963 again
'Hang on a minute' Susan interjected, '1938? Twenty-five years ago?
How did you remember the conversation so accurately?' I explained
that I had been asked to write an interview with Angell for a 2016 edited
collection, and so had travelled back in time. Attending the dinner had
been Angell's idea. I was just back from the event, and was now on
an extended vacation in 1963. I had said a last goodbye to John, and
there was a television programme I wanted to catch (the one that had
shown me how I could visit Angell for the interview).[23] Susan gave me
a pained smile. 'What nonsense! Well, I have some important work on
the Sterling zone that I have to finish'.

Notes

1. Kenneth Younger, 'The Great Illusion', *The Listener*, 10 January 1963, 51–2.
2. Norman Angell, *After All. The Autobiography of Norman Angell* (London: Hamish Hamilton, 1951).
3. See the discussion in Norman Angell, *Peace with the Dictators? A Symposium and Some Conclusions* (London: Hamish Hamilton, 1938). Also: Norman Angell, 'Get Effective Defence and You Get the League', *The New Outlook*, 10 January 1936, 15–17.
4. Norman Angell, 'The International Anarchy', in Leonard Woolf (ed.) *The Intelligent Man's Way to Prevent War* (London: Victor Gollancz, 1933).
5. This argument was developed by Angell before World War 1 in Norman Angell, *The Great Illusion. A Study of the Relations of Military Power in Nations to their Economic and Social Advantage* (London: G.P. Putnam's Sons, 1911); Part I; and Norman Angell, *The Foundations of International Polity* (Toronto: William Briggs, 1914); 81ff.
6. Angell, *Great Illusion*, 27–8, 48–9.
7. Norman Angell, *Fruits of Victory* (New York: Century, 1921), 293.
8. Angell, *Fruits of Victory*, 61, 299.
9. Norman Angell, *Patriotism under Three Flags. A Plea for Rationalism in Politics* (London: T. Fisher Unwin, 1903).
10. Norman Angell, *The Public Mind. Its Disorders: Its Explanation* (London: Noel Douglas, 1926).
11. Angell, *Fruits of Victory*, 61–70; 300–1.
12. Philip Noel Baker, *The League of Nations at Work* (London: Nisbet, 1927).
13. Helena Maria Swanwick, *Collective Insecurity* (London: Jonathan Cape, 1937).
14. Angell, *Peace with the Dictators?*
15. Harold Wilson used this term in a speech on 1 October 1963.
16. Norman Angell, *The Unseen Assassins* (London: Hamish Hamilton, 1932).
17. Norman Angell, *Why Freedom Matters* (Harmondsworth: Penguin, 1940).
18. Norman Angell, 'The New John Bull', *The Political Quarterly*, 1936, 7(3), 311–29.
19. See Angell, 'Get Effective Defence and You Get the League'.
20. For examples of Angell seeing war with the dictators as a risk worth taking see Norman Angell, 'Japan, the League and Us', *Time and Tide*, November 1931, 1302–3; and Norman Angell, *This Have and Have-Not Business. Political Fantasy and Economic Fact* (London: Hamish Hamilton, 1936).
21. Norman Angell, *The British Revolution and the American Democracy* (Toronto: McClelland, Goodchild and Stewart, 1919).
22. John F. Kennedy, *Why England Slept* (New York: Wilfred Funk, 1961 [1940]).
23. The first episode of Dr Who, 'An Unearthly Child', broadcast on 23 November 1963.

22
Functionalism in Uncommon Places: Electrifying the Hades with David Mitrany (1888–1975)

Jens Steffek

JS: Good morning, David – may I call you David? I am unsure how to address a dead man.

DM: David is fine, reminds me of the good old days on Earth. Officially it would be Shadow David down here, but never mind.

JS: OK, David, great. I am here to have a chat with you about your vision of functional international governance, which was path-breaking and had so much influence on subsequent scholarship. Our readers would be thrilled to hear your views on current developments, in Europe and beyond ...

DM: I'm sorry, what did you say? I got a bit distracted. What is all this shouting and laughing over there? All about women and eels.

JS: Oh, I think that is one of our folks trying to interview Thucydides. Hades insisted we come down here as a group. No single admittance to the underworld unless you want to stay, he said.

DM: I think these guys are seriously off topic. Let us go for a walk and I'll show you around. I guess you haven't been here before.

JS: This is very kind of you but I actually wanted to talk a bit about functionalism, you know, and regional integration and all that ...

DM: I got that. And this is another reason why we should go for a walk. Just follow me uphill.

Mitrany and the interviewer walk in silence until they reach a barren mountaintop. From there the view is breath-taking. In the twilight, a vast lake with shimmering blue water stretches to the horizon.

JS: This is awesome, David, and so peaceful.

DM: The lake is actually artificial, and I am proud to say that it is part of my work down here. I founded the Styx Valley Authority, the SVA for short.

JS: You did what? You dammed the river Styx?

DM: Not only the Styx. All major watercourses of the underworld are part of my scheme, including the Phlegethon, Acheron, Lethe and Cocytus. The whole system. Like in the Tennessee Valley, you remember. I studied that scheme back in the 1930s when I was a fellow at Princeton, and it became my blueprint for international agencies doing development work.[1] When I arrived here, the Hades was an unpleasant marshland, all dark and muddy.[2] The wandering souls were stumbling over their own feet. And I knew immediately what had to be done.

JS: What is this huge lake good for, actually?

DM: Down at the Styx dam there is a power plant that I needed to electrify the underworld. Now we have electric heating and light everywhere, we drained the ugly and unhealthy marsh, and on top of that we have some nice lakes for outdoor activities. And I can report that the humans on the other shore of the Styx are also quite happy with the public works we did. The Peloponnese is a rather remote region of Greece, you know.

JS: There are living human beings on the other side of that lake?

DM: You should have read some travel literature before coming down here. The Styx marks the border between Earth and the under-world. It functions a bit like the iron curtain dividing Europe back in my day. No living human being and no dead soul is able to cross the Styx without special permission, and permits are rare. But now we have learned to work together on practically useful tasks, despite all the differences that divide us.

JS: How did you bring together the living and the dead?

DM: Well, that's a long story. Hades of course was very much against it in the beginning. Identity politics, you know. The living and the dead, he said, they are just too different and they are not supposed to mix. Charon feared for his job when he heard about the dam project and started lobbying. On the other side of the river there were also quite some concerns, I heard. Zeus jealously watches the boundaries of his empire and he said damming the Styx was a constitutional issue. It affected the original territorial agreement because it filled some airspace with water.[3] Boundaries are an obsession, no matter where you go.

JS: How did you overcome their resistance?

DM: By way of demonstration. You know how pragmatic I am. I asked Shadow Tom (Edison, J.S.) to build a little pilot facility to showcase the benefits of our electrification project. Of course we made sure that Zeus and Hades were the first ones connected to the grid. And once they switched on the electric lights in their palaces they were all for it.

JS: But how did you manage to involve living human beings in running your SVA?

DM: Joint government of the living and the dead gave me a headache in the beginning. I didn't want just Hades and Zeus striking their despotic deals; I wanted to get some knowledgeable people from both sides involved. But where would we meet with them? They are not allowed in and we can't go out. A good Korean soul came up with a clever idea. We now convene on top of the Styx dam, exactly at the old borderline. We built a kind of pagoda on the dam and we sit on our side, and they sit on theirs.

JS: Was the Korean fellow Kim Jong-Il?

DM: Certainly not, that nasty man was taken straight to the Tartarus.

JS: Electricity for the underworld, David, that really surprises me. Modernization does not seem to stop anywhere.

DM: Well, I learned my lessons about the power of technology and progress in the upper world and now I apply them down here. They are universal, as I always said.

JS: As a political scientist I am very curious to learn more about the system of governance that you installed in your SVA.

DM: Long story, again. I said to Hades, look, what I need is a functional agency. I don't want to get enmeshed in all sorts of power struggles and animosities between the political factions down here. And I can reassure you that we have a lot of factions in the underworld – dead souls are arguing over the silliest of things.[4] So I said to him, I need experts to do the job, pragmatic people who have seen something of the world, no matter where they lived back on Earth. Hades then suggested that we get some philosophers directing the works. He thought they were the most qualified souls you can get. I don't know if Plato told him that. Anyway, I had to get theorists involved but a smart move of mine was, if I may say that, to place them on an advisory board. I have John Dewey presiding it and I got Henri de Saint-Simon and Auguste Comte. But of course they are arguing all the time, as I predicted …

JS: … so what did you do?

DM: The philosophers draw up their annual report that nobody reads – if they get something published at all with their vicious peer review system. But then there is also our executive board, and so who really does the work in the SVA are practically-minded souls. I have a superb selection of them, David Lilienthal, Freiherr vom Stein, Julius Nyerere.[5]

JS: I wonder if there was no resistance against this modernization project, I mean, it must have been a huge change for the Hades but also for the living folks on the other side. No complaints, no worries?

DM: Well yes, admittedly some environmentalist souls claimed that the water of the Lethe was not the same any more after we built the dams and sewers and power plants. The magic was gone, they said, and they made a huge fuss about it.

JS: And were they right? I mean, the magic of the Lethe, was it gone?

DM: I can't seem to remember.

JS: ???

DM: That was a joke. You really need to read some classics, young man.[6] Of course we had to react, and we did it properly. We set up a scientific commission to study the properties of the Lethe water and it turned out to be superb; microbiologically pure, well-mineralized – what else can you ask for. Actually, the quality was so great that we decided to commercialize it in the upper world. We sell it in bottles as Italian mineral water to generate some income for future projects down here.[7] You see, my years in business left some traces on me.[8]

JS: Wow, David, that is all fascinating, but I really would like to talk a bit more about political science. You know that, after you passed away, the world became more sceptical of big public works and state planning. How about you?

DM: I have heard about that. But of course planning works if it is done properly and on the right scale – just look around you. And if it is coordinated transnationally, of course. I never believed in those national five-year-plans that stop at the border. This is never going to work because your neighbour's plan will always upset yours. Why do you think I should have abandoned my faith in planning and public works?

JS: Well, because we have come to think the world is too complex to anticipate all the effects that one project has, and that markets know better than some technocrats what the people really need.

DM: Excuse me, but I think you have been brainwashed by the neoliberals. Of course you need reasonably free markets and private initiative and all that. I always was a liberal and you know that. But at the same time you need public regulatory institutions to keep markets in check and you need a welfare state to take care of the people. Look at the financial crisis since 2008, look at the levels of inequality that you now have in so many countries. Do you really think that a hands-off approach is an alternative?

JS: No, but I do think there is a difference between this old-school planning thing and how we go about things nowadays.

DM: So, how do you go about them now? I am not sure I fully understand the difference.

JS: We do not do this central planning and steering any more, all that top-down stuff, we have multi-level governance.

DM: So, what exactly do you mean by 'multi-level' governance?

JS: Kind of policy coordination, you know, more horizontal, in networks across many levels.

DM: Sounds a bit like what I suggested back in the 1940s and 50s, if I may say so. I actually had my quibbles with centralization. So much power in one place, one central government, this is not a good idea. What you need is devolution, territorial and functional. And try to keep the pushing and shoving and horse-trading out, all the political power games. That is functional government.

JS: No, but we do see things differently today. It is not the same, it is not functionalism. We realized that experts cannot solve all our problems.

DM: But who can?

JS: Err, well the solution is basically negotiated, all in the network you know, and we want to bring the people in.

DM: You bring the people in? How do you do that? Eight billion people, or what do you have now, they meet for breakfast and talk? Are you kidding me? I also wanted to bring the people in, but my approach was different. Just those affected by whatever the public authority did, and those who knew about an issue. If you want to improve agriculture you need to consult the peasants, for example. And that can even create new transnational loyalties. Like I once said: everybody feels a sentiment of humanity, but few act upon it, because action has to be linked to concrete steps within the range of everyday life.[9]

JS: Today we have the Internet, most people can directly connect with each other. Karl Deutsch loves it.

DM: This global electronic network sounds extremely interesting but they are not installing it down here. Officially for technical reasons but I presume that Google and Amazon are not too interested in dead men without credit cards. But if politics is all taking place in a network without any nodes, so to speak, who decides then? I mean, at some point you need to take a decision also across borders. Take the financial crisis, who took the crucial steps? Who is the spider in that web?

JS: Well, of course, in the end deciding something is then more of an intergovernmental thing.

DM: So it is still national ministers who decide and people out there talk about it. That sounds somewhat conventional, if you ask me.

JS: People do not just talk in private, I mean, it is all more public and politicized now, world politics.

DM: Politics is more politicized now? I am not sure I understand what you mean, and I am even less sure that I will like it once I understand it.

JS: You know, David, there is more contestation today, people take to the streets against global governance if they don't like it. No permissive consensus any more. We had these huge protests against the WTO – that's the successor of the old GATT – back in the late 90s.

DM: I observed that – but what happened in the end? Did governments dissolve the WTO in response? No, they didn't.

JS: Err, well, you have a point there.

DM: I am actually not sure that this politicization thing works. Wrong approach, in my view. De-politicize things and you will get substantially good results, not the other way round. Look what happened to the European Union over the last decades. To my mind this is a disaster.

JS: Why a disaster? After all, the EU has grown and it seems it mastered the Euro crisis, even if it might be a bit early to tell.

DM: I am following European integration from down here, you know that it was a bit of my intellectual baby, even if the federalist have won in the end: they built a superstate with headquarters in Brussels and integrated a zillion policy fields, whether that makes sense or not, and all the benefits are for the club members, nothing for the rest of the world. They are just reproducing the old logic of inside and outside.

JS: I see that there might be disadvantages to the federal scheme. But then the EU wants to become a global player, and it probably needs to ...

DM: This is exactly what I feared would happen. You have a regional international organization, pretty humble at the outset, with a clear territorial remit but with a rather unclear mission. And then that beast grows stronger. It starts behaving like a traditional great power, trying to mark a sphere of influence, as we see now in Eastern Europe. They tell the people: you are either with us or with the Russians, you need to choose. What happened in Ukraine followed precisely this logic.

JS: Ok, the EU certainly made some mistakes in the Ukrainian crisis, but it was Vladimir Putin who escalated the situation.

DM: Putin has the mentality of a 19th century politician, sadly enough. National grandeur, imperialism, obsession with territorial security, all these perversions of the political mind. But I hoped that at least the EU could find a more constructive way of engaging him. You have so many common issues with the Russians to work on constructively. And what did the Europeans do instead? Sanctions. As if that ever worked.[10] But there are alternatives. What we need is a flexible institutional architecture in Europe, various constellations of states working together on whatever affects them. Imagine a free trade area between Russia and the EU, with Ukraine in the middle and part of it. And from there we could develop new projects in other fields where collaboration pays. Imagine a Black Sea authority, with Russians, Romanians, Ukrainians, Turks, Georgians etc., or imagine a Dnepr basin authority. Lull the damn nationalists, give them something useful to do together and they forget their ideological bullshit. Sorry for the explicit wording.

JS: I see that you are really aggravated.

DM: Of course, because I grew up in Eastern Europe. I lived through two world wars and one cold war. And I thought I had found something like a recipe to get over the pernicious dynamics of nationalism and power politics that produce only losers. You know I'm Jewish but I never travelled to Israel in my whole life. I like the idea of a Jewish homeland but I would have been forced to speak out against Israel's nationalism.[11] We have to fight nationalism wherever it raises its ugly head. After 1990 I had some hope that things would change for the better, at least in Europe. To see such confrontation happen all over again is frustrating, to say the least.

A horn is blowing in the distance.

JS: This is our signal, David, I am afraid my time with you is up. I need to head back to the upper world.

DM: You'd better not miss your travel group. But wait a second, I have got something for you.

Mitrany hands a little amphora to the interviewer.

JS: Thank you so much. What's in there?
DM: Mineral water from our new plant at the Lethe. I hope you enjoy it.

The interviewer opens the amphora to take a sip.

DM: Not now!
JS: Why not?
DM: Type up our interview first.
JS: What? You said your experts analysed the water.
DM: That's right. But did experts ever tell me I'd go to a place called Hades when I'm dead?

Notes

1. On the Tennessee Valley Authority (TVA) see David Mitrany (1946), *American Interpretations: Four Political Essays*, (London: Contact Publications). The TVA as a blueprint for international cooperation is mentioned in David Mitrany (1954), *Food and Freedom*, London: Batchworth Press, pp. 33–4.
2. See Aristophanes (1908 [405 BC]), *The Frogs*, translated by Gilbert Murray, (London: George Allen & Sons), pp. 34/5.
3. After their victory over the Titans, the three sons of Cronos drew lots to divide the universe among them, Hades came to rule the underworld, Zeus the air and Poseidon the seas; see Homer, *Iliad*, Book 15, lines 187–94.
4. On 'hot dissension among all the dead' see Aristophanes, *The Frogs*, p. 59.
5. David E. Lilienthal (1899–1981) was a board member of the TVA and its Chairman from 1941 to 1946; Heinrich Friedrich Karl Reichsfreiherr vom und zum Stein (1757–1831) was a Prussian minister and reformer of the civil service; Julius Nyerere (1922–1999) was the first Prime Minister and later long-term President of independent Tanganijka/Tanzania.
6. To learn that according to antique mythology the Lethe was the river of oblivion the interviewer could have read, for instance, Virgil, *Aeneid* 6, 705 ff.
7. For evidence see http://www.acqualete.it/it/homepage/homepage.htm.
8. Mitrany worked as international affairs adviser for Unilever from 1943 to 1960. On the nature of this appointment see Sir Frederick Pedler (1976), 'Mitrany in Unilever', *Millennium* 5(2): 196–9.
9. Mitrany here probably quotes a paper of his delivered to the International Conference on Mental Hygiene in August 1949, p. 12, *Mitrany Papers* (London School of Economics and Political Science), box 35.
10. He seems to be referring here to David Mitrany (1925), *The Problem of International Sanctions*, (London: H. Milford/Oxford University Press).
11. David Mitrany (1975), *The Functional Theory of Politics*, (New York: St. Martin's Press), p. 61.

23
Dialogue with Arnold Wolfers (1892–1968)

James W. Davis

This is the fictional account of a chance meeting in the Fall of 2014 between James W. Davis and Arnold Wolfers in the Stiftsbibliothek, a UNESCO World Heritage Site located within the Abbey of St. Gallen, as the latter was observing a medieval handwritten copy of a text by Thomas Aquinas.

Arnold Wolfers: (speaking to himself out loud): I was arguing about the continued relevance of Aquinas – not to mention Augustine and Dante – in 1956.

James Davis: Professor Wolfers?

Arnold Wolfers: Yes. How did you recognize me?

James Davis: Welcome back to St. Gallen! You were born here, weren't you?

Arnold Wolfers: In 1892.

James Davis: 122 years ago. Amazing.

Arnold Wolfers: But you haven't answered my question!

James Davis: Of course. Well, I've been re-reading the collection of essays you published as *Discord and Collaboration* and recognized the argument on the importance of political theory to our understanding of international relations. You made the point back then that trends were pointing to the emergence of a 'new medievalism'.[1]

Arnold Wolfers: That's right. But tell me, you aren't from St. Gallen. Nobody here would be reading an essay I first published in 1956!

James Davis: Oh, but you're wrong! Or sort of … I'm not Swiss – originally from the United States – but I hold the chair for International Relations at the University of St. Gallen and have assigned your book in a seminar

	on political responsibility. By the way, my name is James Davis.
Arnold Wolfers:	It's a pleasure to make your acquaintance, Mr. Davis. Things have certainly changed in St. Gallen. When I completed my *Matura* at the local Gymnasium, one more or less could only study book keeping at the local trade school. That's why I set out on my journey through the Universities of Berlin, Lausanne, Munich and Zürich. And of course, there were almost no courses devoted to the study of international politics. I wrote my dissertation at Zürich in Law. I came to the field of international politics much later. The same was the case with my friend Hans Morgenthau, who studied Law and *Staatswissenschaften* – which I guess is best translated as 'Government' – in Frankfurt, Munich and Berlin.
James Davis:	In many respects the world has changed since you left St. Gallen; in part because of the transfer of ideas from the Continent to the New World. Actually, I think that the 20th Century intellectual history of our field is underappreciated on both sides of the Atlantic and that there are some interesting paradoxes that someone should spend some time examining. For example, in the 1950s you argued that the foreign policies of the Anglo-Saxons differ in important regards from those of the Continental powers and that we therefore should spend more time studying English and American thinking about world affairs. But owing in large part to the influence of the German-speaking émigrés, American scholars of international relations became more interested in further developing the ideas of Continental authors such as Machiavelli, Kant or Grotius than in understanding and elaborating the foreign policy traditions inspired by such figures as George Washington, Thomas Jefferson, James Madison, Alexander Hamilton, or later, Woodrow Wilson. Meanwhile, many, or perhaps most, European scholars rejected on moral grounds much of the very same Continental thinking the Americans were busy learning.
Arnold Wolfers:	Which itself is an argument for the importance of linking philosophical and empirical discussions of international relations!

James Davis: I agree. Meantime American foreign policy practice continues to puzzle academic observers in Europe as well as the United States, even though many of the architects of America's post-war foreign policy were of European origin. I am thinking of people like Kissinger, Brzezinski, or at lower levels of the government, Fritz Kraemer and Fred Iklé, who, you probably know, also grew up in St. Gallen.

Arnold Wolfers: Well, you have only succeeded in identifying the outliers – those Americans whose foreign policy styles were most intelligible for Continentals.

James Davis: And maybe therefore rejected by so many American Liberals as unprincipled, if not immoral?

Arnold Wolfers: Perhaps. But it is important to stress that there has always been a debate between Machiavellians and anti-Machiavellians on the Continent. But I do think you are right. The intellectual history of the field is a subject that deserves more systematic analysis, although not at the expense of understanding the real world of international politics. Tell me, what are international relations scholars talking about today?

James Davis: Quite a bit and yet not very much. There are those who are trying to understand the dynamics and implications of contemporary developments – globalization, the rise of China, jihadist terrorism, or Russia under Vladimir Putin – and those who are more interested in developing abstract theory. Only rarely do the two groups seem to meet in any meaningful way.

Arnold Wolfers: The relationship between theory and practice has always been a topic of much debate, but how could you possibly understand international politics without theory? And how could you develop theory without an understanding of real political developments? The choice is not between theory and no theory, but between disciplined analysis and crude hunches pursued by those who think they can 'play it by ear'. But if you've read *Discord and Collaboration*, you must know this.

James Davis: The relevant question it seems to me is not whether or not one needs theory, but how theory and practice interrelate. Is theory intended to explain previous political choices, inform current ones, or both? If the latter is the case, then theory is causing behaviour as much as it is explaining it, which runs counter to many standard accounts. As long as men and women in positions of authority can think – I know, it often seems a rather heroic assumption – and have some room for choice, then theory is perhaps best conceived as the elaboration of concepts, often at a very abstract level, which permits a better understanding of the situation and suggests options for moving forward?

Arnold Wolfers: That sounds a bit like a Marxist understanding of theory, although I am not completely opposed to the formulation. There is something of a dialectic between theory and *Praxis,* to stick with the German term. But it is an altogether open question whether, or to what degree, there is room for choice in the conduct of a state's foreign affairs.

James Davis: The assumption of those who land on the side of explanation is one of very limited choice. It's what leads to the assertion that international politics is timeless, governed by objective laws that haven't changed since the classic philosophers of Greece, India or China tried to intuit them, to paraphrase your friend Morgenthau. And yet it does seem that the world has changed in fundamental ways since Morgenthau wrote his 'Six Principles of Political Realism'. In many regards the world today looks more civilized than it did in the middle of the last century. And international relations are no longer the sole purview of the nation state.

Arnold Wolfers: Once again, you've packed quite a lot into a few sentences. For one, what on earth do you mean by 'civilized?' As for the arguments about change, well I've heard them all before. Not that I don't see any possibility for fundamental change – that's why I was arguing for the continuing relevance of medieval writings about political systems. We need to be careful about assuming that the nation state is the only durable form of political organization. There is nothing absolute or unchanging about the value men attach to the state or

	state interests. That said, I am more often puzzled by what I regard to be an astonishing persistence of tradition than I am by widespread evidence of change.
James Davis:	I know … the term 'civilized' is no longer politically correct, but I assumed you more or less knew what I meant thereby. If we have to define every term we use, we will never get anywhere.
Arnold Wolfers:	*We* might, and probably do, share a similar understanding of 'civilized' behaviour. But more often than not such terms, if they have any meaning at all, mean quite different things to different people. The importance placed on this or that value – and a description of civilized behaviour would encompass some discussion of values – differs from individual to individual and from group to group. Remember, Lenin argued that the expulsion of landowners and capitalists from Russia was the precondition for civilization! The revolution as a sort of *mission civilisatrice*.
James Davis:	From Marx to Lenin! And I thought you were a Realist?
Arnold Wolfers:	A thinking Realist.
James Davis:	Which brings me back to the role of theory and the possibility for change. Isn't quite a bit of the continuity we observe in international relations a result of persistent anarchy?
Arnold Wolfers:	In a certain sense yes. But I never regarded anarchy as a description of the real world, rather as an abstract and initial working hypothesis. Remember, Hobbes's discussion of the state of nature is a thought experiment. He states quite clearly that there had never been a time where individual men actually did live in an anarchy of that sort. I have always been suspicious of theories that try to explain state behaviour solely on the basis of environmental factors. Likewise, the role of personal traits and factors internal to the state are often exaggerated. Foreign policy, or even international politics, must be understood and explained from the two perspectives – actor and environment – simultaneously.
James Davis:	But doesn't that make prediction extremely difficult?

Arnold Wolfers: Difficult, but not impossible. The accuracy of predictions will depend on the degree to which internal and external compulsions exist and are strong enough to transform the actors into what I once called 'automatons lacking all freedom of choice'. Historically, this is rarely the case but statesmen are often tempted to argue that their environment was so extreme as to leave no room for choice.

James Davis: Again, you confuse me. On the one hand you stress the astonishingly high degree in continuity of international relations across time and space. On the other hand, you warn against underestimating decision makers' room for choice.

Arnold Wolfers: Two comments are in order. First, we need to differentiate between the job of the theorist and that of the decision maker. The former is interested in uncovering general patterns, the latter in promoting the state's values in specific circumstances. For this task, and this is my second point, theory is not an adequate substitute for intuition, experience and good judgment. Whereas it is the duty of the theorist to point out that certain 'necessities' of international politics restrict the statesman's range of choice, it is the duty of the statesman to exploit an even restricted range of choice in pursuit of the state's values.

James Davis: You tend to speak of values rather than interests. Contemporary theorists who would regard themselves as Realists tend to shy away from a discussion of values and focus instead on the state's interests, security being chief amongst these.

Arnold Wolfers: An unfortunate development, but one I feared and warned against. To assert that the history of international relations is nothing other than pure power politics is once again to confuse a theoretic concept with empirical reality. Anyone who has a passing familiarity with history knows that survival is rarely at stake. This is especially true for the major powers, whose relative security allows them to devote their foreign policy to the pursuit of other values. Security is one among a plethora of values and states can aspire to enjoy security in greater or lesser measure.

But again, you should know this if you have read *Discord and Collaboration.*

James Davis: I'm afraid the tendency to assume that theoretical concepts can substitute for historical or cultural knowledge today is widespread. One of the most outspoken contemporary proponents of what we have come to term Structural Realism, John Mearsheimer, argues that history plays but a small role in influencing the contemporary thinking and behaviour of states; that structural theories by definition cannot put too much weight on history. At quite a different level of analysis, proponents of rational choice theories of decision making tend to be interested in explaining specific, time-bound events – a particular war, the outcome of a particular negotiation, or perhaps an election – largely abstracting it from historical context and taking the relevant actors and preferences as given.

Arnold Wolfers: Once again, I think we need to be clear about the utility of theory. Theorists may find it useful to begin from the working hypothesis that all states are enemies and thus must strive to enhance their security, but even then we do not know how they will attempt to do so. Some might choose armaments, others neutrality. Understanding why the Swiss have a long tradition of armed neutrality whereas other mountainous regions of central Europe were prepared to play the game of expansion or empire – and many were successful at it for quite some time, think of the Austrians under the Habsburgs – requires a focus on more than just the structure of the system. Actually, it was the choices of individual leaders that produced the very structures on which this fellow Mearsheimer is basing his analysis. And as for what you call rational choice, I am sceptical of claims that the national peculiarities of people from widely divergent cultural backgrounds are irrelevant when they are trying to hammer out an agreement. Again, the assumption of uniform rationality makes sense for the purposes of creating a strong working hypothesis, but in my day, I regarded the tendency of Americans to engage in moralism as a handicap in efforts to negotiate with allies and adversaries alike.

James W. Davis: And yet you never shied away from a discussion of morals or ethics in international relations.

Arnold Wolfers: The two are quite different ... moralism and ethics. As Max Weber reminded us, personal morals are a poor guide when it comes to identifying the options that are available to a politician in the specific circumstances in which he finds himself. This is not to say, however, that he bears no responsibility for his actions. When the state's existence is not at stake – and as I already said, I believe such situations to be rare in history – every additional increment of security is purchased by sacrificing other values. It is fair to question whether in terms of agreed ethical standards, a less destructive choice should have been made.

James Davis: And where should we look for these 'agreed ethical standards?' International law? The United Nations Charter?

Arnold Wofers: I'm not sure, which is why I decided to come back to St. Gallen. The ethical standards according to which one would have judged the foreign policies of the Prince Abbot of St. Gallen during the Middle Ages were quite different from those according to which I judged American foreign policy during the Cold War. Something changed with the emergence of modern nation states and the triumph of nationalism as a political ideology – not only in the nature of the actors but the ethical standards according to which we could reasonably judge political decisions. Understanding the nature of these changes and the processes that produced them seems fundamental to understanding international politics.

(The church bells begin to ring)

James Davis: (Looking at his watch) Professor Wolfers, I'd love to continue this discussion but I'm afraid I have to run. My seminar starts in 15 minutes.

Arnold Wolfers: Of course. But what is the topic?

James Davis: We're reading Henry Kissinger's latest book, *World Order: Reflections on the Character of Nations and the Course of History.*

Arnold Wolfers: Kissinger? Is he still alive?

Note

1. Arnold Wolfers (1962), *Discord and Collaboration: Essays on International Politics,* (Baltimore: Johns Hopkins University Press). In this fictional encounter, Wolfers repeats many of the arguments found in this collection.

24

E.H. Carr (1892–1982)

Michael Cox

Gazing out across the quad of Trinity College where he had once been an undergraduate before the First World War ('a much different and more hopeful world' he mused) Edward Hallett Carr was in a pensive mood. And for good reason. Thatcher had just been elected in the UK and there was every chance that Reagan would annihilate the Democrats in America in the following year. A 'New Cold War' on the horizon he wondered? Worse. The Soviet Union to which he had devoted 35 years of his academic life looked decidedly moribund. Some on the right were even predicting that the system might fail altogether over the next decade. 'Most unlikely', he felt. Still, it was a concern. And to cap it all, that spent ideological force called liberalism which he had predicted had no future back in the 1930s and 1940s looked to be brimming with energy and life. Indeed, it was difficult to pick up a copy of the London Times (his old newspaper) and not find yet another article by either Hayek or Friedman or one of their epigones like Paul Johnson (a one-time socialist) or Arthur Seldon (didn't he study economics at the LSE?) denouncing socialism in all its forms while celebrating the wonders of the free market. 'What was the world coming to?' he mused.

'And to cap it all, there is this character called Michael Cox coming to interview me about IR – whatever that is'!

Knock on the door. Enter Cox.

Cox: Thank you for giving up your time to see me, Professor Carr.

EHC: Professor. Uhm. I haven't been called that since my Aberystwyth days.

Cox: Well, it is Aberystwyth that I really wanted to talk to you about.

EHC: Fine, but I am not sure there is much to tell. I arrived unwelcome and unwanted by the then benefactor of the Chair – David Davies; that was in 1936. He worshipped at the altar of the League of Nations and I did not. Ironic that I got the job really. And as you know, he then resigned from the College in anger. And when the war broke out in 1939 I remained in London writing editorials for *The Times*. Davies objected to that too. Anyway, I gave up my Chair in 1947 – partly for personal reasons and partly because I was now immersed in an entirely new project: writing the early history of the USSR for the publisher, Macmillan. I worked with Harold Macmillan (the future Prime Minister).

Cox: I'm bound to ask then: why did you take the position in the first place? Aberystwyth was a small seaside town located on the western edge of a small nation. A five-hour train ride away from the seat of power in London. And the Chair was named after Woodrow Wilson – a politician you were known to dislike for being both an American and a liberal idealist.

EHC: That is true. But, to be blunt, there was nothing else. The only other Chairs of International Relations at the time were occupied by Charles Manning at the LSE (an obscure writer but a clever man) and Alfred Zimmern up at Oxford (a better writer but not quite so clever).

Cox: I notice you use the term International Relations. But what was 'IR' back then? Manning after all was a Lawyer. Zimmern trained as a classicist. And you were a Foreign Office mandarin who had authored a biography of the Russian novelist, Dostoevsky; two books on 19th century Russian radicals (Herzen and Bakunin); and of course another work – your least favourite I gather – on Karl Marx. So what were your qualifications?

EHC: Good question and you're right. There was no such thing or discipline as IR back then. That was largely an American construction after the Second World War created in my view to rationalize their own great power role in the world. Typical of the Americans!

Cox: So?

EHC: Well I suppose I brought my own set of 'qualifications' to the job. I had a First from Cambridge. That was usually enough to secure you an academic job back then. I had also been at the heart of power – not just talking to power – but wielding it. And I suppose I had a proven track record when it came to writing books.

Cox: Was this the only reason you got the Chair?

EHC: I don't think so. There was, I suspect, another crucial factor at play. The Chair may have been funded by Davies. However, the

Principal of the College – Ifor Evans – was determined to make the appointment on academic grounds and not just because the candidate happened to support the League of Nations. Evans was an extraordinary Welshman; indeed, he only learned Welsh while interned by the Germans in World War I. He also had his own views about the world and they did not necessarily coincide with those of Davies. As Kingsley Martin (editor of the *New Statesman*) later confessed in the first volume of his memoirs *Father Figures*, he too had been approached to fill the Chair at one point. He didn't go for it in the end. But he did find out that the last thing Evans wanted was to have a 'Liberal idealist wished on him', presumably by Davies. So I had a key man in my camp when it came to the interview![1]

Cox: But that still begs the question: why move to faraway Aberystwyth at all? There must have been a reason?

EHC: There was indeed. I wanted to write 'big book' on world affairs and my 'fancy chair' as I later called it afforded me time and space.

Cox: Which brings us to your writing, *The Twenty Years' Crisis*, I suppose.

EHC: Well, let's get one thing cleared up right away. That was definitely not my title. That was foisted on me by the publisher to help sell the book. My initial idea was to call the book *Utopia and Reality,* reflecting the deeper purpose of the book which was not to explain why the interwar system was falling apart but rather to expose the utopian nature of liberalism – a perfectly coherent set of principles for the 19th century but an entirely redundant set of ideas in an age of revolution, economic collapse and rapid power shifts. Liberalism was also an ideology, one that the Americans in particular deployed rather effectively to justify their own great power ambitions. And I felt moved to tear away the mask especially as their particular brand of liberalism as articulated by Wilson had an ultimate purpose: namely to undermine British power in the world.

Cox: But if you were so critical of Britain's most important ally why were you so uncritical of Germany? Some have even accused you of being pro-German. Is that fair?

EHC: Some have claimed it. I would not. I was simply being realistic. Like Keynes I thought Germany had been dealt an impossible hand by the victors at Versailles in 1919. I was also sensitive to the rights of German minorities in Central Europe, and in spite of all the talk about protecting their interests, the allies had done very little after the Versailles. Finally, we simply could not ignore Germany's claims to being a great power.

Cox: In other words, you were advocating appeasement?

EHC: Call it what you will. But what was the alternative to peacefully allowing change in Central Europe once German power had been rebuilt under Hitler? There was none other than another war even more devastating than the one that had gone before: a war moreover that would undermine the British Empire and force Britain into a dependency relationship with the Americans.

Cox: But surely you were proved wrong? Hitler was not 'appeased'. His ambitions proved more than merely regional? And in the end Britain and France were compelled to go to war in circumstances much worse than they might have otherwise been if they had taken a much firmer stand earlier.

EHC: Easy to say that with the benefit of hindsight. But it ignores two very simple facts: neither the British nor the French were prepared to make serious overtures to the USSR at the time; and the Americans could not be counted on to do anything. Fear of communism on the one hand and US isolationism on the other narrowed our options to such a degree that we had no realistic alternative but to try and come to some arrangement with Germany.

Cox: But the strategy failed – you will admit that?

EHC: Perhaps so. However, it does not invalidate the more general principle laid down in the book that when faced with rapid shifts in the balance of power no amount of appeals to 'international norms' or the 'international law' will help states craft a strategy. And this is why I disagreed with liberals like Toynbee, Zimmern and Angell so strongly.

Cox: How did they receive *The Twenty Years' Crisis* when it was finally published in the autumn of 1939?

EHC: Badly, very badly. Norman Angell no less called it a piece 'sophisticated moral nihilism'. Toynbee made the more obvious point that my attempt to debunk people like him could not hide the fact that I myself had been debunked by the coming of war. Zimmern meanwhile called me a relativist. And Leonard Woolf quite adroitly characterized me as being as much a 'utopian' as the liberals by assuming that Hitler could be dealt with as a normal statesman heading up a state guided by normal 'realist' principles. It was quite a broadside.[2]

Cox: The war then intervened. You began writing editorials for *The Times* some of which clearly annoyed your political enemies on the right. But during the war you also found time to write three more books dealing with wider international questions, *Conditions of Peace, Nationalism and After* and *The Soviet Impact on the Western World*.[3] These all sealed your reputation as man of the left – a champion if you like of economic planning and a powerful advocate of building a new kind of relationship with the USSR. Churchill meantime denounced you when you attacked British policy in Greece, while Hayek in his polemic *The Road to Serfdom* characterized you as being one of the 'totalitarians in our midst'.[4] How did you respond?

EHC: Simply by getting on with my work. But in a way my 1942 book was an attempt to show that I did not worship at the altar of power. In its own way it was fairly visionary – 'utopian' if you like. And my book on nationalism argued that if we were to create a new international order it was not enough to build yet more international institutions. We had to move beyond the nation state as the unit of world politics. Lastly in 1946 I brought out a second edition of *The Twenty Years' Crisis*. But this only provoked criticism in some quarters because it looked as if I was trying to delete some of the less fortunate passages contained in the first edition. If nothing else, this convinced me that I should keep well away from the new emerging discipline of 'IR' then beginning to take off in the United States.

Cox: And what did you think of the new 'discipline'?

EHC: Not a great deal to be honest. In America the subject seemed to launch itself with an attack on me written by Morgenthau in *World Politics* in 1948.[5] Then I was lumped together with other 'realist' writers like Kennan, with whom I had very little in common. He was after all the author of the doctrine of containment to which I was strongly opposed as being unnecessary and provocative. More generally, the discipline as such seemed little more than a guide book on how the United States should run the world.

Cox: And in Britain?

EHC: Here the situation was, if anything, just as bad, even if those drawn to the subject seemed to have a better grasp of history. But to be honest I took little notice of what was going in places like LSE and Oxford, even less so Aberystwyth where I am told my work was not even discussed – though they were nice enough to invite me to attend a conference in 1969, commemorating the

50th anniversary of the International Politics department (interestingly in David Davies' country house in mid-Wales!)

Cox: Did you have anything to do with writers like Martin Wight or Hedley Bull?

EHC: Not at all. And they certainly did not want to have anything to do with me. Indeed, Bull I think later attacked me, calling *The Twenty Years' Crisis* 'a tract for 1939' but not for world politics in general.[6] Hardly a ringing endorsement!

Cox: And Charles Manning at LSE?

EHC: Well I had got to know Manning in the 1930s. Indeed, I had used his ideas on 'peaceful change' in *The Twenty Years' Crisis*. As I said earlier, he was a clever man. In many ways original and stimulating. But his work (and there was never very much of it) was far too abstract. I was even sent a manuscript of his to review for Macmillan in 1961. I tried to be fair, though warned that the book would probably have little impact. But my main criticism was directed against his central idea of an 'international society'. This in my view was an illusion. Anyway, the book was published in 1963.[7] However, I have no idea what influence it exercised. But given that so much of it is impenetrable I would suspect not a great deal.

Cox: Around the same time you published what turned out to be your most popular (and shortest) book, *What is History?*[8]

EHC: Yes that did very well though provoked another minor storm from more traditional historians who not only questioned my attempt to bring history closer to sociology – Geoffrey Elton was particularly incensed at this idea – but accused me of all sorts of deviations.[9] But then British historians were a conservative, a-theoretical lot overall. Hugh Trevor Roper was especially critical and a little later used the pages of the *Encounter* magazine to launch a broadside against me as someone who always stood on the side of the 'big battalions' and the winners in history.[10]

Cox: Did you?

EHC: No. I just didn't much like counter-factual history. If certain parties or individuals were successful – like the Bolsheviks or even later Stalin – the duty of the historian was to explain why this had occurred, not mull over why something that did not happen had not happened.

Cox: What about the 1960s? Surely the rise of the new left and the growth of a new critical spirit in the West after the dark days of the Cold War must have lifted your spirit?

EHC: Yes it did. Though some of the theorizing on the left – particularly that inspired by Louis Althusser, left me cold. Nor did I have any sympathy at all with the new cult of China on the far left. In 1956 the Soviet leadership had rightly attacked Stalin in an effort to reform the USSR. Now we had so-called Maoists in France and Italy attacking the USSR for having de-Stalinized!

Cox: But then there was another crisis in the making. The Americans may have been pushed out of Vietnam; and there were revolutions throughout the 1970s in the Third World. But as the world economy began to flounder – experiencing both stagnation and inflation in equal measure – the tide in economic terms began to turn rightwards. The post-war Keynesian settlement started to implode. Hayek was awarded the Nobel Prize for Economics. And by the end of the decade, free marketers were driving the agenda. Liberalism had shown much more resilience than you could ever have predicted.

EHC: Well there's no denying facts. But only time will tell what the future holds. But I agree with you – up to a point. The old communist left is in deep trouble and the new left – as Lenin would say – has proven to be more infantile than serious. Thatcher moreover is a serious ideological enemy who, unlike the Tories I used to know, seems to take ideas seriously.

Cox: Another twenty years' crisis in the making?

EHC: Well, we are not in the midst of a depression. Fascism is a spent force. Germany and Japan have been tamed. And then there is the little question of nuclear weapons which clearly have had an impact on the way statesmen think about war.

Cox: And the USSR? Surely there is now broad agreement that as a system it is in crisis.

EHC: So I am told. But how much of this is anti-Soviet propaganda? In fact, what worries me most is the fashion these days – even on the left – to be as critical of the Soviet Union as of the West. It's about time the left stopped talking down the Soviet system and recognized the achievements.

Cox: But perhaps they talk that way because the USSR no longer inspires people?

EHC: But if not a planned economy, then what?

Cox: What indeed? But even the Chinese since 1978 seem to be moving ever so slowly down the 'capitalist road'.

EHC: True. But China will never abandon socialism any more than the Soviet people will abandon the known gains of the October revolution – full employment and social security – for the unknowns of the market.

Cox: But what about the people of Central and Eastern Europe? Perhaps they see things very differently?

EHC: I have no doubt they do. But as I said back in 1919 – self-determination offers no serious basis upon which to build an international order.

Cox: But perhaps the Poles and the Czechs and the Hungarians are less concerned about international order than they are about their own freedom?

EHC: Then, if that is the case, we may be on the cusp at some point in the not too distant future of another – very different – international crisis. Thank goodness I won't be around to see it!

Notes

1. Basil Kingsley Martin, *Father Figures* (London: Hutchinson, 1966), p. 190.
2. For liberal responses to the Twenty Years' Crisis see Peter Wilson, 'The Myth of the "First Great Debate"', in Tim Dunne, Michael Cox and Ken Booth (eds), *The Eighty Years Crisis: International Relations 1919–1939*, (Cambridge: Cambridge University Press, 1998), pp. 1–16.
3. E.H. Carr, *Conditions of Peace* (London: Macmillan, 1942); E.H. Carr, *Nationalism and After* (London: Macmillan, 1945); E.H. Carr, *The Soviet Impact on the Western World* (London: Macmillan, 1946).
4. F. A. von Hayek, *The Road to Serfdom* (London: George Routledge & Sons, 1944), pp. 138–41.
5. Hans J. Morgenthau, 'The Political Science of E. H. Carr', *World Politics*, Vol. 1, No. 1 (1948), pp. 127–34.
6. I discuss Bull's critique of Carr at length in Michael Cox (ed.), *E. H. Carr, The Twenty Years' Crisis* (Houndmills, Basingstoke: Palgrave, 2001), pp. xliii–xlvii.
7. C. A. W. Manning, *The Nature of International Society* (London: Macmillan, 1963).
8. E. H. Carr, *What is History?* (London: Macmillan, 1961).
9. G. R. Elton, *The Practice of History* (London: Collins, Fontana, 1967).
10. For a more general discussion of how Carr's *What is History?* was received by historians after its publication, see Anders Stephanson, 'The Lessons of *What is History?*', in Michael Cox (ed.), *E. H. Carr: A Critical Appraisal* (Houndmills, Basingstoke: Palgrave, 2000), pp. 281–303.

25

Modernity, Technology and Global Security: A Conversation with Lewis Mumford (1895–1990)

Rens van Munster and Casper Sylvest

Despite various proclamations about the 'death of the author', the historian, critic and public intellectual Lewis Mumford (1895–1990) rather looks like a thinker whose time has come. Mumford is chiefly remembered for his literary and architectural criticism and his historical writings on cities. He won the National Book Award in 1962 for The City in History and was awarded the Presidential Award of Freedom in 1964 (which was swiftly followed by Mumford's strongly worded attack on the President's Vietnam policy in 1965).[1] But Mumford's reflections on technological modernity, nuclear weapons and global ecology also deserve a wide audience in the twenty-first century – an age that has reached its own cul-de-sac in dealing with issues of technology and global security. We staged a meeting with Mumford in an effort to recover his ideas for contemporary IR theory. What follows is the edited transcript of how the interview took place in our heads.[2]

Q: Professor Mumford, thank you for responding positively to our request for an interview about your ideas about technology and politics and their relevance for IR ...

LM: Forgive me for interrupting you already at this early stage, but could I ask why you went through all this trouble to contact me?

Q: Well, we think that many of your ideas have great relevance for IR theory today; yet, somehow, the discipline has shown very little interest in engaging your work. We thought this interview was an opportunity to correct that situation.

LM: To be honest, I wasn't sure I should agree to this interview. I was afraid that you would put words into my mouth or carelessly extrapolate ideas from my time to yours.

Q: Yes, that's a considerable risk, as we have to rely almost exclusively on our sixth sense – and your published writings. Still, it may be worthwhile, if we succeed in bringing some of your thoughts to the attention of an IR audience.

LM: I must admit, with some shame, that one of my reasons for accepting your invitation was that I was curious to know what this 'IR' stands for? I was hoping it is short for 'Imagination Reborn'.

Q: It stands for International Relations.

LM: Ah, ok. Back in the day, the field was not abbreviated. I remember it as one of the thriving fields of social science in the post-war decades. I once heard that my old friend Reinhold Niebuhr – who helped me realize that Nazism and the rise of fascism demanded resistance by all possible means – came to be regarded as a sort of founding father in this field.

Q: Indeed, traditionally the discipline has sought to study the causes of war and the conditions of peace in its broadest sense, but today it has developed into a sprawling field that encompasses many subjects, from nuclear strategy to post-modern social theory. Some even argue that the field is fragmenting and that the only common focus point is incessant debate about the way in which we ought to study politics beyond the state.

LM: I certainly won't forget the products of nuclear strategy anytime soon. They stayed with me all the way on the road to Necropolis.[3] But to be perfectly honest, I am not interested in academic disciplines and their identity. The PhD in my view is a symbol of specialization and therefore a marker of mediocrity. I used to hold visiting professorships in many of the best-known universities in the US and students kept asking me what my special field was. I always answered that I was *Professor der Allerlei Wissenschaften*. I delighted in the bewilderment that students expressed.

Q: We are not sure we understand either.

LM: It's a German expression for professor of things in general.

Q: Yes, we know. We meant the part about specialization and mediocrity. Specialization is what drives research, isn't it?

LM: That may well be true, but it comes with great danger. One of the tragedies of the specialization we witnessed during the twentieth century – and of the kind of instrumental scientific rationality that accompanied it – is that big questions recede into the background, if they get asked at all. In the second half of the twentieth century universities became as thoroughly automated as modern industrial production plants.[4] Their mass-products are different – publications, students, publicity, etc. – but they tend to extract from its successful subjects a special kind of submission and acquiescence.

Q: Today, many IR theorists worry that the production of knowledge
        in the field follows clear methodological and theoretical rules,
        which reproduce traditionalist attitudes that serve to uphold the
        interest of the powerful. Critical voices have been calling for more
        reflexivity about the role of intellectuals in creating a different
        world.

LM: That's why I spent most of my career outside the officially sanc-
        tioned corridors of knowledge. In the dull world of modern uni-
        versities, most of the questions asked are indifferent to the central
        concerns of human beings on this planet. Although I don't know
        the academic literature of your field – is there anyone, by the way,
        who can keep up with the amount of scholarship that is relent-
        lessly published? – I am willing to bet that your field is no differ-
        ent. I can't help you with that, but I can tell you what you ought
        to take an interest in: modern technics and the human condition.

Q: To some extent you are preaching to the converted. IR scholar-
        ship is progressively more interested in studying how technology
        shapes the structure of global politics and the interactions of
        states in this system.

LM: That may be, but your phrasing risks missing the point. For what
        is technology? For some it is the material face of science, but
        to my mind that's too simple. Already in the interwar period
        I turned to the German word *Technik*, in order to place technol-
        ogy in a social context.[5] Technology – or *Technics* as I prefer – is
        not only material; it is produced and productive. It changes
        mindsets and modes of living. So you cannot separate the role of
        technology in modern politics from the development of techno-
        logical civilization. It is in the subtle effects on minds, lifestyles,
        routines, politics and ethics that you will find the true character
        and effects of the expansion of *Technics*.

Q: Are you suggesting that technology – or *Technics* – instead of
        being material is really ideational?

LM: No. It is both. We can, if we can re-educate ourselves and muster
        the courage, direct technology for human purposes. It is a human
        construction, and we should never forget that.[6] But there is a logic
        in the expansion of technology that progressively makes this sort
        of change more difficult. Technological artefacts have become
        part of a larger system that has detrimental, even inhuman,
        effects. This collective organization of human individuals for vast
        projects stretches far back into history, to the construction of the
        pyramids even.

Q: Is that what you refer to as the history of the Machine?

LM: I know the word 'Machine' may sound archaic in your digitalized world. But in my time I found it a useful concept to explore the links between social organization and technology.[7] I was interested in the social and bureaucratic structures that enabled societies to undertake vast and complex projects, but I also wanted to show that as a form of organization, the Machine often reduced individuals to expendable components in centralized power complexes. We have come to treat technics as an end in itself and estrangement is the inevitable consequence.

Q: So the Machine refers to a complex, symbiotic and mutually reinforcing process between society and technology. Still, why don't we just throw a monkey wrench into the works of the machine?

LM: We certainly cannot overthrow this system at once. After all, the method of thought it has fostered has been expanding for more than three centuries. The vision that humans should control nature has not only created much of the impetus for new, large-scale and expansive technologies – it is also what continues to give these technologies meaning and direction. In fact, all of the predictions put forward by Henry Adams[8] during the early twentieth century about a near-autonomous technological development producing social acceleration and disintegration have held up. Basically, he was right!

Q: Yes, you have often said we owe Adams an apology. What is there to be apologetic about?

LM: I have had many fierce intellectual and political disagreements over the course of my life and rarely have I apologized to anyone. But Adams recognized early on that the human and the cosmic are displaced by the mechanical. I regret that I did not articulate this much more directly in my early work. I was hopeful – too hopeful, as it turned out – that the insights of modern science and technology could be harnessed for human purposes. Only later did I understand that with the rise of the Machine, individuals increasingly feel impotent, apathetic and submissive – and eventually we allow a whole series of transgressions that jeopardize not only our individuality but also our principles and our democracy. The tragedy of our times is that modern *Technics* has fundamentally changed our experience of space, time and energy without leading to integration and cooperation.

Q: Could you try to be a bit more specific?

LM: Sure, let's take the most extreme example: nuclear weapons. We are still coming to grips with the invention of the atom bomb and the hydrogen bomb. Really, they are genocidal weapons and the fact that they were developed – and that the atom bomb has been used – speaks of a moral abdication on our part. In my view, the immediate cause lay in the practice of strategic bombing during the Second World War.[9] However, a more fundamental cause has to do with the kind of instrumental rationality that produced the bomb – it simply lacks the capacity and moral vision for comprehending, let alone dealing with, the social consequences of its own invention. Nuclear strategy – the most explicit expression of this rationality – is a lethal fantasy, simply incapable of dealing with the reality it has created.

Q: Now, wait a minute! Do you really mean to suggest that renouncing nuclear weapons would have been a more realistic policy?

LM: Yes, not only realistic but also realist and sane. I once wrote that a thousand years separated 1940 from 1930.[10] In fact, this was why I attacked a particular brand of isolationist, American liberalism and argued so forcefully for American entry into the Second World War. Liberals had come to believe, falsely in my view, that reason was supreme and that force had no place in social life. After the war and particularly during the 1950s it became clear to me that another thousand-year leap was in the making. The thermonuclear revolution made it incontrovertible that we had entered a whole new era. The madness I had detected in the invention and use of the atomic bomb reached new proportions. A national security state manned by self-professed realists churned out ever more fantastic ideas, policies, plans and phrases.[11] Tragically, Vietnam was the unequivocal, but perhaps belated, demonstration of this.

Q: At one point, you even referred to these realists as the Genghis Khans of strategy?

LM: Yes, I reserved the label Genghis Khan for *so-called* realists like Herman Kahn. In my view, it is not realist to 'rationally' – and this must be put in scare quotes – contemplate mass murder and genocide. A spasm of military plans to wipe out whole enemy cities – and, it was grudgingly acknowledged, ourselves – did not lead to reflection on the human condition, but produced yet further illusions, like the widespread construction of underground shelters. It was a kind of trance, but a monumentally dangerous one.

Q: Yes. Today, duck and cover exercises are mainly the subject of disarming, Cold War comedy.

LM: Maybe so, but in this case the absurd is married to the dreadful. The same kind of rationality that produced the bomb also came to govern ideas about its place in American foreign and security policy. It became evidently clear that the spread of the nuclear mega-Machine was fuelled by notions of quantity, cause, probability, utility, punctuality and regularity. The result was totalitarian conformity in thought and action with no place for the personal, the unique, the human or for balance, autonomy or wholeness. We became obsessed with external threats to the extent that their internal manifestation undermined our basic, democratic principles. At the same time, we refused to confront the excesses and outrages of our way of life. Instead of confronting the central threat of total nuclear destruction, we allowed the establishment of ever more secretive institutions, manned with specialists divorced from fundamental human concerns, to exercise power beyond democratic control. We also allowed huge vested interests to influence and direct this system of mass extermination.

Q: We are not sure how much of this has resonance today. Wouldn't you agree that the 1950s was an extreme and exceptional period in this regard?

LM: No. I still believe that technology has produced an unconditional need for global cooperation if we are to survive on this planet. We can only come to this realization if we make an effort to improve ourselves as human beings. This is a demand placed on all of us as individuals, but our educational system can make a difference. We must prioritize studies in the humanities and curb the worship of instrumental rationality.

Q: Still, the nuclear age was different. Is it not true that we today live in an entirely different age?

LM: Are you telling me that in your age you finally decided on a supranational political structure that could control these monstrous weapons?

Q: Not exactly. There are still more than 15,000 nuclear warheads in the world, many of them operational and some of them can be deployed on very short notice.

LM: In that case, the nuclear age isn't over. You still live and breathe it every single day.

Q: But the predominant global risk today, as it has been defined in Western national security strategies, is terrorism.

LM: From what you tell me, it appears that many of the energies, institutions and policies developed during the Cold War are simply being recalibrated towards this war on terror. Since the dawn of the nuclear age, the one-dimensional world of the atom has expanded and reproduced itself in different settings, so it wouldn't surprise me if it has continued to do so. We seem to have learned nothing of the past. Sixty or seventy years ago we tried to achieve national security by creating a state of impotence and total insecurity. If I understand current policy correctly, this is very similar to what we see today. The measures we have taken are different – but what they signify and entail has often proven more dangerous than the risks they seek to meet. In this sense there is continuity between the atomic age and the age of terror.

Q: Are you saying that we have focused on the wrong problems in global politics? Or are you saying that the problems are self-made?

LM: I am tempted to answer both questions in the affirmative, but this is complicated. Part of the reason why we have created and allowed security apparatuses to overshadow other aspects of human existence has to do with our intellectual incapacity to defend and emphasize the human. We have become estranged from ourselves. One remarkable symptom of this estrangement is that we focus on our self-created problems of security rather than problems of life.

Q: But if security is not about the protection of life, then what is it?

LM: Problems of life have to do with restoring the human and protecting the planet on which we live. We don't seem to realize that the structures we have created – the Machine – are parasitic on the planet when they escape human control; they change the planet and our habitat. In this one-sided guise, we are self-destroying. It speaks volumes of our alienation that we have only recently begun to realize this.

Q: But does your emphasis on human control not entail a vision – a quite popular vision in the twenty-first century, we might add – that we can direct these processes? We made the Machine, to speak in your idiom, but the more we learn, the more we are able to correct it, optimize it and exploit it. We can engineer the world we want, can we not?

LM: What you're talking about now is not in fact control, but loss of control. I have long stressed that my scepticism of the Machine and systems thinking has another face: the affirmation of organic life.[12] In organic life there is diversity, there are qualities, there are things we value for their own sake. The organic is not measurable, or it can at least not be reduced to the measurable. If we want to ensure that life can be replenished and sustained in all its variety we must preserve our habitat and rediscover ourselves. We must rid ourselves of the 'pathological technical syndrome' in which all knowledge is short in memory and applied for short-term gains.[13] In effect this is contrary to living organisms, to their functions and modes of operation.

Q: We were struck by your appeal to human beings to realize that they are part of what you have called an infinitely complicated and involved ecological partnership of planetary dimensions.[14]

LM: Yes, we have now reached a point where the role of man as a geological agent, as an agent in changing the face of the earth as George Perkins Marsh[15] formulated it in the 1860s, is more powerful than we imagine. We must take responsibility for this. This should not be done with cockiness, haste or a wild illusion that we are god-like. Yes, we have in a sense become guardians of the world responsible for maintaining the balance of nature, but the kind of control we should aspire for must find its inspiration in a broader philosophy of man. In essence, conserving natural resources means conserving human potential and variety. It means an expansion of human purposes. It means discarding our inflated respect for abstract rationality. It means rooting our life in the richness of our history and reality. The keywords must be humility, prudence, wholeness. The phantasms of the Machine – that we can go on like this indefinitely without killing ourselves and our environment – must be substituted by a new moral and political imagination.

Q: But, surely, this is idealism in its purest and literal sense?

LM: I beg to differ. In calling for a cultivation of the imagination, I do not mean that we should masquerade as providence by determining in advance what is possible and impossible. Quite the opposite. We have got to stop the one-sided exploitation of the machine, for profit, power and prestige – and focus consciously on quality of life and the preservation of this planet and its organic variety.

Q: But is such an enormous task even possible?

LM: I see no other option. We must create one-world selves – selves that can match the task ahead of us. Only in this way can we resettle and recultivate the earth as a whole. The challenge of the 1950s that I once described is still (if not more so, it seems to me) true of your predicament: politics is not the art of the possible but the art of the impossible.[16]

Notes

1. See Donald F. Miller, *Lewis Mumford: A Life* (Pittsburgh: University of Pittsburgh Press, 1989), 512–13 and Lewis Mumford, 'Open Letter to President Johnson', 3 March 1965, reprinted in Mumford, *My Works and Days* (New York: Harcourt Brace Jovanovich, 1979), 461–2.

2. This is a fictional interview. In composing it we have relied on the published writings of our 'interviewee' as well as biographical and other writings

about Mumford (including Miller, *Lewis Mumford*; Thomas P. Hughes & Agatha C. Hughes [eds] *Lewis Mumford: Public Intellectual* [New York: Oxford University Press, 1990]). At key points – particularly in relation to the concept of the Machine, his critique of nuclear weapons and the national security state, his proto-ecological understanding of the planet and his call for renewed (political) imagination – we have paraphrased or closely followed formulations that occur in Mumford's work. For a more elaborate (and thoroughly referenced) discussion of Mumford's views on technology, nuclear weapons and ecology in the post-war decades, see our forthcoming book *Nuclear Realism: Global Political Thought during the Thermonuclear Revolution* (Abingdon: Routledge).

3. The phrase 'the road to Necropolis' is taken from Gregory Morgan Swer, 'The Road to Necropolis: Technics and Death in the Philosophy of Lewis Mumford', *History of the Human Sciences*, 16:4 (2003), 39–59.

4. Lewis Mumford, 'The Automation of Knowledge', *AV Communication Review*, 12:3 (1964), 261–76.

5. Lewis Mumford, *Technics and Civilization* (New York: Harcourt, Brace & Company, 1934).

6. Lewis Mumford, 'Authoritarian and Democratic Technics', *Technology and Culture*, 5 (1964), 1–8.

7. Lewis Mumford, *The Myth of the Machine: The Pentagon of Power* (New York: Harcourt Brace Jovanovich, 1970).

8. Henry Adams (1838–1918), American writer and historian. *The Degradation of the American Dogma* (New York: Macmillan, 1919) contains many of Adams' pessimistic forecasts on technology and historical development. See also Lewis Mumford, 'Apology to Henry Adams', *Virginia Quarterly Review*, 38:2 (1962), 196–217.

9. Lewis Mumford, 'Gentlemen: You Are Mad!', *Saturday Review of Literature* (2 March 1946), 5–6; Lewis Mumford, *In the Name of Sanity* (New York: Harcourt Brace and Company, 1954), 63–99.

10. Lewis Mumford, *Faith for Living* (New York: Harcourt Brace and Company, 1940), 331.

11. Lewis Mumford, 'The Moral Challenge to Democracy', *Virginia Quarterly Review*, 35 (1959), 560–76; Lewis Mumford, 'The Human Way Out', *Manas*, XIV (1961), 1–4.

12. See Lewis Mumford, 'Technics and the Future of Western Civilization' (1948), reprinted in Mumford, *In the Name of Insanity*, 34–62.

13. Lewis Mumford, 'Closing Statement', in F. Fraser Darling and John P. Milton (eds) *Future Environments of North America* (Garden City: The Natural History Press, 1966), 718–29, at 725.

14. Lewis Mumford, 'Let Man Take Command', *The Saturday Review of Literature* (2 October 1948), 7–9 & 33–35, at 8.

15. George Perkins Marsh (1801–1882), naturalist, conservationist and author of *Man and Nature* (New York: Schribner, 1867 [1864]; a revised edition was published as *The Earth as Modified by Human Action: Man and Nature* in 1874). See also Lewis Mumford, 'Prospect', in William L. Thomas, Jr (ed.) *Man's Role in Changing the Face of the Earth* (Chicago: University of Chicago Press, 1956), 1141–1152; Lewis Mumford, 'Marsh's Naturalist-Moralist-Humanist Approach', *The Living Wilderness* 71 (1959–1960), 11–13.

16. Lewis Mumford, 'Alternatives to the H-Bomb', *New Leader* (28 June 1954), 4–9.

26

More Fragments of an Intellectual Biography: Hans J. Morgenthau (1904–1980)

William E. Scheuerman

Interviewer: Professor Morgenthau, your recent remarks about your political and intellectual experiences in Weimar Germany, your most important teachers and mentors, and also your activities as a young lawyer are very illuminating, particularly for those of us interested in Realist international theory, of which you are presently the world's foremost theoretical representative. Why only now discuss these matters, more than forty years after your arrival in the United States?

HJM: Remember that I had to *escape* Germany. Of course, one could never forget what happened there. But I have avoided dwelling obsessively on such decidedly unpleasant experiences, and in recent years have frequently travelled back. For those interested in the Weimar background to my work, it should be relatively easy to identify. Many of the main figures in the Weimar debates – the great Hans Kelsen immediately comes to mind – are now also pretty much forgotten in this country. Nobody cares about them, which is unfortunate. So it's perhaps not surprising that I haven't been asked about my education in Germany. In any event, the biggest influences on my thinking have surely not been Weimar lawyers, but instead people like my friend the late Reinie Niebuhr, whose writings have inspired me since I first arrived in America. To be sure, I am more sceptical than Reinie was that Realism needs theological foundations. But I like to think that my work and his more spiritually-motivated contributions are complementary. Certainly, our political

	positions always overlapped, though I think Reinie was a bit slow to see what a huge mistake Vietnam was.
Interviewer:	Some of your comments about the Weimar context are not particularly surprising, e.g., that you early on became enamoured of Max Weber's political thought. But other comments seem unexpected and even startling. You recount visiting Carl Schmitt in his apartment, presumably in Berlin, saying to yourself as you later departed, 'Now I have met the most evil man alive.' But you also describe Schmitt as 'amply endowed with intellectual ability', and a 'man of immense – and intellectually well-deserved – prestige.' As you know, Schmitt joined the Nazi Party in 1933 and tried to make himself into the Crown Jurist of the Third Reich –
HJM:	Indeed. He was a brilliant yet despicable man.
Interviewer:	So how would you explain why an impressive thinker like Schmitt could embrace Nazism? The movement was dominated by intellectual mediocrities and nonentities.
HJM:	That is correct. What you are forgetting is that interwar Germany was an authoritarian and corrupt society, in which many scholars ultimately flocked to Nazism. In some ways Schmitt was quite typical, though he was obviously no run-of-the-mill academic. Your question, I am sorry to say, implicitly rests on an optimistic and indeed rather naive rationalism commonplace among liberals. Do you really believe that education or intellectual sophistication immunizes people from the ugly realities of political life? That it protects them from bad political judgments? I see very little evidence of this. Just think of all the highly educated people who have committed irresponsible political acts in *this* country! The Vietnam War, of course, was engineered by 'the best and the brightest'.
Interviewer:	Nonetheless, given your hostility to Schmitt, are you not embarrassed by the fact that he apparently changed the second (1932) edition of *Concept of the Political* in direct response to your dissertation and the definition of politics you outlined there? This, at least, is what you assert in you autobiographical comments, where you appear to be bragging about Schmitt's debts to you. Doesn't this make you something of an influence on Schmitt? Or was Schmitt's Nazism simply a personal decision, political opportunism perhaps, and thus his theory of politics –

which you claim to have shaped – has no integral relationship to his terrible actions?

HJM: This question also rests on a superficial account of things. Of course, Schmitt was a terrible opportunist; one shouldn't underestimate such contingencies when trying to make sense of individual political choices. But, yes, there was more to his alliance with Nazism than opportunism. What you are ignoring is that there are some fundamental differences between his views about politics and my own. In some of the research I conducted while at Geneva right after leaving Germany, I tried to lay out those differences. I doubt that Schmitt, fortunately, will ever garner much admiration in the US or other English-speaking countries, in light of his deservedly terrible reputation, but if by some weird fluke he were somehow to become fashionable, somebody might take a look again at my own ideas about the concept of the political.[1] The bottom line is that I think Schmitt combined some useful insights – some of which in fact he borrowed from me – with theoretical eclecticism and a disastrous hostility to the idea that moral and political action have to be linked, though admittedly in ways more complicated than liberals typically recognize. Most liberals, as I have regularly argued, succumb to a 'moralistic' politics, while Schmitt and his ilk succumb to the opposite extreme: politics for the sake of politics, politics disconnected from what they nastily deride as 'normativities'. My position, as I outlined in *Scientific Man Vs. Power Politics* [1946] and elsewhere, is more nuanced. Responsible political actors have to tackle not only the fundamental laws of the political sphere, which indeed typically involve conflict and intense struggle, but they *also* simultaneously need to heed binding moral imperatives, without which we face the spectre of moral nihilism. We need to take both politics and morality absolutely seriously, without reducing one to the other. For Schmitt, in contrast, politics and morality inhabit, if you will, altogether unrelated universes, and at times it's not even clear that morality has a place in *any* universe. Let me also mention that I always rejected his notion of the friend/foe divide, which I think probably helped open the door to his rabid nationalism and anti-Semitism.

Interviewer:	Did you follow Schmitt's work after coming to America?
HJM:	Yes, on occasion, as have many others, including another friend I recently lost, the brilliant Hannah Arendt, with whom I sometimes shared my reactions to it.[2] But I cannot say that I followed it diligently or systematically. There have been far more important things to worry about. Have you heard about the arms race? Vietnam? Perhaps we can now move on to other topics. You seem obsessed with Carl Schmitt.
Interviewer:	This might be a good time to ask about rumours floating around about your unusually intense interest in Arendt. As you may have heard, Elisabeth Young Bruehl is working on an Arendt biography,[3] in which she mentions a two-week vacation you took with her to Rhodes, where you apparently proposed –
HJM:	I have not seen the manuscript, but I hope it does justice to Hannah as a great political thinker. Her *Human Condition* [1958] I consider one of the best books written in recent decades. Anyhow, these are personal matters, and really nobody's business, and let me just say – as I've told my friends – that our enduring friendship never became anything romantic because of my own choices as well.
Interviewer:	Another somewhat surprising matter raised by your autobiographical reflections concerns your close ties to the interwar German left. This is unexpected, of course, because Realism is so often seen as congenitally conservative. You praise the prominent Weimar socialist lawyer Hugo Sinzheimer, with whom you worked closely and through whom you became friends with young leftist lawyers and intellectuals like Ernst Fraenkel, Franz L. Neumann, Otto Kahn-Freund and Otto Kirchheimer, all of whom later became prominent leftist scholars. Neumann and Kirchheimer, in fact, later became associated with the Frankfurt School of critical theory. Gerald Stourzh, presently of the University of Vienna, reports that you kept Sinzheimer's photograph on your office desk at the University of Chicago.[4] One of your most important academic advisors, if I understand correctly, was Arthur Baumgarten, who after 1933 became a

communist and later an important legal figure in East Germany. Some of Baumgarten's criticisms of Kelsen seem, in fact, to have inspired some of your own.[5] In short, many of your key teachers were on the political left, and you seem to have mingled freely with Marxists at Frankfurt's Institute for Social Research.

HJM: This is all true. And, yes, it does perhaps suggest a more complicated view of Realism's politics than one generally encounters.

Interviewer: So would it then be fair to suggest, as Friedrich Hayek did in *The Road to Serfdom*, that international Realism is essentially an offshoot of twentieth-century socialism, and that it inevitably reproduces socialism's flaws? As Hayek points out, in the writings of E.H. Carr, Realism and socialism certainly go hand in hand.[6]

HJM: Well, the obvious problem with Hayek's thesis is that most Realists have *not* in fact been socialists. For my part, I have never endorsed a planned economy, though unlike Hayek, I believe that any decent as well as efficient economic system will need to rely on extensive state intervention. Henry Kissinger and others would surely be surprised to learn that Realism and socialism are joined at the hip! Like most classical liberals, Hayek thinks good things all come together: if you preserve the rule of law, limited government and representative democracy, you'll also get a flourishing market economy and economic prosperity. But by now we should know that such things often do *not* go together, and that real-life political actors – unlike Hayek's make-believe actors – face tough and even tragic choices between competing aims and values. If you read Hayek's discussion, what really angers him is Car's willingness to let the great powers gobble up lesser powers. Does that aspect of Carr's thinking, which – by the way – I find no less disturbing, stem from his socialist politics? Not necessarily. The real problem is that Carr is no less ambiguous than Carl Schmitt when it comes to the validity of moral claims. As a moral relativist, Carr cannot consistently distinguish between moral and immoral actions, even though his oftentimes perceptive writings could be taken as a clarion call against the *moral* injustices of the international status quo. Sadly, his crude views of morality have left him vulnerable to worshipping at the altars of the power.[7] He endorsed appeasement in prewar England, and then after the Second World War was mesmerized by the Soviet defeat of Nazi Germany. Since then he has proceeded to churn out a series of knowledgeable but basically apologetic books about the Soviet Union. Like Reinie Niebuhr, I instead have tried to formulate a version of Realism which circumvents such dangers.

Interviewer: So what then, if anything, did you pick up from inter-war socialists like your mentor Sinzheimer? You speak about him at great length in your recent reflections.

HJM: The lessons were mostly negative. Like other socialists, he placed great faith in human rationality, peaceful social reform and respect for the law. He downplayed – as did socialism's nineteenth-century patron saint, Karl Marx – the irrational elements in human nature and politics, and like his comrades in the German SPD, paid a high price for doing so. I always admired Sinzheimer's humanitarian aspirations along with his abiding faith in justice, but it remains naïve and potentially disastrous to believe that one can achieve justice without taking the ugliest sides of politics – which, I believe, rest directly on man's [sic] nature – seriously. Modern liberalism and modern socialism too often have failed to do so, and this is one reason why they risk being devoured by their rivals. How can a political ideology that ignores fundamental truths about human nature and psychology realistically flourish?

Interviewer: Carl Schmitt might have agreed with much of what you just said.

HJM [irritated]:   As would Sigmund Freud, Niebuhr and countless others. There is nothing identifiably Schmittian about my position. You give him too much credit.

Interviewer: In your autobiographical essay you in fact refer to a period of intense youthful engagement with Freudian psychoanalysis, which you also describe as ultimately a 'largely negative' intellectual experience. Yet your

	writings are infused with psychological observations and claims about human nature,[8] though you apparently do not think that you need psychoanalysis to ground them. As you also just mentioned, Niebuhr also relies on what we might loosely describe as psychological observations. Yet he uses the concept of original sin to ground his position, whereas you reject such theological foundations, though at times it sounds as though you are again implicitly committed to defending something like them. So from where in fact do you draw your implicit psychology? And how can it be justified without some more rigourous and systematic defence? You want, I think, to have it both ways: you rely heavily on psychology but do not want to offer any defence or even exposition of it.
HJM:	I have repeatedly discussed what you describe as my 'psychological' claims. To the extent that I depend implicitly on psychology, everything I say should be plausible to those who have carefully observed how people interact with one another, both in the political sphere and elsewhere, where conflict, power struggle and egotism are ubiquitous. And my intuitions have been corroborated by a variety of competing philosophical and theoretical standpoints, though admittedly not by some purportedly modern 'progressive' approaches. Unfortunately, they prefer to downplay the more unsettling features of human nature. Consequently, they cannot explain some of our deepest moral impulses, e.g., our sense of guilt, which as Reinie also grasped, potentially plays a constructive role in spurring us to mitigate the many difficulties of political and social existence.
Interviewer:	We have talked about an astonishingly rich diversity of ideas and thinkers whom you have engaged as you articulated your own views. Might not our conversation inadvertently confirm the suspicion that your 'theory' is not in fact sufficiently systematic or even coherent, that to speak of 'Realist IR Theory' as you have conceived it is misleading? After all, how could *any* theory integrate ideas from sources as disparate as Karl Marx, Max Weber, Sigmund Freud, Carl Schmitt

and Reinhold Niebuhr? How could it possibly hang together? You obviously share some common thematic preoccupations with other Realists – about power, the ethical paradoxes of political action and so on – but do such preoccupations necessarily constitute a theory?

HJM: Well, it all depends on what you mean by 'theory'. For my part, and here again you might point to my central European background, I have rejected the view that IR 'theory' should be directly modelled on the natural sciences. My understanding of science is close to Weber's. He insisted on the distinctive attributes of the social vs. natural sciences, while defending the view that we can still develop rigorous concepts and falsifiable hypotheses which are universally comprehensible and can be evaluated, as he put it, 'even by a Chinaman'. We need to reject a crude scientistic view of political and social inquiry, in essence, without succumbing to a one-sided hermeneutics and the simple idea that 'it's all just interpretation'.

Interviewer: Fair enough. But that still doesn't explain how *your* version of such a theory hangs together. In 1961 you called for a creative synthesis of the 'realistic and utopian approaches to politics in general and to international relations in particular'.[9] More recent Realists – I'm thinking of Kenneth Waltz – have not exactly rushed to heed this call, in part because they seem to believe that it inappropriately fuses normative and systematic-empirical questions. Are they wrong to worry about the underlying soundness of your theoretical project?

HJM: As you know, I have approved frequently updated versions of my textbook, *Politics Among Nations: The Struggle for Power and Peace*, and ever since the (2nd) 1954 edition it includes an introductory chapter devoted to the fundaments of Realist theory, what I call the 'six principles of political realism'. I still stand by everything I have said there; I have not revised this part of the book since '54. Nothing in that summary of Realist theory, in my view, gets in the way of constructive or creative thinking about novel political challenges – first and foremost, I believe, the specter of a nuclear cataclysm that continues to haunt us.[10] That is the great issue of our times, and I would encourage you – and others who may read this – to move beyond your philological preoccupations and try to tackle it.

Interviewer: Thanks for your time, Professor Morgenthau, and also for that final bit of advice.

Notes

1. *The Concept of the Political*, ed. Hartmut Behr and Felix Roesch (London: Palgrave, 2012 [1933]).
2. Letter to Hannah Arendt, dated 14 January 1965 (Hans J. Morgenthau Collection, Container 5, Library of Congress), where Morgenthau describes Schmitt's *Theory of the Partisan* (1963) as 'interesting but unbelievably shoddy, both in thought and exposition'.
3. Elisabeth Young-Bruehl, *Hannah Arendt: For Love of the World* (New Haven: Yale University Press, 1982), 453–54.
4. Confirmed in an email message from Dr. Gerald Stourzh, 10 August 2014.
5. See Oliver Jütersonke, *Morgenthau, Law and Realism* (Cambridge: Cambridge University Press, 2010), 84–93.
6. Friedrich A. Hayek, *The Road to Serfdom* (Chicago: University of Chicago, 1994 [1944]). Chicago: University of Chicago, 2004 [1944], 204–8, 252–53.
7. Hans J. Morgenthau 'The Political Science of E.H. Carr', *World Politics*, Vol. 1, No. 1 (1948), 127–34.
8. Robert Schuett, *Political Realism, Freud, and Human Nature in International Relations: The Resurrection of the Realist Man* (London: Palgrave, 2010).
9. Hans J. Morgenthau 'The Intellectual and Political Functions of a Theory of International Relations (1966)', in *Decline of Democratic Politics* (Chicago: University of Chicago Press, 1962), 77.
10. Campbell Craig, *Glimmer of a New Leviathan: Total War in the Realism of Niebuhr, Morgenthau, and Waltz* (New York: Columbia University Press, 2003); William E. Scheuerman, *The Realist Case for Global Reform* (Cambridge, UK: Polity, 2011).

27
The Return of the *spectateur engagé*: Interview with Raymond Aron (1905–1983)

Ariane Chebel d'Appollonia

AcA: I am very grateful that you have agreed to participate in the *Return of the Theorists'* project. I guess I don't need to explain the fundamentals of these dialogues. After all, you spent your entire life conversing – so to speak – with august thinkers, such as Machiavelli, Thucydides, Kant, Hobbes, Clausewitz, Marx, Comte, Durkheim, Pareto, Tocqueville and Weber.

RA: My pleasure. I indeed learnt a lot from these thinkers, comparing their approaches and contrasting their key assumptions. I analysed, for example, the complex nature of industrial societies in the light of the Tocquevillean interpretation of administrative despotism, combined with the Weberian conception of rationalization and bureaucratization, and with Marxist views on industrialization and capitalist accumulation. My goal was to synthesize their works in order to understand the forces that determine the evolution of society and politics. The complexity of social and political choices requires us to be aware of the plurality of modes of intelligibility. I have always suspected that one-dimensional approaches were too simplistic and far more prescriptive than history allows. As Thucydides ably demonstrated, the course of human history is not linear. There are incessant changes; decisions made by one or a few affect millions of people and launch irreversible mutations; and many of these mutations have unanticipated outcomes. This is why I reject any form of determinism. I hope I provided, instead, a partial corrective to the methodological and political inadequacies of the main theoretical trends.

AcA: You both criticized most of these thinkers yet praised their contributions to a better understanding of the ambivalence of progress. This is evident, for example, in two of your books: *Industrial Society and War* (1958), and in *Progress and Disillusion* (1969). You rejected both Comte's positivist optimism and Marx catastrophic optimism. You also had a complex relationship with Weber. You never subscribed to a globalizing utopia, either eschatological or immediate. Your position was not rationalist, nor positivist, nor relativist for that matter. As a result, you were unclassifiable. This annoyed a lot of people. Some interpreted your eclecticism as a form of scepticism. Others described you as a 'frustrated commentator'[1] unable to commit to a major theoretical orientation because of your historicist mode of thinking.

RA: Well, I don't think I can be held responsible for the frustration of others. It is true that I have always refused to subscribe to one 'Grand Theory' or a global 'System of Interpretation'. I regarded both as either naively optimist or vainly pessimistic. Instead, I preferred the idea of a fragmented historical rationality, one that needs to be addressed through a rigourous analysis of political and social realities. I studied German historical sociology for my PhD dissertation, more precisely the contributions of Weber, Dilthey, Rickert, Mannheim and Scheler. They helped me to understand that social and political events are understandable only within their own particular context, their own *Weltanschauung*. I thus developed my own methodological position based on historical comparisons to explain social phenomena. I criticized both positivist and scientific approaches while attempting to explore the limitations of historical objectivity. One member of my dissertation committee, Paul Fauconnet, asked me if I was perverse or, alternatively, devoid of hope. This was in March 1938, shortly after the *Anschluss*. There were good reasons to be concerned at the time. But I was not desperate – only amazed by the complete lack of political awareness among France's intellectual elites.

AcA: You were indeed quite critical of French scholars and more generally of French intellectual life. It dated back to the years you spent at the ENS. Welcome back to your Alma Mater!

RA: Yes, I spent four years at the ENS. I had mixed feelings about this period of my life. I was slightly frustrated by the parochial attitudes of some scholars. What I was taught seemed to me too detached from human reality. I was convinced that Brunschvicg's Kantian rationalism and Alain's pacifist moralism were inadequate in the face of irrational ideologies and the

destructive political forces that emerged in Europe at the time.
Yet, I had a nice time with my classmates, Paul (Nizan), Georges
(Canguilhem) and Jean-Paul (Sartre). Jean-Paul became very
popular among the *Normaliens* who supported the postwar secular religions I criticized in the *Opium of the Intellectuals* in 1955.
I became, by contrast, *persona non grata*, all the more so after
I opposed what I called the 'ideological delirium' of May 1968 in
the *Elusive Revolution*. Now, I have the honour of a room named
after me. That is quite a loop, don't you think?

AcA: Last time I saw you, I was a PhD student at Sciences Po where
you were giving a lecture. It was in 1983, just before the publication of your *Memoirs*, a book that shot to the top of the bestseller
list in France. Fewer and fewer people at that time still believed
'it was better to be wrong with Sartre than right with Aron'.
When you died in October after testifying in favour of Bertrand
de Jouvenel, you had become 'the center of a sort of national
consensus' as your friend Stanley Hoffmann wrote.[2]

RA: I was actually surprised by the flurry of my post-mortem eulo-
gies. I was deeply touched by what Stanley and other friends
wrote about me. As Pierre (Hassner) correctly guessed, my pref-
erence was for those who rendered me homage with a critical
mind rather than with sentimentality. I always disliked personal
comments. What matters is my work's legacy.

AcA: Speaking of legacy, you were a man of many talents: a philosopher, a sociologist, a political scientist and an economist –
combining journalism and university teaching. You published
40 books and numerous articles. You were elected to major
academies, in France and abroad (including the British Academy,
the American Philosophical Society and the American Academy
of Arts and Sciences). You held guest professorships at Harvard
and the University of Chicago. Yet, after peaking in the early
1980s, your fame declined and you only continued to be
deeply esteemed among limited intellectual circles in France
and abroad. One common explanation is that you were primarily perceived as a Cold War theoretician whose conceptual
framework thus became obsolete over time. Furthermore, the
field of International Relations has remained dominated by
Anglo-Saxon scholars. Some of them place your *Peace and War*
(1962) among the great classics of realism, but they generally
prefer to cite other European realists of your generation such as
Morgenthau, or neo-realists such as Waltz.

RA: First, I never had the ambition to create an Aronian school of
        thought. This does not mean that I was not pleased to have sup-
        porters, especially Anglo-Saxon ones. I may have been a little
        bit 'neglected' for a few decades, as Bryan-Paul Frost[3] put it, but
        I have recently noticed the emergence of a new generation of
        scholars all around the world who seem genuinely stimulated by
        my work. Second, I clearly demonstrated that there is no 'pure
        theory' of International Relations comparable to models of pure
        economics in which an imaginary actor (*homo oeconomicus*) tries
        to maximize his satisfaction. The diplomat and the soldier do not
        have 'rational ends'. Therefore, we cannot analyse their behav-
        iour by mixing variables into a mathematical formula. Nor can
        we endow these actors with a single aim. Politics is much more
        complex than a game between abstract entities. Thus, a realist
        theory of international relations (or neo, or post ... I can wait for
        the neo-post!) is actually unrealistic. As I said many times, no one
        could have deduced the systematic murder of millions of Jews
        by the Nazis as a necessary, or even likely, consequence of any
        theory. The position I have chosen seems to me to be closer to
        reality, more instructive and more productive. It is a conceptual
        analysis of the system's functioning and the various subsystems'
        characteristics that allows the formulation of hypotheses about
        the calculation of forces, the ingredients of power and the nature
        of regimes. Every concrete study of international relations should
        include all the elements that constitute the stakes involved in
        conflicts between states: number, space, resources and regimes.
        In *Peace and War*, for example, I combined all these elements in
        order to provide a theory of action. I refuted the geographical,
        demographic and economic single-cause explanations of peace
        and war. I advocated instead a more nuanced approach by con-
        sidering different perspectives – moralism, legalism, realism and
        power politics.

AcA: As a result, both realists and idealists were upset by your hybrid
        praxeology.

RA: I in fact agreed with some realist premises – such as the
        Hobbesian state of nature in the international realm, the radical
        opposition between domestic and foreign policy, and the role of
        national interests. But realists are mostly concerned with the bal-
        ance of power and military capabilities. Yet, what kind of power?
        And power for what? How can you define a national interest if
        you don't acknowledge a state's ideological preferences? Modern

realist theorists completely misunderstand reality. A truly 'realistic realism', by contrast, should be holistic, taking the whole of reality into account. It should rely on a broader framework that includes the nature of the actors at a given time; the multiplicity of goals; the role of ideologies and values; and other critical variables impossible to quantify such as the search for glory and prestige.

AcA: You argued that a 'true realism' should also be concerned with 'people and morality'. You objected to realists who you thought neglected the importance of values, of ethics. Yet, you were quite harsh in your criticism of supporters of idealism. You referred to them as the 'beautiful souls', the 'noble-hearted people' – with a lightweight mind.

RA: Idealism can be both unrealistic and immoral. It is unrealistic to promote a 'morality of law' without taking into account the balance of power as well as the issues raised by the 'morality of struggle'. The Sermon on the Mount is meaningless for a genuine political actor. It is also unrealistic to try to export democracy like a 'common good' – as illustrated by the current situation in Iraq. I am not convinced that the neo-conservatives were aware of the dangers of implementing regime change in Iraq. Furthermore, a moralizing speech can camouflage a Machiavellian form of diplomacy when it actually promotes double standards: laws for the strong – and yet different laws for the weak. Finally, idealism can turn into a 'War of the Gods', and thus fuel fanaticism, something I analysed in the *Dawn of Universal History* (2002). In sum, I don't believe that imposing values by using force is the best option. On the other hand, there is no sustainable power and no legitimate recourse to force without ethics. In order to transcend these two praxeological problems, I promoted what I termed a 'morality of wisdom'. This, as you point out, satisfied neither the moralists nor the vulgar disciples of Machiavelli. Yet, politics can't be divorced from morality, nor can it simply be reduced to morality. The prudent diplomat is thus the one who combines conviction and responsibility, and who takes into account the likely consequences of his or her decisions.

AcA: You argued that the statesman should be fully cognizant of how a potential or actual adversary sees the world. During the Cold War, you characterized the USSR's behaviour as being driven as much by ideology as it was by a calculation of interests. You thus urged Western leaders to have a more sophisticated containment policy, one that took into account geostrategic calculations *and* an awareness of the ideological character of the conflict.

RA: Know how your enemy thinks! The mental universe of political actors frames their goals, their means and their decisions. To ignore the psychological dimension of politics can only obscure the existential nature of political choices. This often leads to governmental failure and/or military disaster. Look at what happened in Vietnam: the US administration failed to see the actual stakes involved in the war. Its leaders never understood the ideological motivations of the Viet Cong (and thus its tendency to act 'irrationally'). Thomas Schelling, an influential advisor at the time, for example understood the power of inflicting pain. He didn't understand the Viet Cong's willingness to absorb pain. And America's leaders overestimated the capacity of South Vietnamese to defend themselves. These were all miscalculations that led to the military defeat of the superpower US. As for the French, they never understood the ideological forces unleashed by the decolonization process. The fact is that fighting an ideology by focusing on the use of force can be counterproductive: ideologies are rather bulletproof. Years of military action against the Taliban in Afghanistan, Al Qaeda and other radical Jihadists in the Middle East and African countries have produced limited results. Do not misunderstand me: I am not suggesting that we should eschew using force against supporters of these fanatical ideologies. But it is unrealistic to expect a 'triumph of weapons' against them. The tragic irony is that force mostly fuels their propaganda and facilitates their recruitment of new followers. We are actually engaged, once again, in a 'public relations war' in which rhetoric is as important as military capacities.

AcA: What kind of rhetoric? You analysed the relationship between subversion, repression and radicalization in your few writings about terrorism and guerrilla warfare.[4] Yet, you remained quite mute about fanatical fundamentalist religions, even after the Iranian revolution.

RA: Current doctrinal fanaticisms have a lot in common with the secular religions I extensively analysed. Just as the communists vilified the capitalists, Islamic terrorists struggle against an evil called 'the West'. The challenge ahead is to combine rigour in evaluation and prudence in action. Western leaders should neither underestimate nor overestimate security threats; nor should they endanger democratic values by undermining civil rights and civil liberties at home, while promoting a neo-Wilsonian crusade in the name of the 'rule of law' abroad. As I made this clear in *The Imperial Republic* (1973), I have always disliked any kind of crusade. I am aware that statesmen face existential choices in fighting terrorism, and no choice is without costs. Yet, I have some concerns about the so-called tradeoff between security and liberty suggested by the proponents of the 'lesser evil' perspective. Civil liberties and human rights are the most precious and tenuous elements of Western democracies. As I explained in my book, *In Defense of Decadent Europe* (1977), the survival of the 'liberal experiment' depends on the preservation of democratic values through the prudence of statesmen and the responsible behaviour of citizens.

AcA: Speaking of Europe, what is your opinion about the European Union?

RA: It has made progress within strong limitations. I acknowledge the positive aspects of the successive enlargements. The European Union has become a much more 'secure community' and there are significant attempts to strengthen a common defence and security policy without damaging Trans-Atlantic solidarity. As I wrote in *Peace and War*, as long as Trans-Atlantic unity is preserved, all can be saved – especially when dealing with the threats posed by a neo-tsarist Russia. European institutions may have more power today, but are they more effective? Many scholars focus on a new form of 'European governance' but I am not sure they know exactly what this notion entails. There is some hope that a sense of being 'European' can emerge from economic and financial interdependence. Yet, we are far away from a European federation. I am still not sure whether that would be desirable. What I know, by contrast, is that European integration has not devaluated the importance of political sovereignties, with distinct states having different objectives. It seems that European Union member states agree to disagree on a growing number of issues, while trying to create new common policies – a strategy that would generate further disagreements. The bad news is that it undermines the perception of the EU abroad, and fuels anti-European sentiments in many of its member states.

AcA: What about the contribution of the EU as a normative power to the international system?

RA: This is an attractive notion, but there is no normative – or 'soft', or whatever – power – without effective 'actorness'. That requires various ingredients: not only norms based on a 'universal consciousness', but also economic power, political influence, and military capabilities. Even if the EU, one day, could combine all these elements, this would not resolve the issues raised by the question of the legitimacy and legality of the use of force. Efforts to re-legitimize a just war approach are sometimes ambivalent, if not arbitrary.

AcA: Do you believe, however, that international society is becoming less asocial?

RA: Yes – and no. Even in the afterlife I have noted strong aspirations towards more effective world governance, as well as the emergence of an embryonic world conscience. There is a greater consensus today about the need, if not the duty, to protect the most vulnerable populations. There is a sort of planetary diplomacy – but it exists without a genuine planetary community. The United Nation's powers remain limited and, thus, international society remains characterized by the absence of an overarching entity holding a monopoly over the use of legitimate violence. International civil society remains weak despite the active involvement of Non-Governmental Organizations around the world. There is still no equivalent of a tribunal of international society. The creation of the International Criminal Court was a step forward, but it isn't an international organization. The fact that the United States has refused to be part of it illustrates the resilience of national interests perfectly.

AcA: A few months after you died, your essay entitled *Last Years of the Century* was published. In this essay, you recalled what you wrote in 1947: peace was impossible, war was unlikely. What is your sentiment today?

RA: I believe that the current state of the world can best be described as a 'bellicose peace'. Rivalries among great powers have not disappeared although interstate wars are becoming less common. Yet civil wars dominate our consciousness after a lull in the first decade of the new century. I see no significant progress in much of Africa, or in the Middle East. The number of refugees, asylum seekers and internally displaced persons is higher today than it was after WWII. The multiplication of failed states leads to the blurring of the distinction between 'civil order' within countries and a 'state of nature' beyond their borders. Revolts motivated by democratic aspirations still often turn into anarchy or authoritarianism.

Ariane Chebel d'Appollonia

AcA: Is there any room left for the idea of Reason? Can we hope for the 'ultimate reconciliation of the human race' as you wrote in *On War*?

RA: I am not the confidant of Providence. As you know, I don't like to make predictions. But I still like to quote Toynbee: 'History is again on the move'.

Notes

1. Luterbacher, Urs. 'The frustrated commentator: An evaluation of the work of Raymond Aron', *International Studies Quarterly*, vol. 29, n 1, March 1985, pp. 39–49.
2. Hoffmann, Stanley. 'Raymond Aron (1905–1983)', *The New York Review of Books*, 8 December 1983.
3. Frost, Bryan-Paul, 'Resurrecting a neglected theorist: The philosophical foundations of Raymond Aron's theory of international relations', *Review of International Studies*, vol. 23, n 2, April 1997, pp. 143–66.
4. See *La Tragédie Algérienne* (1957) and *L'Algérie et la République* (1958).

28

A Conversation with Hannah Arendt (1906–1975)

Kimberly Hutchings

The conversation is between a young party activist (YPA) and Hannah Arendt (HA). It takes place in Brockwell Park, in the constituency of Dulwich and West Norwood, London on 8 May 2015. This is the day after the UK general election, which returned a Conservative majority government.

YPA: Professor Arendt, Professor Arendt, I am so sorry to be running late, I hope you have not been waiting long?

HA: At least I am allowed to smoke a cigarette here, it's a very pleasant spot.

YPA: Yes, I got caught up in watching the coverage of the election result. It's so exciting seeing politics in action in this way.

HA: You call that politics?

YPA: Well, yes, parties competing for a share of the electorate's vote, unexpected reversals of position. Did you know the man who was Deputy Prime Minister a day ago has had to resign as party leader? Some of the campaigners for his party were crying.

HA: Weeping may be in order, but not I think over failure in a competition over who gets to rule, especially when there is little to choose between the alternatives. You should have been there when Hitler came to power, that was something to cry about. Why are you so excited?

YPA: The results were so unexpected, the pollsters got it all wrong.

HA: That's a common mistake – thinking that politics is predictable. If you are going to continue to be involved in politics you need to re-think a couple of things. First, politics is not about rule. Second, politics is not predictable.

YPA: What do you mean?

HA: If you think about politics in terms of rule, then you are suggesting it is subject to a means-ends logic in which you gain power
in the sense of control in order to bring about certain policy
goals. This means that politics can be reduced to one person or
a group of people with power over others, deciding and determining what happens. But this isn't politics, it is government,
administration, bureaucracy.[1] It closes down new possibilities.
Think about it – what kinds of politics are now possible in the
UK with a majority government in power? In your system this
ensures a totally top-down order in which the majority party can
do what they want and any opposition within formal politics is
not much more than hot air. The only politics there is likely to
be in the UK over the next 5 years will be outside of Westminster.
Maybe in Scotland? Their debates over the referendum demonstrated some genuine politics – impassioned discussion over the
constitution, people coming together to try to create something
new. Not exactly the French or American revolutions, but at least
some echoes of those radical new beginnings.[2] Why did you
want to get involved in politics?

YPA: I want to make things better for poor people.

HA: Oh dear! Where do I start? If you want to help poor people,
work for a charity, don't confuse improving people's material
circumstances with politics, politics isn't something you can do
on behalf of someone or something else.

YPA: I don't understand.

HA: Politics is about power in the real sense, the power generated by
people coming together to create a common world. That power
is always there you know. Even in the most dire conditions at
some level government and rule, however cruel, depend on the
consent of citizens.[3] The exception perhaps being the Fascist
world of National Socialism, in which not only everything was
permitted but everything became possible in a huge, terrifying
and murderous experiment.[4] And when I say 'common worlds',
I mean 'common' not in terms of agreement on some party political manifesto, but in terms of the Greek agora, the American
constitution, the soviet in 1917, 1919 or 1956, and maybe even
the virtual environments that helped people to come together
in the so-called 'Arab Spring'. Politics is an always revolutionary
space in which a plurality of meanings can be articulated, in
which opinions will clash and which is utterly unpredictable in
terms of the outcomes of political engagement.

YPA: But then what's the point?

HA: Oh dear again! The problem of 'points' in the grand, overarching sense to which you refer, is that they become 'ends' for which any means may become acceptable. Of course there are always specific values and goals at stake in political engagement, but these are specific, there is no point to politics as such. Paradoxically, pointlessness is precisely the point. For example, the point of countering fascism and totalitarianism or the point of discouraging the production of Eichmanns. I suppose you have heard about him, have you – an entirely thoughtless apology for a man.[5] Sorry, where was I, oh yes and also the point of the pointlessness of politics is ensuring that human beings are genuinely protected against massacre and torture. I have been a refugee, I know what it is like to be stateless. And I know all the human rights in the world did not help me anywhere near as much as citizenship within a state that, at least to some extent, held the space of politics open.

YPA: Do you think all politics is revolutionary? Aren't revolutions dangerous?

HA: Yes and yes. All politics is revolutionary in that it is about opening up new possibilities, and sustaining that opening into the future.[6] It's about challenging rules and rulers, about people speaking and acting for themselves and not for and on behalf of others. At the same time, of course revolutions are dangerous, both the French and the Russian revolutions started with spontaneous organization against oppressive regimes, with participation and self-organizing bodies acting from the ground up rather than being orchestrated by those that see themselves as the emissaries of historical progress. Both, however, ended in tyranny and worse as the body politic became identified as an object to be re-shaped and manipulated by those that know better than the people on the streets.

YPA: Don't you believe in progress?

HA: How can progress be something to believe in? Only if you are assuming that you somehow have the key to future. I've seen that so often you know. All of the modern ideologies and movements, liberal, Marxist, nationalist, all ending up using the idea of historical progress as some kind of alibi.[7] They justify everything from imperialism to the massacre of millions of counter-revolutionaries to hierarchical and exclusionary notions of the 'people'. Liberal regimes assume a deterministic relation between a politics of freedom and particular ways of organizing the economy. Progress, following Hegel, is supposedly guaranteed by the forces of history. Of course this means either that you don't actually need to do anything, just wait for market forces to sort things out, or that you are fully justified in interfering all over the place to make sure everyone else can catch up with you. I gather there's been even more of this since the end of the Cold War. Isn't there something known as the liberal democratic peace thesis in international relations? Such stuff and nonsense. Some kinds of Marxists of course were even worse. Not only claiming to have identified the key to historical progress, but finding that key in processes of labour and work and obliterating any space for politics. Though there were other kinds of Marxist movement too – do you know anything about Rosa Luxemburg?

YPA: And what about nationalism? I thought you just said that politics in the UK was most likely to be found in Scotland over the next five years?

HA: Yes, nationalism is perhaps the trickiest and most dangerous one of all – because it's not clear how we can do without it in relation to the state as the modern space of politics. I started off as a philosopher you know, I was in love with thought (not only a particular philosopher, although I know what people always say), in particular new phenomenological thinking in the 1920s in Germany.[8] I realized very quickly the dangers of ideas of the 'Volk' and the horrible mistakes that philosophers seduced by nostalgic notions of a pre-modern Germany could make. I also realized, however, that there was no getting away from questions of identity. To most of my fellow citizens in my youth I was a Jew, and as this identity became of predominant importance with the rise of national socialism, it was clear to me that I had to act, to resist as a Jew. I became involved with Zionism and with Zionist ideas and organizations. I knew that Germany, and indeed no other European state, could be relied on to protect my rights, and for this reason I thought and still think that the state of Israel is a crucial project. But like all nation-states it has turned out to be Janus-faced, working to provide a space for the rights of Jewish people, but turning its back on an inclusive civic identity and the provision of a space for politics for all that came within its borders. As for Scotland, only time will tell. Some of the inspiration there does come from the republican tradition that seems to me to be most in keeping with the promise of politics, but we know there are no guarantees against ethnic and exclusionary turns in nationalist narratives, so we can only hope. A constitutional settlement that ensures the preservation of opportunities for all to engage politically is one way of guarding against possible horrors, but in a world of mass media and historicist assumptions even that is not necessarily enough.

YPA: If you don't believe in progress, then how do you think about politics in relation to time?

HA: We act between past and future.[9] We can't recapture the past, let alone change it, and we can't control the future. So politics is in a temporality of risk and chance. Machiavelli was very wise – he understood that politics is always a roll of the dice. But he also understood that cultivating political virtues and sensibilities could enhance the chances of political actors to articulate and bring about their goals. Most particularly if they did so in a republican context in which the space for politics had been institutionalized.

YPA: I thought politics wasn't supposed to be about goals? Are you saying the ideal political actor is Cesare Borgia?

HA: You are being deliberately obtuse. Politics is not about the fulfilment of an overarching purpose, but of course it is about the intentions and visions of political actors clashing within the world we create in common. You must remember that Machiavelli's *Prince* was written for very specific purposes, his true allegiance was to republicanism. I am not saying he was right in everything he argued. In my view he sometimes blurred the lines between what I would identify as the realms of 'work' and 'action'.[10] 'Work' is about the ways in which humans create a world in common. I most often exemplify this in relation to the Greek case, in which work builds the walls and forums of the city, the theatre if you like in which politics takes place. 'Action' by contrast, is the drama itself, in other words politics. It is the creating of a non-material world in common through persuasion and rhetoric, it is made up of the public disclosure of the different goals and visions of plural actors, and it depends on the shifting relation between actors and audience. Action is inherently public and inherently risky, it can't be guaranteed to work in the same way so that you can guarantee that particular surveying techniques will lead to the building of a wall that will continue to stand. Politics (action) is most likely to flourish when the city walls are in place (literally in the Greek case, metaphorically in the modern state). But it can't be identified with the work of the builder. In contrast, for Machiavelli, especially when he's talking about Cesare Borgia, political action is sometimes too closely equated with wall-building as a shutting down rather than an opening up of political space. I think Machiavelli had a tendency to over-estimate the links between political and military virtues.

YPA: Did your resistance to the Nazi regime take a violent form?

HA: Not mine, but I did support the idea of a specifically Jewish army and knew that the Nazi regime could only be defeated in war.

YPA: But later, didn't you complain about Fanon and other anti-colonial thinkers and fighters, that they were wrong to use violence to overcome imperialism?

HA: Yes I did. But these were distinct arguments.[11] I am not a pacifist and it wasn't the use of violence *per se* to which I was objecting. Sometimes the only way of righting a wrong is to use violence. You may remember, for example, that I didn't think Gandhi's non-violence could have worked to unseat imperialism if the colonisers were fascists. But one has to be very careful about what the use of violence entails. Two things are important to bear in mind. First, the longer violence is used the more likely it is that using it will corrupt the ends that it is supposed to serve. I don't deny the necessity of the war against fascism, but that violence carried through to a post-war situation in which violence became enshrined in international politics in an unprecedented way. The invention of nuclear weapons and the cold war policies of mutually assured destruction threatened the annihilation of the whole world.

Second, violence is the antithesis of power in the sense that I mentioned earlier – the power of people acting in concert. The Cold War squeezed out the space for politics, the possibility of questioning and dissent, of experimenting with ways of doing things differently, in the West as well as the East. When various kinds of anti-colonial or anti-capitalist revolutionaries glorified the idea of armed struggle as necessary for revolutionary change they made an important mistake. They started to valourize violence itself as somehow to be equated with freedom. They therefore lost sight of the fundamentally instrumental nature of violence and started to confuse means with ends, thus reducing politics to killing. Politics is not about death it is about birth – natality.[12]

YPA: So their mistake was not so much the use of violence as such but the ways in which it became an end in itself?

HA: There was something else worrying in the celebration of revolutionary violence at the end of the 1960s and the early 1970s. It wasn't only that means were being confused with ends, but that this involved embracing a kind of organicism, in which violence was identified with a sort of energy or life-force. The reduction of politics to means-end thinking is bad enough – as I said at the beginning this is the mistake of identifying politics with rule, and it's often associated with not just *justifying* but also *legitimating* the use of violence in politics.[13] But even worse is the identification of political freedom with some sort of libidinal energy. This takes politics into the realm of what I call 'labour' in distinction from 'work' and 'action'. Work and action are specifically human activities and are both about our capacity to create our world. In contrast, labour is what we share with any other species – the endless effort to sustain and reproduce ourselves. There is nothing genuinely political about the organic processes that necessitate labour. Labour doesn't create anything, it just keeps things going and serves no purpose other than preservation of the species. Back in Greece, they understood the anti-political nature of labour. It was, quite properly, confined to the household. A world in which needs for sustenance and reproduction were met and participants were reduced to their role within those processes.[14]

YPA: Isn't the household the sphere where slaves and women were confined? I gather you have never been particularly enthusiastic about the women's movement?

HA: That's not quite right. I absolutely support women's struggles for equal rights, I have done since my youth in Germany. But I support them as struggles for the equal rights of citizens. What worries me is when rights claims become tied to some peculiar aspect of women's identity, including the aspect of traditionally being confined to the sphere of the household, or the capacity to give birth. You can't act politically if you are already determined to act in certain ways, or embody certain qualities because of your biological or social role. If we want women to be politically equal, then the answer to that is not to take the household into the public sphere, but to take women out of the household. Unfortunately, the modern trend is the other way round not just in relation to women but more generally – politics is increasingly identified with the kinds of economic and welfare issues that the Greeks identified as household matters. Which takes us back to your UK election, where most of the discussion was about allocating money to various kinds of welfare function. Interesting how foreign policy, the role of the UK in the appalling events that have unfolded in Afghanistan, Iraq, Libya and now Syria merited scarcely a mention in the election coverage.

YPA: Do you see the international as a space for politics?

HA: You should probably ask my friend Hans Morgenthau that. It's an interesting question. In some ways my ideal of politics has always been that of the city-state participatory democracy or the self-organizing soviet. These are small or sub-state type structures. As I've already said, I also disagree with Clausewitz, war is not in any way a continuation of politics, it is a destruction of politics, which may sometimes be necessary in order for politics to re-emerge. Clausewitz's view only makes sense if you think of politics in terms of rule. Nevertheless, the international context, as a space for a plurality of actors may also be a space for politics. There is potential for acting in concert, for creativity, for new modes of political commonality to be created at the international level. But, like Kant, I think this only applies as long as there is plurality and as long as states can plausibly be seen as individual actors. I'm not in favour of a world state, even in the face of the possibility of nuclear annihilation. And I see many anti-political forces at work in processes of economic and cultural globalization. As with the state, it seems that international bodies are increasingly focused on household matters, mimicking the rise of the social within the state. And the destruction of the particularity of national and sub-national cultures is deplorable. Rampant consumerism and mass media are between them closing down possibilities for encountering difference or thinking differently.

YPA: But there are anti-capitalist movements, what about the Zapatistas or the 'occupy' movements? What about left populist movements in Greece and Spain in Europe today?

HA: I'm not saying that politics isn't possible any more. I don't really know enough about those movements to comment sensibly. My worry would be that they may repeat the errors of earlier radical movements in terms of historicism, instrumentalism or the glorification of violence. But if they are genuinely radical, self-organizing groups, opening up new political questions and answers, then I am delighted to hear it. I certainly don't think the kind of party politics you have been engaging in holds out much hope for new beginnings.

YPA: I think I may need to go and speak to my anarchist friends.

HA: Promises, promises.

Notes

1. Hannah Arendt, 'On Violence' in *Crises of the Republic* (Harmondsworth: Penguin 1973): 108–111.
2. Hannah Arendt, *On Revolution* (Harmondsworth: Pelican Books 1973).
3. Arendt, 'On Violence', *Op. Cit.*: p. 113.
4. Arendt, *The Origins of Totalitarianism* (2nd Edition New York: Meridian Books 1958).
5. Arendt, *Eichmann in Jerusalem: A Report on the Banality of Evil* (London: Penguin Books 1977).
6. Arendt, *On Revolution, Op. Cit.*: 29.
7. Arendt, 'The Concept of History: Ancient and Modern' in *Between Past and Future: Six Exercises in Political Thought* (London: Faber and Faber 1961): 63.
8. Elisabeth Young-Bruehl, *Hannah Arendt: For the Love of the World* (New Haven and London: Yale University Press 1982): 42–76.
9. Arendt, *Between Past and Future, Op. Cit.*: p. 11.
10. Arendt, *The Human Condition* (Chicago: University of Chicago Press 1958).
11. Arendt, 'On Violence', *Op. Cit.*: 90–97.
12. Arendt, *The Human Condition, Op. Cit.*: p. 9.
13. Arendt, 'On Violence', *Op. Cit.*: pp. 119–120.
14. Arendt, *The Human Condition, Op. Cit.*: pp. 79–135.

29
Interview with John Herz
(1908–2005)

Andrew Lawrence

This interview takes place at City College in New York, where the interviewer taught in the department in which Professor Herz was first professor and then emeritus.

AL: Professor Herz, how has the afterlife treated you? And are you content to look back on a full and varied life?

JH: Well, from my posthumous vantage point, I'm delighted to regain my sight and read the *Times* without glasses. I can also attend concert premiers all over the world; it brings back fond memories of the soirées my parents would host at Düsseldorf, where guests performing included Edwin Fischer and George Szell. But these pleasures are counterbalanced by the persistence of the world's woes – in my youth, our goals were 'bread and peace', and it isn't clear that we have decisively achieved progress toward them since then.

AL: At least the classical realist tradition seems to be enjoying a renaissance these days. While you've written as well as taught extensively in legal theory, comparative politics and political theory, it's fair to say that you're best remembered as a key figure of this approach. Typical in this regard is the assessment of Robert Keohane, who praised your work as the epitome of classical realism.[1] You are often grouped with theorists such as E.H. Carr, Hans Morgenthau and Reinhold Niebuhr, and indeed many of you helped to establish this perspective in the United States after fleeing here before and during World War II. Would you agree with this grouping and characterization?

JH: It is certainly an honour to be grouped with such thinkers, several of whom were acquaintances and friends. But on the one hand, the characterization is perhaps overly narrow, and not just for me. The range of intellectual interests you mention was hardly unusual: remember that the tradition in which I and those others of my generation on the European continent were trained was that of a classical, humanistic Gymnasium education. We read the classics, and did not think of science, history and literature, for example, as being completely unrelated but rather as different expressions of humanistic inquiry and endeavour. Excessive compartmentalization of disciplines and sub-disciplines – evidently a growing tendency here in the United States and elsewhere – is one that I would caution against.

AL: Would you say that interdisciplinarity was a characteristic of your cohort of classical realists, particularly as a means of better contextualizing the law's functioning in society?

JH: To be sure, with Morgenthau as well as Carr, George Kennan, and others, I was critical of the dominant mode of study of international relations of the 1920s and 1930s for its wishful tendencies of legalism and moralism, which were especially pronounced in the United States at that time, and have subsequently experienced periodic resurgences.[2] These are all the more ironic, given that the United States failed to ratify Wilson's proposed League of Nations, and still remains a laggard among its peers in ratifying various international conventions and legal norms.

AL: But this commonality of educational and practical *Weltanschauung* notwithstanding, aren't there some salient differences that set you apart from most classical realists?

JH: In my work, to a greater extent than my fellow realists, I think, I emphasize the fragility and intrinsically provisional nature of not just the international order, but of all forms of politics. In this regard, I am perhaps closer to my former associate at Columbia, Robert Cox. In my dissertation, for example, I was already interested in the ambiguity and fragility of state identity, such as is more evident in the wake of revolutions and territorial annexation or change.[3] I don't wish to suggest that there is no scope for international law, treaties, and the like, or that 'anarchy is what states make of it'. For example, I believed at the time (and would still maintain) that the League of Nations had the scope of more effectively confronting and opposing Mussolini's invasion of Ethiopia, which would most probably have changed Hitler's subsequent calculus of risk in pursuing war.

AL: So, like your *Doktorvater*, Hans Kelsen, you envisioned that international law could play a real role in shaping international orders?

JH: Yes; but unlike him, I was at pains to emphasize the 'lesser ideal-ity' of law – its norms need to be historicized, contextualized in a certain time and place – which change, and thus undermine the normative claims of the law that is their product.[4] Moreover, the threat of fascism and war that drove me to the United States underscored for me the importance of guiding research with the imperative of warning against incipient dangers and formulat-ing practical responses to them. In this regard, too, my approach differed from Kelsen's, and perhaps most other fellow classical Realists.

AL: Of course, this experience is one you held in common with Morgenthau, Kissinger and Kelsen, among many others writing on international politics alone; but it seems that your work is distinguished from theirs in its greater emphasis on theorizing and developing normative responses to contemporary problems and issues for the benefit of all of humanity. Would you say this is more of an intellectual or ideological difference?

JH: Well, realism strives to bridge the divide between the intellectual and the ideological, but my realism is indeed qualitatively differ-ent from Kissinger's on both counts. With Morgenthau – a fellow student of Kelsen's, a colleague and friend for whom I always had the greatest respect and admired for the very public stance he took against US escalation of the Vietnam War – my difference is of a different nature. He found the *ur*-cause of international conflict rooted in a supposedly universal human desire to seek power over others, the so-called *animus dominiandi*. With so many counterexamples furnished by history, I never found this strongly universalist claim convincing, and so sought to explain conflict with reference to specific attributes of the international environ-ment, which often instils fear and insecurity in political actors.

AL: So is this primarily a difference in interpreting psychology, or history?

JH: Perhaps both, in that Morgenthau's reading of history was overly confined to Europe's past; for example, he confined his analysis in *Politics Among Nations* largely to state-focused interests and conflicts in the centuries preceding World War II. He chose not to adopt my suggestions for adding discussions of the rise of multi-national corporations, of growing environmental and population issues, with their attendant crises of poverty and overpopulation. In my view, it is not possible to fully comprehend the lamenta-ble rise of terrorist attacks in the post-Cold War period without reference to these conditioning factors.[5] Factors such as these suggest how contingent the practice of the balance of power actually is, something that we realists in general have tended to overlook.[6]

AL: Would you say that your professional experiences in the United States were also a factor in shaping a distinct outlook? On the one hand, it seems that you've adapted better than most had done. You've enjoyed a welcoming and convivial academic life both at City College and Graduate Center from the 1950s to 70s …

JH: Yes, many fine colleagues: apart from my dear friend Tom Karis, Henry Patcher, Ben Rivlin, and those *Jungspunde*, Marshall Berman and Ned Lebow …

AL: On the other, though, the transition to US academic life could not have been easy; the racism that drove you from Germany apparently also found expression in denying you a position at Harvard …

JH: That may be true, but the racism to which you refer fell far harder on others, and did not significantly impede my US career. On the contrary: I will remain eternally grateful to the helping hand stretched out to me and many other refugees of fascism, in particular by black colleges and black scholars. As you know, I got my first teaching job at Howard University, where I taught from 1941–5 and again from 1948–52. I was hired by the great Nobel Prize winner, Ralph Bunche. To be sure, our experience as exiles was sharpened by the experience of witnessing the colour-based discrimination directed at our colleagues, students and friends.[7] It was perhaps with an awareness of this consciousness that Bunche had asked me to write an article on Nazism for the *Journal of Negro Education*.[8] I know that my sense of gratitude was shared by my old friend (and distant relation), Ossip Kurt Flechtheim, who returned to Germany after the war to help establish political science at the Freie Universität Berlin. Many, perhaps most other, refugee scholars felt such loyalty to their historically black adoptive campuses that they remained there until the end of their careers, typically joining the Civil Rights movement as well.[9] These historically black schools' humanity and generosity should not be forgotten.

AL: Did this sense of community extend to an intellectual as well as a personal level, as at City University?

JH: Without question: my colleagues' major contributions to scholarship should not be forgotten either. In addition to Bunche, other illustrious colleagues at Howard included Vincent Browne,

Glendon Schubert, Anthony Dexter Lewis, Bernard Fall, Earl M. Lewis, Harold Gosnell and Robert Martin, and the university could already boast of such luminaries as W.E.B. Du Bois, Franklin Frazier, Alain Locke, Rayford Logan and Merze Tate, among others. It also founded the antecedent publication of the path-breaking IR journal *Foreign Affairs* – arguably the world's first IR journal – under the title *Journal of Race Development*, founded in 1910, which the editors renamed the *Journal of International Relations* in 1919 before giving it its current name in the following decade. The clear normative and moral orientation opposing fascism and imperialism was a distinctive element of this cosmopolitan milieu.[10] And I have no doubt that my black students understood the nature of state-directed oppression in Europe better than most of their white contemporaries on other campuses would have done.

AL: It was during these years at Howard that you completed *Political Realism and Political Idealism*, and the preface of the second edition refers to a shift in your perspective from an emphasis on 'political idealism' to that of 'political realism'. From the end of WW II and the founding of the UN, to the book's publication, just after the outbreak of the Korean War, it seems that world politics indeed would prompt this shift.

JH: That may be so – but I sought to articulate a political ethics that had relevance beyond the immediate circumstances of its writing, even as these circumstances must necessarily change. I hope at least that it succeeds bridging what is in fact a deceptive and artificial divide.

AL: The book also seems to be a plea against the ideological excesses of the early Cold War. By defining liberalism broadly, to include 'all "socialism" that is not "totalitarianism", all "conservatism" that is not authoritarianism or mere defense of some status quo', are you also attempting to articulate a 'common ground' position from the perspective of democratic socialism?[11]

JH: The US political climate at the time was hardly hospitable to such terminology, which in any case is vulnerable to regressive forms of sectarianism ...

AL: But perhaps with so broad a church there's also the opposite risk of losing analytical clarity?

JH: Perhaps, but it didn't seem so at the time. Admittedly, true liberals have become a dying breed, and many, like the *sogenannte* Democrats writing for *Commentary*, much less Samuel Huntington, hardly qualify.[12] It's not what you think, but how you think, that should matter to liberal realists.

AL: Precisely: what strikes me as one of the most fruitful aspects of the book is that you combine politics, history, economics and psychology in order to deepen your understanding of realism as a disposition that recognizes ways that the basic factors of power and security present obstacles to seemingly 'rational' solutions to given problems.[13] For example, and very much in the spirit of Keynes, you advocate a middle position between the polar-opposite 'idealisms' of a pure command economy and a pure market economy ...

JH: Needless to say, these more interventionist measures didn't last. Just because they are more just, sensible, and economically more successful, doesn't mean that they will be adopted or adequately maintained, as the 'idealistic' excesses of the Reagan-Thatcher neoliberal counterrevolution have shown.

AL: I agree. But this multidisciplinary aspect also makes it harder for me to grasp the meaning of 'idealism'. At first, you implicitly define it as a view that does not recognize factors of power and security as obstacles to the achievement of solutions, but later you suggest that human behaviour could be based in other, less 'natural' human motivations.[14] Neither of these exactly fit this example of neoliberalism, however. Further on, you suggest that idealism expressed a denial of the existence of irrationality in the world, as a variety of 'rationalistic' philosophy that presumes reason to be already operative 'in' the 'facts' of a given situation.[15] This definition, it would seem, captures a key dimension of both foreign policy and domestic economic policy – at least, in most of Europe and North America over the past few decades, as well as describing the policy orientation of the World Bank, WTO, etc. The very distinction between short-term and longer-term interests, characteristic of much classical realism, seems to have practically vanished from contemporary mainstream discourse.

JH: Yes, this mindset combines temporal and cultural parochialism, and perhaps historical amnesia – forgetting that economic crises and mismanagement can and do recur.

AL: I'd like to pursue the question of whether the exclusive pursuit of economic growth and profit, *mutatis mutandis,* is not in itself another example of the idea with which you are most often associated, that of the security dilemma. But first, let's confine the definition to your original focus on military security, whereby the very attempts by one power at achieving greater security are perceived by others as a threat, thus escalating a destabilizing dynamic of growing insecurity.[16] It seems that this idea, or theme, is too often taken out of the broader context of the book's endeavour of establishing an ethics of liberal realism (or realist liberalism), missing the idea that it is the dilemma itself that poses the threat, not any other political actor per se. You'd agree, for example, that Mearsheimer's claim that the 'implication of the "security dilemma" is that the best defense is a good offense' is a misreading of the larger ethical framework?[17]

JH: I would say rather that it is a non-reading, and an 'offensive' one at that. Quite clearly, I argue that to adopt the view equating what should be with what is likely, and deeming any efforts to the contrary as impractical and utopian, so that only 'realist' tendencies should prevail as standards for action, without regard to the valuations and ideals of Political Idealism, would mean the ultimate ethical victory of the power-political, fascist and related values over those of liberalism, humanitarianism and pacificism, for example.[18] Ideals can be realized, against cynicism, fatalism and unthinking assertion of will.

AL: Your earlier cautionary remarks against utopianism would seem inimical to these attempts at overcoming the security dilemma. Yet in *International Politics in the Atomic Age,* you come close to arguing the opposite. There, you contend that whereas in the pre-atomic age, 'any advocacy of policies based on internationalism instead of power politics, on substituting the observance of universal interests for the prevalence of national interests, was considered utopian, and correctly so'. Yet in the atomic age of the ever-present threat of nuclear annihilation, 'the "ideal" is bound to emerge as a very compelling "interest" itself'.[19] By the late twentieth century, conventional wisdom had assumed that utopias are always dangerous and misguided, since they necessarily raise false hopes and generate disillusionment and pessimism. Is this not always the case?

JH: Just as international orders, power balances and international law are all fragile and shifting, so too is the distinction between utopian and pragmatic or realist thinking. Utopian thinking, properly scrutinized in a self-critical and reflexive manner, plays an indispensible role in rethinking the nature of the necessary and of the good life.

AL: *International Politics in the Atomic Age* has proven to be your best selling work, and part of its enduring achievement is that it addresses – and helps to educate – existential issues that transcend nuclear war (although of course this threat is still with us). You distinguish between the first phase of a 'holding operation' that seeks mutual accommodation between the superpowers (necessarily entailing greater tolerance for internal dissent) and focuses on regional problem solving (such as those concerning a divided Germany, Korea and China, and the Middle East), and a second phase that adopts a universalist perspective and set of policies that decisively remove the factors contributing to the security dilemma in the first place. You define this perspective in uncannily prescient terms: Whether it is a matter of exploiting 'a subsoil or submarine oil deposit, or whether it is one of exploiting – and quite possibly exhausting – fishing supplies ... the universalist "general" view not only asks whether this lends itself to the profits of individuals ... but also, and above all, what it means in regard to the future availability of the respective resource in terms of global needs.'[20] Do ensuing events vindicate this temporal division and the need for a universalist perspective?

JH: Certainly the latter. My plea for further development of survival research – combining the interdisciplinary cooperation of the social sciences with other scientific disciplines – has become if anything increasingly necessary, to overcome obstacles to effective action combatting global warming and biosphere degradation.[21]

AL: But isn't the aesthetic dimension an equally important part of survival – in which case, it could be termed 'thriving research'?

JH: ... or simply, after Schiller, 'aesthetic education' – albeit under duress. Yes, this is also important, and not in the least contradictory. The life of politics may indeed be one, not of logic, but of experience.

Notes

1. Robert O. Keohane, 'Theory of World Politics', in Robert O. Keohane (ed.), *Neorealism and Its Critics* (New York: Columbia University Press, 1986), p. 199.
2. John H. Herz, 'Political Realism Revisited', *International Studies Quarterly*, 25 (1981), p. 183.
3. John H. Herz, 'Beiträge zum Problem der Identität des Staates,' in *Zeitschrift für öffentliches Recht*, v. 15, 1935, pp. 241–68.
4. John H. Herz, 'Das Recht im Stufenbau der Seinsschichten', *Internationale Zeitschrift für Theorie des Rechts*, 9:4 (1935), p. 291.
5. John Herz, 'Letter to the Morgenthau Conference', in Christian Hacke, Gottfried Karl Kindermann and Kai M. Schellhorn, (eds), *The Heritage, Challenge and Future of Realism: In Memoriam, Hans J. Morgenthau (1904–1980)* (Göttingen: V & R Unipress, 2005), p. 27.

262 *Andrew Lawrence*

6. John H. Herz, *Vom Uberleben. Wie ein Welbild enstand. Autobiographie* (Dusseldorf: Droste, 1984), p. 251.
7. John H. Herz, 1993. 'Black Schools Took Refugee Scholars In', *New York Times* letter to the editor, 3 April 1994.
8. John H. Herz, 'Alternative Proposals to Democracy: Naziism', *The Journal of Negro Education*, 10:3, Racial Minorities and the Present International Crisis (Jul. 1941), pp. 353–67.
9. Cf. Gabrielle Simon Edgcomb, *From Swastika to Jim Crow*, Malabar, Fl., 1993.
10. Muse, Clifford L., Jr. 'Howard university and US foreign affairs during the franklin D. Roosevelt administration, 1933–1945.' *Journal of African American History* 87 (Fall 2002): 403–15.
11. John H. Herz, *Political Realism and Political Idealism. A Study in Theories and Realities* (Chicago: University of Chicago Press, 1951), p. 135.
12. Mario Keßler, 'John H. Herz', *Des Blättchen: Zweiwochenschrift für Politik, Wirtschaft* 9. Jahrgang (IX), Berlin, 2. Mai 2006, Heft 9; Cf. Samuel P. Huntington, 'Conservatism as an Ideology', *The American Political Science Review* 51 (Jun. 1957), pp. 454–73.
13. Herz, *Political Realism, op. cit.*, p. 18.
14. Ibid, pp. 34–5.
15. Ibid, p. 128.
16. Ibid, p. 7.
17. John Mearsheimer, *Tragedy of Great Power Politics* (New York: W.W. Norton, 2001), p. 36.
18. Herz, *Political Realism, op. cit.*, p. 131.
19. John H. Herz, *International Politics in the Atomic Age* (New York: Columbia University Press, 1959), p. 311.
20. Ibid, p. 315.
21. John H. Herz, 'On Human Survival: Reflections on Survival Research and Survival Policies', in Ervin Laszlo and Peter Seidel (eds), *Global Survival: The Challenge and its Implications for Thinking and Acting* (New York: Select Books, 2006), pp. 9–26.

30

Interview with Charles P. Kindleberger (1910–2003), the Reputed Progenitor of Hegemonic Stability Theory

Simon Reich

Kindleberger:	Please call me Charlie. I was most comfortable with people calling me that.
Reich:	Well Charlie, you certainly enjoyed an extraordinary life, working at the US Treasury, the New York Fed and the Bank for International Settlements in the 1930s, then the Washington Fed, the OSS, the US army in Europe in the 1940s. You were one of the architects of the Marshall Plan before joining MIT where you stayed for almost three decades. So you lived through the Great Depression, two great wars, the Cold War, the fall of Communism and died around the time of the two invasions – of Afghanistan and Iraq.
Kindleberger:	It was, indeed, quite a ride. I died over a decade ago – and this isn't even the first time I have been called back from the grave. The fifth edition of probably my most famous book, *Manias, Panics and Crashes*, was published in 2005, two years after my death.[1] I worked on that one. Robert Aliber published a later version after the Great Recession, to remind people of the continuing relevance of my work. So I am accustomed to reaching out from the afterlife.
Reich:	Well I thought it was a good time for a chat, in view of the fact that America is still dealing with the consequences of the Great Recession.
Kindleberger:	The Bible says, 'seven years of feast and seven years of famine'. And from this side of the grave, I appreciate the real meaning of that phrase. After a few years of filet

mignon when I first arrived, in the carnival days before the sub-prime housing crisis hit, it has been nothing but potatoes for the last seven years. So I'm hoping that, at last, as America's unemployment level approaches five percent, there is a steak in sight.

Reich: Well, let's begin with the issue of the Great Recession. What's your take?

Kindleberger: I could see that coming, even from way down here. It had all the ingredients. Bubbles happen when people get greedy and there is no longer a relationship between the price of investments and their underlying value. Regulatory mechanisms are largely abandoned – like President Clinton's repeal of Glass-Steagall. But nobody initially complains because everyone powerful is making money. Ponzi schemes like Bernie Madoff's proliferate and nobody powerful questions it, often because they are direct beneficiaries. It is only when the ensuing malfeasance and widespread corruption becomes irrefutable and damaging – like the behaviour of banks in selling bundles of ruinous mortgages – that a panic ensues. Only then does it finally dawn on us that we've destroyed any mechanisms to curtail this behaviour, and we've even fewer options for dealing with its consequences. A crash becomes inevitable: markets fall and unemployment rises as the underlying lack of value becomes evident. I must say though, you have to be impressed with how the American banks and investment houses created such incredible carnage – an exemplary example of moral hazard – and got away with it. None of the bankers went to prison, all of the banks and finance houses got bailed out (except those poor chumps at Lehman Brothers because the US Treasury was so slow to react) and they even managed to make money out of the crisis by storing away taxpayers' cash given to them to add liquidity to the system. You've got to admire their barefaced effrontery! Of course, Bernie Madoff got to be the unlucky stiff of whom they made an example. Guess he stole from the wrong people.

Reich: Moral hazard has become a real problem. But you've always argued in favour of having 'a lender of last resort', a stabilizer in times of crisis who'll underwrite the system. You said so both in *The World in Depression* and in *Manias*. Doesn't that inevitably mean that huge economic actors will cheat but get bailed out because they are 'too big to fail'?

Kindleberger: As if my blood doesn't boil enough on this side of grave, you have to go and ask me about that! It was hard enough developing my ideas without any recourse to those formal economic models. I had to endure derision at times because I preferred what I affectionately referred to as 'literary economics, as opposed to mathematical economics, econometrics, or (embracing them both) the new economic history'.[2] Yet what I subsequently learned to my cost – after publishing my books – was how economists and political scientists can abuse some simple, powerful ideas. It is, I now accept, harder to do that with a formula – although I've been very amused by that brouhaha over Reinhart and Rogoff's purported misuse of data. They thought they'd proven people like me wrong when they claimed that high levels of public debt irreparably damaged growth rates. It turned out that their results were full of data omissions, questionable methods of weighting, and elementary coding errors.[3] You don't have that problem when you stick to historical writing. So much for that! Even a dead man has to enjoy a few of life's pleasures.

Reich: So what irks you so much?

Kindleberger: Well, where should I start? Let's begin by talking about the idea of 'the lender of last resort'. I plainly said that I got the idea from Walter Bagehot a century earlier, although the poor chap rarely receives his due credit.[4] My work at the Treasury in the 1930s led me to strongly believe that the world needed a stabilizer during times of economic crisis. As I said, I believed that the Great Depression happened because the British then lacked the resources to play the role of stabilizer and the Americans refused to do so. So I offered five functions that a stabilizer should perform, one being the world's lender of last resort.[5] Nobody ever actually chose to test if my argument was true, which I can now admit was quite a relief. But little did I know when I wrote that in 1973 what would happen: First, political scientists started ignoring most of the five functions I wrote about and focused on just one – being the lender of last resort. It was as though nothing else I wrote was of consequence. Secondly, they completely ignored the context in which I wrote: the fact that I had quite clearly stipulated that this stabilizer role was one to be employed *during economic crises* like the Great Depression. Instead, they adapted my argument to embark on a huge body of work that analysed, and advocated, American 'leadership' in routine times, as a justification for all kinds of work – hegemonic stability theory, elements of power transition theory and consequently regime theory – but in a way inconsistent with the rudiments of my work. My focus was on the production of public goods in times of crisis, not routine ones. I thought that Bob Gilpin summed up the difference very elegantly when he said, 'Stephen Krasner and I each appropriated Kindleberger's basic idea that a political leader was needed to create and manage an international liberal economy. However, each of us made several modifications that placed Kindleberger's insight within a state-centric intellectual framework of political analysis and thus fashioned a state-centric version of the theory of hegemonic stability'.[6] I like their work but think that the word 'appropriated' was used quite liberally.

Reich:	And this upsets you?
Kindleberger:	Well, I know you living people think that all publicity is good publicity, and that it doesn't matter what they say about you as long as they spell your name correctly. But I come from a former age when you were judged by your words and deeds. I'm known as the progenitor of hegemonic stability theory because the two Roberts – Gilpin and Keohane – encouraged everybody to believe that.[7] Many others have repeated that claim. Last time I checked on Google, my *World in Depression* had been cited over 2,600 times. That's nice, but all that everyone cites is page 305 where I list my five functions. Nobody ever seems to read the book! In fact, I didn't use the words hegemony or hegemon once in the book, nor did I do so in my noted 1981 essay on domination and

leadership where I discussed how the Pax Britannica and Pax Americana provided public goods through collaborative leadership.[8] And, as I emphatically made clear, I never liked the term.[9] Indeed, the only time I used it in *Manias* was when I mentioned that Bob Keohane did so. Can you imagine being world famous for being the founder of an idea – in fact a whole body of theory – which you didn't actually formulate? Every Tom, Dick, realist and liberal cites me on this in the first half-dozen pages of their book or paper – for something I never said!

Reich: So what would you like to be known for?

Kindleberger: Well, I would prefer that people remember me for two things. The first is that the world needs a stabilizer in a crisis, one that pursued broadly expansive monetary policies rather than the kind of austerity measures often advocated by acolytes of Milton Friedman and the Chicago School. Markets are not self-correcting: they need to be regulated. In a crisis, classic assumptions go out of the window and reduced spending only exacerbates the problems of illiquidity and underconsumption. Of course, I acknowledge that moral hazard is a risk that arises from even the suspicion that a stabilizer exists: Banks and financial houses take speculative risks if they even think the government will bail them out. But that can be combated by appropriate regulatory policies. And the alternative is short-term austerity policies leading to longer-term depression, and economies imploding as a result.[10] Better to deal with the big problem of prospective depression and then introduce prudent rules later, rather than putting faith in self-correcting markets. I think that the Dodd-Frank Wall Street Reform and Consumer Protection Act of 2010 was an honest effort to do that after. But some of its key provisions got watered down and even some of those that survived never got properly implemented.[11]

Reich: And the second thing?

Kindleberger: The second thing I would like to be remembered for is my role as one of the architects of the Marshall Plan. I worked in the Office of Economic Security Policy, setting up the Economic Cooperation Act of 1948 under George Marshall. He was an 'Olympian' in his vision and his moral quality.[12] He truly demonstrated leadership in both dimensions, a commodity nowadays in short supply. Yes, in those days we understood what leadership entailed: It didn't mean squabbling over partisan issues, like who was responsible for that awful mess in Benghazi. It meant enhancing our global legitimacy, even when we made choices that others didn't like. At Bretton Woods, for example, the British led by Keynes opposed Harry Dexter White's plan for the creation of the International Monetary Fund. But, as I said in *Manias*, 'The U.S. view prevailed; the Americans had all the money'.[13] So we didn't have to be popular. Indeed, in contrast to some recent revisionist interpretations, we often were not.[14] But we did have to be credible and to genuinely appear benign – something we've failed to do since turn of the century, even when we've tried to.

Reich: So does America still lead?

Kindleberger: Well, lots of academics and policymakers claim that America is an 'indispensible nation' or 'the world's policeman'. They proclaim that without us demonstrating leadership on a routine basis, the world will be war-ridden and impoverished. But, as I made clear throughout my career, I didn't like anything that approximated despotism.[15] And I don't see evidence of American leadership today. This has little to do with the specific policies of President Obama or George Bush the Second, for that matter – although W's decision to ignore the UN, create the illusion of weapons of mass destruction and to invade Iraq fostered a sense of domination rather than leadership.

Reich: So what makes a country a leader?

Kindleberger: Well, it's dependent on both a fair degree of legitimacy *and* a preponderance of economic resources. I believe that extraordinary degree of American influence for which these people still pine had run its course by 1970.[16] No, as I argued over three decades ago, we have tried to substitute domination for leadership for quite some time. We often simply declare ourselves to be the globe's leader. We rely less on the kind of moral authority shown by people like Marshall and more on

	invoking the biblical imagery of ourselves as 'the shining light upon the hill' – language that sounds pretty amusing from this side of the grave.
Reich:	So how do you think America has adjusted?
Kindleberger:	Well, in short, we haven't. We often declare our behaviour to be in everyone's interest when it appears self-serving. Our ritualistic invocation of the sanctity of free trade is often discarded in favour of a clarion call for fair trade when powerful domestic constituencies are at risk – like George W. Bush's imposition of a steel tariff just before I died. His justifications were so transparently fraudulent that even the WTO – an organization we helped create – found the backbone to stand up to us. Talk about hoist by our own petard! And we sanctimoniously voice support for the virtues of global finance, accusing others of financial cronyism – like we did to the Asians during their financial crisis in the 1990s. That hubris certainly came back to slap us in the face a decade later when our banks and investment houses' illicit dealings turned out to be the source of global instability. Yet nobody seems to have conceded the point on our side, let alone addressed the issue of our hubris, even though Bob Keohane announced in 1984 that we were in a post-hegemonic era. The only thing that has changed since I first made my original point over three decades ago is that America now has less of a capacity to dominate. We have huge debts, are slipping in terms of global innovation, have stubborn underemployment, create low-paying new jobs and have the lowest labour force participation rate since 1978 – the year I first released *Manias*. Nobody has caught up with us yet because we still have a big market and the world's reserve currency. But the competition's clearly doing so, and America's political willingness to adjust during periods of routine growth has been negligible. We gift unwarranted tax breaks to corporations, spend too much money on defence and run massive macro-economic deficits *in stable periods*. Less true leadership in routine times means we are less able to play the role of a stabilizer in times of crisis because we're too broke.

Reich: So how do you evaluate America's role during the Great
                  Recession?
Kindleberger: Well, I was right when I said in the 1980s that neither
                  Japan nor Europe was ready to assume the role of a sta-
                  bilizer in a crisis. Of course, the Japanese subsequently
                  went into a tailspin and the Europeans focused on the
                  regional development of their peripheral countries
                  rather than assuming a global role. That wasn't a bad
                  idea, except they let their weakest economies cheat on
                  their agreement that they would maintain a modicum
                  of economic discipline. And it wasn't as if nobody
                  knew they were cheating: Apollo and Chaos could see
                  that from here! The Germans did play the role of a
                  regional stabilizer but they lost a fair bit of legitimacy
                  by taking a high-handed approach, which feigned
                  ignorance as to what these countries had been doing
                  and then demanded the kind of crushing austerity that
                  will ensure they are despised in these countries for a
                  generation. In contrast, the US looked good for a few
                  years after the fall of the Berlin Wall. Clinton's balanced
                  budgets and support for tech innovation seemed to be
                  working. But we didn't invest that in that grand vision
                  and Bush blew much of it when he tried to impose his
                  own. I think Obama is quite different: he did a pretty
                  good job of playing the domestic lender of last resort –
                  with his bailout of the banks and his TARP program.
                  But I think he should have done more: like ensuring
                  that the banks lend out the money he gave them, and
                  spending much more in infrastructure to create jobs.
                  Measures like that would have done a lot to shorten the
                  crisis at home by increasing domestic liquidity.
Reich: And what about the US' role internationally?
Kindleberger: Well, I think the Fed did pretty well with all those credit
                  swap lines it created with fourteen foreign central banks
                  in the early period of the Great Recession. Bravo! But
                  then it stopped acting like a comprehensive stabilizer
                  and some things started to happen that I could not
                  have foreseen back in the 1980s: first, the Fed decided
                  it had a new job – buying mortgage bonds. But that
                  only helped banks; it didn't increase liquidity. Then
                  the Chinese threw their weight behind stabilizing the

	system. Thirty years ago its economy was the size of Indiana's. Today it is the second largest on earth and hurtling towards the largest in terms of GNP. I couldn't have imagined that even a decade ago when I died.
Reich:	So what do you think of the Chinese?
Kindleberger:	Now I know that China is often demonized as a free rider or 'irresponsible stakeholder'. Some of this criticism is justified. They are very strategic. They also have their own manias and their own problems with cronyism at home. Have you noticed their massive amounts of public sector debt and rows of empty houses in ghost cities? Not good. And I find it funny that many want to believe that they have a master plan to take over from us as the dominant power. The same people who often see American policy as utterly incoherent consider the Chinese to be highly rational, coordinated and strategic. But then again, the Chinese are massive savers, have huge levels of foreign reserves and an unending appetite for buying other countries' foreign debt. They certainly spent lots of money in the critical period of the Great Recession: shrewdly at times on investing in financial services firms in America and natural resources in Africa and Latin America; less tactically at times in increasing imports and exporting capital, and in making some terrible investments like Morgan Stanley and Blackstone.
Reich:	How to you characterize their behaviour?
Kindleberger:	Well, it honestly confounds me. What is interesting is that in the Great Depression the British were willing and unable, the Americans able and unwilling. So I concluded that a crisis needs a stabilizer, *one* stabilizer. On reflection, that may have been a bit rash of me. After all, while I discussed lots of historical instances of manias and panics in my books, most of my analysis, and that of the slew of work in American International Relations theory that followed me, was based on a single example – the Great Depression. The Great Recession seems to have worked differently from my expectations. The Americans spoke authoritatively but didn't actually act as a stabilizer in some crucial areas. Their internal debates were largely about how to save their

own economy. Perhaps there was an assumption that the US economy is so structurally important that by focusing on its welfare, there would be a cumulative beneficial effect. But nobody in the US seemed to be talking about public goods. And despite the scope, scale and magnitude of the crisis, many newly emerging countries – particularly in Asia – prospered while even some relatively poor countries in Africa got by without too much pain. I think this was largely the consequence of American behaviour as a domestic lender of last resort coupled with strategic Chinese behaviour intended to stabilize the system. The Chinese seemed to be willing and, within strict limits, able – if only for their own benefit.

Reich: So what does that say about your work?

Kindleberger: Well, I always argued that the system needed one stabilizer but here there appears to have been two – the US and China. They seemed to have confounded my assertion by sharing responsibilities without actually cooperating to achieve them and by following their own interests.[17] It's what Davis Bobrow and Mark Boyer called an 'impure public good', one where there isn't a match of policy goals – and I guess cooperation isn't required.[18]

Reich: And so what do you conclude?

Kindleberger: Well, we all want to be right. That is part of human nature. Even us spirits feel that way. But eternity gives you plenty of time to contemplate, and I remain a pragmatist even in the afterlife. If I was wrong, and the product of my error was ultimately beneficial in stabilizing the global economy, then I am willing to 'live' with that.

Notes

1. Charles P. Kindleberger, *Manias, Panics, and Crashes: A History of Financial Crises*, 5th ed. (with Robert Aliber), (Hoboken, NJ: John Wiley and Sons, 2005).
2. Charles P. Kindleberger, *Manias, Panics, and Crashes: A History of Financial Crises*, 4th ed. (with Robert Aliber), (Hoboken, NJ: John Wiley and Sons, 1996), pp. 7–8.
3. John Cassidy, 'Rational Irrationality', *The New Yorker*, 29 April 2014, http://www.newyorker.com/online/blogs/johncassidy/2013/04/the-rogoff-and-reinhart-controversy-a-summing-up.html.

4. Walter Bagehot, *Lombard Street: A Description of the Money Market* (London: John Murray, 1917); Norman St John Stevas (ed.), *The Collected Works of Walter Bagehot* (London: The Economist, 1978), vol. 9, p. 267.

5. Charles P. Kindleberger, *The World in Depression 1929–1939* (Berkeley: University of California Press, 1973), p. 305.

6. Robert Gilpin, *Global Political Economy* (Princeton, NJ: Princeton University Press, 2001), p. 99.

7. Robert O. Keohane, 'The Theory of Hegemonic Stability and Changes in International Economic Regimes, 1967–1977', in Ole R. Holsti, Randolph M. Siverson, and Alexander L. George (eds), *Change in the International System* (Boulder, Co: Westview Press, 1980), pp. 131–162.

8. Charles P. Kindleberger, 'Dominance and Leadership in the International Economy: Exploitation, Public Goods, and Free Rides', *International Studies Quarterly*, 25 (2), 1981, pp. 242–254.

9. Charles P. Kindleberger, *The World in Depression, 1929–1939* (Berkeley: University of California Press, 1986), p. 289 Note 1; and Charles P. Kindleberger, 'Hierarchy Versus Inertial Cooperation', *International Organization*, 40 (4), 1986, pp. 841–847.

10. Charles P. Kindleberger, *Mania, Panics and Crashes*, p. 205.

11. Richard Smith, 'A Critical Assessment of the Dodd-Frank Wall Street Reform and Consumer Protection Act', 21 October 2010, http://www.naked capitalism.com/2010/10/a-critical-assessment-of-the-dodd-frank-wall-street-reform-and-consumer-protection-act.html (accessed 12 May 2014).

12. Charles P. Kindleberger, *Marshall Plan Days* (New York, NY: Routledge, 2010), p. 85.

13. Charles P. Kindleberger, *Mania, Panics and Crashes*, p. 263.

14. G. John Ikenberry, *Liberal Leviathan: The Origins, Crisis, and Transformation of the American World Order* (Princeton, NJ: Princeton University Press, 2011), p. 10.

15. Stephen Meardon, 'On Kindleberger and Hegemony: From Berlin to M.I.T. and Back' (2013). Economics Department Working Paper, Series. Paper 4, http://digitalcommons.bowdoin.edu/econpapers/4.

16. See Charles P. Kindleberger, 'Dominance and Leadership in the International Economy', especially p. 248, and Charles P. Kindleberger, *Manias, Panics and Crashes*, p. 202.

17. For evidence on this point see Carla Norrlof and Simon Reich, 'American and Chinese Leadership during the Global Financial Crisis: Testing Kindleberger's Stabilization Functions', *International Area Studies Review*, March 2015, pp. 1–23, http://ias.sagepub.com/cgi/reprint/2233865915573638v1.pdf?ij key=LJrI8wePiziePaz&keytype=finite.

18. Davis B. Bobrow and Mark A. Boyer, 'Maintaining System Stability: Contributions to Peacekeeping Operations', *Journal of Conflict Resolution*, 41 (6), 1997, p. 726.

31
Karl W. Deutsch (1912–1992) Interviewed

Andrei S. Markovits

Andy: It's great to have you back, Karl. I really have missed our many conversations in your office at Littauer, your cozy study at your lovely house on Lakeview Avenue, and, of course, our sporadic meals in fine restaurants in Berlin, Vienna and other European cities. What would you say is the single-most important change in the world of politics, economics, culture – any and all of it – which you have noticed since your untimely but temporal departure in 1992?

Karl: First, great to see you, Andy. You still look the same though your formerly long reddish-blond curls have become all grey and a tad less dense. You could lose a few pounds but on the whole you seem in fine form which makes me very happy. As to my response to your question: please, there is no hesitation for me whatsoever that the Internet and everything pertaining to it has completely altered the world that I knew so well. It is without any doubt in my mind *the* single-most significant and game-changing invention since the printing press. And I must say that I am very happy to see that the Internet has changed things in a Deutschian way, both in terms of its empirical reality and its normative implication. As to the former, it has enhanced our access to data million-fold, if not more. In terms of the quantity that we now can access, it's a dream come true for me. You remember how much I loved data, the more the better, because I fully understood that only via data can we enhance knowledge, improve insights, truly attain understanding in a meaningful way. Remember the thousands and thousands of computer cards and printouts and tapes in those many yards of filing cabinets that I had stored in my second Harvard office at the Vanserg Building where you then worked for more than fifteen years and that was the basis for many of my studies and publications, including our joint work on global modelling and the fear of and trust in science? All of this stuff is a minor fraction – one measly app – on your smart phone, which you can summon with one push of your finger. Amazing, don't you think? And remember how I would often go off on tangents in my seminars with ideas and insights that came to me totally unplanned and at the spur of a moment in our class discussions and then I would ask you or others to go verify my musings by trekking into the bowels of Widener Library to find evidence for what I had said and that this would often take days of hard detective work of tracking and searching and finding – well, this is now done with one Google search, at most two. 'To google': Remember how I always invoked the power of language as a crucial signifier for social reality? Well, here you have it: yet another new verb in the English language which has become part of global speech. That the barriers to the access of the most varied kinds of data in the most amazing quantities have all but disappeared warms my heart no end. The game-changing nature of this technology has impressed me so much that I have just enrolled, so to speak, in an intensive private tutorial on typing taught by the twelve-year old child of my next-door neighbour so that I, too, can soon type words and concepts and ideas into the search engines of my tablet and smart phone at will and whenever anything strikes me without having to rely on our beloved Mrs. Neumark [Evelyn Neumark, Karl Deutsch's longtime secretary at Harvard University to whom he always referred to in this manner, never by her first name] who had to type literally everything – from letters of recommendation and memos to the dean, to text that became my book and article manuscripts – that I wrote long hand on my lined yellow legal pads, which always rested on my knees. It is amazing how these new game-changing devices have become de facto bodily extensions of today's young people. The normalcy and intimacy with which my great grandchildren's daily lives have become defined by these devices is much more powerful than mine was by, say, a pencil or a fountain pen. I did not use such while taking a shower in Prague the way today's young people most certainly use their smart phones as a matter of course. Come to think of it, we did not shower in those days in Prague. We took baths. But let me say something also about the normative implications of all this and why they so much conform to my own personal preferences and hopes. Look, this stuff has vastly democratized knowledge proliferation and thus has created a massive inclusion of ordinary people that simply has no precedent in history. And what, after all, is democracy if it is not the constant inclusion of the formerly excluded and the ever-increasing empowerment of the formerly disempowered all by dint of enhanced knowledge and ever-growing access to data. A Deutschian dream, as it were, has come true. Look at the interconnectedness of the world: time and space have become all but irrelevant in terms of sharing knowledge and information. Other than in North Korea – I rest my case as to what kind of thuggish regime and murderous leadership you need these days to remain untouched by this massive advancement in the means of production to use one of Marx's applicable jargon, and, trust me, this resistance will soon fail, I guarantee it – there are virtually no more spots on earth that are not interconnected with every other spot on earth. On the bus to Harvard Square I saw this kid watch a German Bundesliga match on his smart phone in real time. When some odd corner kick occurred, he forwarded this immediately to his friends via Twitter. Unthinkable even a decade ago! Clearly, this technology has changed the proliferation of cultures, codes and norms. As to its political ramifications, its power of mobilization – remember how much weight I attached to this in my work, especially in the late 1950s and throughout the 1960s – is huge both in quantity and quality. Just think of the so-called Arab Spring, how things jumped like sparks from Tunisia to Egypt then onward to Turkey, to Syria. The outcomes have varied and not all seems to be turning out as I would have liked and hoped. But maybe we can talk about this a bit later. Here I only want to confirm that the mobilizing – and thus democratizing – capabilities of these micro-technologies is immense. By making all knowledge acceptable to everybody all the time, knowledge itself – which was always hoarded and preserved by the powerful for their own, often nefarious, purposes, has become democratized. MOOCS – massive open online courses – be it in the UDACITY or COURSERA or any other version: Stanford and Harvard better beware! You may well have unleashed forces which, at some point, might undermine your very raison d'etre which, after all, was to convey knowledge to folks. You actually did that but only to a tiny sliver of the population thus giving you the aura of lording over a coveted and rare good that bestowed distinction on a few, thus enhancing the value of your identity as the source of such power and privilege.

Andy: It is clear, Karl, that, as I fully expected, you love the Internet and see its contribution to our world largely in a positive light. Still, might there be some negatives that you would care to share with me?

Karl: Yes, I do see serious negatives all centred on the issue of maintaining the privacy of individuals. Here I perceive a two-pronged danger: one by the state, from above; and the other by society, from below. The former problem centers on all the revelations concerning the NSA scandal. I mean I realize that among any state's foremost duty is to guarantee the safety of its citizens as best it can. Security is every bit as much a civil right as are freedom, equality and justice. And I fully understand that the United States and many of its Western allies face an indomitable enemy in Islamic jihadism, which has proven its lethality on many occasions and that will not shy from using any means – including the deployment of weapons of mass destruction such as chemical, biological, maybe even nuclear agents – to harm the West, America in particular. Thus, vigilance is clearly called for and perfectly legitimate. What is much less legitimate and truly worrisome is the obvious abuse of power that the NSA as an agency – most certainly a number of its agents, perhaps on their own, perhaps not – enjoyed deploying it simply for its own sake, just to demonstrate that they could and that nobody was going to stop them. What worried me in this instance is the evident delight in a clear abuse of power for its own sake, just to demonstrate omnipotence. I mean bugging Angela Merkel's, arguably one of the most pro-American German and European leaders of the past decade, private cell phone constituted not only a display of arrogance and hubris, it also bespoke complete stupidity. The costs of this will remain immensely high over quite some time for American diplomacy and foreign policy. But in addition to this inherently Big Brother-like dimension of the Internet, there is also something in it that Bill Maher, this wonderful comedian whom I have just discovered, called 'Big Girlfriend' referring to the instance when the (now former) owner of the Los Angeles Clippers, Donald Sterling's racist remarks made in the privacy of his home to his girlfriend was surreptitiously recorded by her and placed on the Internet causing a national, no international, sensation.

Andy: Karl, are you kidding me? What is this? Have you now also become au courant with our crop of late night television comedians? What next? Developing into a major interpreter and connoisseur of gangsta rap?

Karl: Andy, you remember how one of my least-known personal passions has always been to stay up late and watch late night television, preferably some great crime show, or even a Western or two. In any case, back to my point: Don't get me wrong: I am not defending Sterling's putrid racism and am delighted the way the NBA reacted to him and to the whole sordid affair. But truth be told, Sterling made these ugly remarks to his girlfriend and they would never have become public with the same timeliness and social potency prior to the advent of this new medium called Internet. In a sense, I am almost more concerned by this invasion – indeed negation – of privacy in civil society than by the state. I mean anybody can now video and audio record anybody else in any situation, place that on the Internet for the entire world to see. There are absolutely no social norms, no acceptable rules and limits guiding this new forum of discourse. This is scary stuff when you think about it. And there is one more dimension of the Internet's civil-society based qualities that have come to frighten me and that disappoint me: the unbridled meanness in tone that total anonymity accords any Internet participant. As you well know, as an eternal optimist and an avid disciple of the Enlightenment, I always thought of people being basically good and decent and caring. However, the sheer cynicism, manifest ill-will and ubiquitous Schadenfreude that one encounters on any message board, no matter how innocuous the subject, is truly remarkable and quite upsetting to me. And there is another wide-ranging Internet phenomenon that surprises me: that of 'pillarization'. Remember the great work of my dear friend and colleague Arend Lijphart on 'consociationalism', and that of my equally fine colleague and friend Gerhard Lehmbruch on 'Konkordanzdemokratie', which described so well the structural framework of the politics of countries like Austria, the

Netherlands, Lebanon, Switzerland and a few others where massive vertical pillars – Lager, (armed) camps as they were so aptly called in German, veritable sub-societies – confronted each other and could only cohere via an intricate system of elite accommodation that is best characterized by the key ingredient informing all of postwar Austrian politics called 'Proporz'? Remember these camps with their own newspapers, own institutions, own clientele, own discourse, inimical to all outsiders, totally inner-directed and self-satisfied in their own milieu? American politics seems to have been this pillarization's exact opposite. Much of American public life – with the huge exception of the racial divide – appeared to have been blessed with what we used to call cross-cutting rather than cumulative cleavages. Well, this no longer seems to exist. Indeed, the Internet has reinforced a certain ideological centrifugality that divides America into 'blue' and 'red' states, which I actually see not so much as geographic entities but rather as states of mind and mentality and outlook and preferences. There now exists in the United States the Lager of MSNBC and Huffington Post on one side; and of Fox and the Drudge Report on the other – and the two worlds rarely, if ever, interact other than by bitterly denouncing and berating each other. I just looked at some Pew Research Center surveys that fully bear out this pillarization of American society. Dialecticians always had it right and this continues with their assessment of the Internet: while it has created a hitherto unprecedented global community and integration on the one hand, it has by dint of this very fact also fostered the proliferation of niches, of mini-communities, of micro-cultures that can happily live in their own world completely oblivious to the many others surrounding them. This is what the British sports sociologist Roland Robertson has so aptly termed the ubiquity of the 'glocal'.

Andy: Wait a minute, Karl, you read stuff in the world of sports sociology? Are you serious?

Karl: Of course, never underestimate the catholicity of my interests. I read everything and anything from which I can learn. And I devoured your work on comparative sports cultures which you have produced prolifically since I was last in touch with you, and I noticed that you mentioned Robertson's scholarship with great admiration. So I had Mrs. Neumark check out one of his books from Widener and bring it to my home where I read it with great enjoyment and to my benefit. You know quite well that I never ever stopped being a student. Thus, the learning process continues unabated. But back to the increasingly persistent divide in American society and politics. Of course, the pillarization of American politics and society is not (yet) as bad as it was in the first Austrian Republic of the interwar period where these political pillars had their very own private armies, one of which I had come to know so well as a teenager when my mother, who hailed from Vienna, took me to that city for regular visits during our school holidays from my Gymnasium in Prague during which I would often see my uncle Julius, whom I always called O.J. short for Onkel Julius, and who was, as you well know, the leader of the Schutzbund, the Austrian Social Democratic Party's and the working class's fighting force.

Andy: Karl, tell me your views on the European project about which you already wrote insightful stuff in the 1950s, especially in the context of the North Atlantic Alliance.

Karl: Look, despite the obvious birth pangs that sometimes are ugly and about which I will say a few things in a moment, one can only look at this project in the *longue durée* to speak with the great Fernand Braudel. Anything else is not only silly but actually irresponsible in my view. I mean, my God, we are talking about one of the – if not *THE* – most interesting and unusual state-building processes in human history. Of course there will be setbacks and of course the positive outcome – of a politically totally integrated, peaceful, democratic, wealthy and happy Europe from the Atlantic to, well where? the Russian border, perhaps? – is far from guaranteed. But to anybody with my history whose life has been deeply shaped by the two World Wars that ravaged all of Europe, the fact that deadly enemies like the French, the Germans and the Poles, to name just a few, have become de jure equal citizens of a new state-like entity with no borders and a shared currency and common laws that define their daily existence and activities, is nothing short of sensational, indeed still a bit unbelievable. I mean how many states can you mention that were created completely peacefully and with absolutely no coercion but voluntary compliance? Last I looked Romania and Bulgaria and Croatia and Slovenia joined the European Union not by dint of the EU's army conquering them but by their volition – indeed eagerness – to join this new state-like entity that their elites, at least, rightly perceive as the correct – indeed sole – option for their peoples' future. Of course, one need not be a committed Marxist to understand that coercion can be applied by many other means apart from military intervention. I understand that economic relations also involve power and as such are far from equal with obvious winners and losers. It is precisely for this reason that I am particularly upset by Germans who moan and groan about how bad the EU has treated them and their country when every schoolchild can see that Germany and the Germans have thus far been the EU's most emphatic winners. This is not to say that even the Germans did not have to forego certain aspects of their former de jure sovereignty and autonomy to become the engine of the European project. Yes, there now exist levels of jurisdiction, for example, that supersede national autonomy and sovereignty. That is what a federation – even a confederation – entails. At this stage, the EU is not even a fully-accomplished Staatenbund, let alone a Bundesstaat which, at least in my estimation, would be the sole measure of the project's complete and ultimate success. When my colleagues and friends like Dankwart Rustow, Robert Dahl, David Apter, Daniel Lerner, Shmuel Noah Eisenstadt even Samuel Huntington, envisioned the successful end result of the state- and nation-building process, they did so, despite all their important epistemological and methodological differences, with a West European version in mind, most particularly France. Truth be told, I did as well. In the meantime, I have become a convinced acolyte of David Laitin's brilliant insight of seeing the European state building process as an 'Indianization' of Europe, in other words seeing the chaotic and vastly different, yet cohering and democratic India as Europe's teleological model, not some kind of continent-spanning replica of an ideal-type France. Have there been major backlashes against this massive development? Of course, and how could there not be. Are they pretty and acceptable to me in their ugly revival of all kinds of fascisms that brutally ruined Europe and uprooted my own life? Surely not! But as I said at the outset in my responding to your question, any substantial analysis of this immensely complex process based purely on a *courte durée* accountability – to invoke Fernand Braudel once again – will not only lead to erroneous results but also to pernicious policies.

Andy: How do you see the field of political science and its current state at leading universities both in the United States and elsewhere?

Karl: On the whole, I am very pleased with the huge development that our discipline has experienced over the past 50 plus years. Think about it: When I started out as a young assistant professor at MIT, nobody in international relations or in comparative politics used any numbers. These were largely descriptive fields with very little of the analytic rigour that they now rightly demand. And I will always remain very proud for having been in the forefront of introducing quantitative methods as a matter of course in any serious academic work in both of these sub-disciplines in our field. I was never really at the core of what came to be known as the behavioural revolution of our discipline but I will always remain delighted and honoured to have been one of its important players on the margins – a friend and fan as it were. I also welcome the rational choice revolution that became so prevalent, particularly in the United States, much less in Europe. It really created an epistemologically and methodologically rigorous manner to conceptualize crucial topics of research in comparative politics and international relations. I also welcome the related phenomenon of modelling which, as you so well remember, I was working on in the 1970s, especially on the issue of 'reduction of complexity' that I tackled with Bruno Fritsch but which, alas, never gained the traction that I hoped it would. If there is one thing that I dislike about the current atmosphere in the practice of modelling and rational choice is that some of its practitioners have assumed almost a Leninist zeal for it, meaning that anything that does not engage in their orthodoxy is simply excommunicated from the field, from being legitimate political science. As you well remember, I always hated any and all orthodoxies and this one is no exception. What makes political science such a wonderful discipline is precisely its big-tent nature, its eclecticism, its catholicity. Let us keep it that way. This is all the more important because I also fear that some of our colleagues have been suffering from an inferiority complex vis-à-vis economists and have devised research strategies that one could easily call 'economics light'. There is clearly no need for this, especially at a time when much of cutting-edge work in economics happens in something called 'behavioural economics', which is immensely keen on using data, concepts and approaches from fields like anthropology and psychology. Lastly, let us remember that I always used numbers in very particular social, historical and political contexts. Numbers to me, their mastery and their wizardry, were never ends of themselves. They were always a clear means to understand non-numeric phenomena, i.e. how people lived, strove, hoped.

Andy: One of your most personally endearing but also intellectually compelling qualities has been your optimism. Do you still have that, Karl?

Karl: In his magnum opus *The Better Angels of Our Nature: Why Violence Has Declined*, my eminent Harvard colleague Steven Pinker argues cogently and with vast empirical evidence that, viewed in the long run, the process of civilization has tamed humans and consistently rendered them substantially less violent than they had been. Although the current world is far from perfect, Pinker demonstrates convincingly that on the whole we torture less, we engage in fewer acts of cruel punishments, we have fewer frivolous executions, we have less slavery, we rape less, we beat fewer children, we abuse animals less, we have fewer wars in which there is total disregard for human losses – in short, we are much less brutal, callous and cruel than at any previous stages in human history. As you correctly argue in your own work on human-animal relations, one can clearly discern a constantly increasing empathy and compassion in the public discourse as well as behaviour of humans over time. At the beginning of his *Democracy in America*, Alexis de Tocqueville offered a fine conceptual framework as to how the discourse of compassion will inevitably grow in liberal democracies – and only in those. In Chapter I of his book which appropriately reads 'That Manners Are Softened as Social Conditions Become More Equal', Tocqueville argues that equality in social conditions and – above all – a better acquaintance with formerly distant groups lead to a compelling growth in the civility of manners. Originally, one only has compassion for and empathy toward members of one's inner circle, one's immediate environment. But once one's horizon expands by virtue of economic relations and political interaction – by virtue of what I had termed 'social mobilization' and a clear consequence of what I saw as the key components of 'social communication' – one realizes a commonality with others that one never thought one had. One comes to regard them as equals, which means that one empathizes with their fate. One develops a growing sense – even urgency – of compassion. But this can only flourish via the free exchange of ideas and movements which means that one of the key prerequisites for this growth in compassion is a liberal democratic order. Being more humane and more compassionate means also ipso facto that one is more democratic because one understands the disempowered, one identifies with them, and one ultimately wants to give them voice and not compel them solely to loyalty or force them to exit to invoke the lasting work of my dear friend Albert O. Hirschman. As you can see, I have not changed at all in that I continue to remain the perennial optimist. I must say that nothing in my work, life and legacy has filled me with such pride and delight as my optimistic view of human life and history. This is not to say that I have ever been naïve and wide-eyed, and not realized the horrors that humans can – and do – inflict on each other, alas with regularity. But precisely in the aforementioned LONGUE DUREE of things, human decency will always vanquish human turpitude. And that is a good thing! Be well, my friend, thanks for this lovely chat, and promise me that you will continue to love life and live it to its fullest!

32

International Theory Beyond the Three Traditions: A Student's Conversation with Martin Wight (1913–1972)

Ian Hall

It is May 1960. Jim, an eager but somewhat anxious student, has an appointment with Mr Martin Wight, then Reader in International Relations at the London School of Economics (LSE), and soon to become Dean of European Studies and Professor of History at the University of Sussex. Wight's 'Why is there no International Theory?' has just been published.[1] Together with 'Western Values in International Relations', which later appeared alongside the reprinted 'Why' essay in Diplomatic Investigations *(1966),[2] the article represents the fruit of at last four years of Wight's research on the 'international theory' to be found in the intellectual history of the West. Jim is worried, however, that it seems to contradict some of Wight's earlier arguments, in lectures that Jim heard at LSE, and, in the course of the conversation, inquires how Wight's thought on international theory and the 'society of states' is evolving after his initial experiments, in those lectures, with the 'three traditions'.[3]*

Jim: Mr. Wight, thank you for making the time to see me, especially at the end of term, which I know is such a busy time.

Wight: You're welcome, of course. From your note, I gather that you're a bit confused about something I have recently published.

Jim: Well, yes, I am rather. I just got my copy of *International Relations* in the post and it contains an essay of yours, 'Why is there no International Theory?'. When I read the title, I have to say I was surprised. I attended all of your lectures last year – the ones about the three traditions – and you gave the distinct impression then that there was quite a bit of international theory out there. I suppose I'm struggling a bit to reconcile what you said then with the title of the article. Have you decided there aren't 'three traditions', after all?

Wight: Ah, I see the problem. And the answer, I suppose, is yes and no. The title of the article is provocative, of course, but a great deal turns on what you mean by the phrase 'international theory'. I wanted to highlight the contrast between the quantity and quality of political theory that we have and the relative lack of international theory. Political theory, of course, concerns the doings of – and within – the polis. There is plenty of that about, from Plato onwards, in what the Americans call the 'canon'. What I meant by 'international theory' is a tradition of speculation or argument about the doings of, and doings within, the society of states. As you'll know from the lectures, there is a lot less of that about. My friend Butterfield blames that on Plato – he thinks *The Republic* placed limits on political theory and political theorists, confining them to the discussion of matters within states, rather than between them, thereby preventing the emergence of international theory.[4] He may be right.[5] But what I found, when I was writing the lectures in Chicago, for Morgenthau's class, and then updating them here,[6] was that some political theorists – and more statesmen, philosophers, historians, lawyers, and others – have strayed beyond the boundaries of *res publica* and left some remnants of 'international theory' for us to study. Those remnants are what I discussed in both the lectures and the article.[7]

Jim: Ah, I see. So it is not that there is no international theory, just that there isn't much of it to be found. And you did find it – and it fits into your three traditions.

Wight: Mmm. I thought it did. Now I'm not so sure.

Jim: You're not sure? Why?

Wight: Well, to be honest, I wonder whether squeezing all the different assumptions, beliefs and arguments you find in the history of international theory into three traditions does them justice, even when you add more categories, as I did, like 'inverted Revolutionism', and so on.[8]

Jim: Oh, I see. What's the alternative?

Wight: Good question. One way to do it would be to concentrate on the theory in particular texts or the theory belonging to particular thinkers. That was the approach I used in the other lectures I have given on international theory, which you might have heard.[9] But I've also been thinking that it might be better to explore international theory in terms of what Arthur Lovejoy once called 'unit-ideas'.[10] He famously argued that understanding the history of ideas in terms of 'isms' was unhelpful – he described 'idealism, romanticism, rationalism' and all the rest, in a wonderful phrase, as 'trouble-breeding and usually thought-obscuring terms'.[11] He proposed instead tracing these 'unit-ideas' through history – looking at what different philosophers or statesmen or lawyers have said about a particular concept or topic. Of course, we have to be mindful of Collingwood's warning that what the Greeks meant by 'polis' is not what moderns mean by 'state',[12] but I think there might be some merit in looking at longitudinal themes instead of traditions.[13]

Jim: I see. How would that work, in practice? Don't the historicists have a point – political theory is not a succession of different answers to the same question, but rather a series of answers to different questions?

Wight: Again, yes and no. The questions and answers do change over time, but each answer is shaped by the ways in which past thinkers approached similar questions. It is hard to think that Hobbes' international theory, for example, would have taken the form it did had he not been an avid reader (and translator) of Thucydides.

Jim: Right, so there is some justification for looking – how did you put it? – longitudinally.

Wight: I think there might. I tried doing a bit of this in the pamphlet I wrote after the war for Chatham House, *Power Politics*.[14] In a way, that little book was a kind of glossary of concepts – great powers, for instance, alliances, or vital interests – which set out what philosophers, lawyers, statesmen, and the rest thought about these elements of international society. I've been working more recently on something else that takes a similar approach – an essay for this new British Committee on the Theory of International Politics that Butterfield is convening, with American money, of course. It's presently called 'The Whig Tradition in International Theory and Western Values', but I might just give it the title 'Western Values in International Relations'.[15]

Jim: Yes, that sounds snappier.

Wight: Perhaps. In any case, the essay looks not at traditions, but instead at the ways in which different thinkers approach different concepts over time: international society, order, intervention and international morality. And I've been thinking that I might look at some others too: the balance of power,[16] of course, but also concepts like international legitimacy.[17]

Jim: That's very interesting. So you think you might set the 'three traditions' aside and just concentrate on these – what did you, or Lovejoy, call them, 'unit-ideas'? I can see the merit in that approach. But it might be dull for students, who liked the old approach. We used to spend hours after lectures trying to see if this or that thinker would fit into one or other of your traditions. And of course we spent lots of time debating where you yourself might fit. That was hard! You were always wary of giving your own position away. What was it you said in that very last lecture: you found 'own position' relative to these traditions of yours 'shifting round the circle'. You said your 'prejudices' were Rationalist, but that you see the appeal of the other traditions.[18] That made it hard. Some of us were convinced you were really a Realist. Some thought you were a Rationalist – and a few of us thought you might even be a Revolutionist. Weren't you once a pacifist? And I gather from one of your former students that you once had a portrait of Professor Laski on your desk ...

Wight: Ha! I'm surprised that anyone noticed ...

Jim: I think they are just curious – and looking for help in working out what they themselves think.

Wight: Well, it is true that I was once a Revolutionist of sorts, as many people are when they are young. I was attracted to some aspects of socialist thinking, especially to its critique of European colonialism – and, yes, I did have a picture of Professor Laski on my desk. He taught me a great deal and I helped update a textbook of his for publication, just after his death.[19] But at the same time – this is in the 1930s, you understand – I was a bit of a Grotian, believing that the League of Nations could bring about some kind of order and justice in international society. When that failed, I turned to pacifism for a time,[20] and I became more of a Realist about some things, recognizing that 'power politics' seemed to be, in the 1940s and early 1950s, at least, the preferred way to conduct international relations for most states, totalitarian or democratic. I wanted Rationalism to win out, of course, but I had to admit that Realism seemed to be winning.

Jim: Do you still think that? That Realism is winning, I mean.

Wight: I'm not so sure. The Cold War has taken a terrible toll on the old ways of doing business in international society, as the

Second World War did too. War is no longer limited as it once was by international law. Diplomacy today is often more of a shouting match than an attempt to achieve balance and a modicum of agreement. The United Nations is little more than a stage for demagogues to denounce one another. The Soviets profess an ideology that looks forward to the collapse of international society and the sweeping away of the Whig tradition and Western values that underpin it.[21] And new states like India and Indonesia denounce these ideas and values as cover for imperialism and neo-colonialism.[22] It is hard to see how Realist 'power politics' can be overcome in these circumstances. As I wrote in the *International Relations* essay, I'm not at all convinced – as Bertrand Russell and his Campaign for Nuclear Disarmament seem to be – that nuclear weapons scare the superpowers so much that they will refrain from fighting wars.[23] And I'm sceptical about Revolutionist claims that all it needed is a bigger say for public opinion or that the end of the state will herald something better. The fundamentals of international relations remain unchanged, but the desire to sustain the notion of the 'society of states' doesn't seem to be there. Or, at least, I can't perceive it at the moment.

Jim: Gosh. I had no idea that you were so pessimistic.

Wight: I'm not! But I do think I have an obligation, as a scholar, to be realistic, in the everyday sense of the word.

Jim: Surely things could change, though, couldn't they? Do you have any advice for those of us, like me, that want to see things get better?

Wight: Yes. I've always seen education as an attempt to broaden minds, rather than train them or, worse still, to indoctrinate them. So I'm not sure that I can provide much guidance to you about what to think or how to act ...[24]

Jim: Why not, if you don't mind my asking? You know an enormous amount about the history of international relations and I'm told you spend lots of time at Chatham House, so you have a sense of what politicians and diplomats think and how they do and should behave. Surely you're in a better position than most to help us work out how to approach the world?

Wight: When you put it like that, I suppose you have a point. But I have always been sceptical about the idea that universities can provide a practical training in how to conduct international relations. And since you've finished your degree now,

I suppose I can say this: I've also long been sceptical about Professor Manning's idea that International Relations – as a field of academic study – can and should produce better politicians, diplomats or bureaucrats.[25] But then nor, I suppose, can History – my preferred field. Some time ago I reviewed Rowse's funny little book, *The Uses of History*, and I believe now what I wrote then, that 'historical knowledge is an ingredient of political judgement, not a substitute'. Historians can, after all, be as 'silly as anyone else' in their political views – look at all of those who praised Mussolini, and even Hitler, back in the thirties.[26]

Jim: OK, I accept all of that. But surely scholarship can be some kind of guide for practice?

Wight: Of course. But the point of a liberal education is to introduce students to the great minds and texts of the past, first and foremost, not merely to teach tricks! On this, if not on other things, I agree with Oakeshott.[27] Now, I must get back to my marking. It never ends at this time of year. It has been a pleasure talking to you, Jim, as always.

Jim: Of course. Thank you for your time, Mr. Wight.

Notes

I am very grateful to Robert Ayson for his advice on an earlier draft of this dialogue and to the editors for the invitation to write it.

1. Martin Wight, 'Why is there no International Theory?', *International Relations* 2(1) (1960), pp. 261–281.
2. Martin Wight, 'Western Values in International Relations', in Herbert Butterfield and Martin Wight (eds), *Diplomatic Investigations: Essays in the Theory of International Politics* (London: George Allen & Unwin, 1966), pp. 89–131.
3. These lectures were later reconstituted from the original notes and published as Martin Wight, *International Theory: The Three Traditions*, edited by Gabriele Wight and Brian Porter (London: Leicester University Press and the Royal Institute of International Affairs, 1991).
4. Ian Hall, 'History, Christianity and diplomacy: Sir Herbert Butterfield and international relations', *Review of International Studies* 28(4) (2002), pp. 735–736.
5. Wight agreed with Butterfield's view, arguing that the belief that 'every individual requires the protection of the state' has 'absorbed almost all the intellectual energy devoted to political study' ('Why is there no International Theory?', p. 38).
6. The 'three traditions' lectures were first delivered at the University of Chicago in 1956–1957, when Wight filled in for Hans J. Morgenthau, and taught his class on international theory.
7. See especially Wight, 'Why is there no International Theory?', pp. 36–38.
8. Wight, *International Theory*, pp. 108–110; pp. 254–257.

9. Wight used this approach in his lectures, delivered at the LSE in 1959–1960, on *Four Seminal Thinkers in International Theory: Machiavelli, Grotius, Kant and Mazzini*, edited by Gabriele Wight and Brian Porter (Oxford: Oxford University Press, 2005).

10. Wight cites Lovejoy in 'Western Values in International Relations', p. 91. See also Ian Hall, *The International Thought of Martin Wight* (New York: Palgrave, 2006), pp. 153–154.

11. Arthur O. Lovejoy, *The Great Chain of Being: A Study of the History of an Idea* (Cambridge, MA: Harvard University Press, 1964 [1936]), p. 5.

12. R. G. Collingwood, *An Autobiography* (Harmondsworth: Penguin, 1944).

13. Wight used the phrase 'longitudinal themes' in the context of discussing the History curriculum he drew up in the early 1960s, as Dean of the School of European Studies at the University of Sussex. See Martin Wight, 'European studies', in David Daiches (ed.), *The Idea of a New University: An Experiment at Sussex* (London: Andre Deutsch), p. 110.

14. Martin Wight, *Power Politics*, Looking Forward Pamphlet no. 8 (London: Royal Institute of International Affairs, 1946). An expanded edition, including chapters Wight had updated during the 1950s and 60s, was published posthumously: *Power Politics*, edited by Hedley Bull and Carsten Holbraad (London: Leicester University Press and Royal Institute of International Affairs, 1995 [1978]).

15. Ian Hall, 'Martin Wight, western values, and the Whig tradition in international thought', *The International History Review* 36(5) (2014) pp. 961–981.

16. See Martin Wight, 'The balance of power', in Herbert Butterfield and Martin Wight (eds), *Diplomatic Investigations*, pp. 149–175 and 'The Balance of Power and International Order', in Alan James (ed.), *The Bases of International Order: Essays in Honour of C. A. W. Manning* (London: Oxford University Press, 1973), pp. 85–115.

17. Martin Wight, *Systems of States*, edited by Hedley Bull (Leicester: Leicester University Press, 1977), pp. 153–173.

18. Wight, *International Theory*, p. 268.

19. Harold J. Laski, *An Introduction to Politics*, revised edition by Martin Wight (London: Allen & Unwin, 1951).

20. See especially Martin Wight, 'Christian Pacifism', *Theology* 33(193) (1936), pp. 12–21.

21. Wight, 'Western Values', pp. 93–95.

22. See Martin Wight, 'The power struggle within the United Nations', *Proceedings of the Institute of World Affairs*, 33rd session (Los Angeles, CA: University of Southern California, 1956), pp. 247–259.

23. Wight, 'Why is there no International Theory?', p. 45.

24. There is a debate about how politically-engaged Wight was. Some think he disavowed all interest in practical politics (see, for example, Michael Nicholson, 'The enigma of Martin Wight', *Review of International Studies*, 7(1) (1981), pp. 15–22, and for a more positive view, Robert Jackson, 'Martin Wight, international theory and the good life', *Millennium: Journal of International Studies* 19(2) (1990), pp. 261–272), while others note his involvement in a number of causes (see Hall, 'Martin Wight, western values, and the Whig tradition').

25. On C. A. W. Manning's international thought, see especially Hidemi Suganami, 'C. A. W. Manning and the study of International Relations',

Review of International Studies 27(1) (2001), pp. 91–107, and on Wight's views on this subject, see Hall, *International Thought of Martin Wight*, pp. 88–97.

26. Martin Wight, review of A. L. Rowse, *The Uses of History* and R. G. Collingwood, *The Idea of History, International Affairs* 23(4) (1947), pp. 575–577.

27. Robert Jackson, among others, has argued there are close similarities between Wight's thought on this subject, and that of his LSE colleague, the political philosopher Michael Oakeshott. See especially Jackson's *The Global Covenant: Human Conduct in a World of States* (Oxford: Oxford University Press, 2000) and his *Classical and Modern Thought on International Relations: From Anarchy to Cosmopolis* (New York: Palgrave, 2005).

33
John Rawls (1921–2002)

Huw L. Williams

1952 – Victoria Coach Station, London
Our scene is set on the London to Oxford bus, pulling out onto Buckingham Palace Road, where a gently mannered American, with large glasses and an open, friendly face, has been joined by a young man, who, among other things, really should cut his hair. The American has established that his travelling companion is an unreconstructed Marxist and that he has a throbbing bottom, courtesy of a slip, precipitated by him running for the bus. This, the American gentleman surmises, must account for the young man's brusqueness. The young man, for his part, has discovered he is sitting next to a political philosopher spending some time at Oxford, which he finds inspiring, despite his colleagues' tendency to fall asleep while he presents his work.[1] As we join the conversation, the American realizes why he recognizes the unpronounceable name of his fellow traveller's home town.

'Aberystwyth … isn't the University famous for International Politics?'

'Yes, the first department of its kind in the world. I expect they'll still be using that line in another fifty years! Much interest in the subject yourself?'

'Of course. When you've served in a war it rather focuses the mind on these issues.'[2]

'You've seen action, have you? Do you mind my asking what that was like?'

'Well, it would be enough to say that it changed my perspective on life altogether.'

'Do say, in what way?'

'For one thing it gives you a greater appreciation of the fragility and arbitrary nature of human life. Why I survived and others didn't, there's no telling. I might say *there but for the grace of God*, if only it hadn't shaken my faith to the core.'

293

'You are religious, are you?'

'Well I certainly was, before the war. I had intended to be a minister, but it is rather more difficult to maintain your faith in light of what we experienced.'

'I tend to agree with Marx on religion. But there we go, I tend to agree with Marx on most things ... And what else do you think the war taught you?'

'I'm not so sure it taught me anything specific, rather it encouraged me to look at the world in a different way. It certainly made me ask what it is that influences people to acquiesce to deeply unjust views of the world.'

'And do you have any answers yet?'

He smiles.

'Well, I'm working on it, in a way. One conclusion I've come to is that it is imperative for us to think through what we can reasonably hope for in a just society. Without a clear sense of what that might be, it just seems far too easy for us to lose our way morally, and create political orders that are anything but just. It is unjust regimes in particular that not only cause misery and suffering for their own people, but are most likely to bring the great evil of war into the world. If we can reason properly about what a just and unjust society is, and make it clear so that citizens can understand what proper moral, political standards are, then we may stand a better chance of keeping dangerous ideologies at bay. And who knows, if there are enough of these moral orders, then maybe even peace is possible in the long run.'

'So you don't think international politics is defined by its particular structure or a particular conception of mankind? Rather that it rests on the internal order of states?'

'To a large degree, yes. Personally I'm rather inspired by Kant's vision of international politics, and the idea that an ever increasing federation of likeminded states can form the basis for a moral and peaceful international order.'

'Not exactly a good time to try and make an argument like that, is it?'

'Is there ever a good time to be talking about the transformation of political reality? I'm sure you would agree that if everyone took that attitude, I doubt very much you and I would be sitting here talking the way that we are, having benefited from a university education.'

'Very true. So tell me what you've got in mind in terms of articulating this concept of a just society. I'm not sure it's the best time to be trying something like that either. Hasn't Wittgenstein told us that philosophy should leave everything as it is?'

'Well, I'm not so sure that this latest type of philosophy leaves no space for changing things.'

'How so? Do tell. The idea of a Marxist interpretation of Wittgenstein rather excites me!'

'Well, I wouldn't go that far. But my sense is that as a political philosopher one thing I can do is try to articulate certain values and feelings that are implicit in our everyday lives and our everyday language, so to speak. That is to say, it seems obvious to me that we have certain ideas about what justice means, and a philosopher can try and identify and articulate these ideas in the most reasoned and convincing way possible – make it clear to us all what we have in mind when we talk of a just society, and hold these ideas up as moral norms that politicians and citizens should aspire to.'

'So what you are saying is that political philosophy doesn't have to be talking "nonsense", as some would have it, but that it can work at identifying and making clear to us the values we already have? That doesn't sound very revolutionary to me.'

'Well, not everyone wants revolution! I admit, I'm no Marxist, but I believe that the sense of justice that is part of our political culture is one that has in it deep egalitarian tendencies, both in terms of equality of rights and equality of resources. If we are able to articulate the everyday sentiments that are implicit in our common understanding then we not only make clear what they are, they actually serve as normative goals for our society. So simply by making sense of our political world and our political culture we provide the foundation for change and reform, even if this is not our explicit aim.'

'Ok, so how do you plan on articulating this idea of justice?'

'Well, I haven't thought it through in detail as yet, but my starting point is that when we talk about politics and concepts of justice we're talking about a realm of morality, and so our approach to thinking about them should reflect our moral philosophy as a whole. Now as I've been suggesting, I'm not averse to the idea of beginning with the implicit normative ideas we hold about the world – let's call them our "considered judgements". What we should be aiming for are theories that allow us to articulate and also evaluate these judgements. Bring out, as it were, what we really think justice is, for example – but in a critical way so that we don't just accept our inherited ideas but apply our own reason to them.'

'Sounds like you're stealing from Aristotle. You know, that idea about *endoxa* – that we should begin with the inherited ideas of our forbearers.'

'Yes, I can see that. If that helps you get a sense of what I'm trying to say. But I'm not sure I'd be "stealing" – I mean isn't that why we read great philosophers, for inspiration?'

'In which case we don't really need to look further than Marx ... Anyway, just to recap, what you're aiming to come up with is a theory of justice that takes these considered judgements as a reference point, tries to formulate them systematically, and do so in a critical way that ensures we've produced something that isn't merely an ideological reification of our inherited beliefs, but something that reflects our own rational reconstruction of these ideas.'

'Rather eloquently put, may I say.'

'I have my moments.'

He shuffles uncomfortably in his seat.

'Ok, so I think I'm following ... what's this theory going to look like?'

'Well, I only have a few broad ideas at the moment, but as we're discussing it, maybe I can try them out on you?'

'Please, go ahead. In for a penny, in for pound.'

'Well what you've got to imagine is a sort of social contract scenario.'

'How predictable.'

'Not Marxist enough I suppose ...?'

'Precisely.'

A deep breath.

'Well, you have a group of people who've come together to decide on the terms for their society, and we construct the situation so that the resulting principles are ones that reflect our sense of justice. These people have no idea who they are, or where they are placed in society, so this encourages them to create rules that ensure they have enough freedom and resources to pursue the life they wish to lead. It's basically fair because they can't skew circumstances to fit their own particular preferences.'

'You're expecting entirely ignorant people to make decisions about the founding principles for our society?'

'We're not talking about *real* people. This is a theory, remember, that we want to be in equilibrium with our everyday understanding of justice. Think of it as a thought experiment that tries to model the way we think about justice. So each person is rational in a self-interested way and wants to ensure that the set-up favours them – they have the basic facts about their society – and everyone wants a decent chance of doing what they want to do. But then the fact they don't know where they'll be in society captures the way in which we have a basic sense of fraternity – rational self-interest is circumscribed by the collective idea that everyone merits a basic chance at fulfilling their ambitions. Protecting everyone's rights and resources in this way is an expression of the idea that society is a collective project for mutual advantage.'

The young man, for once, seems to be deep in thought, his pulsating posterior now accompanied by a pain in his brain.

'This contract you're dreaming up ...'

'I was actually thinking of calling it the *General Position*. And perhaps the individuals will be behind a *curtain of ignorance*.'

'Hmm, not very original. Perhaps we should draw a veil over those suggestions ... Anyway, it reminds me rather of the way my brothers and I would settle the distribution of cake. Whoever held the knife and did the division would be the last to select their piece of cake. Not knowing which piece you'd get would ensure a fair cut.'

Another pregnant pause.

'How about this? Rather than these rather prosaic terms like *General Position* you could call it something rather more catchy. *Cake Theory*. That would definitely get you published.'

The American pauses, obviously trying to choose his words carefully.

'It's not that I don't like it, but I think the idea you have there is not quite the same. That is to say, with the cake, you have a pretty good idea already what a fair outcome should be, and you've created a procedure to ensure that outcome. In trying to ensure social justice we're dealing with a very complex situation where you can't predict what an explicitly fair outcome is in the same way. In other words, we're creating a procedure that we can agree is fair without knowing the exact outcome it will produce. Pure procedural justice, if you like.'

'Well, that seems overly complicated to me ... I'm telling you, if you think in terms of brothers fighting over cake you're halfway there. Do you have brothers?'

'Two, as it happens.'

'Sisters?'

'No', he sighs, 'I did have two other brothers but I'm afraid they died when we were young.'

'I am sorry, that's terribly sad.'

'Yes. Unfortunately they both died from diseases they contracted from me.'

The young man, for once, seems lost for words.

'That must have been terribly difficult to come to terms with.'

'I don't know if one does. It lives with me every day.'

'I'm sure. It must have affected you deeply.'

'Yes. I suppose, as with war, one gets a sense of the fragility and arbitrary nature of life. You question why some suffer and others don't, why some are lucky and others are not, why some are born into some circumstances and not others, what we mean by people getting their just desserts ...'

His voice trails away. After a long silence the young man moves the conversation on.

'So those selecting the principles, what do they come up with?'

'Well, I haven't formulated a final version yet, but I'm assuming there'll be the two.'

'Just the two?!'

'Well, I think a couple of well framed principles of justice can capture what is important in such a theory. Firstly they would want a primary principle, with precedence over the other, securing their basic liberties – freedom of body, mind, faith and so forth. Those freedoms that secure a personal sphere of action protected from others and the state. The second, I imagine, would be some combination that would provide them with a real chance to move on in life and pursue their own idea of the good life – my thought is that you'd need equality of opportunity, so everyone can compete for the same roles in society if they wish and are capable of doing so. You'd also need a distribution of resources that allows even the worst off a real chance of trying for these opportunities.'

The young man pauses, and for the second time he has a think. He would make a Communist of this American yet.

'So, these principles of yours; they're aiming at mitigating the contingencies of life. They're looking to ensure the basic liberties and resources of all individuals. So why are they the basis for a social contract for only one society? By your own lights this original position should apply to everyone in the world. I mean it's not some poor fellow's fault if they're born in the colonies, or some former colony, which has suffered under the Imperial hand of Britain. And surely he's got the same basic needs and rights as we have? It seems to me we need to be looking at a world order where everyone has the same liberties and resources.'

'I'm not sure it's that simple ... regrettably it's only a handful of years since we've been butchering each other. Overturning the states system and instigating a transnational egalitarian society seems a little farfetched, don't you think?'

'Well, we need goals to aim at; otherwise we'll only stay still, and the main point is that by your own rationale the extension of the principles to the entire world is what your theory dictates. I think you have misunderstood yourself, old chap.'

'I wouldn't disagree with your first point, but these goals need to be congruent with reality. I suppose in principle it would be ideal for every person to have the same rights and resources, but the international context is a different one to the domestic context – a different moral realm, if you like, where different circumstances prevail and different moral reasoning and considered judgements are relevant. So, as for misunderstanding myself, I'm a little less convinced, I'm afraid.'

'Well do share your vision.'

'I wouldn't say I have a particular vision as such, but as I say, I think political philosophy must speak to our present condition to be of any use or validity, and I don't think international politics is an exception – even if the motivation to address its destructive elements is even more pressing. In that sense I feel the same approach must apply: we should look to a theory for the international realm that speaks to our considered judgements, and elucidates a vision that presents us with a sense of justice that we see as fitting in this context. In that case I'd tend to think it would be representatives that would be in an international general position, agreeing on principles for the relations between states.'

'So, no world state, no global government or utopian order?'

'Well, as you said, we need something to aim at, so there should always be an element of utopianism, and I think any ideas about politics that posit some moral values are always utopian, as they will never be *entirely* reflected by or realized in reality. It's about identifying those utopian values that are *realistic* and broadly attainable – and as I was saying before, constructing a theory that's in equilibrium with our considered thinking on the subject today. If you look at recent efforts with the United Nations and the Universal Declaration of Human Rights, I'd say there's plenty of utopian elements that can be agreed upon – those principles might even be too utopian. And maintaining a society of states doesn't mean we can't aim at these ideals and attain something better.'

'How can you say that when we've seen what they're capable of?'

'But isn't that essentializing the nature of states? Surely as a human construct they are as liable to change and reform as any other part of our social lives? If we can think of states in a moral way, as expressions of political communities with conceptions of justice that ensure they function properly and to the benefit of their citizens – surely if we can conceive of this we should and can work towards it? As I said before, if we can construct domestic orders that are just, or at least reasonable and peaceable, then a lasting peace is a real possibility.'

'I can see why you're a fan of Kant ...'

'Absolutely – I'm more than happy to steal his ideas in this regard, as you so generously put it! That said, I'm not entirely convinced that we must aim at a federation of *republican* peoples. I wonder if a domestic order that has a public, political conception of justice that respects all individuals is sufficient. I mean to say, not all societies have the same emphasis on individualism and egalitarianism, but so long as they provide a minimum of freedom – and allow people to leave – then you've got a decent chance of creating a reasonable, morally aware state. Enough of these and you might avoid war, so long as liberal states live by their own principles and tolerate other types of reasonable political orders.'

It's the young man's turn for a deep breath. One more try.

'Ok, I can see that just domestic orders, or decent ones, might promote a just global order, but what about inequalities of wealth and the relative suffering in some parts compared to others? Surely that undermines stability, and doesn't it create some sort of obligation on behalf of richer states – especially those who have exploited poorer parts of the world – to help out and ensure more resources? If your principles don't apply to individuals, surely we should apply them to states in some sort of way – ensure they have equality of opportunity and resources, as it were. Don't you think your representatives would want a distributive principle?'

'You're not inclined to let things go, are you!'

'I can't help it. I'm a born radical. In the blood you see.'

'Well, you may think I'm just an old fashioned, stuck-in-the-mud conservative, but it just seems inconceivable to me that you apply ideas and principles of redistributive, social justice, to a realm of relatively discrete sovereign bodies. That's not to deny that the domestic and international are closely woven together – for one thing you need a just world order to guarantee freedom and rights in the domestic realm. And it's not to deny either that there is extensive economic interaction, or that states' actions impact on each other in this sense. But if we are going to think about ensuring all states have enough resources and capabilities to be stable and protect the interests of their citizens, we have to think about issues other than fiscal assistance and the like.'

'So just leave everything as it is, is it? Let the weak of the world fall prey to the will of the strong and allow economic exploitation and domination to continue?'

'Well, of course not. There are some aspects of economic interaction in the international realm that are amenable to and demand the creation of laws and regulations that create a level playing field, of course. And as we've seen with the Marshall Plan, there is always a place for special measures and aid to help countries build or rebuild themselves. But think about what is being aimed for there, and I'd suggest applying it globally. One is not looking to instigate a form of transnational welfarism where the elite, economically dominant few provide the pennies for the dominated and powerless majority. That would be as problematic as a welfare state where the productive assets are in the hands of the few. You want to create self-sufficient, robust states that have the political institutions not just to support a just or decent way of life, but to allow the political community to be economically robust with a certain level of capability. States are self-sustaining in a way that just doesn't apply with individuals and our thinking should reflect that. Neither should we divide our thinking about the economy from that of politics. Politically robust, fair and just states will likely be states that are transparent, democratic and thriving enough to stand on their own feet and be productive in their own ways. Yes, I'm sure we could articulate a duty of justice of some sort, but that would be for assistance, not permanent redistribution. A world where certain countries constantly redirect some of their wealth to other countries is surely one that will be riddled with genuine inequality and dependency.'

The young man's head and bottom are now throbbing equally. Luckily for him they are pulling up to the bus station in Oxford. It is all he can do to muster up some sort of reply, and part on amicable terms.

'Well, it looks like we've arrived.' He senses a little relief in the American's voice.

'It's been good to chat. If you think you're up to being dragged across the coals once more I'll be at the Rose & Crown tonight – my uncle and his band have a set there. You might like it – inspired by some American music, he claims.'

'That's kind of you, although I'm not sure I'll make it. I'm rather tired and have a bit to think about after our discussion. It's been an education – truly.'

'Glad to be of assistance. And remember, if you're going to get anywhere with your ideas, you need a better name. Like I say, cake theory, or even better, A Theory of Cake.'

'I'll give it some thought … But you don't think A Theory of Justice captures it?'

'With a name like that, your work will never catch on.'

Notes

1. A story including HLA Hart that Rawls recounted publically.
2. See Thomas Pogge, *John Rawls: His Life and Theory of Justice* (Cambridge: Polity Press, 2007) for these stories and other biographical detail.

34
The Spirit of Susan Strange (1923–1998)

Louis W. Pauly

Friends, colleagues and students of Susan Strange gather every year at the annual meeting of the International Studies Association. It has long seemed to me that she haunts the meeting, where to this day an award in her name is regularly given to 'a person whose singular intellect, assertiveness, and insight most challenge conventional wisdom and intellectual and organizational complacency in the international studies community'. In 2015, the meeting was held in New Orleans, just after the Mardi Gras celebrations. Although I may have enjoyed a bit too much bourbon the night before the meeting began, I swear she returned for a long chat.[1]

Lou: I knew you wouldn't miss this ISA meeting! You always enjoyed a good party.

Susan: It's true, but there has been no shortage in my new digs.

Lou: So you ended up in the good place.

Susan: A double surprise. I really did think that a final good-bye meant lights-out, and I was hardly an angel during my terrestrial time. After I got my bearings and cast off my natural scepticism, which was not easy to do, the key was to charm St. Peter. Piece of cake.

Lou: How did you do it?

Susan: I asked him questions about himself, about what he had learned, about what he thought about all manner of things. But I especially asked him to educate me about who got what in this new life and how we might make things a bit better. Men are so easy to steer. St. Peter remains an incurable romantic who enjoys being taken seriously.

Lou: Even after all of these years, even after all the trouble you once caused at an ISA meeting by calling on women to stop complaining and get on with their work, you still dabble in gender stereotypes?

Susan: I remain convinced that women are more realistic and better able to adapt to changing situations. I also remain fascinated by the life of the mind men idealize, by the 'theories' you dream up and consider so important and exclusive, by your dreams of utopia. Women, especially ex-journalists and mothers – I had six children, know what really matters.

Lou: What really matters?

Susan: Making hay while the sun shines.

Lou: Come on, you were a serious scholar of international relations, a pioneer in the field of international political economy, and a great critic of established orthodoxies.

Susan: That doesn't mean one shouldn't have fun. I enjoyed disturbing the peace, and I especially enjoyed irritating people who thought they wielded power, especially so-called intellectual power.

Lou: Why did your targets continue talking with you? And why did so many become your friends?

Susan: Long ago I discovered that it was better to tame dragons than to slay them. Make the gatekeepers friends. Better to have them open the gate willingly than to have to break it down. Acknowledging one's own imperfections, of course, is a helpful complementary strategy.

Lou: Sounds like you are beginning to recall your principal method of research in your chosen fields.

Susan: You are right about that. Ask big questions, identify a real problem, find the people who can help you figure it out, and go talk to them. Most importantly, however, pay more attention to what decision-makers do than to what they say. Read what others have written. Doubt conventional answers. Question authority. Avoid grand theory. Use your intuition to seek your own counter-intuitive answers. Look beneath the surface of things, but don't ever pretend that you have found the Truth – at least until you get past St. Peter's gate.

Lou: I think you anticipated the 'practice turn' in social theory that has only recently penetrated IR and IPE.

Susan: My practice was to avoid the kind of abstraction that many of my friends over the Channel enjoyed.

Lou: Your own analytical approach led you to anticipate the monetary and financial mess the world finds itself in. In *Casino*

Capitalism, published in 1986, you predicted repeated and ever-larger financial crises on a global scale. In 1998, *Mad Money* starkly concluded that finance calling the tune meant the subservience of real economies, an accelerating loss of control by states over the economies and societies they still claimed to govern, the inexorable concentration of power in border-spanning corporations, an associated rise in corruption as firms sought policy favours everywhere they operated, and vastly increased economic inequality.

Susan: Given my current position, I will resist my humanly temptation to claim much credit. Maynard Keynes, Karl Polanyi, Charles Kindleberger, Hyman Minsky, Fred Hirsch, Jacques Polak and any economic historian not blinded by ideology had a sense that this was coming. Only the 'grand theorists' of economics and international relations missed it.

Lou: Your modesty seems excessive to me. You were way ahead of your time, not least in writing so much about the subject in remarkably accessible language.

Susan: I will accept the compliment and challenge the next generation of scholars to do better.

Lou: If a young scholar wanted to take you as a role model, what should he or she do?

Susan: Get lucky.

Lou: Anything more specific?

Susan: Study with professors who want students not to be disciples but to think for themselves; get experience as a journalist; get more experience writing about policy at a place like Chatham House; find a mentor like Andrew Shonfield; ask questions in an area where dynamic change is underway but scholarly views are not yet fixed (in my case, the international monetary system at a time when the Bretton Woods arrangements were falling apart); go to ISA meetings and meet people with whom you disagree; and *never* retire but do what you can to open up a salary line for the next generation.

Lou: No regrets?

Susan: A few, but only one that you know about. Don't be so driven, so concerned to make the most of your brief life, that you ignore what your body is telling you. Early diagnosis of unusual pains can sometimes lead to effective treatments. As St. Peter reminded me, I could have had another ten years.

Still, I had a good and exciting life on your side of the great divide, and it is really lovely on the other side.

Lou: I suppose we could call that divide a structure. That brings me to your best-remembered contribution to IPE during its early days, your analysis of structural power at the global level. What were you getting at?

Susan: A segue from the sublime to the banal; but OK if you want to go there. By the mid-1980s, I came to the conclusion that the field called International Relations, with its great love of abstract systemic theories, was missing the boat. The great debate between so-called neo-realists and neo-liberals seemed to me like Herman Hesse's *Glass Bead Game*: fascinating only for over-educated academics who spent their lives in quiet seminar rooms on leafy campuses but irrelevant for students who wanted to understand what was really happening in the world. Particularly irritating for me was the commonplace idea that American 'hegemony' was declining, and with it the prospects for future world order. I know this irritated my friend Kindleberger too, but one of your colleagues is interviewing him for this book, so I'll let him explain his own misgivings.

Lou: What were yours?

Susan: I conceded that, ever since the war, changes had occurred in the relational power of the United States. Certainly I found this quite evident when I observed bilateral relationships over the decades. I had seen such changes clearly over many years, and wrote about it in my journalistic work, eventually culminating in 1971 in my first book, *Sterling and British Policy*. Structural power, though, was something quite different. To discern it, one had to look beneath the surface of things. This entailed a certain way of looking at the world, one that couldn't be taught as a parsimonious theory or simplistic paradigm. My 1988 textbook, *States and Markets*, was designed to introduce students to IPE, not as a master discipline, and certainly not as a sub-field of IR, but as an open-ended framework for the analysis of power as it actually manifests itself. I wanted them to observe the world around them, think for themselves, and argue with one another. Specifically, I wanted them to puzzle over the fact that power defined in relational terms was obviously spreading and dispersing internationally, but that the international economy was not coming apart – to the consternation of proponents of theories of hegemonic decline. I wanted them to open their minds to the possibility that deeper structures of power were simultaneously eroding the traditional prerogatives of territorial states but binding together national, regional and trans-regional markets, now often dominated by large business firms. To understand that system accurately termed global corporate capitalism, and the still-extraordinary role of the United States and American corporations within it, my central argument focused on four principal structures: the structures of security, finance, production and knowledge. They all interact to create the 'rules of the game', the game that students might reasonably expect to shape their own lives, for better or for worse.

Lou: Structure remains a slippery word. How did you define it?

Susan: With common sense. Deeper forces pushing and pulling readily-observable political struggles. Underlying social arrangements – reflecting organizing values, interests and ideologies – that shape the political actions and interactions of human beings. Structural power makes invisible the social forces underneath.

Lou: What specifically did you have in mind when you spoke about structure?

Susan: A particular type of structure, the one I observed from various angles all my life. A hierarchy of power. And my image was the image of a pyramid, specifically a four-sided pyramid.

Lou: David Lake wrote a book on hierarchy in international relations after you died.

Susan: Yes, I know. Focusing on 'exchange' between something he calls 'dyads', the book annoyed me from the moment it arrived in the celestial library.

Lou: Why? He is a clear thinker and elegant writer.

Susan: Aside from exemplifying a typically bloodless American academic approach to issues of domination and subordination, nowhere in its 232 pages will you find Susan Strange cited!

Lou: Well, he does take a bow in your direction in the preface.

Susan: Right. Where he says, 'Some readers will undoubtedly find my account of international hierarchy insufficiently social'.[2] No kidding.

Lou: So give us a deeper sense of what you personally thought about the implications of structural power.

Susan: Have you ever been to a casino?

Lou: Yes, but only to play the slots.

Susan: Then you know that the machines, like the house as a whole, cannot lose over the long run. Contemporary financial markets are casinos that are underwritten by the states. States provide their stock-in-trade, money. Their rationale for doing so is to sustain real economies, but the casinos have become ends in themselves. The croupiers are taking home the proceeds, and their ability to do so is reinforced by three other main structures: the global production, security and knowledge structures. No one forces you to lay down a bet inside a casino. But visitors soon find themselves tempted into playing games over which they have no real control.

Lou: Do you think the casinos can persist?

Susan: Not for long, but I see that as an empirical question. When I was a girl, the casinos did collapse. But they did not do so during the global financial crisis of 2007–9. For the time being, those four power structures are durable – but that does not mean forever. And it certainly does not mean that life inside the casino is pleasant or fair.

Lou: Can it be made more pleasant and fairer?

Susan: A belief is still commonly shared among those showered during their earthly lives with what my new friends call 'blessings'. It is the belief that the wielding of all instruments of coercion, from military to financial, can and should be subject to a certain degree of control by legitimate and accountable political authorities. They commonly consider the measurement of just such degrees of control to be the measurement of the quality of the human condition. As my Gramscian colleagues explain, ideology can mask the loss of control and obscure deterioration in the local and global communities within which human beings actually live. As one of my oldest friends Bob Cox famously said, such a mask can be called a theory, and theory always serves someone and some purpose.

Lou: Do you simply mean she who has the power makes the rules?

Susan: No need for political correctness around me; I was a proto-feminist. Not many 'shes' really had power when I started my career. But to the point, your formulation is too instrumental. In fact, Max Weber and I were discussing this just the other day. He still thinks that a sense of legitimacy differentiates authority from power: the two-sided belief that the wielder of power in any and all of its forms is entitled to command and that the recipients of commands have an obligation to comply.

I tend to agree with him that might makes right only in the short run but that right makes a deeper kind of might in the long run. In any event, the distinction is key to understanding the social and political implications of deep structural change.

Lou: Like changes in financial markets?

Susan: Yes, just like the pecuniary developments I closely observed when I was a less spiritual person.

Lou: But you were always spirited.

Susan: I enjoyed my spirits, but only when shared with friends.

Lou: OK, then, let's go back to the casino where those spirits are plentiful and talk about the actual machinery of international finance that your notion of 'structure' evoked.

Susan: Fine. In my early studies of the International Monetary Fund, I did try to describe the mechanics employed in attempting to tame international finance in the post-1945 period. Regulation was possible! I could have claimed that it failed miserably, but I was open-minded. (Pause.) Yes, I was. Don't look askance! Well, at least I was a still-hopeful, if slightly disappointed, scholar inspired by Keynes. I noted that during its infancy the IMF – the supposed arbiter of a fixed but flexible exchange-rate system in a world of segmented and nationally regulated financial markets – was simply placed on ice by the United States. It might have been thawed and revived someday! Alas, by the early 1970s, its time had passed and the post-war monetary system was overwhelmed by resurgent market forces. In other words, myopic American policy preferences swept away all plausible alternatives. I know, Americans of all stripes still like to imagine themselves as reluctant nannies facing unpleasant trade-offs, but really, they didn't even try.

Lou: We might argue about that, and certain other teachers of mine might evoke the notion of 'domestic structures' binding policymakers in the United States and elsewhere. But I'm interviewing you and not them. So, please go ahead.

Susan: You interrupted my train of thought.

Lou: There is a first time for everything. I think you were about to explain how the Keynesian spirit, faint as it was by the mid-1970s, finally left the American body-politic.

Susan: Right. We are all shaped by our youthful experiences, and mine left me with a deep interest in the implications of international finance for democratic systems of government. Related questions became urgent later in my life as many elements of a truly global economy began to come together. Big banks and multinational corporations were more than symbolic of that economy, which is why my research, especially with my business-school colleague John Stopford, came to focus upon them.

Lou: And the questions motivating the research that led you and Stopford to publish *Rival States, Rival Firms?*

Susan: What did the rise of a new global financial and managerial elite – increasingly freed from the obligations of local civil societies – mean for the stability of a system resting on the structural power of the United States, one supported by the willing deference of key followers? John Ruggie claimed that the post-war system reflected the compromise of embedded liberalism – open markets resting on the stabilizing capacities of democratic welfare states. What Stopford and I discovered instead was disembedded liberalism – global corporations on the move, eroding their own social foundations, and devastating a border-spanning physical environment incapable of protecting itself.

Lou: Are you a Marxist?

Susan: No, Marx over-thought the subject. My recommendation was just to look around, sense the presence of power and follow the money as you ask the central questions: Who rules through what structures, and in whose interest do they rule? My longtime friend and occasional sparring-partner, Jerry Cohen, drew a couple of helpful distinctions in *The Geography of Money*, to which I literally gave my last puff. Like other things, the price of money is determined by demand and supply. On the demand side, there is a profound contemporary blurring of the nature of monetary power within many states and among most. On the supply side, however, the world moved from multipolar to unitary, and is now again becoming more multipolar. In emergencies, like the one experienced between 2007 and 2009, the United States still had the power to stabilize an increasingly fragile system. But the long-run drift is toward a less US-centered and even less state-centred system, and for a future financial emergency to be unmanageable. Not for nothing did James Carville, an astute student of power, dream of coming back from the dead not as a president but as the global bond market.

Lou: So are you saying that at long last the erstwhile advocates of the thesis of declining American hegemony are right?

Susan: Ah, the Ozymandias question. Eventually they will be right, everything in your world ends someday. But I am not yet ready to go that far. The United States still has vast if varying degrees of structural power in each of the four areas I highlighted before. The entire pyramid, however, now rests on shifting sand. Globalization, in its various guises, is eroding the unique kind of systemic authority once claimed by the United States. At the same time, allies and followers are being shocked out of their passivity by the ineptitude, arrogance and self-righteousness of America's leaders.

Lou: I think you were riding this particular hobby-horse many years ago.

Susan: Guilty as charged. Always fascinated by power, I sought every opportunity to get close to it, to study it, and even to try and influence those who had it. That meant staying close to Americans ever since my time in Washington in the 1950s writing for *The Observer*. To tell you the truth, I became quite sick of the bull-headedness of the many American power-wielders I got to know over the years in both policy and academic circles. Even into the 1980s, however, I saw no alternative to American leadership. I confess to losing hope before I slipped the surly bonds of Earth, first because of the corrupting influence to what used to be called moneyed interests inside American society, and second because of my research on the changing and increasingly de-centered global corporate economy.

Lou: Eventually, you came to describe the result as the 'Westfailure system'. What did you mean by that?

Susan: For my old IR professors, for the old-before-their-time neorealists, and for the still-walking-around Henry Kissinger, a political system based on territorially defined and delimited states was and is foundational. Sovereignty, no higher authority, anarchy, self-help, voluntary inter-state cooperation at most. Bollocks! Blind, misguided faith in a past that never existed and can in no way comprehend what is really happening today. Back to my pyramid. At most, a security structure dominated by states forms only one side. It cannot stand on its own, which is why I considered IPE superior to IR and not the other way around. Global, not inter-national, structures of production, finance and knowledge keep the pyramid standing. But the symbiosis of a security system based on territorial states coupled with an economic system based on globalizing markets was a transient phenomenon. It was a product of the unique position of the United States in the late twentieth century. Four obvious failures now confront those I left behind: the failure to control the proliferation of horrifying weapons, the failure to sustain a stable system of credit-creation, the failure to protect a physical environment conducive to the health of the human species, and the failure to create a more equitable social system capable of fostering global political stability.

Lou: What can be done about it?

Susan: Pray.

Lou: I never thought I'd hear you say that. Anything else – please!

Susan: Here's a clue: What if global markets are really just tables at the casino, where at least the possibility of iterated, non-zero-sum games is replaced by the certainty that each game is rigged and, in the long-run, that only the house can win? And what if the owners of the house are becoming what the marvellous Chrystia Freeland, who reminds me of myself, has called a new class of plutocrats – more numerous than their predecessors in the gilded age, a new class essentially accountable to no one but itself, and with technocrats at various levels of governance essentially responsible to it?[3]

Lou: What?

Susan: We may not be quite there yet, and booming markets have a tendency to shroud such questions, and even to push them off the public agenda entirely. But busting markets may be counted upon to bring them back. Before my exit from your company, it became clear to me that so-called advanced countries and their citizens were already engaged in a struggle aimed at re-regulating global corporate markets. In other words, they were questioning how political authority could actually be reconstituted. The private face of structural power, wielded for self-regarding purposes, had become too obvious – and that was even before the names Adelson and Koch had become infamous! A political authority to make markets serve the interests of humanity at large is required, and it cannot be reconstructed inside old national boundaries.

Lou: What happens if it cannot be rebuilt?

Susan: Have your read Jared Diamond's *Collapse*?

Lou: Yes, but I recall a bit more optimism in your own thinking.

Susan: True. I'm still a mother, and mothers can't be pessimists. So let's just boil it all down. We are talking about values and preferences. The critical debates focus in on the quality of economic growth and not just its quantity, the purpose of production and not just its sources, the justice of market outcomes and not only their drivers. The basic problem in the world I left behind was that the traditional authority of the nation state was not up to the task of managing mad money, global corporations and rapid technological change. The leaders of those dying social and political structures, however, were not willing even to think about handing the job over to unelected, unaccountable, arrogant and myopic global bureaucrats. The students of my students need to help invent a new kind of polity, but they cannot yet imagine how it might work. I wish them the best of British.

Notes

1. It is uncanny how much our conversation reminded me of the published work she left behind. For a comprehensive overview, see Roger Tooze and Christopher May, eds, *Authority and Markets: Susan Strange's Writings on International Political Economy*, (Basingstoke, UK: Palgrave Macmillan, 2002).
2. David A. Lake, *Hierarchy in International Relations*, (Ithaca, NY: Cornell University Press, 2009), p. xi.
3. Chrystia Freeland, *Plutocrats*, (New York: Penguin, 2012).

35
Questioning Kenneth N. Waltz (1924–2013)

Adam Humphreys and Hidemi Suganami

Professor Hani Magus and Dr Umesh Harpy are in the midst of a viva. The candidate is Kenneth Waltz. His work turns out to be one of the most successful doctoral theses in the history of IR but the examiners are giving him a hard time. Some years later, the two examiners visit Professor Waltz, now a leading IR theorist, for an interview.

The viva

Harpy: So, Mr Waltz, your answers so far have clarified a number of ambiguities we found in your thesis. Still, one key question remains. On this, I should tell you, Professor Magus and I have differing interpretations; so you must tell us which of us has got it right. The question is this: what *are* you saying? [*Professor Magus looks alarmed by his colleague's bluntness.*] Is it (1) that there are three places where we can look for the causes of war – man, the state and the international system – and that they are *equally important*; or (2) that, of the three places, the third one is *the most important*. My interpretation is that the thesis of your thesis, if I may put it that way, is the latter; you, Mr Waltz, are clearly a 'third-image' man, to use your own terminology. But Professor Magus thinks that you are arguing for (1), or at least that that is what you should be arguing for. Of course, it occurs to me now that you may be arguing something else; for example, that – and call this (3) – which of the three locations is the most important varies from one case to another. So what do you say, Mr Waltz? We really need to know.

Magus: Please don't feel we are cornering you, Mr Waltz. We do not demand one hundred per cent clarity or consistency; even the

313

best PhD theses I have examined over the years had many problems. We are really trying to find out where the balance lies in this very interesting work you have produced; is it, let's say, more about three different places where we may find important causes of war or is it more about the particular importance you find in the anarchic structure of the international system?

Waltz: Thank you. Let me begin by going back to one of your earlier questions and stress again that the choice is not between mono-causal analysis and multi-causal analysis. Explaining anything in terms of just one cause – well, that won't do and I am not advocating that at all. I am a multi-causal man. The question then is which of the many causes of war are the most important. Maybe there is some ambiguity in the thesis as I have presented it. But my thinking goes like this: (1) the three locations are all important but for different reasons, (2) we should appreciate the specific reason why each of the three locations is important, and (3) the reason why the third one, the anarchic structure of the international system, is an important cause of war is not often appreciated in current discussions about the causes of war and the conditions of peace.

Harpy: Mr Waltz, do you always think in three steps? Sorry, that's meant to be a joke.

Magus: Er ... yes, I think you are touching on something very important in what you've just said, Mr Waltz. So, please expand.

Waltz: Thank you. I assume that we all want to live in a more peaceful world. So, we discuss the conditions of peace but agree that we must first find the causes of war. That's sensible, in my view. But when we search for the causes of war, it is easy to be influenced by our preconceptions about what's wrong about the world, especially when such preconceptions suggest that the problems of the world can be remedied. I am aware of two very dominant preconceptions of this kind: Christian pacifism and liberal reformism.

Magus: I see; that's very interesting. Please go on.

Waltz: Well, if you are a Christian pacifist, you will say, 'There won't be any war if you all become like us: pacifists'. Or, if you are a liberal reformist, you will say, 'War will be fought less frequently if more countries of the world become more liberal – because war is after all an anathema to liberal values; it undermines them'. Under the influence of such doctrines, there is a general tendency, I reckon, to suppose that the main causes of war are to be found either in the way we are individually or in the way we are governed inside our states. I am not at all saying that these are stupid ideas. But we tend to forget one very crucial fact: no world peace can ever be permanent when all the states of the world live under anarchy, which is the state of war of all against all. Indeed, under such a system, there is a constant possibility of war – in other words, the system is inclined towards war, which may break out anywhere, at any time. My thinking therefore runs as follows: even though there are important causes of war to be found in 'man' and 'the state', we must pay more attention to 'the international system'; people come and go, states come and go, but as long as we live under international anarchy, we are stuck in the state of war; although one war might end, another will surely start.

Harpy: That's impressively eloquent.

Magus: Indeed, that clarifies a lot. And I did in fact notice an important discussion in the conclusion of your work. You don't always think in three steps but sometimes you invoke a dichotomy. I am thinking here of the distinction you draw between 'efficient' and 'permissive' causes of war. Am I right in thinking that this is very important in constructing your position?

Harpy: Sorry, I may have missed that point. Maybe you'd like to explain that, Mr Waltz.

Waltz: Professor Magus, I am very glad that the dichotomy attracted your attention. When I began my research and started reading a wide variety of theoretical works on international relations and war, I was struck by the fact that there is something common in these works: they all think of the world as comprising three layers – man, the states and the states-system. That's why I classified major theories of the causes of war into three kinds. But when, towards the end of my research, I began thinking for myself about the causes of war, I realized that there is an important distinction to draw between (1) what explains the outbreak of a particular war and (2) what makes perpetual peace an impossible dream and makes war a constant possibility. In other words, I thought that many theorists had missed an important distinction between what explains the *occurrence* of a *particular* war and what explains the *recurrence* of war. I intend to pursue this theme further at a later stage.

Anyway, what explains the *outbreak* of a particular war is, to put it simply, 'acts of states', which basically means things committed, or omitted, by individuals acting in the name of their states. These acts bring about a particular instance of war and they are therefore what I call 'efficient causes' of war. Being acts performed by individuals representing states, they are located at the levels of 'man' and 'the state'. But what explains the *recurrence* of war is the fact that there is nothing to stop states from fighting one another. This is what I call the 'permissive cause' of war and it is found in the anarchic structure of the international system. International anarchy is important because this is the one that *permits* war to happen anywhere, at any time; and this tends to be neglected by many people who reduce international phenomena to their particular instances. But I want to avoid that kind of reductionism and go for a structural explanation – bearing in mind, of course, that it's the acts of states, and therefore of statesmen, that force us to fight particular wars.

Magus: Well, as my colleague Dr Harpy said, you are impressively eloquent and, I must say, quite persuasive. There are a few issues, though, I feel you may need to clarify further to tighten your argument a bit. Let me just very tentatively indicate a few as they occur to me; they are not questions that you have to answer for now but you may want to think about them.

Harpy: Please, Professor Magus: do go ahead.

Magus: Well, you said you are thinking in terms of a dichotomy; but I am wondering if you may not be conflating two things in your argument. I mean, isn't there a difference between what you are calling – er, what was it? – the impossibility of perpetual peace and – er – what you were calling the recurrence of war? It seems to me, though I haven't yet thought this through, that there is a difference between something being *merely possible* and something *actually recurring*. And if you are saying that war is always a possibility because there is nothing to prevent it, why does this quality of there being 'nothing to prevent war', if I may put it that way, arise only in the international system and not, say, in human nature? I remain somewhat puzzled but, as I said, these are fairly complex issues …

[There is a moment's silence …]

Harpy: There you are, Mr Waltz; your work has certainly been very thought-provoking. Unless you wish to add anything to what you have already given us in your answers, or you have any thoughts on what Prof Magus is – er – wondering about, you may consider that we have completed our examination.

Waltz: Thank you. I have nothing to add to what I have said in my response to your earlier questions.

Magus: Very well, then; if you could leave the room for a while and wait in the lounge, one of us will come and collect you when we have reached a decision. Well done and see you in a while.

[*Waltz exits*]

Harpy: So, what would we say? A clear pass?

Magus: I suppose. He certainly is eloquent. All right; what if we said 'a clear pass' for now? But we advise him to consider some of the points I was raising at the end if he wants to publish his thesis as a book. We could write that into our report.

Harpy: Great. Let's call him in.

Late 1967. In Professor Waltz's office.

Harpy: Professor Waltz, you've become widely known for your arguments about the stability of the Cold War. I was struck by your confidence, so soon after the Cuban Missile Crisis, in describing the Cold War as stable. I am even more struck now by your claim that we'll miss it when it's over ...[1]

Magus: Indeed. I'm not sure I agree with that!

Harpy: ... but I'd like to talk about the extent to which you are now engaged in debates about domestic politics and how it influences US foreign policy. Does this mark a change of direction for you? After all, despite what I recall to be your insistence on multi-causal analysis, your thesis, later published of course as *Man, the State and War*, has very much given you a reputation as – er – how did we put it at the time ...

Magus: As a 'third-image' man.

Harpy: Right, as a third-image man or, as you might put it yourself, a structuralist.

Waltz: Well let me start by emphasizing the importance of your own phrase: multi-causal analysis. Because I wouldn't want anyone to think I'm a structural determinist: I'm not.[2] In the history of international political thought, the third image has largely been neglected. Rousseau, of course, understood its importance, but because it's a permissive, rather than an efficient cause, its importance is easily underestimated. And that applies in policy circles as much as it does in political philosophy: states that ignore the incentives created by the anarchic structure of the international system are liable to get themselves into trouble.

Harpy: This seems to lie at the heart of what you've been saying recently. In *Foreign Policy and Democratic Politics* you defend democratic governance and even defend the US political system as being particularly well set up for responsible foreign policy, but in your recent article 'The Politics of Peace' you're highly critical of US policy, most notably in Vietnam, and even suggest that a change of government might be required in order to extract the US. Could you explain your thinking?

Waltz: Yes indeed. The simple point we need to appreciate about the Vietnam war is that we can only understand what is at stake by thinking in third-image terms: we need to recognize that whatever outcome is reached it is not going to affect the global balance of power. What then, is the US interest in it? I believe that international politics sets traps for the powerful. When survival is no longer on the line it is easy to forget that the dangers remain constant: this is why we need to focus more on the third-image. Of course, I've argued that bipolarity is stable, but it is stable only if the superpowers recognize the incentives confronting them. President Johnson, like Wilson and Hoover before him, desires, though in different ways, to control the world. This can't be done and even if it could it would be dangerous. Can we always be sure that the leaders of strong states will be wise? And if they claim to act in defence of justice, how is justice to be objectively defined?

Magus: I share some of your concerns here. If we live in a pluralist world, how indeed is justice to be objectively defined? But I'd like to understand the logic of what you're saying more fully. You argue that the anarchic structure of the international system, which is what third-image analysis is concerned with, creates incentives for states …

Waltz: … and those incentives are clearest for two states which far overshadow any other …

Magus: ... Absolutely. But my point is that despite your insistence about the incentives anarchy creates, states, even powerful states, can still act foolishly ...

Waltz: Exactly. That's the danger we face at the moment. That's why I'm concerned about the present direction of US policy.

Magus: Well it's certainly a very suggestive framework for thinking about US policy: it is, how should I put it ...

Harpy: Heuristically powerful?

Magus: Well it's certainly thought provoking. But my question is about the relationship between the first and third images. If anarchy is as powerful as you suggest, Professor Waltz, what is the likely consequence of a state, even a state as powerful as the US, acting foolishly?

Waltz: Well, it is likely to be punished. It will suffer the consequences.

Harpy: But who can punish a state as powerful as the US?

Magus: Dr Harpy asks a good question. And I think the problem is quite a deep one. After all, even if the US is not so powerful as to prevent a balancing coalition from being formed, the formation of such a balancing coalition would surely require that other states respond rationally to the incentives created for them? But if the US can be foolish – and I am right, aren't I, to read you as suggesting that US policy in Vietnam *is* foolish? – surely other states can be foolish too? In other words, doesn't the operation of structural incentives depend on – one might say that it is reducible to – the choices of states and statesmen?

Waltz: You're right to suggest that all three images are in a sense intertwined: as I've argued previously, they are lenses on a more complex reality. But I still think it's helpful to treat the system level on its own merits and to ask what incentives it creates. One can certainly never cater for the actions of a Hitler or the reactions of a Chamberlain.[3] But luckily we are not just relying on the right man (or even woman) being in the right place at the right time. Given the mutual antagonism between the superpowers, the US cannot risk getting it wrong and sensible people recognize that. It is not just an external pressure but it enters into how we think and, I hope, will shape who we elect next year. One of the virtues of a bipolar world is that the incentives it creates are so clear. That, at least, is something to be thankful for.

Harpy: That's very interesting. Your implicit acknowledgement that we always have to work with a partial picture is, I think, very

	important. But listening to you now highlights to me something I've wondered for a while: to what extent is your position at heart an ethical one?
Waltz:	What do you mean?
Harpy:	Well, it seems to me that part of your argument is that it is foolish for the US to become entangled in Vietnam because doing so goes against the structural incentives, and I think Prof Magus is right to ask where those structural incentives emerge from. But you also seem to suggest that some wars are more acceptable than others and, moreover, that that, too, reflects the anarchic structure of the international system. In other words, we all want to live in a more peaceful world, but you recognize that, anarchy being, as you would put it, a permissive cause of war, some wars are unavoidable: states have to defend themselves. But that also means that some wars are avoidable: they are wars of choice, perhaps pursued with good intentions, but avoidable nonetheless.
Waltz:	Absolutely. That is where anarchy creates a trap. In the absence of any higher authority, who is to say which wars of choice are justified and which are not? The danger of seeking to set the world to rights is that it does more harm than good. Where national interests are not at stake, what is to guide us?
Harpy:	Do you wish, then, to give us a theory of the national interest, or perhaps of US national interests?
Waltz:	No, or at least not yet. [*Waltz glances at his pocket-watch.*] Developing a theory is a significant undertaking. Before embarking on such an enterprise one would need to know, for a start, what a theory is and is not. That would require significant preparatory reading in the philosophy of science.
Magus:	I'm interested in the philosophy of science myself, though I've found it hard to get absolutely clear on how all the various positions are distinguished from one another. But let me ask: if what you're offering us isn't a theory of US national interests, what is it?
Waltz:	Well, at the moment I think of myself as being engaged more in analysing US foreign policy than theorizing it, though I explored some of what would have to be the constituent parts of a theory of foreign policy in my recent book. But an analysis is not a theory: I'm putting theoretical ideas to work to explain the risks of our current course of action, not creating a theory.

Harpy: That sounds like an important and most interesting distinction. Could you explain a little more what a theory can and cannot offer us?

[*Waltz looks at his watch again.*]

Waltz: Well, I have some ideas, but I'm afraid I'll have to get back to you on that. I've very much enjoyed our discussion, but I'm late for a class …

Notes

1. Kenneth N. Waltz, 'The Politics of Peace', *International Studies Quarterly*, 11.3, Sep 1967, p. 199.
2. Kenneth N. Waltz, 'Letter to the Editor', *International Organization*, 36.3, Summer 1982, p. 680.
3. Kenneth N. Waltz, 'The Stability of a Bipolar World', *Daedalus*, 93.3, Summer 1963, p. 906.

36
Frantz Fanon (1925–1961)

Rita Abrahamsen

It is December 2011 and left-wing radicals and postcolonial theorists alike are commemorating the 50th anniversary of Frantz Fanon's death and the publication of his most famous and controversial book, The Wretched of the Earth. *As part of the celebrations, Fanon (1925–1961) agrees to come back from the heaven of dead thinkers to do an interview with The Postcolonial Critic (PC), a 'cutting-edge IR journal'. They meet in Paris, as Fanon is keen to return to the country where he studied psychiatry and philosophy in the early 1950s, before he took up a position at a French psychiatric hospital in Algeria and ultimately joined the Front de Libération National (FLN), the Algerian resistance movement, working for their newspaper* El Moudjahid *and acting as their ambassador to several African countries.*

PC: Bonjour, Monsieur Fanon! Thank you so much for agreeing to meet with us. It is a great pleasure and a tremendous honour, as your work has been such an important inspiration for postcolonial IR and our journal!

FF: The pleasure is all mine! And thank you for your kind words and for sending me the issues of your journal. I had the occasion to read some of the essays on my journey here, and I have to say I found them most interesting, if at times a little curious …

PC: Curious?

FF: Well, for a start, it has always baffled me that there could be a discipline that called itself International *Relations* but which almost systematically ignores the most important international relation of all – the colonial relationship! I mean, come on, how can one even begin to theorize the international and the relationship between states without starting with the fundamental inequalities built into this system by colonialism? And by race? To me, this is the fundamental deceit of IR; it began as a discipline of the powerful and it remains, *au cœur*, a discipline of the powerful! So, of course, I have been very pleased to see that IR is finally paying more attention to the Third World – and yes, I still insist on calling it that, *le tiers monde*, to hold on to its revolutionary potential – and I think IR is a much richer and more diverse discipline after its discovery of other parts of the world and of more postcolonial ways of thinking. Although, I do sometimes still wonder what took you so long … But never mind, I'm heartened to see that IR scholars are finally coming around to engaging the colonial legacies and the persistence of inequalities and racial hierarchies.

PC: And what do you think about the way your own work has been invoked in IR?

FF: Well, it is rewarding and even a little flattering to be 'discovered' as a critical thinker and a theorist after all these years. I mean, when I wrote *The Wretched of the Earth*[1] I was a revolutionary and an activist. I was all about action and change, not philosophy and theory as such. That's why I sometimes find your journal a little curious; it seems on occasion more interested in theory for the sake of theory rather that with the actual condition of the wretched of the earth and the urgency of changing it!

PC: But … Excuse me for interrupting, but don't we need to do both at the same time? Isn't it necessary to disrupt the epistemological violence that a Western-centric IR has committed against the subaltern, and does this not require attention to theory as well as practice?

FF: Yes, you're right … Absolutely right … And I do of course touch upon this in my books, but I've always been a man of action and of struggle, and even now I remain impatient, impassioned! There is so much that remains to be done!

PC: Your writing is certainly bursting with passion and impatience, and reading your books is such an extraordinary, such an unsettling, experience. I mean, it's not the normal academic discourse of scientific detachment and distance. It's so raw, so intimate, perhaps even angry. Many have picked up on the anger, and therefore dismissed your work as outright dangerous and as encouraging violence. And after all, you were expelled from French Algeria in the late 1950s, and became one of the French secret police's most wanted persons, surviving several assassination attempts. But, let's leave the issue of anger and violence for a little later, because I think we first need to explore your thinking about race and identity. As you might be aware, this is a topic that is finally gaining more attention in IR. Could you explain how you arrived at your thinking about race and identities, particularly in *Black Skin, White Masks*?

FF: As you know, I grew up in Fort-de-France, the capital of Martinique, in the 1930s, which meant that I grew up associating with France. My family was part of the emerging bourgeoisie and hence I was one of the privileged few that was educated at the *lycée*. This meant I grew up speaking about 'our ancestors, the Gauls', I identified with 'the explorer, the bringer of civilization, the white man who carries truth to the savages – an all-white truth'.[2] So strong were my feelings for France, that in 1944 I boarded a ship and joined the Free French Army on the European front, where I was wounded in battle and awarded the *Croix de Guerre* for bravery.

But, the France that I discovered was not the France of my imagination! Instead, I encountered the fact of blackness.[3] I discovered that in the white man's world, the black man is but an object among other objects. Encountering the white man's gaze, I found myself trapped in a racial epidermal schema and a historico-racial schema. Everywhere I went, I was haunted by my blackness; battered down by tom-toms, stories of cannibalism, intellectual deficiency, fetishism, racial defects, slave-ships ... I felt shame, nausea – endless nausea – and, yes, anger. No matter how intelligent, how refined, how well read, I realized that the black person is unable to escape his or her blackness. I was sealed in a crushing objecthood!

As you know, I was inspired by Sartre's discussion of the Jew and anti-Semitism.[4] But much as I found this helpful for understanding race and racism, I came to the conclusion that the Jew was over-determined from within, by the ideas other people have of him, and so he can transcend the body. The black person, by contrast, is over-determined from without; a slave not of the ideas people have of him, but of his very appearance.

In this situation, there are two options: reject yourself and become white, copy the white man's habits, his clothes, his loves and his hates – become white or disappear. Wear a white mask. Or, define yourself and your blackness against the white man, in opposition. The challenge is that even the latter option remains within the terms of the Other's construction of blackness – a reactive action – and this is why at the end of *Black Skin, White Masks* I wonder how it will be possible to escape the inferiority complex and abolish alienation. There is a constant need to stress that the black person has his own foundation, to continually engage in this act of creation.

PC: Many people have suggested that there is quite a different reading of racial difference in *The Wretched of the Earth*. Here, your description seems to be much more Manichean.

FF: Indeed! And I know you mean that negatively, and that such views are considered rather passé in this age of fluid, postmodern identities, but you have to remember that the colonial world *was* Manichean. When I wrote *Black Skin, White Masks* I had mostly experienced alienation as a black middle class intellectual in France. When I wrote *The Wretched* in ten intense weeks before my death in 1961, I had witnessed at close hand the brutality and dehumanization of colonial oppression in Algeria. Yes, we spoke of assimilation and human equality even then, but while working as a psychiatrist at the Blida-Joinville Hospital in Algeria I came to realize that those ideals were impossible inside the colonial order. Impossible! The violence was not accidental to the colonial system. It *was* the system! The colonial world was a world cut in two, its dividing line marked by barracks and police stations. The two zones were opposed, but not in the service of a higher unity – like assimilation or civilization. Instead, obedient to the rules of pure Aristotelian logic, they both followed the principle of reciprocal exclusivity. No conciliation was possible, for of the two, one was superfluous.[5]

So, I'm sorry my dear, but this is not simply some nice multicultural scheme of mutual recognition and the enjoyment of 'ethnic food', or sending cards that say 'Happy Holidays' instead of 'Merry Christmas'. Unlike in Hegel's account of recognition through the master/slave relationship and its ultimate resolution in mutual recognition, the colonial relationship is and remains a life and death struggle. The colonial master is not seeking recognition from the colonized; he doesn't see him as human, but as part animal, part of nature – and hence the colonized *cannot* become a subject. The black person has no ontological resistance in the eyes of the white, and the only way he can become a subject and realize his freedom is through violence. In the colonial situation, there is no room for fragmented or ambiguous identities; tactically and politically, you need a unified identity and clear position to defeat the total oppressor. For your journal, this might appear as terribly 'essentialist', but the celebration of contingency and ambivalence is a luxury not awarded to the colonized.

PC: But it does make it sound as if you are encouraging violence. Isn't this a very dangerous position to hold? I mean, many people today want to dismiss you as primarily as a theorist of violence. Some even call you a prophet of violence ...

FF: It's nonsense to say that I advocate violence, or even violence for the sake of violence.[6] For heaven's sake, I worked with both torture victims and their torturers as a psychiatrist at the hospital during the Algerian war of independence. I know better than most people the costs of violence, its long lasting traumas and deeps scars – for victims and perpetrators alike. But let's never forget that the colonial situation was one of violence, it cannot be denied or wished away. I believed then, and I believe now, that colonialism is violence in its natural state, and it will only yield when confronted with greater violence. In a situation where there is no civil or political sphere, no political relationships, violence is a liberatory act because it resists colonialism's absolute power, which has been internalized by the colonized.

So, my argument is that counter-violence is necessary for survival and for the emergence of a new humanism. I know many don't like this, and that some contemporary interpreters of my texts would rather overlook this in favour of a focus on how my work speaks to issues of hybrid and fragmented identities. And that is OK, but in the colonial situation, violence was necessary for the new man to emerge. The native, as I called him then, was angry, bitter, battered-down and de-humanized, and I understood the desire to take the colonizer's place. Violence is a therapeutic act! I argue that – absolutely – but what I do not do at any point is to advocate violence for the sake of violence. On the contrary, I argue that without a change in consciousness, anti-colonial violence will merely lead to a new form of barbarism. As you may recall, I warned that a new independent nation, a new Algeria, could not emerge from one barbarism simply replacing another, of one crushing of man replacing another crushing of man.

PC: Indeed! Some of your warnings in *The Wretched* about the pitfalls of nationalism and the dangers of independence turning into another form of oppression seem almost too prescient. Looking at parts of Africa today, what do you think? Has independence been betrayed?

FF: Oh, that's a tricky one! Clearly, the struggle is not over! Just look at the poverty, look at the exclusions! In some ways it was easier before, during colonialism, when the bad people were on one side, and the good on the other. Now, after national independence resistance is much more complicated, and it is more global. I mean look at France! Being back here I realize with horror that the promise of assimilation and equality – *la mission civilisatrice* – still assumes within itself a logic of inferiority. Look at the headscarf debate, for example, and the way in which race is being seen as a threat to western identity in all the talk about Islamic terrorism. I'm reminded of Sartre's preface to *The Wretched*, where he said that Europe too needed to decolonize, to look at itself if it can bear it.

But to get back to Africa; I always knew that the struggle was going to be a long and difficult one for the former colonies. The challenge is to pass from the first stage of the independence struggle to a new consciousness of liberation. Just independence – a new flag, new street names, new statues of great men – well, that risks becoming just a kind of neocolonialism, and it was disappointing to me how quickly and how comfortably many black elites filled the shoes of the colonial oppressor. Their ideals of national unity, liberation and freedom abandoned with remarkable alacrity, and the 'political kingdom' proved to be nothing more than a means for the few to get rich on behalf of the many. So in my attempt to theorize the revolution, I stress that independence needs to be followed by a second transformative stage that involves the people, a liberatory ideology and the creation of a new consciousness. But the awakening of the people cannot be achieved overnight. Independence is not a simple historical break from colonialism, but it requires a complete new consciousness, a new person! That's why at the end of *The Wretched* I argue that if we want to take a step beyond Europe, we must innovate, we must be pioneers! For Europe, for ourselves, for humanity, we must make a new start, find a new way of thinking, and endeavour to create a new person! And just to answer you earlier veiled criticism, this is not a Manichean world, but a new world.

PC: I can't help but notice that you say 'person', and not 'man' ...

FF: Oh, all that gender and sexuality stuff ... Yes, I'm a bit sore about that! It's probably true, but 'man' also means humanity. And thankfully, I don't think we have time to talk about that now. I must get back ...

PC: OK, just one final question: You have been called a Marxist, a psychoanalyst, a Satrean, a Hegelian, a Lacanian, a negritudist, a Pan-Africanist, a postcolonial theorist, a prophet of violence ... So many Fanons! How would you characterize yourself?

FF: HA! And you could add a sexist and a misogynist, and even a premature post-modernist! Yes, there is no shortage of labels, and each comes with its own condemnation! To be honest, I'm not all that concerned with these characterizations and labels, but what I do find interesting is how the interpretation of my work has shifted over time, as a reflection of the broader ideological changes and fashions within academia. For example, the early editions of *The Wretched* described the book as a 'revolutionary handbook', whereas the blurb on the 2000 edition makes no references to such concepts and political struggles but chooses instead to describe me as a founding father of postcolonial theory.[7]

It's kind of amusing, but I can't complain about that. As I say in *Black Skin*, I do not come with timeless truths! I do think it is important to stress the historical specificity of my writing, but I also think that each generation must discover its mission, fulfil it, or betray it. And as long as people can find relevance and inspiration in my work, as long as I can continue to disturb and unsettle, then that is a good thing. Then, perhaps, I can help make of others what I wanted my body to make of me: a man who always questions!

Notes

1. Fanon, F. *The Wretched of the Earth* (New York: Grove Press, 1968) was written in 10 weeks and first published in 1961, a few days after Fanon died.
2. This passage is from *Black Skin, White Masks,* first published in 1952 (Boston: Grove Press, 1967).
3. 'The Fact of Blackness' is a chapter in *Black Skin, White Masks.* Fanon seems here to be reflecting mainly on this chapter.
4. Sartre, J.P. *Anti-Semite and Jew: An Exploration of the Etiology of Hate* (New York: Schocken, 1995 [1948]).
5. This passage draws on *The Wretched of the Earth* (1968: 29–30).
6. Hannah Arendt, in *On Violence,* accuses Fanon of advocating violence for the sake of violence. Jean-Paul Sartre's preface to the first edition of *The Wretched* also stresses its violent message.
7. On this point, see Nigel Gibson 'Is Fanon Relevant? Toward an Alternative Foreword to "The Damned of the Earth"', *Human Architecture. Journal of the Sociology of Self Knowledge* 2007 5(3): 33–44.

37
Deep Hanging Out with Michel Foucault (1926–1984)

Iver B. Neumann

IBN has won a ticket in the lottery to visit the so-called Afterglow, a pocket of the non-corporeal afterlife realm where leading intellectuals hang out, and has decided to spend it on an interview with what was once Michel Foucault.

IBN: You once told another interviewer that the happiest moment in your life came when you were run over by a car and thought you would die.[1] Well, here you are. Happy now?

MF: No. My head is still working at full speed, and I don't even have sex to divert me.[2] I have become more cerebral than ever, and believe me, it's boring.

IBN: Congratulations on your English, though. During your years at Berkeley, students complained.[3] I suppose you get no more of that?

MF: I get lots of practice around here. Some of the recent arrivals here are Americans, and they are, of course, monolingual. Even Heidegger, with whom I have spent quite some time in conversation, has reneged on his view that philosophizing can only be done in Greek and German, and is putting his nose to the grindstone. Not that he really gets any other system than his own for that. You could do with some accent-polishing yourself, by the way.

IBN: Indeed. I'm particularly ashamed of that since my own language [Norwegian, IBN] and English were mutually understandable as recently as a millennium ago. So except for the boredom, what is it like being, ah, I suppose 'dead' is the word, although it sounds a bit too final, perhaps 'respawned'?

MF: I try to fight the loss of my corporeal existence by focusing on the good stuff, like the unbeatable conversations. Pity that Plato isn't here, though, I would really have liked to discuss his ideas on the state with him. With the re-investment I did in ancient Greek to pursue the first volume of my history of sexuality, I even think the exchange could have been rooted in his own concepts, although I certainly do hope his English would have been better than my Greek.[4] You may recall that I embraced his general understanding of the state as I believe he formulated it in *The Statesman,* politics as the weaving together of the strands of life as a privileged social concern.[5] Such a conception spawns a key problem, which is what the relationship between the one and the many should be, and it's around that problematique you will find most if not all of my interventions.[6] There is a line, I think, from all that to Durkheim's understanding of the state as a merging of the separate cadre that is the early state with subjects – what eventually becomes society. These are at least the dominating intertexts in my own work on the state, and it would be nice to have that exchange. However, Durkheim is not so easy to talk to on this. He is a classic authoritarian, and thinks I have misunderstood capitally by focusing on the costs of the merger between state and society. Where I see surveillance, control and debilitating norms, he keeps on insisting on all the good that comes out of an ever-present socially minded state, like some latter-day social democrat. He is right in spotting that his own work on the state was important for me and that I stood much of his thinking there on its head, but he refuses to discuss the Christian genealogy that I suggest, with the welfare state being not only the result of the good citizen but also of the idea that a human lamb must have a pastor. Clausewitz is much easier, he engages my inversion of his idea of politics as an extension of war by other means head on. Durkheim is just too fond of his politico-religious project of sacralizing a human drive towards a world state. Quite stubborn, too, even the existence of his very own propaganda books against Germany during the First World War cannot make him see that the world state he wanted was a France writ large and that all that is gone now. Well. He is still a forefather, and an important one. Durkheim, Mauss, Lévi-Strauss and I still play whist every Friday. It's all in the intellectual family, really.

IBN: But you hardly refer to them in your written work?

MF: Of course not, only an ignoramus would not spot the influence. The no-reference is, after all, a French tradition of long standing, didn't you know?

IBN: Let's return to Plato, I would have thought that his description in *The Republic* of the perfect state of things, with boys taken from their parents and trained by what we translate as the state in the most detailed way would be an example of discipline?

MF: The vision is there, and since this was a model that captures his thinking and so a certain contemporary discourse, I could have opened my book on discipline with that, really, instead of giving the example of a 19th-century English public school. Well, that's all in another lifetime. As to Plato, he simply decamped. Sublimed, as we call it here. Went on to yet another plane of existence. I bet it is ideal, at least for him [sniggers]. Plotinus insists that he is still in contact, but that I can only take note of. Dante was absolutely beside himself when it was clear that Plato had decamped. Here they both were, in a place that is not unlike the place that Dante described, and while Dante was quite pleased about that, he was also disappointed that there seemed to be no heaven for him to go to. Took him the better part of half a millennium to get over it, really, and just as he was about to, Plato goes and leaves for what Dante now believes is, after all, heaven. Bad luck.

IBN: What do you make of your reception?

MF: Let me say at once that I only have arrivals down here to go on. From what I hear, there has been a lot of 'what did he mean' debates. That was to be expected, but it is bad news nonetheless. I went out of my way to spell out how I was truer to the project in hand and to the quest for what I call truth – truth as understood by me – than to consistency, that I was always making a point of trying out new possibilities, and of course that makes for inconsistencies, which was part of the point. *Ni Dieu, ni maître.* I said it again and again, take what you can use for your own project and get on with it, look at the local sequences, beware of the trans-historical. But no. The other issue is simply a thorn in my side by comparison: Bourdieu just joined us. Speaking to him, I understand that he has taken a lot of my stuff, rationalized it, and applied it to what he thinks of as strategic action. That's all right, I suppose, but the way he seems to bend over backwards to hide where he got most of it from strikes me as silly. The boy from Bearn always going on about not really fitting in, but always ready to rip off the very people he is fighting. Typical ressentiment. The only consolation is that I'm not doing all that now.

IBN: Well, it seems to fit what you just referred to as the French no-reference tradition quite well. Are you still doing knowledge/power?

MF: No.

IBN: Then what?

MF: Feyerabend always wanted to be a cabaret singer, and singing is something we can do down here. We're doing scat, mostly. No, no [laughs heartily], I think you misunderstand me, I mean singing in harmony. Jazz stuff.

IBN: No more scholarship?

MF: You don't pay attention. I still stick to the adage of acting locally. The power relations between energetic beings are really not that complicated. Why, with my favourite carnal focus missing, there's little for me to study. I've turned to aesthetics full time.

IBN: I hope you do not mind that I return to the issue of power/knowledge, though. Your earlier studies of discipline have, as you know, become part of the basic tool kit of social history and theory. I see little reason to go over this mode of power, since life in total institutions and your theorization of it are so well …

MF: I must, if you allow, stop you. If what I have heard is true, I have been misunderstood regarding a basic point. I made remarks to the effect that life had become like life in prison. I even said that the point of being critical was not being ruled so much and to break out of a prison of our own making. In French, we like to speak in metaphors. The Americans are more literally minded. Some people, especially criminologists, have felt it necessary to privilege their own field of study by assuming that our lives ARE prison lives. Now, that's rather different from saying that they are LIKE prison lives. It is a fundamental misreading, for if life had been prison life, then discipline would have been the dominant mode of power everywhere – everywhere in the physical world, that is. There would have been little point for me to do all that work on governmentality, for example.

IBN: Well, as long as you use that penal vocabulary, I suppose misunderstanding is inevitable, but let's talk about governmentality. As far as I understand what was going on in the 1970s, your work on the ins and outs of governing from afar was actually a response to critics?

MF: A rare case of critics actually helping me with my thinking, yes, for it made me add a third mode of power to the two that I had worked with before, which were sovereignty – the always present mode of power where we are gaming and the result is not given beforehand – and discipline, where that game is heavily rigged by the total institution that orchestrates it.[7] The critique was really quite simple-minded: why do you ignore subjects when you do your analyses of discipline? Of course I had to, the whole point was that there was no big brother behind it all, no subject, only totalitarian thinking that conjured up the practices, only institutions like the asylum, the prison, the boarding school. Again, I went out of my way to avoid that misunderstanding. I started my book on *epistēmes* with a dictionary that was never written, my book on madness with a ship that never sailed and my book on prison with a penal system that was never built, and what did the historians say? But that Chinese dictionary did not exist! There was no such thing as a ship of fools! Bentham's panopticon was not realized for almost two centuries! 'No shit, Sherlock', as Dewey said to me the other day. I wanted to tease out the power of ways of thinking, and the historians did not get it, not even the third time around. Even Peter Burke, whose work I enjoyed, made that mistake. Wrote a retort based on the arcane idea that I really thought the ship of fools had existed, ha! ha! And still, the critique carried a deeper truth, for I was never good on individuals. Individuation, yes. Individuals, no. In my books on Hérculine Barbin and Pierre Rivière, it is true, I am more interested in using them as examples of how gender and crime is constituted than in them as persons.[8] Personae, not persons, that was the limitation. My work on governmentality did not really make amends for that, for my interest remained in individuation, but at least I was able to get at a much wider set of individuating practices by introducing the idea of the conduct of conduct.

IBN: Your reception in my corner of academia has first and foremost focused on governmentality, but there is also a general interest amongst postcolonialists. They are also dissatisfied with the missing individuals.

MF: That was bound to happen. Already when Edward [Said, IBN] published *Orientalism*, he included that passage on how, in the case of Western academic representations of the Orient, the writings of a few individuals had been important.[9] I have no quarrel with that. Dumézil always talked about monuments, of how certain texts are key to understanding discourse, and that's true enough.[10] You know, I hear that discourse analysis has taken off, but I hatched the idea only *post festum*. Once I had a break in Tunisia and started to think through what I had really done in *Les Mots et Les Choses* [English translation *The Order of Things*, IBN] I concluded that the idea of an age's *epistēme* was really too muscular, too totalizing, too much like Lévi-Strauss' idea that there are latent structures underlying entire societies.[11] I wanted something more specific, which could capture not the utterances, but the specific social setting that could make utterances possible, and the answer was discourse.[12] The *Archaeology* [*of Knowledge*, IBN] was really all an attempt to come to grips with what, with hindsight, was to become my version of a general break with structuralism. Individuals were not the focus here, utterances were. I was out to capture what made it possible to say something, as opposed to what was said, and how that gave rise to a doxa that constrained the one in his dealings with the many. So Edward's critique was fair enough, for he was out to capture a very specific contribution made by very specific people. I was not. I am glad you raise the question of methodology, though, for that was one of my many *bêtes noirs*. The hunt went on, *epistēme*, discourse, assemblage, *dispositif*, but it was all an attempt at getting to the specificity of social constellations.

IBN: To press the postcolonial issue, you certainly made an attempt to take that hunt beyond Europe, most famously, perhaps, by seeing hope in the Iranian revolution?

MF: I must admit that I was flattered when *Corriere della Sera* wanted me there as a correspondent, but I went also exactly because I had focused so much on the Western tradition that I thought I owed it to another tradition to go. And I was curious, not least because there were many Iranian intellectuals exiled in Paris. What I saw there was excitement, the feeling that something new was being created. It was not unlike the bathhouses in San Francisco in that regard, new community on unknown ground. It all went wrong, but then again, human history is rife with false beginnings. From what I hear, though, globalization has really taken off and you all have to relate to other traditions on a regular basis now. A very important change. When I was in Tunis, the memory of colonialism was still so fresh that local energies had not really been released there and in Paris, except for Fanon and some of the students, like Mudimbe, there was not really all that much happening. The rights that have been established in our own tradition have counterparts elsewhere, and we have to open up to that.[13] So, I was a bit too excited there to begin with. Although it is an error on a par with my short flirt with communism, I have no regrets. If critique is the art of not being governed so much, it must include an element of speaking truth to power, and that truth has to come from experience; reading experiences, lived experiences. Sometimes, the truths will be off. There is a sense in which the process is more important than the result. It is, I think, a calculated risk of the parrhesiastic calling to fail sometimes.[14]

IBN: I see from the hourglass sign on my lottery ticket that my time is almost up, so, since you dwell on your mistakes, might I ask you to round this out by mentioning what you think are your greatest successes?

MF: Ah. From what I hear, outside of history, the basic genealogical approach of asking why exactly something becomes a problem within this or that social constellation seems to have caught on. That insight was Nietzsche's, but I take great pleasure in having lent a hand there, for if you ask question in that way, you are already on your way towards doing something critical. And then there is the other end, the effects of it all, the importance of asking not only why people do what they do and if they know what they do, but also if they know what that which they do, does. Very few people do. But that is all methodology. If you meant in terms of substance, I think that knack for looking at seemingly historical stuff in order to criticize the present panned out particularly well when it came to globalization, and also for biopolitics. It is rather nice to look back and see that the questions about the governing of health and life that I asked thirty years ago are now being asked as if for the first time.

Notes

1. David Macey, *The Lives of Michel Foucault* (New York, NY: Pantheon, 1993).
2. Michel Foucault, 'An Ethics of Pleasure', *Foucault Live* (Interviews 1966–84), edited by Sylvestre Lotringer (New York: Semiotext [1982] 1989), pp. 257–277.
3. When I [IBN] translated Michel Foucault, 'Omnes et Singulatim: Toward a Critique of Political Reason', *Power: Essential Works of Foucault 1954–1984*, edited by James D. Faubion, (Harmondsworth: Penguin, [1980] 2000), pp. 298–325 into Norwegian, I checked the provenance of the text to find out whether the translation should be done from the English or the original French. A librarian at Berkeley confirmed that the written original was in French but that the original performance of it was in English so broken that it was hard to follow.
4. Michel Foucault, *The Uses of Pleasure. The History of Sexuality, vol. 2*, trans. Robert Hurley (Harmondsworth: Penguin, [1984] 1985).
5. Foucault, 'Omnes et Singulatim'.
6. 'At the basis of Foucault's concerns, one always finds the question of the dissolution of order, even if this remained unspecified as a topic'. Arpád Szakolczai, *Max Weber and Michel Foucault: Parallel Life-Works* (London: Routledge, 1998), p. 232.

7. 'The S&M game is very interesting because it is a strategic relation, but it is always fluid. Of course, there are roles, but everyone knows very well that those roles can be reversed'; Foucault quoted in James Miller, *The Passion of Michel Foucault* (New York, NY: Simon & Schuster, 1993), p. 263.

8. 'Nietzsche was saying how little a man is responsible for his nature, especially in terms of what he considered to be his morality. Morality has been constitutive of the individual's being. The individual is contingent, formed by the weight of moral tradition, not really autonomous'. Foucault quoted in Miller, *The Passion of Michel Foucault*, p. 283.

9. Edward Said, *Orientalism* (London: Penguin, 1977).

10. Georges Dumézil (1898–1986) was a leading proto-Indo-Europeanist and mentor of Foucault's, instrumental, among other things, in securing a job for him at Uppsala University and a chair at the Collège de France [IBN].

11. 'Both Foucault and the structuralist are not interested in whether the phenomena they study have the serious sense supposed by participants. Thus they reject the view, shared by pragmatists such as Dewey, hermeneutic phenomenologists such as Heidegger, and ordinary language philosophers such as Wittgenstein, that in order to study linguistic practices one must take into account the background of shared practices which make them intelligible'. Hubert L. Dreyfus and Paul Rabinow, *Michel Foucault: Beyond Structuralism and Hermeneutics* (Brighton: Harvester, 1983), p. 57.

12. 'The status of practices was at the heart of the famous exchange between Foucault and Derrida that started with Derrida's lecture on Foucault's *Madness and Civilization* (reprinted in Derrida 1967) and ended with Foucault retorting to his former student that in his work, "discursive traces are reduced to textual traces [...] the original is allocated to what is said and not-said in the text, so as not to put discursive practices back into the field of transformations in which they were carried out"'. Quoted in Didier Eribon, *Michel Foucault*, transl. Betzy Wing (London: Faber & Faber, [1989]1992), p. 121.

13. Foucault defended the right of the Baader-Meinhof-related French lawyer Klaus Croissant to travel freely across Europe, while also falling out with Deleuze and Guattari's stance on the issue, which Foucault felt condoned terrorism. Michel Foucault, 'Va-t-on extrader Klaus Croissant?', *Dits et écrits 1954–1988*, vol. III 1976–1979 (Paris: Gallimard, [1977] 1994), pp. 361–365; David Macey, *The Lives of Michel Foucault* (New York, NY: Pantheon, 1993), p. 393.

14. Foucault is referring to his final work here, which concerned the emergence of the practice of speaking truth to power (Gr. *parhessia*), see his lectures at the Collège de France 1982–1983 and 1983–1984.

38

Interviewing Pierre Bourdieu (1930–2002) about Pierre Bourdieu and International Relations

Anna Leander

AL: Thank you so much Professor Bourdieu for agreeing to talk to me. I will not take more than 15 minutes. As I wrote you, I am contributing to a book entitled *The Return of the Theorists*. We are interested in finding out, among other things, how important thinkers of the past see their contributions to International Relations. I would therefore like to ask you about your contribution to scholarly International Relations. First, I would like to ask you about the way your 'field' concept has been used to study professions ...

PB: *Scholarly* International Relations [sneer]?! IR certainly is 'scholarly'. I can think of few other academic disciplines so prone to 'scholastic fallacy' and so afflicted by 'scholarly hubris'. Yet its effect is far-reaching. The epistemological problem we call 'state' is perpetuated, no, aggravated, and made almost irresolvable. The consequences are disastrous: wars, violence, poverty and ecological disasters. If you ask me what contribution I would *want* to make to this so-called scholarly discipline: I would like to be part of its demise. It is such a pity that I did not complete my manuscript about the state. That would have made the point far more clearly.

AL: You do know that they published your lectures on the state posthumously,[1] I assume? Also, it seems to me that there is no shortage of references to your state theory in other parts of your work, including, for example, in your work on the university or on the social structures of the economy.[2] But could we get back to the way 'fields' have been used to study, for example, diplomats or NGO professionals?

PB: You have actually read what I have to say about the state and still want to return to the field concept to understand my contribution to IR? This is surreal! Worse than I imagined.

337

AL: Would you mind explaining what is so wrong about this? As most IR scholars, I have read Didier Bigo, Yves Dezalay, Frederic Mérand, Michael Rask-Madsen, and so on. I have even written about fields myself. Are you saying we all misunderstand you?

PB: [Deep sigh] No, no. That is not the point. I appreciate the work you are doing – it is not a contribution to what you call 'scholarly IR', but to a radical reformulation of so-called IR, or perhaps its demise.

AL: Would you mind explaining what you mean?

PB: As I have argued so many times, the state is an *epistemological problem* [articulated with pathos]. The problem is that we accept the state's claim to monopolize symbolic violence which we therefore also contribute to ensuring. Through its role in forming our language, our lives, our laws, and even our innermost feelings about the supposedly most private aspects of life – including love and family – the state is penetrating our most intimate thoughts. It is shaping our behaviour.[3] The public 'interest' or 'good' in the name of which this is done is that of specific people. It used to be the interest of the nobility and the bureaucracy into which it had transformed itself; today it is increasingly that of companies and so-called market actors.

The trouble with what you call scholarly IR is that it locks the door on this kind of critique of the state as an epistemological problem. It assumes the state. In the process it naturalizes and enshrines its monopoly on symbolic violence. Worse, it is constantly committing the scholastic fallacy of assuming that practice functions according to the logic scholars have pinned down to explain it. In so doing, it undermines attempts at contesting the symbolic violence of the state. And since (as all scholars[4]) IR scholars suffer from hubris and are persuaded that their knowledge is superior to all others, they propose their 'expertise' with a certain missionary zeal. I hope that you now see why I think it is vital to tackle the state as an epistemological problem and why I would therefore have appreciated it if more people had worked on my state theory.

AL: I am still a bit confused about the question of fields though: did you say that you did not think studying fields could be a contribution to IR?

PB: No, that is not what I said [deep sigh]. Did you say that you read my work?

What I said was that I thought my theory of the state constituted a far more important contribution to scholarly IR. Of course, one can study fields and look at how they work across all the conventional inside/outside, public/private, civilian/military or economic/political divides and get much out of doing so. You can even use field analysis to demonstrate direct attention to the ways in which the state works as an epistemological problem. You can draw on it to show how the imprint of the state shapes a production of capital in the field, how it fashions the ontogenetic aspects of the *habitus,* and how state capital is consequently mobilized in the contexts of struggles and strategies over positions and dispositions in the field. Clearly, this is not bad. If you do this you can move quite far in the analysis of what you term 'professions' and in the analysis of the way hierarchies and domination are established in these contexts as well as more generally. However, not only does this kind of analysis require a lot of empirical work, it also demands that you are indeed capable of treating the state as an epistemological problem. Because, if you are not doing that, you will not be able to see the state effect in your analysis. This is why I think that my understanding of the state is my most fundamental contribution to IR and why I am therefore also surprised that you can engage in a conversation about that contribution without putting it in the most central position but instead keep moving away from it and onto other kinds of issues.

AL: I see your point. Thanks! So if I were to summarize this: you are saying that you think your work on the state is your core contribution to IR because the state is the structure that shapes ...

PB: Structure?! Certainly not. This is why attempts to summarize and simplify usually do more harm than good. The simplified is usually the simplistic. It distorts.

AL: I am afraid I am not following you. What is so wrong with talking about the state as a structure? You often refer to structures, don't you? Everyone knows your definition of the habitus as a structuring structure or your self-definition as a structuralist constructivist. So what is so mistaken about extending the use of the idea of structure to the state?

PB: This is precisely why I so dislike the *Anglo-Saxon* [slowly articulated with disdain] way of working with theory and concepts. They take definitions out of their context as if they could make sense without it. This is totally absurd in general. It is as if one took a scalpel – no, a butcher's knife – and then cut out some organ or a piece of the brain and expected it to do its work without the context from which it has been severed. No serious theorist can or should encourage his thinking to be treated in this manner. Theoretical work is (or, more appropriately, should be) about generating dispositions for thinking along new paths. It is about opening up avenues; not closing them by positing so-called definitions as roadblocks. This is why I like to talk about thinking tools and open concepts. At least on this Foucault and I agree.

AL: I would like you to return to what you find so objectionable about terming the state a structure. Do you think you could elaborate a little?

PB: Certainly. I hope you realize the importance of getting the preliminaries in place though. You are right that I refer to structure in many places in my work. I don't do it though in the way you suggested. I use structure when I want to draw attention to the historicity of the practices I analyse. As you probably are aware, I am rather annoyed with approaches that seem to assume that what they term practices are, somehow random and free-floating or liquid. I have for example written quite extensively on my disagreement with so-called 'symbolic interactionism', 'constructivism' and 'post-structuralism' precisely on these grounds. While I share many ideas of the exponents of these trends, I find their over-emphasis on the malleability and alterability of practices unacceptable. It reveals a very shallow and ahistorical understanding of sociology, language, aesthetics, materiality and theory. It fails to direct attention to the way in which history is enacted and reproduced. Indeed this is a core theme of my work. The force of law stems from the historical construction of law as a field with exclusive competence over justice which covers a seemingly ever-increasing range of issues.[5] The historically grounded power of French nobility is enacted in its reproduction as a 'state nobility', allowing it to continue to dominate society through and after the revolutionary turmoil and the establishment of the republic.[6] Or conversely, the lack of social mobility in French suburbia or the eradication of traditional Kabyle values in the face of the market economy can only be comprehended if the enactment of specific historical constructions is taken into account.[7] I could elaborate with more examples and in much greater detail. The point is that when I invoke structure it is precisely to direct attention to this historicity. I find it absolutely essential to do so as part of the *Realpolitik* of Reason any responsible academic must engage in.

AL: Could you explain what you mean by *Realpolitik* of Reason?

PB: Of course. Knowledge production plays a very special role in the reproduction of social domination. It produces the categories through which we think, argue and act. As I have shown innumerable times our rationality and what I call our strategies re-enact these categories. This is why I have insisted that the distinction between strategies and habitual actions is misleading. Our strategies also express habitual patterns of thought. The strategies we follow are reflected upon, but that reflection is structured by the structuring structure that I term *habitus*. This is why a *Realpolitik* of Reason is so important. It can call into question these categories and make their work visible. This making visible has nothing to do with digging out something hidden or perhaps inventing it as it has become so common to claim. Rather, it is about putting words on things that are glaringly obvious but that no one mentions. Perhaps they don't even see them? The child who calls out to say that the emperor is naked in Andersen's story is perhaps the best analogy.

AL: Do you have any thoughts on what issues the *Realpolitik* of Reason should focus on at present?

PB: Yes, obviously I do: it should be directed at showing the power of markets, that is, of the neo-liberalism that I wrote about as a 'cunning imperialist reason'.[8] While it is essential to be aware that the state as an epistemological problem (yes we are back to the outset of the interview), it is perhaps even more important at the present juncture to be aware that alternative orders, and especially the order of the neo-liberal market, may have even more nefarious consequences for knowledge. As you probably know, the implications of the trend towards allowing markets and market mechanisms a steadily growing role in ordering knowledge production became a core preoccupation for me towards the end of my career. At the time, this trend was only emerging. Since then it has become vastly more powerful. The consequences I observed and cautioned against at the time (including the illusion that the market can provide a governance of knowledge marked by impersonal neutrality and divine objectivity) have only made themselves more strongly felt since then. The effect is that the governance of knowledge is increasingly serving 'the production of ignorance', to borrow Philip Mirowski's excellent expression. This also has far-reaching implications for the way the state as an epistemological problem can be approached. Not only has the overarching role of market orders and quasi-market forms of knowledge governance refashioned the way states are linked to knowledge production and therefore transformed the manner in which the state is an epistemological problem. Even more centrally, the turn to markets is seriously eroding the protection states have provided for knowledge production in universities and schools, and hence the conditions of possibility for critical knowledge development itself. It seems to me that both sides of this development – the growing role of market orders including *inside* states and the way they are altering the conditions of possibility for knowledge production – have not received anything close to the attention they deserve in IR. On this front a *Realpolitik* of Reason is really needed.

AL: Don't you think that sounds a bit judgemental? I thought you said you did not know much about IR. Also is it not a bit odd that after beginning this interview by saying that you thought your knowledge could at best contribute to the demise of IR, you are now lecturing IR scholars about what they should be studying?

PB: I sincerely hope you are right that I am being too 'judgemental', as you say. These issues are far too important to be ignored. All the better if IR scholars are already working on them. With regard to the second part of this question, I would like to elaborate: I see no contradiction here. Indeed, if IR scholars followed my suggestions and focussed on the state as an epistemological problem, this would necessarily lead them to focus more on the role of markets in that problem and its articulation. Both these moves would necessarily lead either to the demise of IR as conventionally conceived or to a radical re-examination of what IR is and can be. I am in other words pursuing the same line of argument as at the outset of this interview. But perhaps you are right that I should come out clearly in favour of a reformulation of the so-called discipline of IR. After all, it seems to me that much interesting work is going on in IR. I gather that the fact that you are interviewing me is a sign of that [smirk]. I assume that someone will read this and perhaps pursue the discussion.

AL: Well now it is my turn to hope you are right.

PB: What?! Are you taking my time without even being sure of that? [Irritated voice. Sound of pens and paper being gathered] Well, that reminds me of time. This has certainly lasted for more than 15 minutes.

AL: Uh, well, uh ...

PB: That was what I would call an articulate answer. It would take Latour to make it less precise. I really have to go now. I expect you to send me the interview so that I can go over it before you publish it!

AL: You did not mention this before the interview. Actually I am working towards a tight deadline. I am not sure the editors will appreciate if they have to wait.

PB: Well, I will not appreciate if you publish [mocking imitation].

AL: Well then, I will send it. Please do try to respond quickly though.

PB: This is so characteristically ungrateful. I generously take time from my precious eternity and all I get in return is ill-prepared superficial reading of my work thrown into my face followed by ridiculous talk about deadlines. I keep wondering when your generation will roll up its sleeves, get its hands dirty and do some serious academic work.

AL: Well ...

PB: Sorry I have no more patience for this. Good day now.

Bourdieu hangs up.

Notes

1. Bourdieu, Pierre. (2014) *On the State. Lectures at the College De France 1989–1992.* (Oxford: Polity Press).
2. Bourdieu, Pierre. (2000) *Homo Academicus.* (Stanford: Stanford University Press) and Bourdieu, Pierre. (2005) *The Social Structures of the Economy.* (Cambridge: Polity Press).
3. Bourdieu, Pierre. (2002) *Practical Reason: On the Theory of Action.* (Stanford: Stanford University Press): post-script esp.
4. For Bourdieu's view on academic hubris and its implications see: Bourdieu, Pierre. (2000) *Pascalian Meditations.* (Cambridge: Polity).
5. Bourdieu, Pierre. (1987) The Force of Law: Towards a Sociology of the Juridical Field. *Hastings Law Journal* 38:814–53.
6. Bourdieu, Pierre. (1998) *State Nobility: Elite Schools in the Field of Power.* (Cambridge: Polity Press).
7. Bourdieu, Pierre. (1999) *The Weight of the World: Social Suffering in Contemporary Society.* (Cambridge: Polity) and Bourdieu, Pierre. (2000) Making the Economic Habitus: Algerian Workers Revisited. *Ethnography* 1:17–41.
8. Bourdieu, Pierre, and Loïc Wacquant. (1999) On the Cunning of Imperialist Reason. *Theory, Culture & Society* 16:41–57 and Special Issue: The Cunning of Imperialist Reason. (2000) *Theory, Culture & Society* 17.

39
Hedley Bull (1932–1985)

Robert Ayson

'I'm sorry to be late, Professor Bull. I got rather lost on the way to your office.'

'And you are?'

'Edward Hoskings from Macmillan.'

'Well you'd better come in and sit down then. You're not the first to be disoriented by the Coombs Building. And you've come to see me about ...?'

'Your book. While I was in Australia I thought it would be a good idea to drop by the ANU and pay you a courtesy visit. To get a sense of how you were going with the writing and to see if there was anything we might do to help you.'

'I'm not sure that you can. Help me, that is. All I can ask is for some more patience while I complete the manuscript, amidst all the other things I am doing.'

'Yes, of course. I expect it being late summer you probably have plenty of teaching to prepare for.'

'Oh, not really. In the Research School [of Pacific Studies] teaching is not a major preoccupation. That's a big change from the LSE where I had students lining up to see me, even when I was on leave at the Foreign Office. So apart from a few doctoral students, who occasionally produce passable work, and apart from sharing the running of the International Relations Department with Professor [Bruce] Miller, I am allowed to get on with writing and overseas conferences.'

'That sounds a good set up, Professor Bull, in which case ...'

'But you see, I've had all sorts of demands on my research time. When I returned to Australia to take up my chair here in 1967, I already had lots of writing on the go, especially on arms control. The Nuclear Non-Proliferation Treaty was being wrapped up and we'd been doing some work on that in the Arms Control and Disarmament Research Unit I was running at Whitehall. Australia had some decisions to make about the approach it would adopt to these issues. There was much to say about how Canberra might keep open its nuclear options without creating major problems in a volatile Southeast Asian neighbourhood.'

'I can see how that might move you some distance from your more theoretical study of the problems of international order with us ...'

'Well, yes and no. You've read my earlier book on *The Control of the Arms Race*.'[1]

'Parts of it, yes, Professor Bull.'

'So you are aware of my view that the management of the problems of nuclear armaments has been central to the study of the modern international order? While I don't spend as much time on nuclear questions as I once did, the control of these weapons is essential if major war is to be avoided, and if we don't have that, we can't have any sort of international society.'

'That's going to be the title of the book with us?'

'I'm thinking of calling it *The Anarchical Society*.[2] That's less vulgar than some of the alternatives that have been suggested to me.'

'Yes, but I wonder if readers will be attracted to a book whose title suggests the subject is about anarchy when really it is about order.'

'Those aren't the readers I want. If they can't see that it is possible to have a society without formal government, then I can't see the point of trying to reach them. I will not be adjusting my approach for bone-headed people.'

'I see, but speaking of readers, Professor Bull, is there a date by which time they might look forward to seeing the book in print?'

'Oh I think it will see the light of day if that's what you are worried about. But I'm soon to begin some fairly significant overseas travel and while I plan to write while I am away, I am not sure I can promise ...'

'You are heading to Britain again, Professor Bull? My colleagues at Macmillan often spot you at conferences around the country.'

'Well, Britain is on my agenda. But first I am off to India for several months.'[3]

'That's a very interesting place to visit, I am sure, but won't it be hard to find a decent place to do your writing there, especially with the food and everything? And isn't that a bit of an international relations backwater? I thought that the major powers were a central part of your book, for example.'

'They are. But you underestimate India's importance. The rise of the Third World is a crucial aspect of contemporary international politics.

India is at the forefront of an array of Asian and African countries challenging the West's dominance. It mightn't be long before India joins the nuclear weapons club. And surely you have been following what has befallen the United States in Vietnam?'

'I'm sorry, Professor, I'm not sure I see the connection to the book you are writing.'

'You're not alone. Legions of people in Britain have not adjusted to the world we are living in. But amongst Western countries Australia is especially exposed to the Third World and the need to adjust to its rise. And without such an accommodation any semblance of international order in the late twentieth century won't be possible. This even means coming to understandings with a revisionist power like China.'[4]

'But isn't that tantamount to appeasement?'

'I thought you might say that. Appeasement gets far too much bad press. And what's the alternative? Blundering on in the pretence that after the decline of Britain, France and the other former great powers of Europe, and as the United States withdraws from its commitments in Asia, that Western power remains supreme? Instead of relying singularly on American power, I've been busy arguing that Australia's future rests on the fostering of an equilibrium between the United States, the Soviet Union, China and Japan.'[5]

'From the little I know about Australia, wouldn't that be expecting too much change?'

'Perhaps if the old Liberal-Country Party governments were in office here. They had such little imagination I used to worry about where this country was heading. But Gough Whitlam[6] understands the need to adjust to these new demands, even if he doesn't always take every bit of good advice he is given from people here at the university.'

'So you are a strong supporter of independence in Australia's neighbourhood? I saw a piece in this morning's paper that Papua New Guinea was finally about to become a former colonial possession of Australia.'

'Oh, I don't think so. When PNG's independence comes it will be due to impatient opinion in Australia, not because the leaders there want or need it. And, as I often think when I am visiting Oxford, we have much to be grateful for the fruits of colonial expansion. Our Western experience would be a far duller place without it, and we must not judge earlier periods by our own contemporary standards.'

'I'm sorry Professor Bull, you have completely confused me. First you say that the West needs to accommodate the Third World. But then you evince sympathy for the colonial mindset. You support the Whitlam government, which suggests you have progressive views on foreign policy. But if we depicted you as that sort of author, readers would then struggle with your emphasis on order and its reliance on an equilibrium of power. So should we call you a realist?'

'No, definitely not.'

'But you see the balance of power as a fundamental building block of your society which exists in anarchy.'

'The anarchical society, the international society, yes.'

'Mightn't readers see that as a contradiction?'

'They might. But they will come to see the balance of power as a political institution, not a mechanical instrument. If you go back and reread *Control of the Arms Race* carefully you will find a similar argument.'

'Surely your earlier book was not about the anarchical society, Professor Bull. It was about arms control.'

'Why do you see these things as being mutually exclusive? In that earlier work I suggested that the superpowers required mutual understandings to avoid nuclear catastrophe. They may have found themselves in a situation where their forces balanced one another, a geopolitical stalemate as it were. But this accident of history, a fortuitous by-product of their competition, was not bound to persist. To be sustained, it required them to be consciously aware of their need for a set of rules to bind them in a mutual quest for international order. It is very dangerous to see a balance of power, as many American thinkers have a habit of doing, as something that appears automatically because nature abhors a vacuum. Instead we need to see the balance of power as a political institution – just as the détente we have seen in the last few years is the product of deliberate resolve.'

'So rather than setting your book in the realist tradition, perhaps we should be situating it as part of a British-led challenge to American International Relations theory, chipping away at the bastion of realism.'

'I like the last part of what you have just said, but am not entirely comfortable with where you are going in the middle of your comment. In the first instance, your desire to categorize thinkers, above all the one you are talking to at the moment, is troubling. It's also intellectually lazy. Secondly, there is also something off-putting about the idea, if you are heading that way, of a genuinely British approach to international politics, and not just because I have been writing this book in Australia.'

'Sorry to have offended you, but might you explain your reservations to me? You're regarded as an essential member of the British Committee on the Theory of International Politics, and as I understand it some of your book comes from that experience.'

'Yes, you have that part right at least. Some of its most important antecedents lie in my two chapters in *Diplomatic Investigations*, one on "Society and Anarchy in International Relations", the other on the "Grotian Conception of International Society".[7] And I continue to owe a profound intellectual debt to Martin Wight, without whom that Committee would not have been possible. We jointly rail against the hopeless idea that international order is built on formal organizations such as the United Nations when really it rests on informal institutions such as diplomacy, the great powers, and the balance of power. I even think war, when limited by agreed rules, is also one of those institutions. Yet I am not sure my book, which you keep bringing me back to, should be limited by ideas of a British approach to the subject. What's more ...'

'But Professor Bull, you're very well known for attacking American social scientific approaches to International Relations and defending what you call the classical approach.'

'You've clearly not read the article in question[8] carefully enough. A scholar's duty is to be a critic of all ways of thinking and to be imprisoned by none of them. Yes, I did enjoy taking pot-shots at the formal International Relations theorists. As you might know I detest the notion that international order can be evaluated quantitatively. Many an American PhD student is being supervised into a world of false precision, and I delight in informing them that the methodologies they are being pushed into are fruitless. I do not myself see any point in imitating the American predilection for formal approaches like game theory or the dreaded content analysis. But I have great respect for the robustness and energy that many American thinkers bring to our subject, and to the refreshing set of questions they can introduce to the desiccated intellectual lives of many of my British colleagues. If I hadn't gone to the United States early in my LSE career, my own eyes for this sort of thing would not have been opened, and I am grateful to Charles Manning[9] for having set this up to avoid me heading into the military draft as a British subject.'

'So you were an unhappy member of the British Committee.'

'No, far from it. And I do what I can to remain in contact with my British colleagues. We get to go to some nice places too. A workshop at Bellagio is far from a bad way of spending a few days in Italy. But I was not content that as a Committee we should remain insulated from the big and reinvigorating intellectual challenges that were coming from the other side of the Atlantic. So that's why I arranged for someone like Thomas Schelling to address the Committee. And that's also why I insisted on presenting papers on the work of Morton Kaplan[10] and Karl

Deutsch. If there is a British approach, and if it is not infused by these new perspectives, it will wither on the vine. But some of my colleagues, including Martin Wight, weren't so sure.'

'In which case Australia has been a much happier place to base yourself: strong connections to Britain still but also influenced by American thinking and close to Asia where so much is going on?'

'That's an unusually insightful thing for you to say, but I wouldn't give Australia too much credit. I have a line I am saving up for whenever I have the chance to use it. It is so good to see Australia getting over its inferiority complex in relation to Britain, I will say. But then I will add that Australia still has a considerable amount to feel inferior about.'[11]

'That's very amusing, but I hope we won't see too much of that sort of thing in the book. Some of our readers struggle with contrarian viewpoints, Professor Bull.'

'Well then they probably won't like what they find. If they look for a single hypothesis – to use a word I don't employ very much myself – they may encounter several. If they look for me to get to the essences of concepts – something my philosophy education under John Anderson[12] at Sydney warned against – they will find themselves being taken through several alternatives. And if they are looking for a completed argument, they will discover on-going dialectic.'

'That doesn't sound as if the book will be easy going.'

'It shouldn't be. I will make no apologies for that. If the study of international politics was easy, I wouldn't bother myself with it. I'm not here to make a complex and troubled world simple and convenient. I am not a therapist.'

'No, I can see that from talking with you. But can we expect a completed manuscript by a particular date? I mean to say, the contract was issued some time ago.'

'Yes, I signed it well before leaving the LSE. But as I say, I have been busy. And the fact that I am even working on theories of international order is still a surprise to some of my colleagues here.'

'Surely not. You've said enough today to indicate that this area has been an abiding interest for you. And some gossipy person I know at the LSE once told me you had even been planning to do a doctoral dissertation on the subject, something you never completed.'

'Yes, and I take pride in teasing my own doctoral students that the degree they are reading for is not something I ever had to do. I actually didn't even really start the doctorate, although I seem to recall scribbling "International Anarchy" down on one of the yearly forms as my proposed topic. But when I arrived here in Canberra, I was greeted as a strategic studies expert. And given your unusually detailed knowledge of goings on at the LSE, you will know that I was appointed Reader there at one stage with a special focus on Strategic Studies. So not long ago, when I gave a seminar here in the Coombs Building on international order, I got some quizzical looks from some of the scholars here, including people connected with the Strategic and Defence Studies Centre. Desmond Ball,[13] one of my most able students, swore at me in that wild colonial-boy way of his. So even those who have worked with me don't necessarily know what I am most interested in and how it seems to fit together.'

'Would that not be different back in Britain?'

'That's the second time you have shown some real insight. After India I will be spending some time back at Oxford.[14] They don't necessarily understand my interest in Asia, or in the Third World there. But Britain is probably where my work stands a better chance of evolving, especially now that I am expecting to move into deeper work on questions of international justice. Order, with which justice is often battling,[15] may well have had its day.'

'So you might be tempted to come back?'

'Perhaps. But if some longer-term possibility came up, I'd need to discuss it with my wife Mary. We'd have to think about what a move back there would mean for the children. I'd also be giving up wonderful working conditions here for lots of teaching and less money.'[16]

'Yes I can already see this would be a great place to write. And before you set sail on the new work on justice I was just wondering about *The Anarchical Society*, as you're calling it. Is it premature, Professor Bull, to talk about a date at which we can, at Macmillan, confidently expect a manuscript to arrive? We have had some very good readers in place for some time now ready to look at what you have produced.'

'It is definitely not premature to talk about a date. But I also know that Professor Miller is keen to talk with me this morning about overseas leave. There have been some complaints that I am planning to spend too much time abroad, and so we have to keep the administration at bay. You'll find your own way out, won't you?'

Notes

1. Hedley Bull, *The Control of the Arms Race: Disarmament and Arms Control in the Nuclear Age,* (London: Weidenfeld & Nicolson for the Institute for Strategic Studies, 1961).
2. Hedley Bull, *The Anarchical Society: A Study of Order in World Politics,* (London and Basingstoke: Macmillan, 1977).

3. Bull was Visiting Professor at Jawaharlal Nehru University in 1974–5.
4. Hedley Bull, 'The New Balance of Power in Asia and the Pacific', *Foreign Affairs*, 49:4, July 1971, pp. 669–681.
5. Hedley Bull, 'Options for Australia', in Gordon McCarthy (ed.), *Foreign Policy for Australia: Choices for the Seventies*, (Sydney: Angus and Robertson, 1973), pp. 137–183.
6. Prime Minister of Australia, 1972–5.
7. See Hedley Bull, 'Society and Anarchy in International Relations' and 'The Grotian Conception of International Society', in Herbert Butterfield and Martin Wight (eds), *Diplomatic Investigations*, (London: George Allen & Unwin, 1966), pp. 35–50; 51–73.
8. Hedley Bull, 'International Theory: The Case for a Classical Approach', *World Politics*, 18:3, April 1966, pp. 361–377.
9. Montague Burton Professor of International Relations at the London School of Economics, 1930–1962.
10. Political science professor at University of Chicago; author of *System and Process in International Politics* (1957).
11. For the use of this line, published two years after Bull's death, see Hedley Bull, 'Britain and Australia in Foreign Policy', in J.D.B. Miller (ed.), *Australians and British: Social and Political Connections*, (North Ryde: Methuen Australia, 1987), p. 127.
12. Challis Professor of Philosophy, University of Sydney, 1927–1958.
13. Subsequently Professor and (from 1984 to 1991) Head of the Strategic and Defence Studies Centre, Australian National University.
14. Bull was Visiting Fellow at All Souls College, Oxford in 1975–6.
15. See Hedley Bull, 'Order vs. Justice in International Society', *Political Studies*, 19:3, September 1971, pp. 455–463.
16. In 1977 Bull became Montague Burton Professor of International Relations at Oxford. On his career and thinking, see Robert Ayson, *Hedley Bull and the Accommodation of Power*, (Basingstoke: Macmillan, 2012).

40
Jean Bethke Elshtain (1941–2013): A Women's Refuge, Baghdad, Summer 2015

Caroline Kennedy-Pipe

Caroline: Professor Elshtain, thank you for meeting me here in Iraq. It is a pleasure to meet the author of *Women and War*. I bought that book many years ago in a second-hand bookshop in New England. I had attended APSA in Boston and was enjoying a holiday with my family; whilst browsing in the bookshop, I happened upon *Women and War*. I still have that copy although it is now littered with comments and rather dog eared from my use and that of my students! Now in a quirk of fate we are both here in the ruins of Baghdad at a seminar on 'Women after War'. It is really your views on the current crisis that I wish to discuss today.

So in your book *Just War against Terror* you argued for an ethic of responsibility, and the need/the imperative for sometimes responding to significant political events. That is, you have always advocated a responsibility to act, obviously 9/11 was in your view just such an event, which required robust action against those who both conspired and instigated the attacks on your homeland. How now, sitting here, do you think that those wars waged by the United States have actually helped those we wish to keep safe, let alone those who we wished to liberate?

Elshtain: Well, what remains even now with all that has happened in Iraq is that the wars themselves were 'Just' whatever the outcome may be. The challenge is and remains, as we see with ISIS, that Islamic fundamentalism cannot and refuses to be limited by reason. Whatever the US did or did not do to allay the concerns of the radicals, it could not and did not rid itself of its essential principles – those of democracy, freedom of speech, equality and so on – the very qualities loathed and challenged by fundamentalists. As patriots, however chastened we may be by the consequences of these wars, we cannot and should not repeal our commitment to the defence of the United States and personal freedoms around the globe.

Caroline: Yes, we need to discuss patriotism and your concept of the chastened.

Elshtain: Indeed and we will, but the wars were in essence 'Just' because we did not fight to conquer or destroy countries for our own selfish purposes. These were defensive wars precisely about protecting our ways and our ability to keep our homes, and our kith and kin free. War in my view, as you know, can and should be an instrument of justice.

Caroline (who is looking around the rubble in the compound, the listless women and children and the stray dogs): But on what basis has justice been served by these American wars?

Elshtain: Bad states, rogue states need to be restrained and even disciplined for their actions in the international system – these states usually have a democratic deficit and nothing close to what we would recognize as a civil society. In contrast, the US is in so many ways the standard bearer for an ideal type of state. Therefore it needs to be defended against those who would do it harm; yet it also needs, indeed is required, to act as a force for good in the world. So national sovereignty is an achievement rather than a presupposition. We presuppose God is sovereign but we cannot assume a nation state is sovereign until it demonstrates its ability to be independent from the protection of another state, to treat its citizens decently and to foster a vibrant civil society: sovereignty as responsibility. You know this idea has been at the heart of my work. This 'decency', if I can use an old-fashioned word, marks a state as a mature member of the international community. Something analogous is true for the person – persons are not born as mature members of society but they can grow with encouragement to become such. This is the chance we gave Iraq – to become decent. We removed an unjust regime, gave people protection and the chance to build a civil society and to behave in a responsible way in the international system.

Caroline: But that was surely just a shield for a type of chauvinism and indeed the worst kind of a return to war purely for American interests? We know that Saddam did not have nuclear weapons and that was the original pretext for war.

Elshtain: Your problem is that, as a European, perhaps understandably because of your troubled history, you are wary of my kind of patriotism and sceptical of its virtue. You seem to view patriotism as simply instrumental or the product of a manufactured cynicism. This is simply not the case in post-9/11 America. Political sovereignty is a great historic achievement. It has helped to bind millions of people to a particular 'place' and to create a civic home for which the people themselves have a responsibility. In its constitutional form, it provided and provides for a type of civic identity that is not and should not be reduced to terms of race, gender, ethnicity or religion … it recognizes that there are certain dignities that belong to human beings as such and that the state can either honour or dishonour these. So in short my conception of sovereignty – a chastened sovereignty if you will – offers in my view about as good a deal as human beings can reasonably expect in a world beset by conflict and confronted daily by the prospect of wars of all sorts.

Caroline: Surely this is a problem. By what rubric does a sovereign state have to act in a benign way towards its own people? On what basis do you make this claim?

Elshtain: In my view we cannot assume a nation state is sovereign until it demonstrates its ability to be independent from the protection of another state, to treat its citizens decently and to foster a vibrant civil society: it is sovereignty as responsibility.

Caroline: But I cannot think of a definition of sovereignty in which a state treating its own people decently – (and what does that actually mean?) is a requirement of sovereignty. Can you? The central problem of modern sovereignty and of course a challenge to the heart of your so-called chastened sovereignty is that the ideal of self-government (the modern preoccupation) conflicts with the requirement of good government (the ancient concern). So surely the trick is to ensure that self-government by the people and good government coincide but the question you do not answer in your work is how to achieve this fusion.

Elshtain: The US Constitution does a pretty good job .... I suggest you read the XIV Amendment ...

Caroline: Yes, the protection of US citizens is certainly there; yet the challenge running through your work in the post-9/11 period is you acknowledge the nastiness and brutality of war and conflict – but it seems as if anything, indeed everything, torture of a certain variety, war, the killing of women and children (and I will, if time permits, return to feminism) is justified in the defence of America and its citizens. Indeed your type of American patriotism means that after 9/11 the nuances and complexity of some of your earlier views is almost lost in the call to arms – as, for example, your justification and seeming endorsement of torture.

Elshtain: I harbour few illusions about the nature of the world or any view that a utopian world government is likely any more than say nuclear disarmament – the world is ugly and war even more so. There are tough choices to be made, but yes war can lead to a greater degree of justice. To quote Arendt, 'Politics is not the Nursery'.[1] Politics is about the tension between the world we would wish to see and the world which exists. Our reality is one in which there are social and political evils and our role is to confront that evil. To quote another inspiration of mine – Niebuhr – Christians must use the power of power politics even if we dirty our hands in the process.

Caroline: So like Morgenthau you believe in power?

Elshtain: We, the powerful, must respond to attacks against persons who cannot defend themselves because they, like us, are human beings, hence equal in regard to us, and because they, like us, are members of states, or would-be states, whose primary obligation I repeat is to protect the lives of those who inhabit their polities. We must also act against evil where it exists. We have to pursue international justice. All people I think have a claim to have coercive force/violence deployed on their behalf if they are victims of the many horrors attendant upon radical political instability. In this less than ideal world and in the absence of any effective international body to act as a guarantor, the one candidate to underwrite this principle is the United States. There are good reasons for this. One is indeed the superior nature of our political system and the fact, like it or not, that we are the sole remaining superpower. The fight against German fascism and Japanese militarism put us in the world to stay. Therefore, America bears the responsibility to help guarantee international stability, whether much of the world wants it or not.

Caroline: But this does not seem much like chastened politics to me; America everywhere?

Elshtain: You wilfully misunderstand the position. This does not mean that we can or should rush around imposing solutions everywhere in a giddy fashion. It does however mean that we are obliged to evaluate all the pleas for justice and relief from people who are being preyed upon, whether by non-state enforcers (like terrorists) or by state-sponsored enforcers. (My own background is pertinent here. I come from a small people – the Volga Germans – who would have been murdered and terrorized had they remained in Russia. The escape to the United States, even the hardships of the journey meant ultimately a sanctuary and protection).

My Christian realist position is one that accepts the inevitability of action in a plural and divided world. I do not deny that this brings moral costs that we must bear.

Caroline: Well, let us return to the idea of costs. Let us take the issue of torture and your stance which has, to put it mildly, caused some controversy. You have written so much about your belief that a democratic and civil society must protect the dignity of humans, you have written on abortion and the treatment of the elderly. So it seems to me that your endorsement of certain torture practices and your rejection of other forms of torture are, even in your own terms, ambiguous.

Elshtain: I attempt to distinguish between what is awful but *must* be done and what is unacceptable and *must never* be done.

Caroline: You must see though how your finely grained differentiation between different types of physical and mental abuse of those detained in places such as Abu Ghraib and Guantanamo is at best confusing. Why, for example, can guards slap and shout and humiliate? You famously (or perhaps infamously) asked whether a 'slap' constitutes torture. Why is it acceptable to place another human being in solitary confinement and impose methods such as sensory or sound deprivation? Your endorsement of such practices is even more puzzling to me when we consider that you have placed ideas of the body

at the centre of much of your work. You have drawn power-
fully on your own experience of polio and the effects of that
disease on your own body and also spoken of giving birth to
your own first child at the age of nineteen. You have created
powerful images of the male body as straight, hard and fit
for combat, yet, post-9/11, you have endorsed the degrading
of the bodies of those detained. You have spoken of female
bodies as life-giving and life-affirming and yet again women
are tortured – their life-giving bodies defiled and destroyed.
Yet, even more than this, it is not just the endorsement
of torture, troubling though that is, it is the false premises
which underlie your justifications ...

Elshtain: Well let me interrupt you. 'Torture' is indeed an unpleasant
feature of war ...

Caroline: I notice that you are using your fingers to indicate that you
are putting 'torture' in quotation marks, So, why the 'torture'
in parenthesis? Why not just plain torture?

Elshtain: You know, we do have to recognize that the ruthless, the
fanatical and those who would do us harm need to be
stopped. Sometimes, distasteful as it may be, intelligence
gathering, however rough the methods, may keep us safe.
Far greater moral guilt falls on a person in authority who
permits the deaths of hundreds of innocents rather than
choosing to 'torture' those who are guilty or complicit. In
my book *Woman and War* I quote Marisa Masu: 'Each Nazi
I killed ... shortened the length of the war and saved the lives
of all women and children'.[2] I go on to say that many may
of course see in this pithy formulation as only a base rationalization for violence, but that is too simplistic and it fails
to do justice to the problem of 'dirty hands' and indeed fails
to recognize the necessary moral ambiguity of any action in
and on the world.

Caroline: Yes but again you parade the ambiguities of such action: you
also have endorsed the idea that those who torture may be
placed on trial and have to account for their actions. Yet,
this seems bizarre because as Nancy Shearman has argued,
'torture is rarely solo work'.[3] It takes the actual institutionalization of torture, the doctors, the interrogators, and the
chain of command to make it happen. This surely reflects on
the very essence of the state that permits and endorses such
practices not just the individual ordered to torture.

Elshtain: I always used to say in my classes that Americans did not have living memories of what it meant to flee a city in flames. As I watched tens of thousands fleeing from New York City on 9/11 and I sat and wept, I recalled thinking 'no more, now we know'.

Caroline: But that is a side step, though an elegant one, from addressing my point. Yes of course that day – that terrible day – is imprinted on so many people but the idea which underpins your endorsement of torture and indeed that of many others is that of the so-called 'ticking bomb'. The idea that torture may compel a terrorist to confess/inform on his comrades about to launch a massive, imminent and lethal attack is not credible surely. Isn't this a vanishingly unlikely scenario?

Elshtain: How do we know? I have argued endlessly against any notion that we can predict outcomes in International Relations. Dreams rarely come true. But the world is full of horrors and underneath much of what is wonderful is so much that is not. We must be prepared to counter those who, for example, would behead our own citizens to make a point. Let us not forget the Daniel Pearls and now many others executed. For what crime exactly?

Caroline: Yes but this is what I feel is missing from your views after 9/11 and it is perhaps the most important principle in international relations. I am talking about prudence.

Elshtain: What do you mean 'missing'?

Caroline: Perhaps I mean hidden rather than missing. I cannot see in your work and in your recent public statements any acceptance of the idea of prudence. This surely for a theorist of International Relations of your ilk must be a guiding force. So, if prudence is the ability to judge the rightness of a course of action from a range of possible alternatives on the basis of its consequences, there was surely little prudence demonstrated in the rush to war after 9/11. Certainly the current tragedy in Iraq and Syria, the suicide bombers, the hostage taking and the creation of an Islamic pseudo state has all stemmed from that intervention.

Elshtain: If action had not been taken after 9/11 we would have failed in our duties to our fellow countrymen. The common good was threatened by those attacks.

Caroline: I understand the need for revenge, I understand the need for action, my point is that the consequences have been (look around you) not what was expected here or in Afghanistan. Surely we should have exercised in Machiavelli's terms 'prudence'? What we have is a cauldron of instability of extremism and a deeply ideological struggle that will end who knows where. You have written and spoken about the importance of Arendt's approach which she dubbed 'pearl fishing'.[4] You dive in, not quite knowing what will come up ... the important point is to be open to any subject ... my point is that after 9/11 you did not remain open to many of the possibilities of action ... or perhaps inaction?

Elshtain: I think you know that it was my honour to be amongst a group invited to the White House to meet with President Bush, to contemplate, to pray and to find a way of addressing the events and reaction to 9/11. There was no rush to war. There was no hoopla. There was a calm acceptance of the need to act and the need to sacrifice.

Caroline: Well, let us in this context return to Machiavelli. Surely the problem as he points out is that private and political morality do not coincide? Building on this supposition, Max Weber in his lecture 'Politics as a Vocation' dramatizes Machiavelli and argues that once you enter the world of power you inevitably keep company with demons, no matter what your intention might be.

Elshtain: To answer that charge, let me quote Mark Twain: 'rumours of my death have been greatly exaggerated'. 9/11 did not change any of my essential beliefs about power, responsibility or the United States and its place in the world. It just so happens that at this historical juncture my country is the most powerful, the most capable of guarding and guiding justice. Along with that power, as I have always maintained, comes responsibility. We can exercise our power with restraint or we can sit back and let the rest of the world go to hell in a hand cart. The question is not, as I have said, in response to the criticisms of my old friend Nick Rengger, whether the United States is a superpower but what kind of superpower it is and should be.[5] But we should all remember – and this view always has informed my work – there can never be any promise of control over events. We live in a world that threatens to be eclipsed by a moral darkness, terroristic evil is simply wrong but ridding ourselves of it requires and will continue to require a series of tragic encounters such as we see before us here in Iraq.

Notes

I would like to thank Noel O'Sullivan, Nicholas Rengger and Fiona Ritchie for their comments.

1. Hannah Arendt, *Eichmann in Jerusalem: A Report on the Banality of Evil.* (London: Penguin Classics, 2006).
2. Shelley Saywell, *Women in War.* (New York: Viking, 1985), p. 38 quoted in Jean Bethke Elshtain, *Women and War.* (Basic Books, 1987), p. 179.
3. Nancy Sherman, *The Untold War Inside the Hearts, Minds, and Souls of Our Soldiers.* (New York: Norton, 2010), p.147.
4. Hannah Arendt, Introduction to Walter Benjamin, Illuminations. Houghton Mifflin Harcourt, 1968, quoted in Jean Bethke Elshtain, *Women and War,* (New York: Basic Books, 1987), p. xi.
5. Nicholas Rengger, 'Just a War against terror? Jean Bethke Elshtain's burden and American power' in *International Affairs*, Volume 80, no.1, pp. 107–116.

Conclusions

Richard Ned Lebow, Peer Schouten and Hidemi Suganami

Panel 71A

Has There Been any Progress in International Relations Theory Since Thucydides?

57th ISA Annual Convention, 16–19 March 2016

Atlantis

Richard Ned Lebow: As chair, I am delighted to welcome you all to this panel. Thinking that many people would be interested I requested a big room, but had no idea there would be such a large turnout – and at 8:30 on a Saturday morning! Please, those of you in the back, there are still a few empty seats up front and the rest of you should feel free to sit in the aisles or in the back, in front of the windows.

Before introducing our speakers and commentators, I want to note that our speakers have agreed to keep their presentations to less than five minutes. They all have papers that we are posting online.

Excuse me, Hans. I don't think this is the right moment to take a selfie! And where did you get that selfie stick?

Hans J. Morgenthau: I agree it is out of character, but Karl asked all of us for self-portraits. He is going to post them on something called 'You Tube'.

Karl W. Deutsch: That's right. I'm uploading the pictures and creating a link to a Dropbox for the papers. I want to see how many hits they both get, and from what countries, whether the pictures and texts get forwarded to others, and what kinds of comments readers leave. It's all part of a research project.

Richard Ned Lebow: I see. I've arranged for a group photo after the panel and you can post that too if you like.

As I was about to say, we will begin with Thucydides, the most senior of our panellists, followed by Thomas Hobbes. Next come three well-known twentieth-century theorists: Hans Morgenthau, Karl Deutsch and Hedley Bull. Our two commentators are Peer Schouten of the Danish Institute for International Studies and Hidemi Suganami of Aberystywth University. Thucydides, Son of Olorus, the floor is yours.

Thucydides: I am accustomed to speeches, but to those of others that I try to report as accurately as possible, adjusting them on occasion to highlight key tensions or deeper truths. This morning I am going to represent myself, and I am not only going to read my remarks in English but to adopt a modern style of presentation. My account of the Peloponnesian War uses the sophist mode of presentation. What appears in the authorial voice does not reflect my considered judgments but rather comprises introductory remarks that I deliberately undercut in the narrative that follows. Sophists used tensions and contradictions to lead readers to deeper understandings. Today I will speak only in the authorial ekphrastic voice and my words can be taken at face value. That said, I am new to thinking this way, and have had to read an enormous amount of theoretical material and history since giving my interview for *Return of the Theorists* eighteen months back.

Perhaps foolishly I offered my account as a 'possession for all time'. I did so because human nature is unchanging and the kind of hubris responsible for the Archidamian and Peloponnesian Wars will manifest itself again and again. It may not always produce the chain of events that provoked these conflicts, but it is a real possibility. So too in democracies is the threat of demagogues rising to power by appealing to the fear, greed and pride of citizens ever present. And in all societies, regardless of their form of government, we should expect that passion will make reflection difficult, that hope will often trump reason, and that people will exaggerate the skill and cleverness of their leaders while minimizing that of their adversaries.

These verities provided fertile themes for our poets, who conveyed wisdom in plays. They differ from today's scholarly texts in that they make use of emotion and reason. As Aristotle understood, they combine, especially in tragedy, to bring about a catharsis, which can facilitate the most productive kind of learning. Tragedy is a genre of story with an established and well-understood structure. I adapted it to politics, knowing that my audience would respond to this structure and expect certain things from my narrative. I expected tragedy to endure, which was a great mistake, as it comes and goes, and more often the latter. My point here is that the kind of wisdom my culture developed is conveyed through stories, and better yet performances that engage the community. But change was already in the air and everything is different since Plato; Nietzsche is absolutely right on this score.

Your goal is conceptual knowledge, what Aristotle refers to as *epistēme*. Tragedy and my account of the Peloponnesian War seek to convey practical reason, or *phronēsis*. It is deliberative but directed toward action. It leads to knowledge about what is worthwhile in life, and provides the incentive to educate the desires to act in accord with these goals. *Phronēsis* is the product of an arduous educational process that must begin in childhood and gradually allow emotions arising from the affection we develop towards good friends and role models and reflections about them and our life experiences to shape the psyche. It finds expression in the taste for more complex pleasures, recognition of the need of deferred gratification and of the value of self-restraint. *Phronēsis* applies equally to foreign policy because it is the produce of human goals, calculations and actions. Like Socrates, I believe that the same principles and dynamics that govern the psyche govern the polis.

I offer this long-winded introduction to my remarks to make you aware that I bring a different perspective than most of you to the question of this panel. I am less interested in *epistēme* than *phronēsis*. From my perspective, what you call International Relations theory is valuable only to the extent that it helps leaders, assemblies, and in your time, public opinion, formulate appropriate goals and means of achieving them. With this benchmark in mind I can attempt to answer the question.

The question presumes that there was some knowledge of international relations in my epoch. This is certainly belied by the policies of Corcyra and Corinth, and of Athens and Sparta, and the *stasis* [civil war] to which this led in Hellas. Only Hermocrates and Syracuse rise to the occasion. Political life does not look much different in your day. Leaders and peoples, motivated by fear, interest and honour, have repeatedly acted in ways that diminish their security, wealth and standing. Your demagogues make Cleon look restrained and Alcibiades merely frivolous. But here I am willing to defer to your greater knowledge of contemporary affairs.

Was there good knowledge about international relations at the time, and if so, why did it have seemingly little impact on the course of events? I think the answer to the first question is largely no. The tragedies of Sophocles and Euripides and the comedies of Aristophanes, which have the potential to encourage *phronēsis*, were not written until late into our civil war, and in some cases afterwards. They were a response to these events, as was my account, which modern translations annoyingly insist on calling a 'history'. Plato's *Republic* and other relevant dialogues were also reflections on this disaster. He and I went in opposite directions in what we supposed were the best strategies for rebuilding civilization. All of us hoped that tragedy or philosophy could lead the way to more peaceful and happier societies, although we were uniformly pessimistic about this prospect.

Looking at your era, and the history leading up to it, our pessimism was fully warranted. In every part of the world, except those dominated by a single power, it is a saga of inflated ambitions, poorly conceived initiatives, and, at times, unlimited violence. The understanding of human affairs and international relations that we Greeks developed has had little impact. This is so, for many reasons, I think. For over a millennium, these writings were lost to European culture. When rediscovered, they were not always properly understood. My fellow panellist Hobbes owes us all an explanation on this count. Later, the Germans treated Greek texts as Rorschach Tests and projected their political and psychological needs onto them. The tragic understanding of politics and its associated view of life did not take deep roots in any Western culture. Efforts by our esteemed panellist Professor Morgenthau had little effect. American readers especially came away from his book with the wrong lesson that power was everything. Subsequent American realists read the Melian Dialogue in support of their misguided conclusions when I intended it to be understood as a pathology.

As Marx – whom I'm told is in the audience – would expect, many discourses are intended to justify and sustain existing power relationships. In the mid-twentieth century, Professor Morgenthau suggested that this was true of American International Relations theory. More recently, it has been shown how the concept of hegemony, so central to realist and liberal theory, has little empirical basis but offers ideological justification for American exceptionalism and dominance. Sadly, this kind of theory makes tragedy more, not less, likely.

I do not pretend to have the competence to evaluate quantitative research, rationalist approaches, feminism or post-structuralism. This is due in the first instance to my lack of training, but also to the opacity and often crudeness of these narratives. We Greeks aspired to produce *literature* and to make it appealing to a wide audience, including those most likely to influence policy decisions. Your search for *epistēme* is inaccessible and uninteresting to policy elites or the general public. I gather that some contemporary scholars also maintain that it is irrelevant.

I am disappointed, but not surprised, that the world is not that much different from the one I knew. I am surprised that the International Relations theory enterprise has gone in a direction that makes it less, rather than more, relevant to the problems you face.

Richard Ned Lebow: Thank you Thucydides. I now cede the floor to our next panellist, Thomas Hobbes.

Thomas Hobbes: I am honoured to be part of this gathering, and wish to thank you all for your gracious invitation and attendance. It is also a great pleasure to meet my fellow-panellists. I am particularly pleased to have the opportunity to converse with Thucydides; the task of translating his great *History* into English was something from which I learned a great deal, though I suspect we depart from each other on some quite crucial points. I am gratified also to have had the leisure to read the works of the other panellists. One of the strange things about Eternity is that you have plenty of time. At any rate, I commend Professors Morgenthau and Bull for having understood more of what I had to say than many scholars seem to have managed, though I regret to say that they seem to have gone badly astray on a number of points. Professor Deutsch seems a charming man, albeit a misguided one. His mind recalls to me somewhat that of my old adversary Sir Robert Boyle, whose mania for experimentation knew no bounds. I trust, however, that our conversations today will be more convivial than those I was forced to be engaged in with Mr. Boyle.

When I was fortunate enough to spend time at the Royal Court in the 1660s, I was much vexed by those who considered themselves great wits; so much so that upon my arrival at Court, my revered Monarch Charles the Second was wont to jest 'here comes the bear to be baited!' [Laughter]. I wonder if the same will be true today? I hope not, tho' I fear it will be so – since as I remarked in my earlier discourse in this volume, the vanity of scholars knows few limits, and I suspect that this is little changed – even as so much else appears to have been transfigured. Moreover, as much as I enjoy laughter, it is necessary always to remember that it is often occasioned by vanity, being an expression of one's perceived superiority over another. As such, it can generate resentment as much as conviviality. In truth, laughter captures much in our world: it is pleasant and dangerous at the same – and it shows an important truth: the need to appreciate relations between things that are not immediately apparent, to examine their implications for how people behave, and assess how we ought to behave in turn.

Nonetheless, I relish intellectual battle as much as I fear and wish to avoid actual battle, so I am pleased to enter the lists in this chamber.

Perhaps, indeed, I may take these initial musings as a beginning for my words today. I have always sought to develop a vision of politics based on reason. The proofs of geometry remain to my mind indisputably one of the highest achievements. However, this does not mean that political knowledge is the same as what I often call natural history, or what many in your studies today seem indiscriminately to lump together as 'science'. A proper understanding of the role of reason must embrace the insights of the sceptics as well as the rationalists, without falling into the arms completely of either. I regret to say, that a failure to recognize this seems to be all too common at this gathering, which you refer to as the ISA, at least if my observations of your continual disputes about 'method' are to be relied upon.

If you will permit me to continue a moment on this subject, and if I may speak freely, I must say that this tendency toward oppositions seems to occupy too great (and too destructive) a position in your discussions. If you wish another illustration, I this morning attended a panel where my views were discussed; a speaker referred several times to 'Hobbesian realism', though without defining properly what, if anything, the words signified and contrasted it to an examination of what he termed 'subjectivity'. At the time, I was sorely vexed at this patent misrepresentation of my views, but civility demanded I forebear, lest frustration get the better of me. I wish now, however, to make clear in person what should be apparent from even the briefest glance at my writings: a proper understanding of politics must understand the place of the passions (what some of you here seem now to refer to as 'emotions') as well as reason. The one does not exclude the other. To my mind, recognizing the importance of the passions does not relieve one of an obligation to think logically about the implications of this insight; to the contrary, it demands the application of reason to this end. And if I may say so, I would invite those who wish to do so to examine carefully my *Leviathan*, where I undertake this task.

As I demonstrate there, and throughout many of my works, these issues of belief and emotion are not disconnected from the question of knowledge and knowing (of 'method') with which I began these remarks. For example, what many now call my 'materialism' is in part a response to political, not just scientific, challenges. It rules metaphysical speculations about God's will or ultimate values beyond this world outside of the court of proper knowledge. These remain legitimate questions of private faith for individuals, but not of politics and policy. If people will recognize (and be *taught* to recognize – the task of many of you in this room) the practical as well as the analytic merits of ontological materialism, and see themselves, their actions, and their aspirations through its lens, they can agree on fundamental principles (such as survival as the highest good and death the greatest evil) and build a shared theory of authority, legitimacy and action. As I mentioned in my earlier conversation, although I have not applied this reasoning to 'IR', its implications can be reasoned out fairly clearly. This to my mind is an example of political knowledge, rightly reasoned. It is pursued in my *Leviathan*, and remains as true today as it was when I wrote it. Should others disagree with my reasoning and conclusions, I challenge them to follow carefully the logic I there expound, and to demonstrate how I err. For my part, I stand by reasoning and its conclusions unflinchingly. Those who truly wish to understand the conditions of peace, I believe, must do likewise.

Richard Ned Lebow: Thank you Mr. Hobbes. It was a singular treat to hear directly from two of our field's great thinkers. We will now listen to theorists close to our time whom at least some of us present have had the privilege of knowing, even studying with. May I start with you, Professor Morgenthau?

Hans Joachim: Let me express my gratitude to Ned Lebow for his

Morgenthau: successful efforts to bring me back to life, which I must admit raises some questions in my mind about the critique of 'scientism' I advanced in some of my writings. Although I still think I was basically right to worry about a misplaced faith in science and technology as a cure-all for tough moral and political dilemmas, I have to admit that it certainly feels good to be alive again. In any event, I would like to thank the medical researchers and technicians who made this minor miracle possible.

But let me turn to the topic of the panel. (And let me also note that I am very happy it is not a dreadful APSA panel. So far, I am happy to report, I have avoided such hellish experiences in the afterlife). Unfortunately, I feel obliged to express some scepticism about both the premise on which the panel seems to be based, and also about some of the views expressed by my esteemed colleague Thucydides.

I simply do not believe that we should describe Thucydides as a *theorist* of international relations. This is not meant to be disrespectful; as will become clear from my comments, I have always admired his great masterpiece on the Peloponnesian Wars. But I have been asked to respond to a very specific question, and to do so I will need to clear up some confusion.

As I have said on numerous occasions, Thucydides is best read as a historian with a philosophical bent, who indeed relied on what we might describe as implicit theoretical claims, but whose intellectual endeavour always remained fundamentally different from that of a theorist of international relations. Thucydides, like the great Ranke, employed some latent theoretical ideas to make sense of a specific constellation of historical events. He did so, as I stated some years back, in order 'to provide the standards for their selection and to give them meaning'. But a fully developed international theory was never his main concern. Not surprisingly, even when he points in the direction of such a theory, its elements are incomplete. This, by the way, was the reading of Thucydides that Martin Wight also offered in his important essay, 'Why is There No International Theory?', which I endorsed immediately upon its publication in a piece of my own on the same question. Of course, theorists also rely on history, so at times the division between the two scholarly tasks becomes blurred. Yet theory – what I have tried to do – simply should not be reduced to history, however philosophically or theoretically minded. As I have noted in a different context:

> [w]hat distinguishes such a history of international politics from a theory is not so much its substance as its form. The historian presents his theory in the form of a historical recital using the chronological sequence of events as demonstration of his theory. The theoretician, dispensing with the historical recital, makes the theory explicit and uses historical facts in bits and pieces to demonstrate his theory.[1]

What I have done – and with all due respect to Thucydides – this *does* perhaps represent a certain intellectual advance, is pursue *theory*, and that means that I have tried to understand the general principles of politics and how those general principles relate specifically to international politics. What are the fundamental regularities of politics, and how do they play out given the peculiarities of international society, e.g., the 'national interest defined in terms of power, the precarious uncertainty of the international balance of power, the weakness of international morality, the decentralized character of international law', and so on? Of course, there is overlap with Thucydides' approach, yet the orientation is a different one. And of course my writings have unavoidably included discussions of particular historical examples, since I have found it useful to rely on them to illustrate my ideas. When doing so, I have in fact followed Thucydides' example in one decisive way: the assessment of any specific historical or political context, I believe, must always depict the various political actors as objectively as possible, as representing 'different incarnations of the same species of man, endowed with the same virtues and vices, equally capable of great and mean deeds, of wisdom and folly', something both he and Herodotus did successfully in their great histories. This is what I once described as striving for a 'charitable understanding', and I believe it is crucial to all sound political analysis.

Let me also emphasize, since I have been misunderstood here as well, that my commitment to a general theory of international politics should not be conflated with the views of those who think political science should be modelled on the natural sciences. That's a real mistake, for reasons I cannot explore today. Compared to hard-line advocates of that position, Thucydides and I are in fact allies. But that overlap should not lead anyone to miss the differences between his endeavour and my own.

One additional comment on this issue, if I may. In his remarks today, Thucydides reminded us the classical distinction between conceptual knowledge, *epistēme*, and practical or deliberative knowledge oriented towards action, *phronēsis*. I am no classicist, and though I have always admired not just Thucydides but also Aristotle (whose writings I have regularly taught in seminars), I have never had the time to garner the requisite exegetical and philological expertise. However, it still seems to me that what I have tried to do as an International Relations *theorist* – and perhaps herein lies another difference between us – still falls primarily under the rubric of abstract conceptual or theoretical knowledge, though I do assuredly believe that such knowledge can have positive practical benefits. Yet it is still not quite the same thing as practical wisdom or judgment, which is closer in spirit to the classical conception of *phronēsis*, and which political actors – and especially statesmen – need to acquire. But that is a different kind of knowledge from what scholars and especially theoreticians aim for *as scholars*, which is also not to say that scholars should be systematically precluded from acting as political creatures, as I have in opposition to the Vietnam War and on other occasions. These are complicated issues. In any event, here I remain indebted to the great Max Weber, who would perhaps have questioned whether the classical idea of *phronēsis* can provide guidance in the modern world – given what he famously described as 'Entzauberung' (or 'disenchantment') – in the manner it did for the Greeks. At the very least, modern moral scepticism and relativism make things messier than perhaps Thucydides (or, for that matter, Aristotle) appreciated. Lastly, I would again simply emphasize that Thucydides' version of *phronēsis*, if that in fact is how we best should understand his project, takes a distinctive *historical* form, and whatever its other strengths, that unavoidably circumscribes its theoretical scope.

Now, just to be clear, I have always considered Thucydides a notable *Ur-Realist* of sorts, and his views about human nature, the irrepressibility of power and political struggle, and the fundamental importance of interest to understanding political action anticipated some of my own ideas. But, as I have been saying, a fundamental difference remains: as a *historian*, Thucydides was doing something different from what I always intended.

I would love to present Thucydides with a copy of *Scientific Man Vs. Power Politics*, but apparently it is now out of print. If I understand correctly, books are now being replaced by little buzzing electronic devices? For those who bother to look, in fact, I interpret the Melian Dialogue in somewhat more complicated terms than many other realists. What I have said is that Thucydides' account of the Melian dialogue should not be read as historical fact but instead as a literary tool for expressing a fundamental truth about the nexus between justice and power: 'even if assuming the reality of justice, we are incapable of realizing it', which is hardly the same thing as denying the existence or at least desirability of justice, something I have never sought to do. As the Melian Dialogue so vividly illustrates, however, people 'have always thought and acted as *though* justice were real', even when it is obvious to objective bystanders that such claims are in fact misbegotten. One of the sources of the tragic nature of human existence is precisely the fact that we can never fully achieve justice, even though we are obliged to try to do so. Both Thucydides and I understand this crucial feature of all political existence: the quest for justice and the lust for power are unavoidably intermingled, which makes the quest for justice much more complicated and paradoxical than either his countrymen or my own ever acknowledged.

Richard Ned Lebow: Thank you, Professor Morgenthau. Karl Deutsch is next.

Karl W. Deutsch: Thank you, Ned. It gives me great pleasure to look around the room and see some of my former students, and even more, to see how they have thrived. It is equally satisfying to see our discipline move forward, as indeed it has. I know my faith and optimism in social science put me at odds with the other panellists, so let me explain the basis of my beliefs.

Much of my career was devoted to the study of nationalism. While still a student in Prague I was familiar with the work of Otto Bauer, the leading Austro-Marxist thinker on the subject. In America, I read Carleton J. H. Hayes and later, the works of Hans Kohn and Rupert Emerson. My *Nationalism and Social Communication* builds on their historical insights and advances our understanding by using concepts from cybernetics and quantitative research. It offers a more rigorous understanding of the phenomenon of nationalism, and one that sheds new light on the causes and timing of nationality conflicts within countries. In the sixty-plus years since my book was published, there has been a veritable explosion of research on nationalism, much of it using new concepts and research methods. Computers and advanced statistical techniques enabled my successors to amass and manipulate amounts of data of which I could only dream. Today's researchers can use more variables, make more exhaustive horizontal and vertical comparisons, and begin to probe the way in which so-called structural features interact with those of context like path dependence and agency. The potential of even bigger data analysis will open up further avenues of research.

To be sure, progress has not been linear. I was an early supporter of the Correlates of War (COW) project, and still believe that my friend David Singer was on the right track in attempting to transform our extensive qualitative understanding of war and its causes into variables that could be measured and compared. It brought badly needed rigour to the enterprise at every step of research from identifying possible causes of war to collecting and assessing data about them, and above all, to the process of inference. Admittedly, the inductive fishing expedition that followed was not a particularly productive enterprise, but much has been learned since then. The project has many more variables, the data is more carefully coded, and researchers are using it in more sophisticated ways.

The same is true of the *World Handbook of Social and Political Indicators*, published in the early 1960s, and the product of my collaboration with Harold Lasswell, Bruce Russett and Hayward Alker. We collected international data in the age before governmental data were computerized and the Internet and Wikipedia existed to make it accessible. The fact that the project now looks primitive indicates just how far social science both in its methodology but also in its epistemology has progressed and what is now possible, especially with the help of new technologies that continue to impress me. I recently read of a nice study that used nighttime satellite images of India to identify rural districts that were receiving public services and that facilitated the study as to how this issue correlated negatively with political protest and violence. Such research was unimaginable in my day!

Social media are the most recent communications breakthrough. When my former student and long-time friend Andy Markovits interviewed me for his book, I told him that this new complex arguably constitutes the most exciting and potentially revolutionary development since the printing press. For International Relations scholars it has endless possibilities, and I am hoping to be in Atlantis long enough to start my own project. This is why I am collecting selfies, in the hope of tracking global intellectual networks and comparing them to those of the Enlightenment, which I will have students reconstruct from correspondence among eighteenth-century thinkers. If anybody is interested in participating in this research, do come and see me after the panel. The only problem I foresee is the bandwidth here in Atlantis, given the use we are all making of the Internet. [laughter from the audience]

Printing produced a secular, liberal world, although, as always it is under siege. In my day, nationalism and fascism were the biggest threats. Today it is nationalism and religious fundamentalism, and as in the past, repressive political regimes of different ideological persuasions. Science and social science working together have the potential to overcome these threats in the long-term. In every decade throughout the twentieth century the number of scientists doubled, so too did the number of books published, and of equal importance, the number of people capable of reading them. With English as the lingua franca and the development of electronic media, information will accrue and flow at a rate that would be impossible for printed matter. Information of such quality and quantity will also be more difficult to suppress. Communication is the highway of progress, and the dissemination of research findings about poverty, prejudice and war all have the potential to reduce these scourges of humankind.

Have we progressed since the time of Thucydides? The answer is unambiguously yes. I propose that we take a survey of everyone in this room to discover what they think, and to break it down by age cohort. Hard data are more convincing than the idiosyncratic musings of an old man.

Let me return to Thucydides, whose account of the Peloponnesian War is one of the great works of history and literature. I read it as a university student for the first time and was deeply moved. I'm honoured to share the podium with all of the participants, but especially with a man of such extraordinary stature. There is much to learn from his book about war and its causes, and the causes of political order and breakdown more generally. I also believe that its format makes it accessible, and even fascinating, to a wide range of people who would never consider reading an article in the *Journal of Conflict Resolution*. For the same reason, I have always enjoyed reading Livy and the great works of Czech, German and English literature. They open the hearts and minds of great thinkers and profound authors to their readers, and, one hopes, the latter's own hearts and minds as a result.

We should nevertheless not shy from treating Thucydides' exquisite narrative as a storehouse of data from a different historical epoch. By my count, he describes twelve attempts at deterrence and compellence. We can code these encounters as successes and failures – mostly failures, I fear – and read the speeches and narrative to grasp the reasons why this is the case. These reasons can also be coded and become the first step in the creation of an international data set covering first the Greek and then the Roman worlds. We can run regressions to see if deterrence succeeded and failed for the same reasons it did in the nineteenth and twentieth centuries, and also study differences in the causes of war. There are great possibilities here for interesting dissertations.

Richard Ned Lebow: Thank you, Karl. What is this? You want me to do a selfie too? OK, but later. I now turn the floor over to Hedley Bull.

Hedley Bull: Thank you chair. I'd like to begin my remarks with an objection preceded by an observation. Professor Deutsch, I've been defending your work for years among my colleagues in the British Committee on International Theory, insisting that you've been one of the leading American theorists who have brought new insights and rigour to the dilapidated study of international politics. Your work on political community I rate as especially significant. But I must say that your obsession with collecting the trivia which you call data, and your foolhardy dedication to the vacuous charms of content analysis, leave me wondering whether I should have saved my breath.

My objection is to the question we've been asked to consider in this panel. I was very happy to accept the invitation to be here today to rub shoulders with some of the thinkers whose work I've read and sought to understand, and whose approaches I have agreed and disagreed with. But to ask any of us whether International Relations theory has progressed since the days of our colleague Thucydides strikes me as the begging of a patently unanswerable question.

This objection might appear odd to those of you who know that one of my first suggestions to any new students of International Relations is that they read the classics on the subject. This is what my mentor Martin Wight had me do when I got to the London School of Economics, and it has stood me in very good stead. Far better a morning reading Hobbes than a year consulting the Correlates of War. But

I do not require students to do this because I believe that earlier thinkers belong to a continuous line of theorists who are dealing with very similar circumstances to those our current world faces. Happily for them, they did not have to contend with some of the accidents of history we have to deal with, including the arrival of nuclear weapons. Unhappily for them, this also means that they lacked one of the most important material factors that have inclined our generation to accept the urgency of avoiding catastrophic war.

Similarly, it is wrong for us to fault those earlier thinkers for arguments – including those about interactions with peoples beyond European civilization – which we would find objectionable today because of where world opinion has taken us. A study of earlier thinkers is valuable *precisely* because we get to see how they were responding to the international circumstances of *their* time, not because they are speaking directly to *ours*. It is only possible to speak of progress, therefore, if we think we are doing a better job of responding to our international circumstances than they were to theirs.

How then are we to make this comparison? It seems to me that in doing so we need some sort of agreement on the purpose of International Relations theory, an issue upon which the question posed for this panel is unhelpfully silent. I doubt that we are likely to achieve consensus on this matter, but let us say that it is first of all by giving an account of international order in terms of a common set of rules and institutions which operate amongst the main members of the given international system. And it is second of all by determining whether the members of that system, who in our case still happen to be states, approach their relations with each other in such ways that we can conclude that they enjoy some measure of international society with each other. And it is thirdly by determining whether there are possibilities for a significant and potentially radical transformation of the current system, including the replacement of the system of states by something politically quite different.

If these are the proper purposes of International Relations theory, I must admit to being doubtful as to whether a better job is being done now than was done in times we know rather more about than the Greek city states period about which Thucydides has been speaking. How much his world amounted to a properly international system is a point of some significance, and something we should take time to ask him while he is here. But our main point of understanding, lest I say comparison, would be the theorists who were writing in the sixteenth, seventeenth, eighteenth and nineteenth centuries about the international relations of the European system and society of states. Should it be found that they did a better job of determining the rules of their system, the meaning and extent of their international society, and the possibilities of its transformation, than we have of ours, then our answer to the question posed for this panel must be in the negative.

And yet even if we were to examine with great care the international understandings of Vittoria and Vattel, and of Grotius and Gentz, the question would in all probability still suffer from its original defect. It seems manifestly evident to me that there was a stronger sense of international society in the practice of European international relations than in that of a more global international relations today. But what was more intense then was so partly because of the exclusivity of that system – more extensive of course than the world of Thucydides, but far less extensive than ours. We are dealing today with international relations in a properly global system of states. So are we to say that we have not made progress when the task set before us is so challenging because of the absence of a common world culture to correspond with the common European culture which inhabited the rules and institutions of that European international society? Or are we to instead acknowledge that we may have a much greater challenge in establishing the foundations of the new international society?

And in seeking to meet that challenge we in fact should be grateful to Professor Deutsch and his fellow social scientific International Relations theorists. Not of course for their methods, which make a fetish out of formal technique. But instead the assumption that a common commitment to scientific reasoning – in place of natural law and the sentimentality that comes with losing empires – can be the basis for that new international society. It might even help transform our system into something else. So without causing any offence to Thucydides here, I say that we need much less of Plutarch and Plato. And in words that may bring a smile to Professor Deutsch, I say that instead we need more Parsons and Pareto.

Richard Ned Lebow: Thank you Professor Bull – and the other presenters. You have done an admirable job of making brief presentations. There was no need to pass along little notes or pottery shards threatening ostracism. I'm sure our two commentators will follow suit. I can't say I envy them the task of criticizing the kinds of authorities from whom we have just heard. First, Dr. Schouten.

Peer Schouten: Before I start, can I ask you to open that window next to you, Nietzsche? It seems to be getting hot in here with all the heated debate. Oh, you're right, that's probably not a good idea here in the Sunken City. Ah well.

Ladies and gentlemen in the room – it is an honour to be with you. As probably the youngest here, I am more than a bit nervous to find myself in such distinguished company – albeit mostly white men, and mostly dead ones at that. I'm quite sure that because of my nerves, I'll appear just as pale in the selfie that will be posted online; and I'm happy the picture won't be able to convey my trembling left hand, with which I am holding on to my glass of water as if it were life itself.

As for this closing panel. If thought, like wine, matures with age, then my comments here are probably devoid of the kind of phenolic complexity that characterizes the contributions of panelists before and after me, but with that caveat, let me use my five minutes as a discussant for two observations on the main question this panel revolves around: that of progress in International Relations theory since Thucydides. I will base my reflections on two ideas that predate our most senior thinker by a couple of centuries: one attributed to Heraclitus of Ephesus and another to Archilochus of Paros. I'll borrow from the first a view on progress in IR; I'll borrow from the second to distinguish between two ways of relating to that view, typically adhered to by two types of IR scholars.

Even if Heraclitus is often called 'the Obscure' because the fragments of his work that have been delivered to us are often oracular and aphoristic in nature, his formulation of *panta rhei* has dominated philosophy for a long time since Aristotle. Time and again we students of international politics attempt to step in historical streams of thought, diving for theoretical gems that can help us make sense of the flow of the river, and, in some cases, the direction the river will take next. But if it is not possible to step in the same river twice, is it then possible to speak of progress, or only of the meandering of history? Is it possible to intervene in the flow of history based on our reading of its course, or is every such attempt futile? So what is the track record?

Centuries of thinking on IR has not led to the dissolution of war and destruction. On the contrary, the quantitative explosion of theorizing in IR over the course of the last century coincided with the largest accumulation of human-made dead bodies in the riverbed of history. The realization is now dawning on humankind that we have entered an era of irreversible destruction to the environment, which we political thinkers have comfortably but insistently bracketed away, operating as we do in the shadow of Descartes. Hobbes, your state of nature is increasingly polluted. In short, if progress in IR on the level of *epistēme* is judged in terms of real-world progress, it's doing a bad job, and we could indeed weep with Heraclitus.

If I see some realists in the audience nodding in agreement at the suggestion that progress in international politics is not possible, my invoking of the second predecessor of Thucydides, Archilochus, might curb your enthusiasm. If modern realists are typical incarnations of his *echinos* or hedgehogs, laughter would only become the *avulpes* or foxes. The intention of Archilochus might have been – as Isaiah Berlin notes in his brilliant essay on the philosophy of history in Tolstoy – simply to point out the moral lesson that the fox cannot, for all his cunning, defeat the hedgehog's one defence. But more interestingly, Berlin has used this distinction to categorize a number of thinkers present here – Plato, Hegel and Nietzsche as hedgehogs, Aristotle as a fox...

If IR is about distilling stable categories and using history as a source of illustrations, as Morgenthau just said, we should all be hedgehogs in this room (and there's a few clear-cut cases that Berlin didn't incorporate present here – yes I'm looking at you, Hume, Rawls, Bourdieu and Waltz). We humans have a natural inclination to attempt and reduce and fit the unknown into known categories derived from previous experience, in order to make it amenable to action, to give it a place in our system of knowing – to give us some sort of ontological security, to use a modern descriptor. We as IR scholars are, and are expected to be, standard bearers of this inflection; and in order to fulfil the vocation of academic analysis of international politics, one has to elevate the urge to domesticate the unknown to a conviction – in other words, IR scholars ought to be hedgehogs. But the charge of history against us as hedgehogs is serious: how can we continue to defend our belief in overarching truth and progress if those have failed to steer us clear from the barbarous succession of real-world events?

If progress is by contrast approached as a fox, there might be some reason for Abderitan laughter. There are some foxes in hedgehog clothing in this room – Ned, you of all people can't hide your red tail since you published your *Cultural Theory*. And indeed the very premise of the current project – to capture the diversity of voices in international theory along the centuries – is a foxy one. If Hans pointed out just now that Weber laments the disenchantment of the world, foxes perhaps wouldn't see it that way: they revel in the multiplicity engendered by the differentiation and fragmentation of understanding across time, and happily plunge in the river of time again and again to discover new partial and unique aspects of its diversity of life. Hedgehogs might only see the swamp of decaying ideas where foxes revel in the intrinsic beauty of the confused blooming of a thousand – no, millions! – of theoretical flowers (articles in PDF can be likened to flowers, with a little effort) that live out their (generally short) lives on the shores of intellectual history. While foxes might be morally relativist, foxiness does not equal some postmodernist end of great narratives: if indeed there are many foxes among twentieth-century poststructural and self-appointed critical branches of IR, our intellectual history knows of many pre-twentieth century foxes, as morally sceptical and relativist as some contemporary poststructuralists. And there are just as many 'posty' IR scholars who defend their monist vision of international politics with a staunchness that ranks them firmly among the prickliest of hedgehogs.

If foxes do have progress, it is this proliferation of epistemic diversity itself – perhaps with Lakatos, it is a matter of valuing different *epistēmes* coexisting and competing. The fox's hunt is for yet another intellectual catharsis, a proclivity which must have driven Weber to explore the diversity of cultural and religious experience himself. So foxes would celebrate – with Karl Deutsch – the availability of the vast digital archives we have at our disposal as progress in and by itself – even if it might be a step back from learning through intense one-to-one dialogue, the practice of which we have shed in favour of spending our time shackled to electrified boxes that emit gloomy light. Weber, Aristotle, wouldn't you love a crash-course on Google Scholar and some time behind one of these magic screens to explore the sheer diversity of fragmented knowledge and ideas now circulating among scholars?

But perhaps with Weber and Tolstoy, the tragedy of IR theorizing is that we are all foxes by nature but hedgehogs by conviction; inclined to find fault in the *epistēmes* of other hedgehogs, only to find our own attempts at producing alternative theories of order in international politics subject to the same dynamic. So progress perhaps depends on whether we manage to combine – without becoming schizophrenic – our duties as hedgehogs with a healthy dose of foxiness.

Richard Ned Lebow: Thank you, Peer; and now Prof. Hidemi Suganami of Aberystwyth University.

Hidemi Suganami: Thank you, Ned. I don't often come to the ISA but the opportunity to meet Thucydides and Hobbes, as well as Morgenthau and Deutsch, and to see Hedley Bull perform again was too good to miss. I am greatly honoured to be invited to offer my thoughts on their presentations.

Let me begin by observing that, even though the question given to the panellists was seemingly simple and straightforward – 'Has there been any progress in International Relations Theory since Thucydides?' – I could not help but notice that they have collectively addressed a number of complex and inter-related issues.

First, there is a question about whether our study of international relations should aim to produce *epistēme* or *phronēsis*. On this issue, Thucydides is clear that he is less interested in the former than in the latter. His culture produced tragedy as a form of story to recount, drama to perform, with the view to engaging the whole community and conveying practical wisdom. Thucydides himself famously emplotted his account of the Peloponnesian War as a tragedy and laments that the tragic vision of human affairs and international relations the Greeks had developed has had little impact in any Western culture. What we now call IR Theory, he insists, is valuable only to the extent that it helps leaders, assemblies and public opinion formulate appropriate goals of foreign policy and means to achieve them; and he regrets that there is now too much emphasis on *epistēme* and on the methods by which to obtain this at the expense of gaining practical wisdom leading to appropriate actions.

To this, Hobbes has added his observation that a tendency towards oppositions seems to occupy too great and too destructive a position in the community of IR scholars. He believes that, if taught properly, people should be able to understand and agree on certain fundamental principles, such as that survival is the highest good and death the greatest evil, and build upon them a shared theory of authority, legitimacy and action. What this means for IR can be reasoned out fairly clearly, he believes, if we follow the obligation to think logically and rationally. Hobbes is seeking to integrate theoretical understanding and practical wisdom.

Second, there is a question about what a *theoretical* form of understanding in IR means as distinct from a *historical* form – a tension also noted by Peer in his observations just now. Morgenthau has made significant observations here: Thucydides was a historian, *not* a theorist, he insists – and, to that extent, the question the panellists were given was misleading – but the difference between history and theory is more one of form than of substance, Morgenthau rightly observes; the historian presents his theory in the form of a historical recital using the chronological sequences of events as demonstration of his theory whereas the theoretician, like Morgenthau himself, makes the theory explicit and uses historical facts selectively to demonstrate his theory.

On the issue of *epistēme* vs *phronēsis*, Morgenthau believes that his theory is in search of the former but *with* practical significance. He observes that this form of knowledge is to be distinguished from practical wisdom or judgment of the classical kind and adds that, in the modern era of moral scepticism and relativism, the Thucydidean idea would be harder to implement.

Third, there is a question about whether IR Theory should aim to produce knowledge modelled on natural science. Hobbes stresses that political knowledge is not like natural science and that, in making sense of politics, we must not forget the place of the passions (or emotions) as well as reason. Morgenthau agrees. Only Deutsch departs from this apparent consensus among the panellists. For him, there has been significant progress in the scientific studies of international relations, especially through gradual sophistication in quantitative data collection and analysis accompanied by the invention of the computer. From this perspective, he suggests that even Thucydides' accounts of the Peloponnesian War can be exploited as a valuable data source regarding the conditions under which deterrence and compellence succeeds and fails.

In this connection, Bull's statements are very interesting. Contrary to a popular impression in the IR community that he is flatly 'against science', he expresses his appreciation of the rigour of rational and logical thinking, present in the work of Deutsch and his fellow social scientists. However, as we just heard in no uncertain terms, he remains very sceptical of the values of their data sets.

Bull rightly observes that theorists of different historical periods, working against different backgrounds, may have had different concerns; and that our theory can be said to be better than our predecessors' if ours deals with *our* questions better than they did with *theirs*. And he is of the view that the purpose of our theory is closer to that of the theorists of the European states system from the sixteenth to the nineteenth century than to that of those of the Greek city states system; it is to explain how order is maintained in the international system, assess how far this system is also a society, and explore whether a different form of political structure may be able to replace or is already replacing this system/society of states.

I was a little surprised to hear him define the purpose of our IR Theory quite so narrowly. Still, Bull has made an important point when he reminded us that we cannot discuss the panel question without deciding what International Relations Theories are *for*; to this it is by now customary to add, *'for whom'*. I also want to remind ourselves here of Bull's remark elsewhere that, much as we may make serious mistakes in international politics if we fail to take note of what earlier thinkers and practitioners had already thought through, we may also err in considering our future options if we allow ourselves to be constrained by the tyranny of extant concepts. It requires no reminding that treating some particular thinker of the past as *the founder* of our discipline can be constraining if it contributes to legitimizing a particular conception of IR Theory, and of its purposes, at the expense of others.

Rather than look back and ask whether there has been any progress in International Relations Theory since Thucydides, therefore, we should engage with a wide range of issues that confront us in our contemporary world and reflect on the philosophical presuppositions and political implications of our ways of engaging with those issues. In so doing, we should not forget to take into consideration the arguments of our predecessors, where relevant, however ancient, critically and constructively. Thank you.

Richard Ned Lebow: Thank you, Hidemi. I now invite participation from the floor. Please make your interventions brief and in the form of questions to one or more of the panellists. We'll take a few questions and then allow the panellists to respond. Let's start with the bearded gentleman standing by the window. I apologize, I do not know your name.

The bearded man: I am Abū Zayd 'Abdu r-Raḥmān bin Muḥammad bin Khaldūn Al-Ḥaḍrami, professor emeritus at the University of Cairo. Might I ask why your panel only comprises ancient and modern scholars? Is there a reason why we Medieval intellectuals – covering a millennium of human history – have not been included? And why have no scholars from the House of Islam been recognized? Is this a temporal and spatial example of what John M. Hobson calls the Eurocentric Conception of World Politics?

Richard Ned Lebow: And next, a young woman at the front.

The woman at the front: H. M. Swanwick, journalist and suffragette. I have spent a delightful conference attending many panels. While I am pleased with how far feminism has progressed since my time, I am shocked at how many all-male panels there still are, including this one. Might I point out that women represent more than half of the population of the underworld?

Richard Ned Lebow: The elderly gentleman sitting in the second row.

The man in the second row: I believe I am called Confucius in this part of the world. [*He takes a deep breath.*] I know what I do not know; and I fear I know less and less about this 'International Relations Theory' of which you all speak. I shall, however, confine myself to one question. While I mean no offense to Master Thucydides, why must we speak of progress 'since Thucydides'? I do not wish to ask why there is no non-Western IR theory; however, if instead we were to ask how IR Theory has 'progressed' since the time of Laozi (who sits beside me), Sima Qian or Nishida Kitarō, where would this lead our discussion?

Richard Ned Lebow: Thank you, all; and yes, the young woman at the back, who appears keen to come in at this point.

The womanat the back: Thank you, Chair; I am Sarah Jamal, a PhD candidate at Aberystwyth. Somewhat aligning with previous questions, I would like to ask the panellists how they feel about their work being considered and used as the 'cannon of IR'. To be more specific, has your work not contributed to what Spivak calls the 'epistemic violence' that IR has propagated throughout the non-Western world? By 'epistemic violence', I mean the erasure of non-Western ways of thinking and being and the use of 'scientific' both as a term and the practice to form cultural and racial supremacy. Do you not think that your work has done violence to the Other by helping construct the notion of 'civilized peoples' and the various inclusions and exclusions that have been a part of that idea, e.g. slavery, colonialism, patriarchy, white supremacy, capitalism, etc?

Some of the audience is turning restless by now, shaking their heads. Others are eyeing them, and someone can be overheard urging restraint to his neighbour.

Richard Ned Lebow: Order, please. I understand some of you are agitated. Thank you. I now invite the panellists to respond to the questions raised so far. Let's start with Karl.

Karl Deutsch: There is *no* contradiction between an all male panel and a profession that is now fifty percent women. The panel is composed of dead thinkers from earlier eras when almost all thinkers and IR scholars were men. I am delighted to see the greater gender balance that prevails today. When I was alive, you could count women IR scholars on one hand: Margaret Sprout, Annette Baker Fox, Margery Perham and Susan Strange come to mind. All distinguished, but a definite minority in what was then a man's world. *Vive la différence!*

Richard New Lebow: Thank you, Karl; Thucydides would like to come in next.

Thucydides: I would like to respond to Kong Fuzi's remarks. No offence taken, to be sure. I did not choose the title of the panel and had no input in who was invited. I am very pleased to see that it signifies my hope has been realized: my account of the Peloponnesian War has become 'a possession for all time'. I make no claim that it is the only such work, nor that such works are all European. Your *Analects*, Kong Fuzi, even if posthumous, certainly qualify.

Richard Ned Lebow: And now, over to you, Hans.

Hans J. Morgenthau: Since the basic laws of politics and the struggle for power operate pretty much uniformly across culture and time, we should not be surprised to learn that many perceptive thinkers elsewhere dealt with the great issues of international politics. If Ned can bring me back to life again for a future conference, I would be happy to participate in a panel devoted to any of the thinkers Confucius mentions.

   And as for Spivak, of whom the young lady has just spoken, I would caution against the employment of loose terms like 'epistemic violence'. [*At this juncture, Frantz Fanon walks out of the room.*] Is that what in my generation we used to call 'ideology'? If so, let's call it that, and then we can have a fruitful debate about its merits and demerits. Otherwise, we risk confusing things. We already have enough violence as things stand in international relations! As you probably already know, I do think the category 'civilized people' is a potentially useful one, as I tried to explain in *Purpose of American Politics*. How are we otherwise to distinguish the great accomplishments of the Greeks or Romans from so many others? Without some distinctions of this type how can we begin to criticize the terrible crimes committed by nations which consider themselves great but in fact are not. The Germans under Nazism were not a 'civilized people'. The Americans in Vietnam behaved in anything *but* a civilized manner. I do not believe the Americans' attempt to decimate the Vietnamese can be attributed to an excess of civilization on the part of President Johnson and his advisors.

Karl Deutsch: I agree with Hans. I would also like to add my belief that science is not an expression of a particular culture or a prop for colonialism, racism or any other objectionable practice. Science has the potential to transcend and unite people and their cultures. People from many cultures have contributed to its advances, and have been recognized for doing so. Bad science was used to justify colonialism and racism, and its practices were exposed by good science. Given your goals [*looking in the direction of the PhD candidate*] you should be supportive of it.

Richard Ned Lebow: And now Thomas Hobbes wishes to respond.

Hobbes: Cultures differ, certainly; as do beliefs, desires, aversions, and much else. Yet reasoning from first principles with systematic logic does not. This is what separates true political philosophy from scepticism (whether ancient or modern) and opinion from knowledge. Without such knowledge, there is likely only to be chaos and dissention – both epistemic and political – and the violence that will likely accompany this chaos will not be 'epistemic': it will be slaughter.

Richard Ned Lebow: Thank you; and finally, Hedley Bull.

Hedley Bull: My concern with the tone of at least one of the questions is the presumption that it is fitting for thinkers from a particular period to use the world opinion of their day to sit in judgement of the thinking of an earlier era. There may also be a case for hesitation in holding western international theory guilty of a sin of omission in not acknowledging the ideas of non-western scholars. A more urgent task, it would seem to me, is to acknowledge that contemporary international order has depended on the established powers of the west coming to terms with the rising powers of the third world. This may be something about which more can practically be done.

Richard Ned Lebow: Thank you, Hedley. I have just spotted Max Weber with his hand raised.

Max Weber: Indeed, thank you. My question is for Karl. You seem to be arguing that the growth of data, information, knowledge and science ultimately provides the basis to defeat three scourges of mankind: poverty, prejudice, war. You also refer to the expansion of the scientific community across the world, amazing advances in technology to generate data, and so on. How do you explain that, despite this truly impressive development, we do not seem to have made any dent at all in eliminating these evils? Nor has any consensus emerged in the scientific community about how this might be accomplished.

Karl Deutsch: It is a great honour to respond to your question, Herr Weber. You are right in distinguishing between knowledge and politics. Take global warming. There is a strong consensus about the problem of carbon dioxide emission and how it might be lowered among scientists but little political will in most countries to do what is necessary. To a lesser extent, the same is true with problems of war and racism. I agree with you that all knowledge is subjective in our – as you so nicely put – 'disenchanted world'. Data does not produce knowledge. It must be interpreted, and this demands conceptual formulations that are inevitably subjective. As I understand your epistemological writings, these subjective findings must be evaluated on the basis of their utility. This is difficult to do if they are never put into practice.

Max Weber: And often dangerous if they are, as twentieth-century attempts at social engineering have revealed.

Richard Ned Lebow: Thank you everyone. And, yes, the gentleman with the long white beard in the third row here. What would you like to add?

The man in the third row: I'm John Dalberg-Acton, 1st Baron Acton. I have only a short interjection in the form of a compliment to the speakers. I've attended a number of panels at this meeting, and in almost all the presenters used audio-visual aids. I was pleased to see none of that nonsense here. I would like to offer the dictum that power corrupts, and Power Point corrupts absolutely.

Richard Ned Lebow: On that note, I bring this panel to a close.

Note

Thanks are due to Michael Williams, William Scheuerman, Robert Ayson, Lucian Ashworth, Sarah Jamal and Beate Jahn for their contributions.

1. Morgenthau, Hans J. (1954) 'The Theoretical and Practical Importance of a Theory of International Relations' in Guilhot, N. (ed., 2011) *The Invention of International Relations Theory. Realism, the Rockerfeller Foundation, and the 1954 Conference on Theory.* (New York: Columbia University Press, pp. 263–268), p. 263.

Index

Printed by Printforce, United Kingdom